Adult Literacy

A Compendium of Articles from the Journal of Reading

MARGUERITE C. RADENCICH

EDITOR

DADE COUNTY PUBLIC SCHOOLS, FLORIDA

INTERNATIONAL READING ASSOCIATION
NEWARK, DELAWARE 19714, UNITED STATES

Director of Publications   Joan M. Irwin
Managing Editor   Anne Fullerton
Associate Editor   Chris Celsnak
Assistant Editor   Amy Trefsger
Editorial Assistant   Janet Parrack
Production Department Manager   Iona Sauscermen
Graphic Design Coordinator   Boni Nash
Design Consultant   Larry Husfelt
Desktop Publishing Supervisor   Wendy Mazur
Desktop Publishing   Anette Schütz-Ruff
                       Cheryl Strum
Proofing   David Roberts

The International Reading Association attempts, through its publications, to provide a forum for a wide spectrum of opinions on reading. This policy permits divergent viewpoints without assuming the endorsement of the Association.

Much of the material contained in this volume first appeared in the *Journal of Reading*, a copyrighted journal of the International Reading Association. Every attempt was made to contact authors of previously published work to inform them of this use of their material. The publisher welcomes correspondence from contributing authors concerning corrections or updated information that can be incorporated in subsequent editions of this publication.

Library of Congress Cataloging in Publication Data

   Adult literacy: a compendium of articles from the Journal of Reading/Marguerite C. Radencich, editor.
       p.   cm.
   Selection of articles published between March 1975 and March 1994 in the Journal of Reading.
   Includes bibliographical references and indexes.
       1. Functional literacy.   2. Adult education.   I. Radencich, Marguerite C., 1952– .   II. Journal of reading.
   LC149.7.A39   1994   94-12295
   374'.012—dc20   CIP
   ISBN 0-87207-122-7

Contents

F o r e w o r d

This compendium of articles is nothing if not diverse. Denise Davis starts the volume with a political call to action urging adult literacy educators to structure their programs to become means to "achieve social and economic equality" by changing the social status quo. Her parting counsel to directors of "emancipatory" and "liberatory" programs for which economic support is lacking is to "maintain the vision and await the revolution and attempt to prepare learners for political options not yet available." Lest the rhetoric of the first article deceives you into thinking the book is a neo-Marxist approach to literacy, be aware that the same volume also contains articles which would make nervous any activists pushing for revolution. For example, Phyllis Miller writes on how to teach employees reading strategies by using annual reports and company correspondence, while Francis Kazemek and Pat Rigg describe adult literacy teaching approaches using the politically neutral poetry of William Carlos Williams and others. In this book, political essays and opinion pieces are mixed with research studies and detailed descriptions of effective instructional techniques.

The dozens of articles contained within this volume are arranged under six organizational headings (that is, theoretical and organizational issues, assessment, general teaching methodology, technology, tutoring, and workplace literacy) which attempt to sort out the diversity. This organization is useful, to some extent, in that it may help the reader find areas that are important to him or her. The organization is illusory, however, if it gives the impression that the reader will finish any section with a clear and comprehensive sense of major issues or learnings in the highlighted area. Brief introductions to each section attempt to frame some of the major foci in the field of adult literacy, but one could not use this volume, all by itself, as a self-study textbook about adult literacy. It is instead, a collection of solid, readable articles on adult literacy which have appeared in the *Journal of Reading* during the last decade or so. As such, the collection offers support materials for several different approaches one might take to teaching or learning about adult literacy. It also makes for interesting browsing since one can literally enter the volume at any point and profitably pause to read.

Adult literacy educators usually find only brief time and opportunity to communicate with each other. Conversations with other educators are often transitory and cut short — a question will be asked in passing, a teaching technique or a cogent idea quickly summarized. Later, if one teacher has the time to sort through a pile of old journals, he or she might locate and pass along a relevant article to share as a conversation follow-up. This compendium of articles will make this process considerably easier. Program directors will be able to more easily share relevant articles with their staffs, and adult literacy instructors now have a book full of articles more accessible to themselves and colleagues. Between the covers of this volume are a file drawer of good ideas. Enjoy them and use them well.

Larry Mikulecky
Indiana University, Bloomington

Introduction

*T*his book originated in a discussion at the 1993 meeting of the Journal of Reading *Editorial Advisory Board.* JR *is a journal of adolescent and adult literacy, and the board members were looking for ways that the journal could address the theory and practice of adult literacy instruction—strategies and tools, assessment and teaching, workplace literacy, beginning adult literacy, and the stages in between—in a comprehensive way without excluding the journal's focus on adolescents.*

Over the years, many outstanding articles on adult literacy issues have been published in JR, *and we realized that they provided an excellent resource. The suggestion was made to gather these pieces into a single book, to allow easy access for both adult literacy professionals and volunteers. The International Reading Association could then use its resources to make the book available to its members as well as to others working in this field.*

I reviewed back issues of JR *and identified articles that focused on adult literacy topics. Janet Ramage Binkley,* JR's *editor, offered some additional suggestions. In order to ensure that the book included the best and most recent thinking on adult literacy instruction—a field that has changed over the past years—most of the articles included in this resulting compendium come primarily from recent years. Some articles were excluded to avoid unnecessary overlap; several important pieces from earlier years were included. We decided to exclude articles on college literacy, an area generally distinct from other adult literacy efforts.*

The resulting selection of articles was grouped into sections, as follows: theoretical and organizational issues, assessment, general teaching methodology, technology, tutoring, and workplace literacy. Each of these sections in the book begins with a brief introduction that provides an overview of the topic and the articles.

Teachers of children clearly have a tremendous responsibility, but how much greater, in a way, is the responsibility of the teacher who serves adults, people who often had given up on a system but have risked coming back. This book is aimed at providing some answers (and more questions!) to help teachers and tutors of adults increase their knowledge about issues related to reading instruction so that they can better address the needs of their students. I hope that the book will serve as the basis for discussion among program administrators, teachers, and tutors, university students, and the adult clients themselves.

MCR

Theoretical and Organizational Issues

> **"The materials of instruction as well as the underlying theories of teaching and learning that were developed during the first half of the century continue to shape people's underlying conceptions of literacy education."**
>
> —LANGER, 1991, P. 11

What paradigms are behind adult literacy programs? Whom do the programs serve? With what success? The pieces in this section address definitional and management issues regarding adult literacy programs.

Langer (1991) points out that "although notions and uses of literacy vary among cultural groups, they also change within groups across time" (p. 12). When I selected the articles for this section, I took a hard look at the authors' theories and notions about the uses of literacy. In the first piece, Ilsley and Stahl provide a provocative essay on the metaphors used to dramatize illiteracy and how they shape our thinking. The piece analyzes the problems of metaphor and of competing stakeholders and concludes that we should always consider literacy in a political context. Shuman writes from personal experience

and corrects the assumptions he held regarding adult reading instruction.

Heathington argues for an expansion of the definition of literacy for adults.

Davis uses a sociological perspective to show how programs in different settings reflect the values of their sponsoring institutions. Learners whose values do not coincide with those of the institutions become resisters. Community organizations are suggested as a viable alternative to existing institutions.

In the next two pieces, Norman and Malicky analyze stages in the reading development of adults. They adopt a constructivist view (Hiebert, 1991) in which learners are seen as active participants in the creation of their own knowledge. In their latter piece, they describe a study that used interviews and miscue analysis to evaluate adults. Results showed that adults use knowledge-based strategies and supported previous findings that adults' reading development begins with the use of language.

The remaining pieces have specific foci. For Ferrell and Howley it is rural programs, and for Hansell and Voelkel, a prison population. As a group, the pieces in this section address the theory and practice of adult literacy programs within changing paradigms of instruction. The variety of settings helps keep a broad perspective.

References

Hiebert, E.H. (1991). Introduction. In E.H. Hiebert (Ed.), Literacy for a diverse society (pp. 1–3). New York: Teachers College Press.

Langer, J.A. (1991). Literacy and schooling: A sociocognitive perspective. In E.H. Hiebert (Ed.), Literacy for a diverse society (pp. 9–27). New York: Teachers College Press.

Theoretical and Organizational Issues

Reconceptualizing the Language of Adult Literacy

PAUL J. ILSLEY
NORMAN A. STAHL
SEPTEMBER 1993

A recent magazine advertisement contained a headline designed to have the same type of advertising punch for the U.S. adult literacy movement as the "be all that you can be" sound bite had for the U.S. Army. The idea behind the ad was to recruit volunteers for The Coalition of Adult Literacy. Produced in 1989 by the National Advertising Council, the advertisement portrayed a crowd of mostly average-looking people in a large picture. Underneath was the eye-catching message "There's an epidemic with 27 million victims. And no visible symptoms."

The application of certain trigger words in the headline was intended to shape the reader's perspective and to recruit volunteers to assist nonreading adults in need. The text of the advertisement was even more gripping, in that it appealed to both altruistic and patriotic instincts. It stated that "millions of Americans are victims of a tragic epidemic," and that "in human terms, the price of illiteracy is staggering. People who can't read, often can't work. They make up 50%–75% of this country's unemployed." Furthermore, it appeared that one need not have special skills to help, because "when you join the fight against illiteracy...it takes no special qualifications. If you can read, you can tutor or help us in countless other ways." Yet as one looks critically at the advertisement, the following components seem out of place:

- Many people in the picture look confused and aimless, as if nonreading adults are that way. Probably some are, though certainly not all, as is true of any population.

- The reference to "epidemic" is strange, if not patently inappropriate, because it sounds as though people who cannot read are sick. Probably some are but, again, so is some of the rest of the population.

- The overworked and careless slogan used by some members of the adult literacy movement that there are "27 million victims" is suspect for two reasons. First, to estimate a number of illiterates requires a solid definition of illiteracy. Is literacy merely the ability to read the printed word? Is it a matter of being functional in the roles of parents, citizens, and workers? Or is it to be equated with "voice" and "power"? The numbers vary greatly according to the definitions of literacy and illiteracy. Second, the word *victim* is a label that applies to people who are on the receiving end of a crime or a disease. Moreover, the word evokes images of a fool or a chump, or someone who has lost control of a situation. Nonreading adults are not victims in either sense of

the word. It is sheer speculation, if not outright prejudice, that guides the selection and use of this term.

- Equating illiteracy with unemployment, or for that matter, crime, drug abuse, or any other social evil, rests on the assumption that the inability to read necessarily makes a person a societal burden, and fails to note the productivity of illiterate, semiliterate, and non–English-speaking adults in factories, on farms, in service industries, in homes, and elsewhere.

- The implication that anyone who can read can help illiterates may well be true, but by itself the statement is facile and irresponsible. Effective volunteer literacy programs are highly complex organizations that rely on the coordinated efforts of a variety of people, including the students themselves (Ilsley, 1990). In a real sense, a person's decision to learn to read is a negotiated affair, not a matter of "helplessness" (Ilsley, 1985a).

- The overall effect of the advertising campaign is that it serves the need of organizations that produce literacy programs, not the needs of nonreading adults.

Unfortunately, illiteracy is often discussed in relation to such striking notions as war, disease, prison, and chronic unemployment both in print and in electronic media campaigns. Similar overzealousness and sensationalism is employed regularly in the speeches of well-12known figures. For instance, when addressing the 1984 National Convention of Literacy Volunteers of America, Barbara Bush (wife of the then U.S. vice president) proclaimed that "adult illiteracy is one of the nation's most insidious diseases." The following year, in his address to the American Newspaper Publishers' Association, former U.S. Secretary of

Education Terrell Bell (1985) argued that "the time is now to mobilize our forces, the corporations, various sectors of government, the military, and, of course, the media against adult illiteracy."

Why resort to pretentious language, inflated statistics, and misplaced metaphors for the purpose of dramatizing illiteracy to the public? Usually, people select metaphors according to their own vested interests in describing a situation or solving a problem. Furthermore, as individuals or organizations develop and in a sense market a metaphor to explain a concept or a phenomenon, they are attempting to create a power base that leads the selected audience to interpret the problem in a way favorable to the goals of the respective group. Indeed, both the public and nonprofit sectors are rather like the private sector, where language is used strategically in advertising and public relations campaigns to compete for market share or in this situation grants, contracts, favorable public opinion, etc.

The more successful if not dramatic the metaphor, the more likely will be the group's emergence into a dominant leadership position. It is the metaphor that becomes known to many. Unfortunately, the highly affective-effective public metaphor on literacy avoids forcing both professional and laypersons to come to grips with a basic definition of literacy (e.g., literacy vs. functional literacy vs. illiteracy, or relative literacy vs. absolute literacy).

At this juncture, the way stakeholders describe adult literacy reflects their position and goals and perhaps even determines their success as an ongoing entity. Hence, educators need to note the language used by government leaders and by the media to describe literacy and illiteracy. In the rest of this article, we present some of the more popular metaphors, followed by analysis of their usage.

The discussion that follows is organized around four metaphors that have been presented regularly in the popular press, in electronic media, and in speeches by both elected and self-proclaimed U.S. leaders. These language devices are what might be identified as public metaphors. They serve what Hayakawa (1978) noted as the affective use of language—designed to invoke strong connotations in the public's collective mind. We cover (in order) illiteracy as a function of school language, illiteracy as a disease, illiteracy as a national enemy in the military sense, and illiteracy as a lack of capital in a cultural banking system. Scribner (1984) in a somewhat similar vein used the development of metaphor to attempt to define literacy. Yet her forms of metaphor (i.e., literacy as adaptation, literacy as power, literacy as state of grace) were presented for scholars by an acclaimed scholar. Thus her metaphors have a rather "private" usage serving a specialized population. The metaphors identified here are drawn instead from the public media and have an impact on us all.

The School Metaphor

By far the most popular and perhaps most ironic of all choices of language to describe adult illiteracy comes from professional educators, who speak of literacy in absolute, quantifiable terms—grade levels, achievement tests, competency exams—reducing the problem to school language. This way of looking at literacy has consequences if applied to literacy programs. What sense does it make to subject people who did not perform well in their school years to the same regimen of rote memorization, isolated skill mastery, punctuality, and obedience?

In contrast, adult literacy education assumes participants will display consistency, ingenuity, cooperation, and efficiency—the kinds of attributes that promote personal success and help to drive an organization or profession in this modern technological culture. Hence, at the very least, pedagogese is out of place in the adult literacy context.

Anyone who has discussed the matter with one or more nonreading adults will agree that the standards by which youngsters are measured in the typical U.S. classroom give way in adulthood to other standards and goals. It is not necessarily true that adult nonreaders, whom we often treat like metacognitively naive youngsters, do not know what they want, as the stereotype would have us believe. Like the rest of us, they would like to achieve their goals on their own terms. When the school language, tests, processes, roles, and norms that failed them in the past appear to be once again unrealistic or uncompromising, adult nonreaders simply avoid them.

The Medical (and Industrial) Metaphor

In response to the societal *disease* of adult illiteracy, the adult nonreader is encouraged to check into a learning *clinic*, where the primary *symptoms* are hypothesized during a *triage-like* intake interview, which is then followed by the in-depth *diagnosis* of weaknesses and strengths (in that order) by a *clinician* or an *intern* and the *prescription* of an individualized plan of instruction. Then through the monitoring of instructional *vital signs*, *prognoses* are made. Once the problem has been controlled, the student-patient is released from the clinic to undergo long-term *therapy* at the local adult education program while on the other extreme the illiterate is declared a *terminal case* as an *undiagnosed* dyslexic or a learning-*disabled* individual.

The medical metaphor, like any, has advantages and disadvantages. Among the advantages is the image that there is scientific precision in teaching adult literacy. The result is the quest for systematic analysis of students, and consistent and efficient programming and instructional evaluation. Goals are clear, accountability is high, and records are kept methodically under such a model. Moreover, the sense of drama contained in labeling adult illiteracy a social disease creates societal awareness and evokes public consciousness raising and charitable participation akin to calling national attention to cancer or heart disease.

As for the negative, there is a difference between curing a disease and promoting health. A premise behind the idea of eradicating illiteracy, as if it were a disease, is that a deficit model is appropriate. Merely by eliminating illiteracy we will have met our goal. However, the medical model is not very attractive to participants. Even if it were possible, rooting out illiteracy from society is not nearly so upbeat a proposal as is the advancement of literacy, which is more purposeful and full of hope. Common sense would indicate that educational programs are more likely to appeal to people when the benefits and ease of attending are presented persuasively rather than when people are shamed or even coerced into programs designed to "eradicate the disease of illiteracy."

Moreover, the medical metaphor places the problem within an individual. Consider the purpose of diagnosis. Once tested, various characteristics of the person—as opposed to his or her context, culture, or society—are identified for treatment. The myth is encouraged that all similarly diagnosed individuals can be treated with the same kind of instruction. Also, when illiteracy is defined as an individual problem, an educator can define deficiencies in ways that remove a student from the decision-making process. Belief in the stamp of industrialization, or the cookie-cutter model, predominates, leading to the unitization, standardization, and compartmentalization of students and their problems. In this way, illiterates are not educated; they are processed. (And people don't like that in medicine, either.)

Finally, the medical metaphor, with its crass implication that people are diseased and that there is an epidemic in our midst, suggests that illiterates are contagious and are to be shunned or feared. Despite the drama implied when the medical metaphor is put to use, it is pretentious and misleading. As the model is questioned at other levels of education, so it certainly should be rethought in adult literacy education circles.

The Military Metaphor

Perhaps it was the Lyndon Johnson–era slogan of the "War on Poverty" that gave rise to the more current U.S. slogan of the "war on illiteracy." In declaring war, the *legions* of volunteers will be *strategically mobilized in a campaign* to hit the *target* populations. Americans will win the *battle* against illiteracy and *conquer* ignorance. In this way, the military metaphor provides the illusion that the *enemy* is a serious *threat* to the nation and that as good Americans, we must find that inner resolve to respond in a bold and forthright manner.

While such militaristic talk highlights the problem of illiteracy for the public, it skirts the harsh analysis that the populace would find of little direct interest. There is no mistaking that those who use such rhetoric are dreaming of a speedy educational Desert Storm rather than a pedagogical Vietnam-style quagmire. Indeed it is all too easy to get caught up in patriotic flag waving (if not propaganda) without realizing that the illiteracy problem is serious and requires an enormous amount of attention and the commitment of resources. Similarly, the unidirectional recruitment campaign makes no estimation of the difficulty of reaching illiterate adults and convincing them to join programs. It will take long-term strategic planning to reach and to serve the target population of nonreading adults properly.

Furthermore, we must ask what a closer examination of military talk says about volunteers and the call to arms. Talk of such a good war suggests there may be the glory of personally conquering illiteracy in a willing and able tutee. Yet, when a person decides to become involved in the "war on illiteracy," he or she must be concerned with the possibility of becoming another of the casualties who fall by the tutorial wayside.

And what does the military metaphor say about the potential students? Just who is the enemy in this war on illiteracy? Is it all of society, for permitting conditions to reach such proportions? Not likely. Social reform is not an important matter in the circles that rely on such rhetoric. Are schools to blame for ineffectively educating a proportion of students under their charge? Hardly, since the action is with the students, and not with school reform (adult literacy and school reform are concepts that are rarely linked). No, adult illiterates themselves are the object of attention, and, though they are not deemed the enemy, they are nevertheless depicted as Kiplingish burdens to society, as unemployable, and as ashamed of themselves, and therefore as likely *targets* for literacy instruction.

Like the medical metaphor, the military metaphor is based on a deficit model. The logic of it leads one to believe that conquering the enemy will bring peace (or peace of mind). That is, ridding society of illiteracy will promote higher levels of employment, better family relations, and even improved worker morale. The American Century will continue past the year 2000.

Yet there is an old saying that "a nation that hates war will never find peace." It is not enough for society to hate the opposite of what it wants. It must instead envision its goal, and then act on the vision. No amount of hating a social condition, such as illiteracy, will bring about the opposite, such as the achievement of a literate society. There is a vast difference between a nation that is not illiterate and one that is literate. Promoting war, calling good people to arms, and encouraging hate of any kind is a limited worldview in any event. While the battles rage on and nonreading adults are caught in the crossfire, the military metaphor is not all it can be.

The Banking Metaphor

In the banking metaphor, assumptions are made about the nature of knowledge and of the way people gain it. Accordingly, knowledge is stored in *vaults* from which *withdrawals* and *deposits* can be made. A person is *rich* when his or her mind is full of facts. In this way, educators from the preschool through the university are like bankers, in that they keep watch over the *currency* of knowledge—or of that knowledge that is *officially approved*. The coin of the realm then is the content, which is taught in school, that appears on standardized tests and supports the belief system of the dominant economic culture. Language, facts, beliefs, and even regional or cultural dialects that are not a part of the official *system* are deemed inappropriate and, on balance, "correctable" (Freire, 1970) to the degree that a corpus of culturally appropriate knowledge is deemed necessary (Hirsch, 1987).

One positive attribute of the banking metaphor can be seen in its hopeful nature. There is comfort in wealth, and a realistic plan to gain economic (educational) security is intriguing to people as well as ingrained in the American national psyche as positive. Better yet, unlike money, knowledge is infinite, and its value relative to the situation. It is all around people, and it is there for the taking. A belief in the banking metaphor is a belief in the goal of education.

To consider the metaphor's prejudicial side, not all knowledge is equally accessible, and not everyone is granted equal entry to it. Some knowledge is sacred and is kept from people who lack the proper credentials to obtain it and hence to use it "properly." Information from the medical, legal, mortuary science, and insurance fields comes to mind as an outstanding example. It takes persistence to secure the linguistic capital or the specific information about a disease, a coffin, or a life insurance policy, unless one happens to have passed the respective rites of passage to be a doctor, an attorney, an undertaker, or an insurance agent. The professions are not typically educative. Indeed, many professional registers and practices are inherently monopolistic and are designed to hinder public access to information that would otherwise be in the public interest.

Since the teaching profession has been historically an acceptable portal into the middle class, teachers have often fallen into the role of the metaphorical loan officer guarding the cultural capital. The question that becomes central to the literacy debate is whether educators should be keepers of the official knowledge, as opposed to facilitators of the critical thinking skills that will empower others who are at present without the accepted currency. Actual capital to offer services, of course, tends to go to those who accept the keeper role, as opposed to those serving in community organizations that advocate change within the system.

Choice of Metaphors

The four common metaphors just discussed are not the only ones now in use. Others favored in public relations circles, if not among professional educators, include gardening, computing, machine language, and communications. All of these metaphors, along with the ones we analyzed above, have at least two things in common. First, they place the selection of solutions above the determination of the problem. In doing so, they categorically remove students from the decision-making process, as if their opinions of what it means to be illiterate or to be literate are subjective, value laden, unsophisticated, or in some other way do not matter. Second, these metaphors are all nonhuman. Reliance on medical, military, and banking metaphors conveys a belief in systems, techniques, and professional expertise—not in the mission, the purpose, or the human processes of learning.

The careful selection of language to discuss any problem requires first considering the full extent of a situation; second, determining what is to be achieved and in what ways; and third, finding the connotations that accurately convey the meaning. Adult literacy educators need not be locked into nonhuman metaphors, despite their allure, unless these truly describe our beliefs. Let's hope the day will come when human language is more compelling than technical and mechanistic language.

There are times when dramatic, emotion-laden language is used to convey a sense of urgency and there are other times when it is used to advance an agenda. In discussions of adult literacy, all stakeholders have a moral responsibility to avoid allowing the "war against illiteracy" to turn into an undeclared war on illiterates. In "conquering the epidemic of illiteracy" we must not view the learner as diseased. It is imperative that society respect the dignity, the rights, and the accomplishments of all people, regardless of their ability to deal with the printed word.

The Problems of Metaphor and Competing Stakeholders

Values and assumptions are inherent in phrases applied to adult illiteracy. The metaphors all too simply present fundamental premises about the nature of illiteracy and those who cannot read. Those most prone to making such statements are probably well-meaning members of the adult literacy movement, such as politicians, community leaders, and educators. Though they may not intend to affront adult nonreaders with their language, their word choice probably follows their own interests—that is, the interests of their respective profession. Educators may wish to spice up the rhetoric with scientific or medical language to provide the clarion call, and politicians may use forceful, vote-winning military language as a function of ongoing campaigns.

Whatever the interest in adult literacy, the resulting choice of words used to describe it is important because the labeling of a problem directs the solutions. To elaborate, if illiteracy is defined in terms of reading deficiency, the solution is to direct the nonreading adult population toward reading instruction. If literacy is defined in terms of citizenship—that is, if what it means to be literate includes the ability to fill out tax forms, drive a car, vote regularly, or use medical services—then the solution is quite different.

The question then follows: Who should label the adult literacy problem? The government? Corporations or other employers? The students themselves? Clearly, in the years since illiteracy has become a media-invested concern, various groups have expressed an interest in defining both illiteracy and the attending solutions, including reading specialists, adult educators, politicians of various stripes, corporate moguls, workplace leaders, criminal justice workers, librarians, religious leaders, newspaper personnel, and more recently, special educators (working with learning-disabled or otherwise cognitively handicapped persons). In each instance, there is a different view of literacy and what it means to be literate, according to the respective stake or investment. There are also expectations of people regarding how they are to behave—for example, to be spiritual, to be law abiding, to be good consumers. Yet in no instance are provisions made to help nonreading adults determine for themselves why they should learn to read. Each of the stakeholders touches but a part of the elephant and describes the beast minimally.

Is there an easy way for professionals to avoid the problems inherent in the overreliance on metaphor to convey understanding, biased or not, about the literacy situation? We think not. Clearly, metaphor provides easily developed affective-level communication that promotes understanding without the necessity to coin new words or jargon unlikely to be found in the working vocabularies of the multitudes, or to write extensive text conveying information to a sound-bite generation dependent upon bulleted, chopped text and 15- to 30-second messages over the airwaves.

Indeed, metaphor may be the most direct form of communicating new ideas or important issues of the day. However, as Hayakawa (1978) warned, the real danger is that metaphor often passes into the language (and we would go as far as to say into the national psyche) as part of the working vocabulary and hence the regularly accepted concepts of complex societal phenomena. When a questionable metaphor, such as one of those men-

tioned earlier, is regularly used, the best hope is that it will in time simply become a cliché and hence inconsequential. Still there is no overcoming the initial problems encountered.

The issue is not so much whether a metaphor is used, but whether it promotes the language of the commons, provides useful, positive elements for public discourse, and reaches the greater portion of the stakeholders. This implies the need to use language that educates, not simplifies, and the need for not just education for illiterate adults but for all the highly educated individuals who serve or want to serve the, nonreaders—namely, those who write the advertising text, those who draft the campaign speeches, those who compose the popular press manuscripts, those who write the nighttime television sound bites, those who develop commentaries for radio shows and newspaper editorials. It also calls for greater communication between literacy providers and literacy advocates so that we come together to speak a common language and convey important ideas and current issues to the populace via agreed upon and readily comprehensible understandings (Ilsley, 1985b). The need for further cross-disciplinary and cross-national forums such as the cosponsored Adult and Adolescent Literacy Forums becomes apparent.

To many, literacy is a phenomenon about which society assumes a common and a universal understanding. Of course, neither assumption is correct. Compare, for example, how literacy is defined in the workplace with how it is defined in a community action center. In the former, the desired result is increased productivity for the company, if not the country, whereas in the latter, it is group empowerment for the poor and oppressed. Viewed this way, the problem with the way most of us rely on adult literacy metaphors is that it allows us all to bridge among specialized fields at the expense of the nonreading adults themselves. So long as popular metaphor provokes either positive or negative images of what it means to be illiterate or literate, and the consequences to a nation, we may miss more subtle though holistic points of the human issues of illiteracy.

Rather than presupposing that illiteracy is an individual problem, we should always consider literacy in a political context. If illiteracy has political origins, it is likely that literacy requires political solutions. Adult nonreaders can certainly participate in determining the curriculum. In this way, literacy education focuses not only on individual instruction but also on group instruction, to the end that participants comprehend the forces and injustice that can oppress entire groups of people. If those of us involved in all facets of literacy education begin to understand the attitudes and the agendas of the various stakeholders (our own included), exhibited through the metaphors and language used, we will have accomplished a great deal. Then and only then will the U.S. be in a position to address the needs of adult nonreaders.

References

Bell, T. (1985, May 23). *Keynote address.* The American Newspaper Publishers' Association, Memphis, TN.

Bush, B. (1984, September 17). *Keynote address.* The National Convention of Literacy Volunteers of America, Chicago, IL.

Freire, P. (1970). *Pedagogy of the oppressed.* New York: Herder & Herder.

Hirsch, E.B. (1987). *Cultural literacy.* New York: Harper & Row.

Hayakawa, S.I. (1978). *Language in thought and action* (4th ed.). New York: Harcourt Brace.

Ilsley, P.J. (1990). *Enhancing volunteer participation.* San Francisco, CA: Jossey-Bass.

Ilsley, P.J. (1985a). *Adult literacy volunteers: Issues and ideas* (Information Series No. 301). Columbus, OH: ERIC Clearinghouse on Adult, Career, and Vocational Education.

Ilsley, P.J. (1985b). Including educationally deprived adults in the planning of literacy programs. In S. Rosenblum (Ed.), *Including adults in the educational process* (New Directions for Continuing Education, No. 26). San Francisco, CA: Jossey-Bass.

Scribner, S. (1984). Literacy in three metaphors. *American Journal of Education, 93,* 6–21.

Theoretical and Organizational Issues

Expanding the Definition of Literacy for Adult Remedial Readers

BETTY S. HEATHINGTON
DECEMBER 1987

We often ask "How do we define an adult remedial reader?" The definition is important. It should help us in providing an appropriate reading program for these adults. If we know, or can define, a situation, we should be able to plan for it. However, many current definitions do not help us to plan and implement programs or understand the needs of the adult remedial reader. This article reviews some current definitions of literacy and suggests that an expansion of the definitions is needed, based on information gained from interviews with adult remedial readers as they describe their needs.

Current Definitions

Consider some of the current definitions of literacy:

• *The reading and writing ability definition* is one of the earliest definitions of literacy, stating that persons are considered literate if they can read and write their names. The U.S. Census Bureau has considered individuals to be literate if they reply affirmatively to a question about their ability to read and write a simple sentence. The requirements for literacy under this definition are modest; extensive skills are not required. This definition gives us little direction in program planning. We simply would have as our objective that the adult would be able to read and write his or her name or a simple sentence. Such a reading program would be a limited one for the adult remedial reader.

• *The years of schooling definition.* Another definition of literacy is years of schooling or grades completed. Some people disagree that this is a valid definition. They point out that just because someone has not completed 12 years of schooling, it does not necessarily follow that she or he cannot read; and, conversely, just because someone does receive a diploma, it does not mean that she or he can read. However, after examining extensive data, Fisher (1978) has stated that the evidence is strong that those who fail to graduate from high school constitute the bulk of illiterates. Further, Hunter and Harman (1979) have stated that when high school

completion data are compared with competency testing data, essentially the same numbers are established. There seems to be a strong link between years spent in school and competencies in reading. The ease of defining literacy by years in school is undoubtedly another reason it is often used as a measure. However, defining literacy by a prescribed number of years spent in school does little to guide the content or process of an adult program.

• *The grade level equivalent definition* is prevalent in educational writings. Dinnan (1980) has described illiteracy as the inability of the individual to function with materials written beyond 5th grade level. In Adult Basic Education, three categories of ability are defined by references to grade levels: Level I = Grades 0–3 (beginning); Level II = Grades 4–6 (intermediate); Level III = Grades 7–up (advanced). Three levels associated with grades in school are also presented by Powell (1977): (1) a preliteracy level during which the individual begins to gain knowledge and use of basic skills in society—namely, those essential literacy skills upon which further learning depends (estimated grade level of K–3); (2) a basic literacy level during which literacy skills can develop further without formal instruction (estimated grade level of 5.5); and (3) a career literacy level during which basic skills plus advanced skill performance are necessary (estimated grade level of 7.5).

The definition of grade-level equivalents forces the adult into a pattern provided for children. It must be remembered that grade-level scores on standardized achievement tests use norms based on testing of specific populations. For example, a 5.0 reading score is what the average child in a 5th grade standardized sample scored on the test. Problems in using these scores with adults, who must deal with very different types of content and situations than those addressed in an achievement test, must be recognized. The content and situations related to reading for an adult are very different from those of a child in the early grades.

• *The competency-based or functional literacy definition* relates to the individual's ability to read real-life materials. At present, competency-based or functional literacy is receiving more attention than the previous definitions. However, Ayrer (1977) has pointed out how difficult it is to define functional literacy: "Everyone knows what functional literacy is but no one can tell you. It's one of those concepts for which there is no single definition which will fit every situation." Hunter and Harman (1979, p. 7) define functional literacy as "the possession of skills perceived as necessary by particular persons and groups to fulfill their own self-determined objectives as family and community members, citizens, job-holders, and members of social, religious, or other associations of their choosing." Kirsch and Guthrie (1977–1978) defined functional literacy as relating to the level of skills needed by individuals or populations to be able to complete a certain real-life reading task. Readence and Moore (1979) list functional literacy skills under five major categories: forms and applications, advertisements, pictorial materials, consumer information and directions, and information and information sources.

In recent years, the competency-based or functional definition of literacy has been prevalent in the United States. In 1970, Louis Harris and Associates conducted a study to assess survival literacy skills, defined in terms of such tasks as reading an application form, a telephone directory, and a classified ad in a newspaper (Hunter & Harman, 1979). The Adult Performance Level (APL) Project also used functional competencies to assess

literacy: consumer economics (reading labels on cans), occupational knowledge (reading job-wanted ads), health (reading first aid directions), community resources (reading a movie schedule), and government and law (reading about your rights after arrest) (Greenfield & Nogueira, 1980).

The competency-based or functional reading definition provides much more direction in program planning and program implementation than do the other definitions. Content for reading classes for adult remedial readers can be specified more clearly. Such a definition has contributed much to an understanding of the adult's needs. However, although it is superior to others, it lacks certain aspects needed for us to fully understand the adult remedial reader. It focuses on the individual's ability to read certain types of adult materials. The definition is directed at reading skills needed for real-life materials; overlooked are the affective aspects of adult reading situations. The current competency-based or functional reading definition needs to be expanded to include affective aspects of literacy. Interviews with adults in a literacy program show us why.

Expanding the Definition

In interviews conducted in the University of Tennessee Adult Reading Academy Program over several years, adult remedial readers have described not only their needs related to reading certain types of materials but also their feelings about reading. These feelings should be addressed as programs are developed, for they can help us in understanding the adult remedial reader. Let us note examples taken from the interviews which demonstrate the impact the affective domain has on the adult remedial reader. In the interview, the readers describe the effects of their inability to read on their lives as related to their roles as workers, as consumers, as parents, as students, in social situations, and in recreational or leisure situations.

As workers. Unemployment and underemployment often concern adult remedial readers. The interviews reveal over and over the embarrassment of an adult who had to take his wife with him so that she could complete the job application form for him, or the adult who stated that his most embarrassing times were when he had to fill out a job application form "in front of all of those people." The interviews reveal the frustration and fear related to employment. Examples include:

- The cook who was afraid someone would find out she couldn't read the recipes.
- The mechanic who was embarrassed when his boss found out he couldn't read the charting sheet.
- The truck driver who was frustrated because he couldn't locate places for deliveries because he couldn't read the road or street signs.
- The chemical worker who was frightened and frustrated because he couldn't read the labels on the chemicals he mixed.
- The worker who was embarrassed because he had to ask fellow employees to read his work orders.
- The worker whose self-esteem was very low because he had to tape-record his work and take it home to be typed or written by family members who could read.

As consumers. Feelings of embarrassment, low esteem, and frustration also plague the adult remedial reader in the consumer area. When faced with such tasks as buying groceries, obtaining health services, securing credit, paying bills, writing checks, reading menus, and a host of tasks taken for granted by most people in a modern society, adult remedial readers are affected in adverse ways. For example:

- They are embarrassed when they cannot read labels in a grocery store and must ask for assistance.
- They feel guilty that they cannot read health-related materials so that they know how to take care of a sick child.
- They are fearful of signing documents for credit buying because they must depend on others to explain what they are signing.

As parents. Many adult remedial readers express concern about their reading as they become parents. They are fearful that their reading problem will have detrimental effects on their children. For example:

- They are embarrassed when their children's friends find out they cannot read or they are afraid such revelations will be made.
- They are afraid their children will ask them to read a book aloud and they will not be able to do so.
- Fathers have expressed their feelings of inadequacy when the mothers can help with homework and they cannot help.

As students. In educational settings, adult remedial readers face frustration and feelings of inadequacy as they attempt to gain knowledge and skills to improve themselves. For example:

- They are embarrassed when asked to read aloud in a classroom. They are uncomfortable and nervous when teachers make such requests.
- They are frustrated when they cannot read assignments or pass tests.

In social situations. Social interactions with family, friends, and work colleagues are sometimes difficult for those with limited literacy skills. For example:

- Many of them are frustrated at being unable to read letters from family and friends. One man could not communicate with a son in a distant state because of his inability to write and inadequate financial resources for telephone calls.

- Many report embarrassment in church activities, specifically Sunday school classes when they are asked to read a passage in the Bible. They report feeling inadequate when they must decline to read in front of social acquaintances.

- For some, social activities taken for granted by many of us create an unpleasant situation. One woman never went to baby showers because she was "afraid they'd play those writing games."

- Many go to great efforts to hide the fact they cannot read. Sometimes close family members, even a husband or wife, are unaware that the person is unable to read. They sometimes report they feel like "half a person" and are ashamed to tell even those close to them about their inability to read.

In recreational or leisure situations. Reading provides pleasure for many people; this pleasure is denied those who lack reading skills. For example:

- One woman reported she was lonely and wanted to read books to fill the void.

- Another woman was frustrated at not being able to read books that "teach things of value in life."

The foregoing comments taken from interviews emphasize that current definitions of literacy, which concentrate only on materials and skills, are lacking. The definitions do not help us understand the frustration, the negative self-concept, the fear, and the embarrassment that plague adult remedial readers. We must expand our definition of literacy to encompass aspects of affect. We must understand that not only does a definition of an adult remedial reader relate to his or her reading skills with various types of materials, but also to using these materials. This information can help us plan better reading programs for adult remedial readers.

References

Ayrer, J.E. (1977, May). Problems in the development of a test of functional literacy. *Journal of Reading, 20,* 697–705.

Dinnan, J.A. (1980). An evaluation of literacy programs for mature adults. In M.L. Kamil & A.J. Moe (Eds.), *Perspectives in reading research and instruction.* Washington, DC: National Reading Conference.

Fisher, D.L. (1978). *Functional literacy and the schools.* Washington, DC: U.S. Department of Health, Education, and Welfare, National Institute of Education.

Greenfield, L., & Nogueira, F. (1980). Reading should be functional: The APL approach. In L.S. Johnson (Ed.), *Reading and the adult learner.* Newark, DE: International Reading Association.

Hunter, C.S.J., & Harman, D. (1979). *Adult illiteracy in the United States.* New York: McGraw-Hill.

Kirsch, I.S., & Guthrie, J.T. (1977–1978). The concept and measurement of functional literacy. *Reading Research Quarterly, 13,* 485–507.

Powell, W.R. (1977, March). Levels of literacy. *Journal of Reading, 20,* 488-492.

Readence, J.E., & Moore, D. (1979, December). Coping with minimal reading requirements: Suggestions for the reading teacher. *Reading World, 19,* 139–148.

Adult Literacy Programs: Toward Equality or Maintaining the Status Quo?

DENISE M. DAVIS
SEPTEMBER 1991

If adult literacy programs in the United States are viewed as a means to achieve social and economic equality and thereby improve society, why do these programs fail to reach most marginal economic and social groups? Are there some adult literacy programs that have succeeded or might succeed in reaching these people? What obstacles lie in the paths of educators involved in the implementation of such programs?

The adult literacy programs found in U.S. community colleges, universities, and adult high school classes are frequently described as serving the "cream" of the adult nonreading public (Hunter & Harman, 1979; Kozol, 1985; Mezirow, Darkenwald, & Knox, 1975). Many of these programs rely on state or federal funding and must therefore adhere to rigid requirements for teacher certification, financial accountability, maintenance of attendance and enrollment records, and course completion figures. Although these factors may help explain the lack of attractiveness of these formal programs to many adult nonreaders, it must be noted that volunteer organizations such as Literacy Volunteers of America (LVA) and Laubach Literacy Action (LLA) face similar problems reaching and retaining students.

Conflicting Values

These issues can be viewed from a sociological perspective. Programs found in community colleges, universities, and adult high school classes tend to reflect the values of the sponsoring institutions, which more often than not coincide with values held by the dominant social class. In the United States, this "dominant social class" is that of the white middle-class male.

These same values permeate the volunteer organizations. Ilsley (1985b, p. 12) suggests that "without attempting any exact analysis at this point, one can state that both organizations [LVA and LLA] uphold strong middle-class orientations in such matters as interpretations and definitions of literacy, the type and method of training provided, and the goals they attempt to reach."

Sociologist Bourdieu (1981) speaks of such entrenched values as the "habitus" of the institution. Institutional values reflect laws and customs accumulated by a social group over the course of history as well as the web of perceptions, thoughts, and actions unique to that institution. Educational curricula reflect what is accepted as knowledge, culture, or linguistic practice by the dominant social group and thus serve to reproduce the values of that group. Bourdieu theorizes that a mismatch between the values of the educational institution and those of specific learners is common. Consider adult literacy programs in light of Bourdieu's theory. Many nonreaders are not members of the dominant social group. Research suggests that a potential learner's awareness of this mismatch in values may result in resistance to an educational institution's programs, not so much because of content but because of the values that institution embodies (Beder & Quigley, 1990; Fingeret, 1983, 1984; Quigley, 1987). This problem seems to apply to programs offered by formal educational institutions *and* volunteer groups.

For example, volunteer tutors are frequently recruited from outside the learners' communities and social groups. Despite their no doubt good intentions, tutors may reflect an attitude prevalent in their own community—that the inability to read represents a deficiency in the learner. Tutors may, as Ilsley (1985a) suggests, include the nonreader in the definition of the problem by saying "You don't know how to read; I can teach you," suggesting that "You are the problem; I am the solution" (p. 38).

Fingeret's (1983, 1984) research clearly challenges deficiency-based theories of literacy. Her work with adult nonreaders suggests that these individuals are neither perceived as deficient by others in their communities nor do they view themselves as deficient. It seems reasonable to assume then that adult nonreaders would be less likely to resist involvement in literacy programs that more closely reflected their own cultural or social values.

In other words, a resister to a program offered by a community college may be quite willing to encounter and learn the same content when it is taught in a community center. In this context, the learner has an investment both in the process of learning and in the community where the instruction is offered.

The Resistance Phenomenon

Quigley's (1987; Beder & Quigley, 1990) analysis of the phenomenon of resistance leads him to note the importance of the resister's values. Also important in Quigley's analysis is the way in which the learner views the consequences of resistance or nonresistance. Quigley deliberately developed his model of resistance through analysis of resistance to education as it appears in literary fiction. This, he asserts, eliminates the inevitable intrusion of the researcher in cross-cultural work—that is, the reactivity between the subjects being analyzed and the process and biases of the researcher. Expanding on Quigley's resistance model and applying it to an analysis of adult literacy programs yields the following conclusions:

1. Resistance may be either overt or subtle, since resisters respond to values imposed upon them in a number of ways. They may enroll in a program but drop out quickly when they perceive a conflict between the program's values and their own. They may quietly conform (or appear to conform) to the values, ethics, and definitions of what constitutes knowledge imposed on them, while waiting to break through institutional constraints. They may stay in educational institutions in order to learn the language of the dominant social group and eventually use this knowledge in educational or political activities designed to strengthen their own group.

2. Resisters may not be resisting the content of the program but may find the values embodied in that program unacceptable. For

example, learning the alphabet in one context may be acceptable but in another, unacceptable.

3. Resisters may find the content irrelevant to their lives. Fingeret (1983) asserts that the ability to read is but one skill that contributes to the exchange of skills in a social network.

4. Resisters are aware of the consequences of resistance and nonresistance. Adults in Fingeret's (1983) research group, for example, knew that if they learned to read, all of the relationships in their social network would shift. Not only would they have less time to participate in their social networks, but their own needs would change.

Adult nonreaders who conform to the educational practices and values expressed by existing literacy programs risk eventual rejection by their own cultural or social groups. Some conform despite pressure from their social, family, or cultural groups because doing so enables them to reconstruct the conditions under which they live, work, and learn.

An Alternative: Community Organizations

Experts argue that the most successful adult literacy programs are those offered by community-based organizations or CBOs (Anorve, 1989; Fingeret, 1983, 1984, 1989; Heaney, 1989; Hunter & Harman, 1985; Ilsley, 1985a, 1985b, 1989; Jurmo, 1989; Kozol, 1985; Zachariadis, 1986). Ilsley (1985b) defines CBOs in terms of six criteria:

1. Community orientation—the program serves a definable constituency, is based locally, and uses indigenous staff.

2. Program independence—the program is independent and autonomous and does not rely on a larger organization (such as a public education system) for managerial guidelines.

3. Underserved populations—the program serves populations who typically do not join more traditional programs because of low reading level or poverty.

4. Student empowerment—program objectives include economic and social self-sufficiency for both students and their communities through measures that promote independence. Here individual achievement and independence are linked with community achievement and independence. Methods by which this is achieved vary considerably, from job-skill training to promoting solidarity among groups effecting social change at the local level.

5. Learner-centered curriculum—the curriculum is based on learners' objectives as opposed to a prescribed set of activities and subject matter. Community-based programs avoid diagnosis, grade-level assignments, and the use of standardized materials. Instead they rely on students' real-life problems and on experiential materials.

6. Learner-centered methodology—methodologies are not didactic nor authoritative in approach.

To be defined as community based, an organization need not necessarily meet all of these six criteria. Heaney (1989) indicates that many modern community-based organizations were originally grounded philosophically in the work of Paulo Freire (1970), who asserts that learning to take control and achieving power are not individual objectives. For poor and dispossessed people, strength is to be found in numbers, and social change is accomplished in unity.

The Freirean liberatory programs that multiplied during the 1970s (Heaney, 1989) gave rise to national networks of liberatory educators who attempted to adapt methods used by Freire in other countries to the ghettos and barrios of North America. These programs occupied storefronts and abandoned schools, for educators in community-based organizations were denied access to funds readily available to schools and community colleges. Yet Heaney asserts that the CBO programs were more effective than those offered by the well-funded institutions, when effectiveness is defined as high enrollment, retention, and completion rates. Heaney states that as long as a program is considered "methodologically distinct but not different in its social and cultural consequences," it is tolerated as a variation on traditional systems of adult literacy education (p. 24). Thus, some CBOs were able to build cooperative relationships with traditional institutions, as well as to apply for government or state funding. These alliances were formed at a high cost to their missions, however, when their emancipatory efforts were blocked by economic sanctions imposed by their institutional sponsors.

Such problems persist today. A visit to a neighborhood CBO serving a community of Spanish-speaking adults in the heart of a large midwestern U.S. city revealed that emancipatory initiatives are blocked if the CBO accepts federal or state funds. The director and one of the founders of this center said she was pondering the eventual consequences of the center's recent acquisition of SLIAG funding (from the State Local Impact Assistance Grant program, jointly sponsored by the Illinois State Board of Education and the United States Immigration and Naturalization Service). Since receiving the SLIAG grant, the center has had to devote much time and energy to meeting federal and state priorities. There are rigid requirements for teacher certification (a problem for this particular center, where former students often become tutors and teachers) and accountability. SLIAG funding prohibits students from doing volunteer work. At this center students have heretofore

taken pride in participating in decision making, as well as in sharing the responsibilities of building upkeep.

The director is grappling with the issue of what has been and will be sacrificed in order to retain SLIAG funding. She remarked that the center had managed with little money prior to obtaining the grant and would survive if its members felt compelled to refuse the funding in future because of state interference with the center's mission. She agrees with Heaney (1989, p. 24) that "cooperation with mainstream educational institutions takes its toll on staff for whom the limited interests of their sponsors dictate priorities and moderate action." There is often little time left for "critical teaching and transforming action" after fulfilling these obligations.

Literacy and Social Change

The missions of successful community-based literacy organizations have typically been linked to issues of empowerment, social mobility, and equality for program participants. In this context, literacy education is focused on humanitarian principles and on raising the ability of learners to participate more fully in a democratic society. Although acquisition of basic entry-level employment skills may be a part of the program, it is not usually the program's sole focus.

By contrast, traditional literacy programs sanctioned and financially supported by the United States government stress literacy for increased workplace productivity and maintenance of the status quo. For many adult nonreaders, that status quo includes a standard of living well below the poverty level.

Federal funds and private donations are readily available for institutionalized literacy programs that typically lack student involvement in goal setting and are laden with institutional values. While some administrators and adult literacy instructors ponder the efficacy of whole language as compared to phonics or skills-based methodologies for teaching adult nonreaders, others express concern regarding the inability of literacy programs to attract and serve large sectors of the nonreading adult population. Ilsley (1985a) theorizes that adult literacy programs such as those offered by many CBOs threaten the established social order because one of their goals is student empowerment.

Community-based organizations are involved in the education of marginalized social and cultural groups, many of whose members belong to racial minorities. Some fear the inevitable social changes that will occur when these groups educate themselves and begin to express values counter to those of the dominant social group.

The United States has traditionally looked for economic returns from its literacy programs. We may do well to ponder the wisdom of Botkin, Elmandjra, and Malitza (1979) who in *No Limits to Learning: Bridging the Human Gap* noted as follows:

> It is neither proper nor necessary to assess such literacy programs in terms of immediate economic returns; while literacy may bring economic advantages in the long run, the most immediate concern is to start a process that leads to increasing human dignity and to breaking the vicious circle of poverty and marginalization (p. 91).

Can we as educators meet the challenge of viewing literacy not only as a technical problem, but as a social and political issue? Will we dedicate our efforts to development and use of superior techniques and methodology for working with adults who are nonreaders? We must without hesitation focus our efforts on eventual resolution of the social and political issues just addressed. We have the energy, means, and enthusiasm with which adult literacy education may be transformed into a vehicle dedicated to the pursuit of equality.

As Heaney (1989) points out, most emancipatory or liberatory literacy programs have been sustained by governments for only a brief time following either a revolution or a declaration of independence. For these programs to proliferate and survive, he counsels that their directors, founders, and teachers must "maintain the vision" and "await the revolution and attempt to prepare learners for political options not yet available" (p. 25).

References

Anorve, R. (1989). Community-based literacy educators: Experts and catalysts for change. In A. Fingeret & P. Jurmo (Eds.), *Participatory literacy education: New directions for continuing education* (Vol. 42, pp. 35–42). San Francisco, CA: Jossey-Bass.

Beder, H., & Quigley, B.A. (1990). Beyond the classroom. *Adult Learning, 1*(5), 19–21, 30.

Botkin, J., Elmandjra, M., & Malitza, M. (1979). *No limits to learning: Bridging the human gap.* Oxford, UK: Pergamon.

Bourdieu, P. (1981). Men and machines. In K. Knorr-Cetina & A. Cicourel (Eds.), *Advances in theory and methodology.* London: Routledge & Kegan Paul.

Fingeret, A. (1983). Social network: A new perspective on independence and illiterate adults. *Adult Education Quarterly, 33,* 133–146.

Fingeret, A. (1984). *Adult literacy education: Current and future directions* (Contract No. 400-81-0035). Columbus, OH: National Center Publications, National Center for Research in Vocational Education. (ED 246 308)

Fingeret, A. (1989). The social and historical context of participatory literacy education. In A. Fingeret & P. Jurmo (Eds.), *Participatory literacy education: New directions for continuing education* (Vol. 42, pp. 5–16). San Francisco, CA: Jossey-Bass.

Freire, P. (1970). *Pedagogy of the oppressed.* New York: Seabury.

Heaney, T. (1989). Freirean literacy in North America: The community-based education movement. *Thresholds in Education. Adult Literacy: Global Perspectives, 15,* 21–26.

Hunter, C.S.J., & Harman, D. (1979). *Adult literacy in the United States.* New York: McGraw-Hill.

Ilsley, P. (1985a). Including educationally deprived adults in the planning of literacy programs. In S.H. Rosenblum (Ed.), *Involving adults in the educational process: New directions for continuing education* (Vol. 26, pp. 33–42). San Francisco, CA: Jossey-Bass.

Ilsley, P. (1985b). *Adult literacy volunteers: Issues and ideas* (Information Series No. 301). Columbus, OH: ERIC Clearinghouse on Adult, Career and Vocational Education. (ED 260 303)

Ilsley, P. (1989). The language of literacy. *Thresholds in Education. Adult Literacy: Global Perspectives, 15,* 6–10.

Jurmo, P. (1989). The case for participatory literacy education. In A. Fingeret & P. Jurmo (Eds.), *Participatory literacy education: New directions for continuing education* (Vol. 42, pp. 17–28). San Francisco, CA: Jossey-Bass.

Kozol, J. (1985). *Illiterate America.* New York: Anchor/Doubleday.

Mezirow, J., Darkenwald, G.G., & Knox, A.B. (1975). *Last gamble on education.* Washington, DC: Adult Education Association.

Quigley, B.A. (1987). *The resisters: An analysis of non-participation in adult basic education.* Unpublished doctoral dissertation, Northern Illinois University, DeKalb, IL.

Zachariadis, C.P. (1986). *Adult literacy: A study of community-based literacy programs* (Vol. 1, study findings and recommendations). Washington, DC: Association for Community Based Education.

Stages in the Reading Development of Adults

CHARLES A. NORMAN
GRACE MALICKY
JANUARY 1987

Can stages be identified in the reading development of adults? The answer to this question has more than theoretical significance since this information could be very useful in planning reading programs for adults.

This article reports a study in which 123 adults, reading at grade levels 1–8, were assessed to determine the strategies they used as they read. Oral reading miscues were analyzed in terms of reading processes and comparisons were made across levels. Results generally revealed two stages of reading development across the levels tested. In the first stage, at reading levels 1–3, the adults relied equally on print-based and language-based strategies as they read, but initially they had difficulty integrating these two knowledge sources. Near the end of the first stage, an increase in integration was evident and this was followed in the second stage, at reading levels 4–8, by a marked increase in the ability of adults to use language knowledge to integrate and to predict as they read.

Stages Among Children

Stages in the reading development of children have frequently been postulated but perhaps the most comprehensive attempt to delineate stages is that undertaken by Chall (1983), who outlined six stages of reading development. Stage 0 is labeled "prereading," and the focus is on meaning, with knowledge-based strategies used to reconstruct stories.

For children, school entrance signals the start of Stage 1, which involves initial reading or decoding and lasts for one or two grade levels. In this stage the reader is "glued to print," focusing on print-based rather than meaning-based processing. Stage 2 is a transition stage occuring at about Grade 3 reading level and is labeled by Chall as "confirmation, fluency, and ungluing from print." The reader begins to integrate print-based and knowledge-based strategies through extensive reading but the major focus is still on decoding. Stage 3, which corresponds to grades 4–9, involves "reading for learning the new." The focus is on meaning and on use of knowledge-based strategies.

Chall's final two stages are also meaning based. Stage 4 occurs from grades 9–12 and involves "reading for multiple viewpoints," and Stage 5 involves "construction and reconstruction" to gain a "world view." While Chall's major focus is on children, she does suggest that Stages 1–5 are appropriate for conceptualizing the reading development of adults.

Jones's Three Adult Stages

Few adult educators have attempted to delineate stages in reading development but Jones (1981) is one exception. He describes three phases which cover a continuum with end points of learning to read and reading to learn. In Phase 1, which involves "using language for reading," the focus is on reading as a language process and on use of knowledge-based strategies. Once the reader has established a basic understanding of what reading is, the focus turns to "refinement of word recognition ability" or print-based strategies in Phase 2. Finally in Phase 3, labeled "reading to learn," the emphasis is on deriving meaning from print with the adult relying heavily on vocabulary and background knowledge.

There is considerable similarity between Chall's Stages 0–3 and Jones's three phases, although Chall does not view Stage 0 as having relevance for adult learners. Neither scheme has been verified by research with adults and in fact there have been few attempts to provide empirical support for any notion of stages in the development of adult literacy. If, as both Jones and Chall suggest, there are instructional implications arising from stages in reading development, the results of research in this area could have considerable significance in planning and implementing programs for adults engaged in literacy programs.

Three Studies of Adults

The possibility of stages in the reading development of adult illiterates was evident in the results of two of our previous studies (Malicky & Norman, 1982, 1983). It appeared that changes in reading strategies were related to level of reading achievement and that it might be possible to identify stages in reading development by analyzing the strategies used by adults at increasing levels of reading proficiency. The purpose of a third study, reported here, was to investigate this possibility.

The sample for the study involved 123 adults reading from grade levels 1–8. They were attending three different literacy programs, one at a vocational center as part of a program in academic upgrading, one at a university as part of a research project, and the final one in a community literacy project sponsored by the provincial government. Hence, a fairly comprehensive cross-section of adults in literacy programs in the area was obtained. Of the 123 adults, 56 were males and 67 were females. They ranged in age from 18 to 63 with the majority in their 20s and 30s.

Each adult read passages increasing in difficulty from a first to an eighth grade reading level. Reading was discontinued when frustration level was reached. Oral reading miscues on all passages except those at frustration level were analyzed using categories from the *Reading Miscue Inventory* (1972): (1) graphic similarity, which reflects print processing; (2) grammatical and (3) semantic acceptability, both reflecting knowledge processing; (4) meaning change; and (5) successful corrections, which are thought to indicate integration of print-based and knowledge-based processes.

A Shift at Level 3 for Adults

Percentage scores were calculated for each adult for each miscue variable and statistical comparisons were made across reading grade levels 1–8. Results revealed a significant change between grades 3 and 4 on three of the miscue variables: grammatical acceptability, semantic acceptability, and meaning change. These results support the hypothesis of two adult stages in reading development. At grade levels 1–3, there was little difference in the ability of adults to use print-based as compared to knowledge-based strategies, but at reading level 4, there was a marked increase in use of language knowledge and to a lesser extent background knowledge to predict words while reading. In other words, an important change at reading grade level 4 involved increased reliance on knowledge-based strategies but little change in relative use of print strategies. Hence, increased reliance on print strategies was not a significant factor in reading proficiency for the adults in this study.

Figure 1
Diagnostic Indicators of Adult Reading Stages

	Adult Stage 1 Print-based processing	Adult Stage 2 Integrative processing
Level of reading:	Able to read material at grade levels 1–3 with adequate comprehension (word identification may be adequate at a higher level).	Able to read material at grade levels 4–8 with adequate comprehension.
Miscue profiles:	Half or more miscues show **graphic** similarity to the stimulus; less than half are **grammatically** acceptable; or the ratio is **50:50.**	At least half the miscues are acceptable grammatically *and* more show **grammatical** acceptability than graphic similarity.

It is important to note, however, that the increased use of meaning-based strategies by more proficient readers was accompanied by an increase in miscues which maintained the author's meaning. Thus, the adults at levels 4–8 not only made greater use of knowledge-based strategies but they were also generally able to integrate these strategies with those for processing print to maintain the author's meaning.

When the results on meaning change were examined more closely, it was apparent that the increase in ability to integrate print-based and knowledge-based strategies, while evident on levels 4–8, began at level 3. What appeared to be happening at reading level 3 was a consolidation or integration of strategies used at earlier levels, with little change in the relative use of either print- or knowledge-based strategies. Correctional behavior, as found in previous studies with adults (Malicky & Norman, 1982, 1983), was not indicative of increased integrative functioning.

Agreement on Two Adult Stages

The two stages identified in this study are similar to those postulated by Jones (1981) and Chall (1983). Adult Stage 1 of reading development is consistent with what Jones referred to as "refinement of word recognition ability" and Chall as "glued to print." Jones notes that the focus for adults at this stage is on word identification, and while that does not preclude use of knowledge-based strategies, it does result in considerable reliance on print. For Chall, this first stage is also print based, and while the adults in our study at reading grade levels 1–3 could not be described as completely "glued to print," they definitely made less use of their background and language knowledge than adults at the second stage of reading proficiency.

The second stage evident in our data, Adult Stage 2, was consistent with what Jones called "reading for learning" and Chall called "reading for new learning." They both described readers at this point as being more concerned with meaning, and this was reflected in our study in an increase in the percentage of miscues with high grammatical and semantic acceptability at Grade 4 reading level. There was also some indication in our data of what Chall referred to as "confirmation, fluency, and ungluing from print." Near the end of our Adult Stage 1, which encompassed reading levels 1–3, a consolidation of reading strategies was evident in the increase in miscues which retained the author's meaning. This ability to integrate print-based and knowledge-based strategies may be necessary before the adult can begin to rely more heavily on his or her language and background knowledge. Without an ability to integrate information sources, an increase in the use of knowledge-based strategies may lead to considerable inaccuracy in reconstruction of an author's meaning rather than to an increase in reading proficiency.

A question which remains unanswered is whether a prereading stage can be identified in adults. A major difference between the positions of Jones and Chall is that Jones feels that a prereading phase is crucial in work with adults who are almost totally illiterate, whereas Chall suggests beginning with decoding. This has important instructional implications, since most current literacy programs, such as Laubach, focus heavily on bottom-up processing, bypassing any prereading stage.

Teaching Adults at Different Stages

The distinction between the two stages of reading identified in this study has implications for planning reading programs for adults. To assist literacy teachers in identifying which stage students have reached, critical differences in reading level and miscue profiles are presented in Figure 1.

Almost everyone would agree that adults at reading levels 1–3 need to develop print-based strategies, but there is a difference of opinion regarding when and how this should be done. Chall suggests that work with illiterate adults should begin with decoding; Jones as well as Rigg and Kazemek (1983) recommend focusing on decoding after the adult becomes aware that reading is communication and knows what written language sounds like.

There is little doubt that the people in our study who were at Adult Stage 1 believed in the power of print-based strategies. This was reflected both in their miscues and in their comments about the importance of "sounds" and "words" in learning to read. Clearly then, some focus in this area is indicated, but in light of the need for adults to integrate print- and meaning-based strategies before they can move to a more advanced stage, it is questionable whether instruction should focus as exclusively or intensively on cues within words as many programs do.

When adults reach Adult Stage 2, at which their major focus is on meaning, Jones and Chall both suggest the need for them to take more responsibility and to a large extent direct their own learning. It is at this stage that adults are able to take full advantage of the extensive knowledge which they bring to the learning situation.

Independence appears to be necessary for this to occur and Thistlewaite (1983) suggests

Figure 2
Patterns of Oral Reading Miscues Among Partially Literate Adults

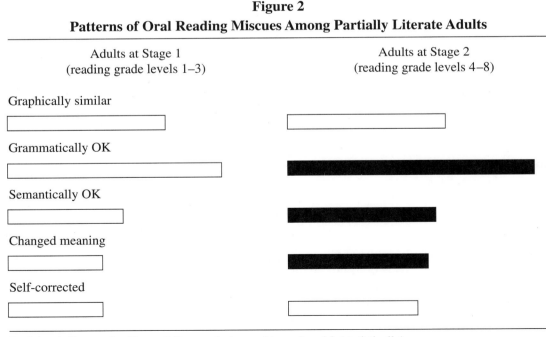

| Adults at Stage 1 (reading grade levels 1–3) | Adults at Stage 2 (reading grade levels 4–8) |

Graphically similar

Grammatically OK

Semantically OK

Changed meaning

Self-corrected

Dark bar indicates significant difference between Stages 1 and 2 (statistically).

that a comprehension-based model of reading provides a means for adults to work independently and take responsibility for their own learning. Without this independence adults may learn how to read but never become "readers."

References

Chall, J.S. (1983). *Stages of reading development.* Toronto: McGraw-Hill.

Jones, E.V. (1981). *Reading instruction for the adult illiterate.* Chicago, IL: American Library Association.

Malicky, G., & Norman, C.A. (1982, May). Reading strategies of adult illiterates. *Journal of Reading, 25,* 731–735.

Malicky, G., & Norman, C.A. (1983). *A comparison of approaches with adult illiterates: Final research report.* Ottawa, ON: Social Sciences and Humanities Research Council.

Reading miscue inventory. (1972). New York: Macmillan.

Rigg, P., & Kazemek, F.E. (1983, Fall). Adult illiteracy in the USA: Problem and solutions. *Convergence, 16,* 32-38.

Thistlewaite, L. (1983, November). The adult disabled reader: An independent learner? *Lifelong Learning, 7,* 16–17, 28.

Theoretical and Organizational Issues

The Reading Concepts and Strategies of Adult Nonreaders

GRACE MALICKY
CHARLES A. NORMAN
DECEMBER 1989

In a recent study, Norman and Malicky (1987) obtained data that provide support for stages in the development of adult literacy. [The report of this study is reprinted in the preceding article.] Two stages were identified for adults reading at grade levels 1 to 8, and these stages appeared to have clear pedagogical implications. What was not evident from the study was the nature of reading concepts and strategies of adults who have not yet reached a Grade 1 level of reading proficiency.

Relatively little attention has been devoted to stages in the literacy development of adults and more particularly to adults who are virtual nonreaders. However, Chall (1983) has outlined six stages in the reading development of children and has hypothesized that these stages are similar for adults, with the exception of the beginning stage. For children

Chall delineated a Stage 0 in which the focus is on meaning and children use knowledge-based strategies to reconstruct stories. She did not hypothesize a corresponding stage for adult illiterates but suggested instead that adults at beginning levels can be more appropriately characterized in terms of her Stage 1, which involves a strong focus on decoding. She describes readers at this stage as "glued to print."

Jones (1981) disagrees with Chall. He feels that the focus of the first stage for adults involves "using language for reading" or, in other words, reading for meaning and using knowledge-based strategies. An examination of most materials developed by publishers for use with adults at the beginning level reveals that they are more consistent with Chall's rather than Jones's hypothesis regarding stages.

The purpose of the study reported here was to explore the nature of illiteracy for adults who have made no or minimal progress in learning to read or write, and to draw implications for planning effective programs for them.

Concepts and Strategies

Several researchers have attempted to determine through interviews how reading is viewed by illiterate adults. When Taylor, Wade, Jackson, Blum, and Gould (1980) interviewed 17 participants in literacy programs in Washington, D.C., they found two general patterns. One group defined reading in terms of decoding proficiency; the other recognized the necessity of integrating the decoding process with comprehension.

Most researchers have found that adult illiterates generally fall into the first group. Gambrell and Heathington (1981), interviewing 28 good and 28 poor adult readers, found a significant difference between the two groups in how they viewed reading. Only 21% of poor readers gave a meaning-centered response, as compared to 79% of good readers. Similar results were obtained by Keefe and Meyer (1980). Of the 100 adult disabled readers they interviewed, 85 perceived reading as processing of words rather than as making meaning. Amoroso (1984) interviewed 44 adults from prison, adult basic education, and alternative high school populations and also found evidence of a restricted view of reading. For most, reading meant operations on words. In a local study by Norman and Malicky (1986), only 2 of 25 adults interviewed recognized the importance of comprehension, but even they viewed it as something apart from reading—e.g., "I can read well but comprehension of vocabulary is low."

None of the studies noted above focused specifically on nonreaders, although it is likely that a small number of adults at very low levels of reading proficiency were included. In addition, few of the researchers related how adults say they read to how they actually do read.

Another line of research has focused on how adults interact with print as they read aloud. In an early study, Raisner (1978) examined the oral reading miscues of adults and found that they focused primarily on print-based cues and made far less use of context. The reading levels of the adults were not reported, so it is impossible to determine whether this was true for adults at all reading levels.

The possibility of differences in reading processing between adults at different stages of development was indicated in two of our early studies on adult literacy (Malicky & Norman, 1982, 1983). In the first, adults in a literacy program who made progress in reading were compared with those who did not. Findings revealed that the no-gain group entered the program demonstrating heavy reliance on print-based processing but limited use of context clues. By the end of the program, this tendency was reversed so that the adults more nearly resembled those in the high-gain group. It was hypothesized that adults needed to rely more heavily on knowledge than on print in order to make gains in achievement.

In the second study, differences were evident between reading strategies of adults at reading grade levels 1–2 as compared to those at levels 3–6. The more proficient readers made more effective use of their knowledge to predict words as they read.

A further study was designed to focus specifically on the question of stages in reading development of adults (Norman & Malicky, 1987). Oral reading miscues and unaided retellings of stories were collected from 123 adults reading at grade levels 1–8 in a variety of literacy programs. Results revealed two stages across these reading levels. In the first stage, at reading grade levels 1–3, the adults relied equally on print-based and knowledge-based strategies as they read. The second stage, which corresponded to reading grade levels 4–8, was indicated by a marked increase in use of language knowledge, with little change in use of print-based cues. However, this study did not include adults below a Grade 1 level of reading achievement and hence did not provide information regarding the strategies of adults who are just beginning to learn to read.

The Adults

Most of the 22 adults in this study were either just entering literacy programs or had been in literacy programs for less than 3 months. Only one adult had been in a literacy program longer, and hence a strong impact of that program on concepts and strategies for reading was considered unlikely. The adults were attending literacy programs in two urban centers and most were urban dwellers. They ranged in age from 20 to 65 with most in the lower age ranges. There were 15 males and 7 females. The group presented a general picture of social and economic disadvantage as reflected in education, employment, and income. Half had either not attended school at all or had gone for less than 4 years. Only two had been to high school. Their parents also had limited education with very few going beyond Grade 6. Only six were employed at the time of the study (even though most were in part-time programs), and only two of these earned more than CAN$10,000 per year.

An examination of backgrounds indicated that 16 of the adults were Canadian born and that of this group, 7 were native Indians. Only one of this native group had gone beyond Grade 3 in school. Of the foreign born, three came from war-ravaged countries and two from poor Caribbean families in which education had been sacrificed for survival. The other two were women of East Indian origin who had had limited educational opportunities prior to coming to Canada. Overall, this group of nonreaders was more disadvantaged than the majority of illiterates as described in the Canadian literacy survey conducted by Southam News (1987).

Assessing Response

Each of the adults in the study was interviewed individually to gather background data and to assess concepts about reading. Questions were adapted from Davis and O'Brien (1985), Paris and Meyers (1981), and Gambrell and Heathington (1981). A series of literacy tasks was used to determine how the adults interacted with print. The first was a task in which familiar print in the environment (store names, product labels, etc.) was presented in three formats: picture context; sign, trademark, or logo in isolation; and typed words in isolation. The adults were asked to tell what each said and how they knew. They were also given a local newspaper and asked to locate and read any parts they could.

The second type of task involved passages containing familiar language of both predictable and unpredictable nature. The predictable, familiar material involved common songs (e.g., "Jingle Bells" and "O Canada"), and the unpredictable material a language experience story generated and dictated by the adult in the testing session.

Finally, the adults were asked to interact with unfamiliar material. Rhymes from *Jazz Chants* (Graham, 1978) were predictable though unfamiliar, and selections from the *Bader Reading and Language Inventory* and *Laubach Way to Reading* provided unpredictable material. The adults were asked to attempt material first without assistance. If they were unable to attempt a piece, it was read first to them orally and then they were asked to try to read it on their own. All but two of them attempted to read at least some of these passages.

Responses on the interview, environmental print tasks, and reading passages were rated in terms of relative use of print-based and knowledge-based information.

Concepts About Reading

When asked why they wanted to learn to read, the adults gave a wide range of answers. Some clearly involved functional literacy— e.g., "if I go places..., so I can read the signs." These reasons seemed to be related to the adults' desire to gain increased control over their lives, and these and several other answers reflected a theme of independence. Said one student, "You feel you could do a lot of things. Like nobody will have to push you or tell you this or that." Some indicated that reading is important to gaining knowledge, but a few recognized the even more profound influence literacy has on our lives—e.g., "This is sorta like a reading world. If you can't read, you're not a part of it, sorta outside."

While their reasons for wanting to learn to read were broad and encompassing, their notions about reading itself were much more restricted. We asked questions such as "Which would be easier to do, read word for word or for the general meaning?" or "When you are reading, what do you do if you don't know a word?" The adults generally gave responses that reflected a concept that print rather than meaning is paramount in reading. On the question about identifying hard words, only two adults gave a response indicating they could use context cues.

Strategies for Reading

All the adults in the study were able to read some of the 24 environmental print items correctly when provided with picture context. The number of items correct ranged from 3 to 20 with a mean of 12.2. The adults did almost as well on the logo format (mean = 11.8) but performed more poorly on the typed print format (mean = 7.4). The relatively high level of accuracy on the logo format suggests that these adults were beginning to use print cues, although certainly the distinctive shapes of the store signs and product labels were of more assistance than the letters and words themselves. On this task, ten of the people performed better on the picture than print format (7-point difference or more), suggesting reliance on picture context (meaning-based) cues. Eleven people performed at a similar level on the two tasks, suggesting use of both print-based and knowledge-based information.

Survey of 22 Adults
Reading at Less Than Grade 1 Level

Mean score in reading 24 environmental print items:

 Picture context, 12.2

 Logo, 11.8

 Print, 7.4

Self-reports on cues used on environmental print task:

 Pictures or experience, 10

 Picture and print, 7

 Print, 4

Nature of oral reading miscues:

 Grammatical in context, 41%

 Meaningful in context, 35%

 Graphically similar to cue, 25%

 Phonically similar to cue, 17%

Performance adequate:

 In a print-based miscue category, 15%

 In a knowledge-based miscue category, 40%

Adequate use of knowledge:

 On predictable passages, 56%

 On LEA stories, 64%

 On unfamiliar, unpredictable passages, 36%

Based on a study of 22 adult urban nonreaders in Canada, age 20–65, 15 male, 7 female, just entering a literacy program or in a program for less than 3 months.

It is interesting to note that self-reports on cues used were relatively consistent with actual performance on this task. Most reported using picture or experiential information ($n = 10$) or both print and picture cues ($n = 7$). Only four reported heavy reliance on print, and this was generally reflected in letter-by-letter naming or sounding. Self-reports to the general questions asked during the interview reflected a far greater print bias than did responses to questions during the environmental print task. Hence, these nonreading adults were much more accurate in reporting their reading strategies when engaged in a specific task and asked to comment on how they did it than when asked more abstract general questions.

When miscues were combined across all passages, there was a clear-cut trend toward greater reliance on knowledge than on print cues. This was reflected in higher scores in the grammatical area (41% of miscues were grammatical in relation to passage context) and in meaningfulness (35% were meaningful in relation to passage meaning) than in categories assessing graphic similarity (25% contained half or more of the letters in the text word) and phonic similarity (17% contained half or more of the sounds in the text word).

When scores for individuals were examined, it was found that over half of the adults met the criterion set for adequacy (40%) on a knowledge-based category, as compared with only 15% who met this criterion on a print-based category. The adult nonreaders in this study were not "glued to print" (Chall, 1983) despite the fact they had reported reliance on print in the interview. Instead, they attempted to make use of the knowledge they brought to the page in their efforts to interact with print.

It was difficult to compare differential strategy use on different materials because of the small number of miscues subjects made on some types of passages. However, there was a trend toward greater use of knowledge-based strategies on predictable and language experience stories than on unpredictable unfamiliar passages, with 56% of the adults demonstrating adequate use of knowledge-based strategies on predictable passages, 64% on language experience stories, but only 36% on the unfamiliar unpredictable passages.

It appears, then, that predictable and language experience materials foster use of knowledge-based strategies. While use of unfamiliar, unpredictable passages did result in somewhat greater use of print cues, only about one-fifth of the adults made adequate use of these cues and half were unable to adequately use either knowledge or print cues on that type of material.

Implications

The results of this study provide support for Jones's (1981) contention that the first stage in reading development of adults involves using language for reading. Only two of the adults in this study focused heavily on print and these were both Lebanese immigrants, one of whom was in a Laubach literacy program at the time. In relation to concepts about reading, quite different results were obtained when adults were asked in general terms about how they read when compared to what they said when completing a specific task or what they did when actually attempting to read various types of passages. The results on general questions were similar to results obtained by others (Amoroso, 1983; Gambrell & Heathington, 1981).

Brown (1980) has suggested that metacognitive deficiencies "are the problem of the novice, regardless of age" (p. 475). However, the metacognitive abilities of the adults in this study were adequate when they were asked to do a specific literacy task and comment on how they did it. This has implications for both researchers and those assessing the literacy concepts of adults entering literacy programs.

In an earlier article (Norman & Malicky, 1986), we suggested that instruction for adults in the early phase of literacy development should focus on whole language rather than on isolated words and letters. The results of this study provide further support for whole language programs. We believe that programs should begin with and take advantage of what the adults already know. Without

prompting, most adults in this study spontaneously relied on their knowledge as they approached environmental print tasks and all types of passages. The material most conducive to use of knowledge-based strategies, however, involved language experience and predictable passages.

Results of this study provide support for the suggestion of many (Jones, 1981; Newton, 1980; Rigg & Kazemek, 1983; Schneiderman, 1978) that the language experience approach be used for adult beginning readers. The unfamiliar unpredictable passages found in many of the widely used beginning literacy programs appear to be less appropriate for adults at a beginning stage of reading development.

Perhaps the most significant implications of this study, however, derive not from the results on concepts and strategies for reading but rather from the nature of the nonreaders themselves. These adults were far more disadvantaged than adults who attend postsecondary institutions and even than most of those who become involved in adult basic education programs. Chronic poverty and unemployment were pervasive aspects of their lives, with many viewing literacy as a means to greater control, increased independence, and also a greater sense of self-worth and belonging. These goals provide further support for a language experience approach, as it begins by acknowledging and valuing what adults already know and provides the opportunity for daily concerns and problems to serve as the content of literacy classes. Language experience stories need to be supplemented by functional literacy activities, however, so that adults can gain control over specific aspects of their lives involving print.

Finally, in order to enlarge self or, in Bhola's (1981) words, to enter the "magical circle of the literate," adult nonreaders need to read a range of other material as well. In the beginning, the use of predictable material such as poetry will foster use of knowledge-based strategies as well as introduce a significant part of the literate culture.

What will be critical as well, considering the degree of deprivation reflected in the lives of most of the adults in this study, is awareness that literacy programs alone are not the solution to the social and economic problems of most adults at beginning levels of literacy. As several writers (Hunter & Harman, 1979; Lind & Johnston, 1986; Ryan, 1985) have pointed out, literacy programs need to be part of a more comprehensive solution; this is particularly true for adults at early stages of reading development.

References

Amoroso, H.C. (1984). *Adult concepts and assumptions about literacy*. Paper presented at the conference of the American Educational Research Association, New Orleans, LA.

Bader, L.A. (1983). *Bader reading and language inventory*. London: Collier Macmillan Publishers.

Bhola, H.S. (1981). Why literacy can't wait: Issues for the 1980s. *Convergence, 14,* 32–38.

Brown, A.L. (1980). Metacognitive development and reading. In R.J. Spiro, B.C. Bruce, & W.F. Brewer (Eds.), *Theoretical issues in reading comprehension* (pp. 453–502). Hillsdale, NJ: Erlbaum.

Chall, J.S. (1983). *Stages of reading development*. Toronto: McGraw-Hill.

Davis, N., & O'Brien, M. (1985). *Literacy programs and their participants in the Halifax-Metro area*. Halifax, NS: Mount Saint Vincent University.

Gambrell, L.B., & Heathington, B.S. (1981). Adult disabled readers' metacognitive awareness about reading tasks and strategies. *Journal of Reading Behavior, 13,* 215–222.

Graham, C. (1978). *Jazz chants*. New York: Oxford University Press.

Hunter, C.S., & Harman, D. (1979). *Adult illiteracy in the United States*. New York: McGraw-Hill.

Jones, E.V. (1981). *Reading instruction for the adult illiterate*. Chicago, IL: American Library Association.

Keefe, D., & Meyer, V. (1980). Adult disabled readers: Their perceived models of the reading process. *Adult Literacy and Basic Education, 4,* 120–124.

Lind, A., & Johnston, A. (1986). *Adult literacy in the third world: A review of objectives and strategies*. Paper presented for the Institute of International Education, University of Stockholm.

Malicky, G., & Norman, C.A. (1982). Reading strategies of adult illiterates. *Journal of Reading, 25,* 731–735.

Malicky, G., & Norman, C.A. (1983). *A comparison of approaches with adult illiterates: Final research report*. Ottawa, ON: Social Sciences and Humanities Research Council.

Newton, E.S. (1980). Andragogy: Understanding the adult as a learner. In S. Johnson (Ed.), *Reading and the adult learner* (pp. 3–6). Newark, DE: International Reading Association.

Norman, C.A., & Malicky, G. (1986). Literacy as a social phenomenon: Implications for instruction. *Lifelong Learning, 9,* 12–15.

Norman, C.A., & Malicky, G. (1987). Stages in the reading development of adults. *Journal of Reading, 30,* 302–307.

Paris, S.G., & Meyers, M.M. (1981). Comprehension monitoring, memory, and study strategies of good and poor readers. *Journal of Reading Behavior, 13,* 5–22.

Raisner, B. (1978). Adult reading strategies: Do they differ from the strategies of children? *Reading World, 18,* 37–47.

Rigg, P., & Kazemek, F. (1983). Adult illiteracy in the USA: Problem and solutions. *Convergence, 16,* 32–38.

Ryan, J. (1985). Some key problems in adult literacy. *Prospects, 15,* 375–381.

Schneiderman, P. (1978). Active reading techniques system (ARTS): A method for instruction of functionally illiterate adults. *Urban Education, 13,* 195–202.

Southam News. (1987). *Literacy in Canada: A research report*. Toronto: Creative Research Group.

Taylor, N., Wade, P., Jackson, S., Blum, I., & Gould, L. (1980). A study of low-literate adults: Personal, environmental and program considerations. *Urban Review, 12,* 69–77.

Some Assumptions About Adult Reading Instruction

R. Baird Shuman
January 1989

Mark has just earned a master's degree in reading at a U.S. urban university in the west coast city in which he has been a public school teacher for the past decade. His career began in an inner-city middle school where he taught English and social studies for 3 years. He soon realized that his students were not in a position to learn much about English or social studies because most of them could not read the textbooks designated for their grade levels.

When Mark was assigned to teach social studies in a high school in the same district, he found his students were still plagued with reading problems that blocked their access to the ideas around which he wanted his course to be structured, and as he had in the middle school, he soon turned himself into a teacher of reading. He felt ill equipped to teach reading, having had only one reading course during his undergraduate education. He decided that if he was to teach successfully, he had to learn more than he knew about the basic skills of communication, so he entered a master's degree program in reading.

Now, with 10 years of teaching and a master's degree behind him, Mark felt better able to meet the needs of his students. He realized that while he was trying to help students improve their reading ability, he had to seek out material in which mature ideas were presented in a form his students could deal with. He knew that he had to engage them intellectually if he was ever to teach them either subject matter or reading skills.

He also acknowledged that some students with more severe reading problems would need special attention. He wanted to create an atmosphere in his classroom that would make his students feel secure and positive in their approach to learning. By now he had overcome the initial discipline problems that face most new teachers, and he looked upon himself as an effective teacher who could make a difference in the way students learn. It was at this point that the school principal asked Mark if he would be interested in teaching two sections of a district-sponsored adult reading class, "Improving Reading Efficiency," that was to meet at a local community college. Each class would enroll no more than 15 students and would meet for one hour two evenings a week for 16 weeks. Mark welcomed the opportunity to work with adults, and before the first session, he wrote down some assumptions about the adult learners he planned to teach. Mark's assumptions, followed by a comment he made about each at the end of the semester, are presented here.

Mark's Assumptions

Assumption 1: These students are well aware of their reading problems and will be eager to remedy them. The reading level of my adult students ranged from Grade 2 to Grade 10. The greatest problem I faced was in getting them to admit that they had reading problems. The fact that they enrolled in this class indicated that they felt a need to do something to improve their reading abilities. The weakest readers, however, were deeply ashamed of their inability to read and did everything they could to mask it, as they had been forced to do throughout their adult lives. Many who could not read a newspaper with real comprehension always carried one with them and sat before class with the paper open, appearing to read it. I made the mistake of calling on some of these apparent readers to read aloud in class and found that they could not do so. My calling on them embarrassed them and I soon learned that when reading aloud is appropriate, it is best to ask for volunteers. If no one volunteers, teachers are well advised to read to the class themselves.

Assumption 2: Teaching classes that are half the size of my high school classes will be easy. I soon learned that although my classes were relatively small, they were extremely complex. The broad range of abilities among my students presented a major challenge. I found that 14 of my 30 students had reading problems directly related to interference from the dialects they spoke naturally. Three different major English dialects—black, Chicano, and Asian American—were represented. Eleven students were nonnative speakers of English, and their native language backgrounds included Romance, Germanic, Slavic, Arabic, Indic, and Oriental languages. Each language group had different identifiable types of learning and reading problems in English. I soon found that although some

of these foreign students had scored low on the pretest, they were adequate readers in their own languages, so their pretest scores were misleading.

Assumption 3: These students will be well motivated to learn. To a large extent this assumption proved reasonable. These students, with the exception of two who attended class to meet the conditions of their probations, had chosen the class voluntarily. The title of the course, "Improving Reading Efficiency," was selected so that those who took it would not have to admit by their enrollment that they were deficient readers. When they registered, test scores were used to divert students who read reasonably well into a course that emphasized increasing one's reading speed and comprehension, entitled "Advanced Reading." Despite my students' inherent motivation, however, I soon realized that some of them had worked at demanding jobs for such long hours during the day that they dozed in class. I assumed correctly that if I could encourage them to move around rather than just sit at their desks, they would be more likely to stay awake and accomplish something.

Assumption 4: These students, because they are well motivated, will present no discipline problems. This assumption was largely correct, although I was faced with having to decide what to do when a student dozed off. Besides providing opportunities for sleepy students to move around, I found that I had to make a conscious effort to keep the room well ventilated so the physically spent students would not be breathing stale air for an hour. I had to move quickly from one classroom activity to another to keep interest high and to add as much variety as I could to the course.

I faced some problems I had not anticipated. As students came to know and trust me, they began to tell me things that I was not comfortable in hearing. I became sort of a father confessor for a chronic shoplifter and was uncomfortable in the role. One student told me that she couldn't stand to hear her baby cry, and she beat it whenever it did. She realized that she needed help, and I suggested how she might obtain it. Many of my students had few people with whom they could talk about their lives and frustrations, so they would come to me using some element of their work as a pretext, but they would then divert our conference into something not related to the course. At times this robbed me of the opportunity to give other students the kind of individual attention they required. I soon had to learn how to get our conferences back on track without alienating students who wanted to talk about their problems. Although I had no overt discipline problems with these two classes, I had to assert my leadership to keep some elements of the situation from deteriorating to the point that learning was affected adversely.

Assumption 5: These students will have a positive attitude toward school. This generalization was true for about half of my students. The other half were school dropouts whose memories of school were unpleasant. Anything that reminded them of their past school experiences stood in the way of their learning. For this group, I had to create learning situations that were far removed from those I would have sought to create in my regular teaching position. Adult students with negative attitudes about school are better at obscuring them than high school students are, but the attitudes can exist, nevertheless. I found as I came to know my students well that many of them had had to work hard to overcome their negative attitudes before enrolling in the course. Several had enrolled because they were called upon to read at

work and could not afford to acknowledge their inability to do so.

Some parents could not help their children with school work unless they could read. Several admitted to me having shouted at or even hit their children when badgered to help them do their school work. They did not want the children to know they couldn't read, so they yelled things like "Do your own damn homework" or "You gotta learn to do your own work, you lazy good-for-nothing!" Giving their children a hard whack immediately diverted attention from the parents' inability to read to the injustice of the punishment and to their children's reaction to it.

Assumption 6: Every adult can read to some extent. Although this assumption proved largely true, I found that two of my American-born students initially were virtually unable to deal with the written word at any level. To try to understand how they coped and how they projected the impression of being able to read, I thought back to the time I had been in a small town in Japan. I could read no Japanese, and the English-language assists I had depended upon in Tokyo and Kyoto were not available to me. I had to depend on nonprint clues for all the information I processed, and I quickly became expert in using every nonprint source available so that I could function in that milieu, in which I found myself to be an illiterate.

The two students who seemed to be virtually unable to read were far from stupid. They had honed their senses to the point of being able to extract meaning from every nuance, from every nonprint source, and they were able to function pretty well as long as they were not called upon specifically to read. In teaching them, I had to start from point zero as far as print media were concerned, but their maturity level was high, so we could have mature discussions. I showed my genuine respect for their intelligence. It took great tact to lead them into reading while never acknowledging to them that I knew they could not read. Other nonreaders can read words but read so slowly and with so much difficulty that they cannot comprehend and are, therefore, dependent upon nonprint sources for their information.

Assumption 7: If I can find interesting books, I can teach anyone to read. The problem word in this assumption is *books.* People with reading problems equate books with defeat. I soon learned that I had to use every means available to me to get students to read from sources that enable one to absorb information without realizing that actual reading is taking place. Because they abound in nonprint clues, I found signs, advertisements, catalogs, automobile repair manuals, cereal boxes, cans of fruit and vegetables, and other such props good starting points for readers who are severely disabled.

I soon learned that my students succeeded best if several of their senses were simultaneously engaged in the reading process. I discovered that if students could listen to a tape of someone reading, could follow the printed text of what the person was reading by running their index finger along the lines of the text, and in time could come to read along with the person on the tape, they were challenged by what they were doing. The situation was a competitive one, but students were competing only with themselves, and they rose to the challenge. A more advanced step in this process is for individual students to play the tape for the first paragraph or two, then to turn the volume all the way down and continue to read the text for two or three paragraphs before turning the volume up again to see whether they have kept pace with the reader on the tape.

Similar Assumptions

People who teach reading to adults commonly make assumptions about their students similar to Mark's. Often it takes only two or three class sessions for them to realize that their initial assumptions are not all valid. Certainly those who teach reading to adults, most of whom have fragile egos and are ashamed at not being able to read easily, have to recognize the assumptions and prejudgments they have made about their students. They have to be vigorous in challenging these assumptions and prejudgments as they face the realities of the adult classroom. Researchers in the field constantly challenge the same sorts of assumptions in order to point the way to new and better ways of dealing with adult literacy than have emerged from the old assumptions educators and the public have held. Encouraging headway has been made in such programs as The Adult Performance Level Project (APL), sponsored by the U.S. Office of Education in the 1970s.

Freire, long an advocate of the oppressed, considers illiteracy to be "one of the concrete expressions of an unjust social reality." He calls illiteracy "not a strictly linguistic or exclusively pedagogical or methodological problem [but rather] political, as is the very literacy through which we try to overcome illiteracy" (1985, p. 10). Undeniably, literacy has generally been defined in our society to suit political ends. Yet, as Kazemek and others have pointed out, it is difficult to speak categorically about what illiteracy is (Freire, 1970, 1985; Kazemek, 1985a, 1985b; Levine, 1982).

Functional Competency

The APL Project concluded that the notion of competency, broadly speaking, is meaningless unless it is placed within a cultural context. The project discovered that functional competency is bifurcated: it involves a set of skills such as reading or writing and a knowledge base as well, such as legal or medical or financial knowledge. Certainly the latter of these two branches in essence represents the philosophical stand of Hirsch in *Cultural Literacy: What Every American Needs to Know* (1987), which has stirred such heated controversy.

The APL Project found that adult competency has as much to do with social requirements at a specific time in the development of a society as with the individual abilities of its populace. The project also discovered that "functional competency is directly related in a mathematical sense to success in adult life." Northcutt calls this "an operating assumption which underlies all APL research activities" (1975, p. 3), and this conclusion seems indisputable when one considers that functional literacy is measured most frequently by three criteria: level of education, annual income, and occupational status.

Levine insists that no empirical measurements exist for deciding which standards might be used to define functional literacy for whole societies. He contends that functional literacy "seems to require a preexisting notion of functionality" (1982, p. 260).

Another misapprehension about adult literacy is that it can develop quickly given the proper circumstances. Kazemek, questions this assumption: "Admittedly, a 30-year-old brings a tremendous amount of world knowledge, language facility, and so forth to the reading and writing processes that a 10-year-old does not." But "learning to read different texts for different purposes and learning to play the whole range in writing take time, experience, feedback, and developing awareness" (1985b, pp. 332–333).

Kazemek insists that adults with literacy problems do not become literate in 6 months. He reminds his reader that Goethe at the end of his life still considered himself to be engaged in learning how to read, indicating that Goethe's definition of literacy was quite different from most definitions today.

An Inner Struggle

Probably no level of reading instruction is more engaging and rewarding than that found in adult reading classes, with their highly diverse populations of students who realize more fully than almost anyone else in our society how important it is to be able to read. Most of these students have not had easy lives. They risk a great deal when they come to an adult reading class. They are willing to do so, however, because they are convinced that learning to read will provide them with the means for a more fulfilling life. As adult students, they come out of the closet, as it were, because many of them have been masking their illiteracy or limited literacy for a long time, and going to classes like Mark's exposes it.

Sometimes the first meeting of such a class is the culmination for them of an inner struggle that has gone on for years. The teacher who realizes the social dynamics at work in classes of adults who have reading problems is in an admirable position to give these people the encouragement they need to be more accepting of themselves and to be more productive in society. Teachers who build on what their adult students know and on the greatly varied life experiences they bring with them will help their students to develop and build on their strengths while they begin simultaneously to pay less and less attention to their weaknesses. In time, through effective tutelage, adults who want to become efficient readers will do so, but often not within the time frame they anticipate or we expect. The key to helping these students learn how to read is to allow them their dignity at all times and to respect the aspirations that have brought them into a setting in which many of them initially feel terribly threatened.

Cervero reminds his readers that adult "literacy is not something that can be measured in an absolute sense, such as body weight" (1985, p. 50). He concludes that "the effort to achieve a common definition would not be a technical process aimed at discovering the objectively best definition of literacy. Rather, it should be viewed as a clash of competing value positions, ideologies, and power structures" (p. 54).

It cannot be denied that adult literacy is, as Cervero and others cited in this article attest, a politically charged issue. The realization of this fact, however, cannot be the excuse for us to forget that those who try to teach adults to read are dealing with individuals whose need is great, whose motivation is real. In the last analysis, what Eugene O'Neill designates "the human equation" will count for them more than any element in their learning of the skills we need to teach them.

References

Cervero, R.M. (1985, Fall). Is a common definition of adult literacy possible? *Adult Education Quarterly, 36*, 50–54.

Freire, P. (1970, May). The adult literacy process as cultural action for freedom. *Harvard Educational Review, 40*, 205–225.

Freire, P. (1985). *The politics of education: Culture, power, and liberation.* South Hadley, MA: Garvey.

Hirsch, E.D., Jr. (1987). *Cultural literacy: What every American needs to know.* Boston, MA: Houghton Mifflin.

Kazemek, F.E. (1985a, October). An examination of the Adult Performance Level Project and its effects upon adult literacy education in the United States. *Lifelong Learning, 9*, 24–28.

Kazemek, F.E. (1985b, January). Functional literacy is not enough: Adult literacy as a developmental process. *Journal of Reading, 28*, 332–335.

Levine, K. (1982, May). Functional literacy: Fond illusions and false economics. *Harvard Educational Review, 52*, 249–266.

Northcutt, N.W. (1975). *Adult functional literacy: A summary.* Austin, TX: University of Texas.

Theoretical and Organizational Issues

Adult Literacy in Rural Areas

Susan T. Ferrell
Aimee Howley
February 1991

Adult illiteracy is a persistent concern, but one that varies with the economic and political climate. In the United States, policymakers express greatest concern when the need for economic development or recoupment seems most pressing. A similar response occurs in Third World countries. There, an even more direct link is made between economic productivity and literacy.

Since many policymakers identify adult literacy as a condition for economic development, their concern is often directed toward the literacy skills of a nation's most impoverished citizens, those with the most visible need to improve their economic well-being. Although many such citizens live in inner-city neighborhoods, many others live in remote rural communities. In the U.S. as well as in numerous Third World countries, the rates of adult illiteracy are highest in rural areas (Behrstock, 1981; Hunter & Harman, 1979). For a variety of reasons, however, literacy programs may be difficult to sustain in rural areas.

This article examines the current status of adult literacy programs in rural areas. Relying primarily on works that consider two topics, adult literacy and rural adult education, the article synthesizes the issues that confront rural literacy workers. We examine four key questions: (1) What goals do rural adult literacy programs espouse? (2) What are the needs of adult illiterates in rural areas? (3) What types of programs are reported to be effective? (4) Which conditions support—or limit—the widespread influence of effective programs?

Goals of Adult Literacy Programs

Why do educators, policymakers, and political reformers all stress the importance of adult literacy? According to Knox (1987), adult basic education—including literacy instruction—serves one of four purposes: to promote economic productivity, to underwrite political change, to effect social equity, or to enhance quality of life.

In the U.S., literacy efforts on behalf of rural citizens most frequently address the first of these purposes. Akenson (1984) traces this theme in his comparison of the Southern Literacy Campaign (1910–1935) with current efforts in the rural South. "Industrial efficiency" was a watchword of earlier programs;

today similar results are expected from programs that prepare rural workers for the "information age." Throughout their history, such literacy efforts have emphasized one outcome: improved rural economies (Akenson, 1984).

Another goal of literacy efforts—particularly in the Third World—has been to support political reform or national unity. Muller (1986) cites developing nations in which governments have used literacy initiatives as a way to instill citizens with a sense of national identity. The work of political activists like Brazilian educator Paulo Freire characterizes this approach. By enabling peasants to give labels to their feelings of oppression and anger, literacy campaigns of this sort involve citizens in the determination of their own political destinies. Recent arguments (e.g., Aronowitz & Giroux, 1985) suggest that such efforts might improve the plight of the underclass in more highly developed nations as well.

Closely allied to the political aim of literacy work is the goal of promoting social equity, a goal that faces a particularly troublesome challenge. Literacy workers have noted that the nation's poorest citizens, whether rural or urban, are those least likely to participate in programs (Quigley, 1990). Consequently, literacy efforts may actually widen the gap between the haves and the have nots. According to some writers, this effect does not occur often—even the poorest citizens acquire incremental benefits as a result of the increased literacy of their more fortunate neighbors. Cameron (1987) reasons that "both participators and nonparticipators gain economically. As programs prepare better qualified and motivated people for occupational advancement, lower level jobs become available for less skilled or less experienced workers" (p. 175).

A final perspective on adult literacy, however, rejects this logic. Proponents like Kozol (1985) see literacy as a worthy end in itself. They interpret literacy—like oral language—as the birthright of all humans, and they stress the role of literacy in cultivating human potential. From this perspective, all political, economic, and social improvements depend on *universal* literacy.

Literacy Needs of Adults in Rural Areas

Though educators attempt to draw a profile of the adult illiterate, generalizing to all such members of the population is unwarranted. Just as communities vary, so do the needs of the people within those communities—both rural and urban. There are, however, some recurring characteristics that can be used to describe the rural adult learner in contrast to an urban counterpart.

Rural residents often do not value formal education (Theobald, 1988). These prevailing attitudes originated at a time when the local economy required that even relatively young children be available for work on farms, in fisheries, and in the mines (Butterworth & Dawson, 1952; Duncan & Moyer, 1981). Moreover, the curriculum offered in schools was not perceived as a means of attaining more desirable forms of work or of improving work skills (for example, see Duncan & Moyer, 1981). Even today, when rural economies are considerably more complicated, rural residents sometimes overlook the benefits of formal education.

As a result of the place accorded formal schooling in many rural communities, rural adults usually have spent less time in school than their urban counterparts (Behrstock, 1981; Sher, 1978). They have completed fewer years in school and these years likely have contained fewer required days (Butterworth & Dawson, 1952). Consequently, rural adults may lag in the basic skills of reading, writing, and mathematics (compare to Noor, 1982).

Rural adults also have access to fewer community services (Bhola, 1981). Because of their lower tax base, rural communities have fewer resources (Sher, 1978); but because of the poverty in many rural areas, such communities actually need extensive services. In addition, geographical constraints make it difficult for rural residents to make use of services that are available (Bhola, 1981). The rural adult who maintains one and sometimes two jobs has time constraints that make it difficult for him or her to travel to urban areas where better services—including education—might be found (Treadway, 1984).

Considering these general characteristics of rural adults, what factors should be considered when developing a literacy program in a rural area? Numerous authors (for example, see Hunter & Harman, 1979; Lucas, 1985; Treadway, 1984) have concluded that rural adults need a program based in the community. A program of this sort is self-generated and -sustaining because it depends on the continuous involvement of the individuals whom it serves (Noor, 1982). A community-based program is owned by its participants and is responsive to their needs.

Not only do rural adults want to be involved in planning and directing education programs, they want education to be relevant to their situations (Noor, 1982). In most cases, therefore, they need programs that go beyond basic literacy to provide continued job training and retraining. Without extensive practical training, rural adults may continue to lack the skills necessary for access to economic and social opportunities within the community. Moreover, some rural residents want community-based education programs that give them access to opportunities outside of their communities. Optimally such programs ensure some measure of job security by increasing the competitive advantage of rural residents (for example, see Nickerson, 1985).

Rural Programs to Improve Adult Literacy

Literacy programs in rural areas vary in accordance with the definitions of literacy they adopt. Chall, Heron, and Hilferty (1987) identify three types of programs that define literacy in different ways. Volunteer programs work mainly with *illiterate* adults. These programs address the needs of adults who read below the fourth grade level. Competency-based programs work with adults who already have elementary reading skills but who need to acquire more advanced academic skills in order to be functionally literate by modern standards. These programs tend to define functional literacy as the minimal skill necessary to receive a high school degree or its equivalent (for example, the GED or General Equivalency Diploma).

Fingeret (1984, p. 23) describes programs of these first two types as "individually oriented." She faults them for approaching adult illiteracy as deficits of individual persons. These programs, she claims, offer instruction that emphasizes reading skills in isolation from their meaningful context.

Both Chall, Heron, and Hilferty and Fingeret distinguish the first two types of programs from community-oriented programs. These seem more consistent with the needs that rural residents express. Rather than ascribing value to just one kind of learning, community-oriented programs assume that adults can determine their own learning needs based on the norms of the communities in which they live. Community-oriented pro-

grams, therefore, provide instruction that may or may not have an academic focus.

A variety of postliteracy opportunities supplement and enhance the effectiveness of the three basic types of literacy programs. Postliteracy programs offer those who are newly literate the chance to continue their education, practice newly acquired skills, and effect positive changes in their lives (Ouane, 1982). Such programs are extremely important for sustaining literacy gains in rural areas, especially when limited economic opportunities keep literate adults from applying their new skills in more challenging jobs. When adult students see literacy as worthy in itself, they may be more likely to maintain and develop their literacy, whatever the local economic situation.

Recognizing that technology increases the potential to reach adults in rural areas, programs both in the United States and in the Third World attempt to incorporate out-of-school strategies using media—films, newspapers, radio programs, records, audiotapes, periodicals, and satellite broadcasts—to reach the target population. In addition, some literacy and postliteracy programs have direct ties to business and industry, and others make use of resources available in two- and four-year colleges (Chall, Heron, & Hilferty, 1987; Hone, 1984).

• *Rural literacy projects in the United States.* Among adult literacy programs in rural areas, some offer a single service (Lucas, 1985). Alaska's *Centralized Correspondent Study Handbook for Grades 1–12*, for example, provides the framework through which rural residents can complete correspondence course work at no charge. Teleteacher, a telephone-based system in Virginia, enables rural residents to have access to academic assistance 24 hours a day.

Other rural literacy programs provide a variety of services (Lucas, 1985). An Alabama program uses a statewide educational television network, learning centers, and home tutors as three different ways to reach adults in rural areas. A weekend program in New Jersey offers a variety of counseling services, sponsors independent study projects, and administers subject area examinations.

Some extensive projects offer a wide range of services to a large clientele (Lucas, 1985). Project Communi-Link, for example, reaches 26 selected rural communities in 14 western U.S. states. An inter-organization linkage system, this project works to help rural communities improve the social and economic well-being of residents through expanded opportunities for Adult Basic Education (ABE) and GED preparation. Two Pennsylvania projects, Regional Utilization of Resources to Aid Literacy (RURAL) and Grass Roots Alternative Diploma Study (GRADS) also exemplify this approach.

• *International projects.* Though interest in promoting literacy is gaining momentum in the developing world, such efforts vary widely in scope, content, and ideological purpose. Noor (1982) claims that many of these programs have a single focus: they are designed to fulfill particular objectives of their sponsors—religious institution, employer, or public service agency. He describes other programs—those directed toward a mass audience—as nationalist in focus and dependent on the support of the political hierarchy.

Literacy programs range from beginning literacy training to postliteracy and continuing education. The majority of students are from among the rural poor. They are often malnourished, have high fertility rates and short life expectancy, and are in poor health (Fisher, 1982). Programs such as ones in India and Thailand focus particularly on educating rural women (Naik, 1982), but many programs that serve women have limited effectiveness. Social conventions in some countries restrict women's access to education and narrow the range of instructional options available to them (Clark, 1983).

Delivery systems vary among regions and, within a region, from country to country. Among such programs, there is use of both trained and untrained teachers, use of varied sites including private households and learning centers, and inconsistency in conducting program evaluations. In some instances there is reliance on technology, as with Pakistan's functional literacy efforts.

One major problem of literacy programs in the Third World is the difficulty in selecting a specific language for literacy instruction (Noor, 1982). Many countries have as many as 300–400 different languages in use. When the program imposes instruction in a language that differs from the native language of its clients, it may be perceived to be irrelevant or—in some instances—suspect (Ouane, 1982).

The hope that improved literacy and postliteracy skills will eventually lead to a change in attitudes and a change in living and working conditions remains part of most programs. According to Muller (1986), countries committed to bringing about change in their socioeconomic system (for example, Vietnam, China, Cuba, Burma, Tanzania, Ethiopia, and Iraq) are more likely to develop and offer successful postliteracy and continuing education programs for newly literate adults.

Conditions for Effective Programs

Literacy programs—even those claimed to be effective—have had a limited influence on adult literacy rates in rural areas. Some conditions limit the scope, and sometimes threaten the survival, of such programs. Inadequate funding reduces the possible impact of literacy initiatives (Kozol, 1985). The funding that does exist may be divided among a variety of agencies, all competing for a share (Chall, Heron, & Hilferty, 1987). These agencies base their claims on the superior effectiveness of their own programs (for example, see Kitz, 1988). This competition makes it difficult for such agencies to coordinate their efforts and, on occasion, results in one agency attempting to undermine the efforts of another (for example, see Chall, Heron, & Hilferty, 1987; Taylor, 1989).

Moreover, the implicit goal of many rural literacy programs—to increase the economic productivity of rural regions—poses a threat to even the most effective programs. Despite this implicit goal, these programs tend to define their effectiveness in terms of increased literacy, not economic improvement. If the advertised economic benefits fail to develop, these programs may lose the support of their external funding sources.

In spite of difficulties, however, some rural literacy programs manage to persist. These programs often share certain features. Hone's (1984) analysis of effective rural programs suggests some reasons why: effective adult programs address local needs, satisfy the expectations of their clients, entail cooperation among agencies, and advertise their benefits in clear language.

Several authors (e.g., Kozol, 1985; Noor, 1982) emphasize an additional source of success. Involving community members in the development, promotion, and evaluation of literacy programs gives rural residents a stake in making these programs work.

References

Akenson, J.E. (1984, November). *The Southern Literacy campaign 1910–1935: Lessons for adult learning in an information society*. Paper presented at the National Adult Education Conference, Louisville, KY. (ED 252 726)

Aronowitz, S., & Giroux, H. (1985). *Education under siege*. South Hadley, MA: Bergin & Garvey.

Behrstock, J. (1981). Reaching the rural reader. *Journal of Reading, 24*(8), 712–718.

Bhola, H.S. (1981). Planning rural vocational and adult education: A multiframework megamodel. *Viewpoints in Teaching and Learning, 57*(3), 91–101.

Butterworth, J., & Dawson, H. (1952). *The modern rural school*. New York: McGraw-Hill.

Cameron, C. (1987). Adult education as a force toward social equity. *Adult Education Quarterly, 37*(3), 173–177.

Chall, J.S., Heron, E., & Hilferty, A. (1987). Adult literacy: New and enduring problems. *Phi Delta Kappan, 69*(3), 190–196.

Clark, E.J. (1983, March). *Improving the status of women in the Third World: A challenge to adult educators*. Paper presented at the Annual Conference of the Comparative and International Education Society, Atlanta, GA. (ED 235 349)

Duncan, J.A., & Moyer, H. (1981). *Agricultural, social and educational change in rural Wisconsin 1953–1973*. Madison, WI: College of Agriculture, University of Wisconsin-Madison. (ED 205 339)

Fingeret, A. (1984). *Adult literacy education: Current and future directions*. Columbus, OH: ERIC Clearinghouse on Adult, Career, and Vocational Education. (ED 246 308)

Fisher, E.A. (1982). Illiteracy in context. *Prospects, 12*(2), 155–162.

Hone, K.A. (1984). *Serving the rural adult: Inventory of model programs in rural adult postsecondary education*. Manhattan, KS: Kansas State University, University for Man. (ED 256 527)

Hunter, C., & Harman, D. (1979). *Adult illiteracy in the United States: A report to the Ford Foundation*. New York: McGraw-Hill.

Kitz, W.R. (1988). Adult literacy: A review of the past and a proposal for the future. *Remedial and Special Education, 9*(4), 44–50.

Knox, A.B. (1987). *International perspectives on adult education*. Columbus, OH: ERIC Clearinghouse on Adult, Career, and Vocational Education. (ED 290 931)

Kozol, J. (1985). *Illiterate America*. New York: New American Library.

Lucas, G.S. (1985). *Non-traditional community-based GED programming outreach efforts*. (ED 254 678)

Muller, J. (Ed.). (1986). *Learning strategies for post-literacy: The Tanzanian approach: A reader*. Bonn, Germany: German Foundation for International Development. (ED 276 842)

Naik, C. (1982). *Education for rural development—A portfolio of studies, volume 2: Education for disadvantaged women*. New York: Unipub. (ED 231 567)

Nickerson, R.S. (1985). Adult literacy and technology. *Visible Language, 19*(3), 311–355.

Noor, A. (1982). Managing adult literacy training. *Prospects, 12*(2), 163–184.

Ouane, A. (1982). Rural newspapers and radio for post-literacy in Mali. *Prospects, 12*(2), 243–253.

Quigley, B.A. (1990). Hidden logic: Reproduction and resistance in adult literacy and adult basic education. *Adult Education Quarterly, 40*(2), 103–115.

Sher, J.P. (1978). *Revitalizing rural education: A legislator's handbook*. Washington, DC: National Conference of State Legislators.

Taylor, D. (1989). Toward a unified theory of literacy learning. *Phi Delta Kappan, 71*(3), 184–193.

Theobald, P. (1988). *The ideological foundations of midwest rural education*. (ED 308 035)

Treadway, D.M. (1984). *Higher education in rural America: Serving the adult learner*. New York: College Board.

Theoretical and Organizational Issues

Views of Personal Literacy Within a Prison Population

T. STEVENSON HANSELL
JEAN A. VOELKEL
MARCH 1992

While educational researchers continue to study the problems associated with learning to read, there is little information available about how incarcerated adults, who are not trained in the field of education, view factors related to their own literacy levels. The population in U.S. prisons represents the single highest concentration of nonproficient readers from among the general U.S. population (Kozol, 1985). Rosenthal (1987) estimated that 50–65% of the prison population was functionally illiterate, in contrast to 10% of the general population. In 1983, an estimate of US$6.6 billion was given as the minimum annual cost of prison maintenance for an estimated 260,000 inmates (of the total 440,000 imprisoned in the U.S.) whose imprisonment has been correlated with functional illiteracy (Kozol, 1985). Functional illiteracy among juvenile offenders in 1987 was even greater at 85% (Rosenthal, 1987).

The number of years spent in the educational system varies considerably between the prison population and the general population. In 1987, 75% of all U.S. prisoners had not completed high school (Rosenthal, 1987), as compared with only 25% of the general population. This suggests that research is needed about the roots of illiteracy and the school dropout rate among prisoners.

Much research has attempted to explain the process by which humans learn to read, define the factors that influence this process, and identify factors that retard literacy. Major investigations have centered around four variables of education: (1) nonschool environment, (2) school environment, (3) the learner's physical characteristics, and (4) the learner's psychological characteristics (Harris & Sipay, 1980). These four were also the center of our own analysis.

Our study examined the opinions of two groups within a prison population regarding their personal literacy development. We addressed two questions:

1. To what factors do the male inmates of a close-security correctional institution in the midwestern U.S. who are enrolled in a prison literacy program attribute their current reading levels?

2. Do inmates who serve as tutors for other inmates view these factors differently from those who are students in the program?

Two Types of Prison Inmates

We studied a group of 32 male prison inmates who voluntarily participated in the Chaplains' Literacy Dynamics Program. One morning a week, seven community tutors provided aid, supervision, and tutoring support for up to 25 tutor inmates who simultaneously supported up to 25 student inmates with individual instruction. The community tutors had been trained with Laubach materials and a variety of other approaches.

Of the voluntary survey participants, 16 were enrolled as students; 16 were serving as tutors. The student group had a lower level of reading ability than the tutor group, as indicated by standardized test scores. The years of schooling completed ranged from 7 to 12 for students and from 9 to 15 for inmate tutors. The age range was 19 to 52. The group's racial mix was 72% African American, 25% Caucasian, and 3% Hispanic. On the day of the survey, the ratio of Caucasians to other racial groups among the inmate tutors was 3:1. Childhoods were spent in various parts of the U.S.; one man was from Mexico.

The survey (see Figure 1) was prepared to address four areas, namely educational, environmental, physical, and psychological variables of reading as prisoners remembered them. The survey consisted of 20 statements to which inmates responded "yes" or "no." Figure 2, which sums up the responses, also shows how the survey statements relate to the four categories of variables. The number of items for each type of variable was reasonably balanced apart from a stronger emphasis on psychological variables.

The statements used as survey items were phrased in nontechnical, nonthreatening language to encourage participation. Because the test group included low-ability readers who may or may not have received assistance in reading the survey, we tried to use words that were easy for adults to read. The Fry Readability Scale indicates that the survey had a readability level of fifth grade. The statements, as well as a final comment that respondents were asked to complete, were formulated to collect personal opinions according to the respondents' perceptions and memories of influences on their current level of literacy.

Figure 1
A Survey About Reading

I am in the Chaplains' Literacy Dynamics Program.

I am a _____ student _____ tutor. (Please put *x* in the correct blank.)

I have finished the 1 2 3 4 5 6 7 8 9 10 11 12 13 14 15 16 grade.
(Please circle the correct number.)

    This is a survey about you as a child. It's about what you remember about learning to read. It's about your family. It's about what you remember about school.

    Your experiences as a child were different from those of the others who are taking part in this survey. So your answers will be different. There are no right or wrong answers. Choose the answers that show what *you* think.

    Some sentences are listed below. Read each sentence. Then think about yourself as a child. If the sentence is true for you, put *x* in the blank beside "Yes." If the sentence is not true for you, put *x* in the blank beside "No." If you would like to tell more about your answer, you may write in the space below the sentence.

What I remember about when I was a child

1. My parents wanted me to do well in school.	31 Yes	1 No
2. Someone in my family read to me.	18 Yes	14 No
3. My teachers liked me and thought I could do well.	27 Yes	5 No
4. I liked to go to school.	17 Yes	15 No
5. I tried hard to do my school work correctly.	24 Yes	8 No
6. Someone helped me when homework was hard.	22 Yes	10 No
7. My friends wanted to do well in school.	23 Yes	9 No
8. I watched television a lot. (If yes, what did you watch?)	25 Yes	7 No
9. I felt tired and sleepy in school.	19 Yes	13 No
10. I missed school a lot.	15 Yes	17 No
11. The other students learned faster than I did.	23 Yes	7 No
12. I felt dumb in school.	13 Yes	18 No
13. There were many books I could read in school.	24 Yes	7 No
14. Reading aloud made me feel scared and nervous.	15 Yes	16 No
15. The books were dull and boring.	11 Yes	20 No
16. The words in books and writing on the chalkboard were hard to see.	7 Yes	24 No
17. It was hard to hear the teacher.	3 Yes	28 No
18. It was hard to understand the words when the teacher talked.	10 Yes	21 No

How I feel as an adult

19. I read as well as I want to.	17 Yes	14 No
20. I want to read better than I do now.	30 Yes	1 No

Please complete the following sentence:

I think I read like I do because _____

_____

If you would like to sign your name, it would help the volunteers of the Literacy Dynamics Program to know you better. No one else will see this paper. If you do not want to sign your name, that's OK.

Thank you for sharing what you think about learning to read.

This survey was administered to prison inmates in November 1989.

Figure 2
Prison Inmate Responses to 20 Survey Items by Category

Types of variables	Survey item number	"Yes" Students	Number of responses "Yes" Tutors	"No"
Educational variables (4)	3	15	12	5
	6	11	11	10
	13	10	14	7
	15	5	6	20
Environmental variables (4)	1	16	15	1
	2	12	6	14
	7	14	9	9
	8	14	11	7
Physical variables (3)	9	11	8	13
	16	5	2	24
	17	3	0	28
Psychological variables (7)	4	10	7	15
	5	16	8	8
	11	14	9	7
	12	6	7	18
	14	11	4	16
	19	6	11	14
	20	16	14	1
General statements (2)	10	8	7	17
	18	9	1	21

N = 32 prison inmates (16 literacy students, 16 tutors). One inmate tutor responded only to items 1–10. Items 10 and 18 (general statements) fit more than one category of variable.

The final comment gave them an opportunity to express their opinions in their own words.

We administered the survey at the beginning of a literacy session, in late autumn. Because of time and personnel limitations, tutors and students completed their surveys independently, following brief instructions. Tutors helped latecoming students, who missed the instructions, to complete their surveys.

Each survey was given a respondent number for tabulation purposes. Respondent 18, a tutor, neglected to answer questions 11–20 and to complete the final statement (these were on the back of the page). Although no provision was made for an answer of "I don't know," Respondent 1 (a student) wrote, "I don't know" as an answer to statement 15 which asked if textbooks were dull and boring.

Question 1: Attributions

To address the first research question (To what factors do these male inmates of a close-security institution attribute their reading levels?), overall scores and open-ended responses were examined by category. As might be expected, no one area (educational, environmental, physical, or psychological) seemed to

Figure 3
Responses to Survey Items Showing Substantial Agreement or Clear Split

Types of variables	Survey item number	Statement in survey item	Number of responses "Yes"	"No"
Statements most inmate respondents agreed with:				
Environmental	1	My parents wanted me to do well.	31	1
Psychological	20	I want to read better than I do now.	30	1
Physical	17	It was hard to hear the teacher.	3	28
Educational	3	Teachers liked me and thought I could do well.	27	5
Environmental	8	I watched TV a lot.	25	7
Physical	16	Words on the chalkboard were hard to see.	7	24
Statements to which responses were split:				
Environmental	2	Someone in my family read to me.	18	14
Psychological	4	I liked to go to school.	17	15
General	10	I missed school a lot.	15	17
Psychological	14	Reading aloud made me feel scared and nervous.	15	16
Psychological	19	I read as well as I want to.	17	14

N = 32 male prison inmates (16 literacy students, 16 tutors). One tutor inmate responded only to items 1–10.

predominate for the total group. In the group of items where most inmates answered "yes," all variable areas were represented. However, where responses were evenly split, the items related most often to psychological variables, as shown in Figure 3.

Up to 10 of the 32 respondents may have had physical limitations. Three reported that it had been hard to hear the teacher and seven responded that it had been hard to see the words on the chalkboard. Furthermore, all three of those who reported hearing problems and five of the seven who couldn't see the chalkboard were in the student group. This suggests that half of the 16 students might have had a physical basis for learning problems and that environmental classroom conditions might have hampered learning (see Figure 2).

However, more frequent responses from the student group included missing school, not liking to attend school, and feeling nervous or scared about reading aloud in school. These responses suggest psychological as well as environmental and physical influences. This interpretation seems supported by the general agreement that "teachers liked me and thought I could do well" and by the free response statements, which are reported in Figure 4. It is clearly possible that the inmates responded that teachers liked them because they had accepted the societal view of themselves as less valuable than authority figures. It also seems possible that these incarcerated

Figure 4
Prison Inmates' Open-Ended Responses About Their Reading Ability

Responses to statement "I think I read like I do because..."

Student inmates' responses
1. I try to read fast and lose track of what I'm reading.
2. reading haven't never been a problem just math. I guess since I have been out of high school so long!
3. I don't understand big words.
4. of missing days in school also not completing my education.
5. because, I am not able to read English as was I want to be able to.
6. I didn't take school as serious as I want to. But now I'am in school taking care of my reading problem.
7. I need help.
8. I need more help.
9. growing up I didn't take it seriously.
10. I didn't take time to read.
11. I do not read that much.
12. I like to read some.
13. —
14. I am learning from my tutor.
15. slow learned
16. —

Tutor inmates' responses
17. I've continued to read and feel the more that I read, the better I'll become at it.
18. —
19. because it enhances my ability to comprehend and understand.
20. it is best for me in the world today. Besides that I love reading God's Word daily.
21. there was a lot of interesting books and I love reading I couldn't get my nose out of a book.
22. I like to spend as much time reading as I can.
23. of all the hard work and the help I had while growing up.
24. I have good reading comprehension and I spell words excellently; also, I give 100% effort to the reading task.
25. of my attitude toward reading.
26. I read books as often as I can.
27. as I grew older in life I started to enjoy reading. This made me want to read anything that I could put my hands on.
28. I enjoy reading.
29. Now I understand the importants of reading and why one should read more.
30. I finally applied myself to learning to read.
31. I tryed to read and got better. I read a lot better today than I did in my younger days.
32. I strive to achieve perfection in any and all social and/or informal, formal endeavors I pursue.

All responses given are shown.

men had had higher priorities than learning to read while of school age.

Question 2: Students vs. Tutors

The results of the survey were analyzed by means of the chi-square statistic through the SAS computer program to determine if inmates who served as tutors viewed these factors differently than did those who were students. When we used the 0.05 level of significance (95% of the samples drawn from this population would furnish the same result), items 2, 7, 14, and 19 (discussed below) showed significant differences between the responses of tutors and students. However, item 7 ("My friends wanted to do well in school") had fewer than five responses in the negative cell and was therefore incompatible with the chi-square statistic.

Surprisingly, on item 2 significantly higher numbers of students (12 of 16) than tutors (6 of 16) said that someone in the family read to them. One interpretation is that student inmates responded to the recent past rather than the preschool frame intended by the survey authors. Students also responded with significantly more "yes" answers to item 14 about being scared to read aloud—11 of 16 students marked "yes" to this item while only 4 of 15 tutors did. This result is not surprising. Inmates who accepted the role of tutor would probably feel more confident about reading than those who elected to be students. Similarly, for item 19 it is understandable that significantly more tutors than students felt that they read as well as they wished.

Interpreted this way, we get little insight from the "yes or no" responses into variables that may have caused differences between the two groups. As noted in Figure 4, however, student responses to the open-ended question "I think I read like I do because..." show

clear differences of focus. Student responses dealt primarily with the past while tutor responses reflected current purposes and intent. A few student statements clearly indicated personal causes for inadequate reading skills:

1. I try to read fast and lose track of what I'm reading.
3. I don't understand big words.
4. of missing days in school....
6. I didn't take school as serious as I want to....
10. I didn't take time to read.
15. slow learned

These statements reflect the psychological factors only. Physical factors are not mentioned.

In light of current criticisms of educational institutions, it is interesting to note that no comments degraded teachers, materials, or the general environment. Again, this is possibly because these men view themselves as being in a position from which they cannot denigrate authority. Comments from tutors support this emphasis on personal responsibility with added emphasis on having clear purposes for reading:

17. I've continued to read and feel that the more I read the better I'll become at it.
20. it is best for me in the world today. Besides that I love reading God's Word daily.
21. there was a lot of interesting books and I love reading and couldn't get my nose out of a book.
32. I strive to achieve perfection in any and all social and or informal, formal endeavors I pursue.

In response to our first research question ("To what factors do male inmates of a close-security correctional institution attribute their current reading levels?"), the data provide interesting insights. Figure 2 shows the range of responses by the total group, clustered by the type of variables involved.

Figure 4 presents the full list of free-response statements provided by the men at the end of the questionnaire. Our interpretation of these free statements is that those men in the student role discussed the past and dealt with problems (e.g., "I didn't take much time to read," "I don't understand big words"). Tutors, on the other hand, focused on the present or future ("I enjoy reading," "Now I understand the importants of reading") and on purposes for reading (enjoyment, improvement, understanding, and salvation).

Better Readers Have a Purpose

To judge from the results of this survey, it appears that those inmates who have developed proficiency see reading as having a purpose: they feel competent enough to enjoy reading, or they feel they can learn about themselves and the world through books. Those inmates who did not develop proficiency may have been influenced by physical or environmental liabilities. They reported that they did not read as well as they wanted to and that they did not work at learning to read while in school. Perhaps they did not try because, as reported, they felt nervous about reading aloud. The anxiety may have carried over into all reading. Furthermore, it seems likely that that anxiety was based on awareness that in fact they did not read as well as their classmates.

Answers to this survey reflect the opinions of the adult male prison inmate literacy program participants on a particular day, based on their individual memories of childhood and school experiences. This sample is not necessarily representative of the entire population of the institution or penal system. These men have chosen to participate in the literacy program and their attitudes may have differed from those of the general prison population. Therefore, caution should be used in interpreting the survey findings to the general population.

A variety of causative factors in the respondents' backgrounds could have influenced their responses. Accuracy of memory should not be discounted. Factual information regarding literacy development and background of the inmate participants was not studied. Given the high percentage of nonproficient readers among incarcerated persons, it would seem that more extensive research and intensive instruction in this area would be beneficial.

While no specific causal factors can be isolated through this study, it seems safe to conclude that better readers in this population have a clearer sense of the purposes of reading. Better readers read for a reason while poorer readers do not see through the trees of words to the forest of gaining knowledge or enjoyment. Teachers and administrators might use this information to find methods and materials to encourage student enjoyment and sense of purpose.

References
Harris, A., & Sipay, E. (1980). *How to increase reading ability* (7th ed.). White Plains, NY: Longman.
Kozol, J. (1985). *Illiterate America*. Garden City, NY: Doubleday.
Rosenthal, N. (1987). *Teach someone to read*. Belmont, CA: David S. Lake.

> " **Understanding is not cued knowledge: performance is never the sum of drills; problems are not exercises; mastery is not achieved by the unthinking application of algorithms. In others words, we cannot be said to understand something unless we can employ our knowledge wisely, fluently, flexibly, and aptly in particular and diverse contexts.** "
>
> —WIGGINS, 1993, P. 200

*I*n his review of assessment, Johnston (1984) issued conclusions that still hold true. He complains that, even though recent research has tended to emphasize process over product, educators and researchers persist in depending on the more conveniently obtained product data. The articles in this section address process as well as product. Metz cites programs that attempt alternative assessment with adults. Padak, Davidson, and Padak detail easy-to-use strategies for informal assessment. Finlay and Harrison discuss standardized tests versus competency-based assessment. Fargo and Collins started out looking for answers on how to evaluate adult beginning readers and, in the process, learned how liberating the right interview questions can be, found ways to redesign research in progress, and developed keener observation of their own teach-

ing. Ash reports on a six-year project to evaluate the tests used in a large-scale merit system. Murphy et al. provide a test designed for health-care professionals to use to identify low literacy levels in patients. Padak and Padak provide guidelines for adult literacy program evaluation in the categories of personal, programmatic, and external factors.

García and Pearson (1991) hold as a basic thesis that the keys to meeting the assessment needs of a diverse student population are a flexible approach to assessment and a dramatically improved teacher knowledge base. The articles in this section certainly encourage flexibility in assessment. And educators who internalize literature of this type do have at least a solid beginning toward establishing a strong knowledge base.

References

García, G.E., & Pearson, P.D. (1991). The role of assessment in a diverse society. In E.H. Hiebert

(Ed.), Literacy for a diverse society (pp. 253–278). New York: Teachers College Press.

Johnston, P.H. (1984). Assessment in reading. In P.D. Pearson (Ed.), Handbook of reading research (pp. 147–182). White Plains, NY: Longman.

Wiggins, G. (1993, November). Assessment: Authenticity, context, and validity. Phi Delta Kappan, 200–214.

A s s e s s m e n t

Issues in Adult Literacy Assessment

ELIZABETH METZ
MARCH 1990

A vast array of adult education programs are offered across the United States and around the world. There are programs offered through state education offices and public school districts. Other programs are provided by volunteers through Literacy Volunteers of America, Laubach Literacy International, and public libraries (Gaughan, 1986; *Literacy: The Key to Success*, 1988). The U.S. government provides literacy programs tied to the Job Training Partnership Act and through the Departments of Agriculture, Defense, Health and Human Services, Interior, Justice, and Labor (Newman, 1986). Private industry also offers literacy classes.

To further complicate matters, some programs are learner centered, some competency based, and some job centered. The instructors may be found anywhere along a continuum from volunteers, who have received only a few hours of training provided by their specific program, to certified professional adult educators. How does one assess literacy under such circumstances? It is very difficult to develop standards when adult learners' needs are so dissimilar and the programs are so varied. One common goal is that the assessment procedure used should integrate both curriculum and student-identified goals and needs. Jeanne Chall states that "there are few tests specifically meant for adults (and) there seems to be a hesitation in using them" (see French, 1987, p. 7). The commonly used Test of Adult Basic Education (TABE) until recently was normed *on children*. Most normed and criterion-referenced tests are scored using grade level equivalents similar to those used for children. French calls this a "legacy from our definition of literacy as a level of achievement" (p. 40).

There are few research-based models available for assessment of the many different programs. French (1987) suggests that informal testing would be one direction to follow which would allow for a more personal perspective. In informal testing the learner can be actively involved in his or her own assessment. While there are a number of viewpoints about adult literacy assessment, no one perspective seems to dominate the field at this time.

Representative Programs

The Center for Literacy in Philadelphia, Pennsylvania, provides a curriculum based on the individual learner's goals, interests, and needs. Their underlying assumptions are that literacy is social and that the learners come with their own goals and objectives. The

Center for Literacy uses planning conferences during the intake session and every 6 months for assessment. Items such as the learner's everyday life, reading and writing strategies, interests, and goals are considered. A portfolio of the learner's accomplishments and current work is also kept (Lytle, 1986).

The U.S. federal prison system reading programs use standardized tests. Each inmate takes the Adult Basic Learning Examination (ABLE) on entry. Although ABLE is used by the prison system, each institution may develop its own basic education program (Muth, 1988). Project LEARN, in Cleveland, Ohio, uses volunteer tutors trained in the use of Laubach literacy materials. Assessment of learners begins at the intake interview, and progress is closely monitored in the early lessons. Project LEARN also uses the Wide Range Achievement Test (WRAT) (Pasch & Oakley, 1985).

Comprehensive Adult Student Assessment System (CASAS) is used in all California programs that receive U.S. Adult Basic Education Act funds. Assessment is linked directly to a list of identified competency statements. Materials used in the program are coded to this list. When learners first enter the program, their needs and skills are assessed through an interview. The program has had difficulty in record keeping and plans to use a computerized management system (Rickard & Stiles, 1985). Given the range of assessment tools highlighted above, field-based personnel continue to note limitations of these instruments and suggest changes.

Towards Alternative Assessment

It appears that both standardized tests and competency-based assessment poorly serve the adult learner. Standardized tests are often related to former failure in school, are intimidating, and give a one-sided view of a multi-sided problem. Since each adult had his or her own reasons for coming to a literacy program, these reasons rarely match up with the skills measured on standardized tests. Competency-based programs also have a similar problem. In such programs, competencies tend to be imposed on a learner rather than the learner choosing competencies that match his or her goals.

Assessment of the adult learner can be conducted on an informal, nonthreatening basis. The cultural, physiological, psychological, and educational characteristics of the learner can be noted through a series of informal interviews over a period of several sessions. Learner interests and goals can be discussed on an ongoing basis by the tutor and learner. Reading level can be determined through an informal reading inventory and the learner's reading strategies can be assessed using miscue analysis.

While these methods of assessment may take more time than a standardized test and formal intake interview, more appropriate information can be obtained. Rapport would be built between learner and tutor, the self-image of the learner would be enhanced as the program would be learner centered, and the goals and needs of the individual learner would be met. Success would be built into the program. Progress would be noted as each goal of the learner is reached, and new goals would be established as part of an ongoing assessment program.

References

French, J. (1987). *Adult literacy: A source book and guide*. New York: Garland.

Gaughan, K.K. (1956). Literacy projects in libraries. *Library Trends, 35*, 277–291.

Literacy: The key to success. A literacy handbook. (1988). (2nd ed.) Utica, NY: Mid-York Library System. [ED 303 180]

Lytle, S.L. (1986). *Literacy theory in practice: Assessing the reading and writing of low-literate adults.* Paper presented at the annual meeting of the American Educational Research Association, San Francisco, CA. 65 pp. [ED 278 675]

Muth, W.R. (1988, September). *Federal prison system reading programs.* Paper presented at National Adult Literacy Symposium, Washington, DC.

Newman, A.P. (1986). *An evaluation of the impact of the Advertising Council's "Volunteer Against Illiteracy" campaign on public awareness of and resources devoted to adult literacy for 1985.* Bloomington, IN: Indiana University. 677 pp. [ED 293 979]

Pasch, M., & Oakley, N. (1985). *An evaluation of Project: LEARN.* Paper presented at the annual meeting of the American Educational Research Association, Chicago, IL. 25 pp. [ED 255 759]

Rickard, P.L., & Stiles, R.L. (1985). Comprehensive Adult Student Assessment System (CASAS) design for effective assessment in correctional education programs. *Journal of Correctional Education, 36,* 51–53.

Exploring Reading with Adult Beginning Readers

NANCY D. PADAK
JANE L. DAVIDSON
GARY M. PADAK
SEPTEMBER 1990

Helping adult basic education learners become competent, avid readers is a major challenge facing ABE teachers and tutors and a major goal for most ABE programs. Understanding these adults as readers is the first step toward meeting the challenge and achieving the goal.

Most ABE programs rely on standardized tests to yield information about reading ability. However, both standardized testing and the results it yields have limitations that restrict its usefulness for ABE instructional planning. Many learners are intimidated by standardized testing, perhaps because they are reminded of unpleasant prior experiences. Moreover, test results do not provide information for planning instruction. An adult who scores in the 5th percentile on a standardized test may indeed need assistance in reading, but the test score does not provide specifics. Does the adult enjoy and value reading? Read for meaning? Have a workable strategy for identifying unknown words?

These problems with standardized tests are aggravated with adult beginning readers, who are even more likely to fear formal testing situations and to score poorly. Furthermore, test-taking fears may counteract attempts to create the positive initial experiences so important to retention in programs. Fortunately, several alternatives to standardized testing can yield diagnostic insights. This article will explain several strategies for exploring beginning adult readers' perceptions about reading and their abilities.

Exploring Ideas About Reading

An intake interview of some sort is usually part of registration or an early instructional session with the adult beginning reader. During these interviews, teachers typically ask about background, interests, and goals (Davidson, Padak, & Padak, 1989): Tell me about your family. Where do you live? Where have you worked? What are you interested in? What do you do in your spare time? Why are you interested in this program? What do you hope to accomplish?

Discussion surrounding these questions provides the teacher and adult with opportunities to learn about each other and begin establishing rapport. Additionally, information shared about interests and background can be useful in planning instruction. For example, Ray told his tutor that he'd probably miss a session in the spring because he had attended every Cleveland Indians home opener for the past 25 years. Knowing about Ray's interest in baseball helped his tutor select interesting materials.

Questions about reading should be asked during intake interviews as well. What readers do during reading is determined, at least in part, by what they think they should be doing. An adult who believes that "saying the words" is the goal, for example, will probably approach reading differently than one who believes that "getting the message" is the goal. Furthermore, mistaken notions may impede the teacher's efforts to help the adult grow as a reader. Interview questions that explore the adult's notions of the reading process and awareness of reading strategies, can provide useful instructional insights.

Questions like these can be useful (Burke, 1980; Padak, 1987; Wixson, Bosky, Yochum, & Alvermann, 1984): Who's the best reader you know? What does this person do that makes him or her such a good reader? How would you explain reading—what would you say that it is? What should readers do? Why do people read? Do you think that you're a good reader? Why? What's the best way to become a better reader? Why?

The adult's awareness of reading strategies can be explored through interview questions such as these: What do you do when you come to a word that you don't know? How do you try to figure it out? What do you do if that doesn't work? Do you ever find that you don't understand something that you've read? What do you do to try to figure it out? What if that doesn't work? What do you do when you want to remember something that you've read? How well does this work?

In evaluating responses to these questions, it's important to differentiate between strategy awareness and strategy use. An adult might mention context as a means to identify unknown words, for example, yet show no indication of using context while reading; the reverse may also be true. Nonetheless, the adult's awareness of his or her options as a reader, as well as ideas about the process of reading, can provide the teacher with useful insights for planning instruction.

Exploring Comprehension Ability

Knowledge about the learner's comprehension ability is critical; after all, comprehension is what reading is all about. Two informal strategies for gaining preliminary information about strengths and weaknesses in comprehension are described in this section. The strategies are based on text read to the adult, rather than reading he or she does independently.

Although listening comprehension and reading comprehension abilities may differ, they also share important features. Both involve sampling, predicting, and confirming. Both depend upon inferences that are based on the adult's prior knowledge and information presented in the text. As such, knowledge about the adult's ability as a listener can be a useful source of hypotheses about his or her ability as a reader. Besides that, if the adult cannot read independently, we cannot examine reading comprehension directly.

(1) Active readers make predictions about what they expect to read and then confirm or refine their predictions based on evidence from their reading. This process allows the reader to construct the author's message, to comprehend. These same thinking processes are involved in listening to an unfamiliar text. One way to explore listening comprehension, then, is to ask the adult to make and evaluate predictions about a text being read to him or her.

The Directed Listening-Thinking Activity (DL-TA) (Davidson, Padak, & Padak, 1989; Stauffer, 1980) is an instructional technique that works well for this diagnostic purpose. In brief, the DL-TA involves asking listeners to make predictions about text content and provide reasons for their ideas. A portion of the text is then read, and listeners are asked to evaluate their predictions in light of what they have heard. They are then asked to speculate about what may be presented next and to explain why they think so. Two questions typically facilitate the discussions: What do you think? Why do you think so?

Responses during a DL-TA can be analyzed to formulate preliminary hypotheses about comprehension. Three aspects of the responses are important: willingness to predict and evaluate, plausibility, and demonstrations of text understanding. Willingness to predict and evaluate provides an indication of the adult's understanding of the reading process. That is, adults who predict and evaluate freely most likely know that their thoughts are important to reading and listening, while those who hesitate may not. The plausibility of predictions can be determined by judging whether the ideas are possible, given information provided in the text. Finally, demonstrations of text understanding are frequently shown in statements such as "I think _____, because it said _____."

(2) Analyzing an adult's retelling is a second way to explore his or her listening comprehension ability. After an unfamiliar text has been read to the adult, the teacher can invite retelling by saying "What was this all about?" or "Tell me everything you remember about what I just read." After the adult has completed an initial retelling, the teacher can ask for further response: "OK, what else?" or "Good. What else do you remember?" Prompts such as these encourage elaboration without providing clues to text content.

The teacher should make extensive notes during the retelling or tape record it. Either way, analysis of the retelling should be based on several guidelines that involve judging the extent to which the adult understood what was heard (Padak, 1987):

1. How fluent was the retelling? Did the adult retell freely or was a great deal of prompting necessary? Was the retelling well

organized? Good fiction retellings recreate the plot in the sequence presented. For non-fiction, maintaining the author's sequence might not be as important as other aspects of organization, for example, recalling which details belong with which major topics.

2. How complete was the retelling? Excellent retellings need not be verbatim accounts of the text—rote memorization is seldom, if ever, a goal for either listening or reading. Instead, the teacher should analyze the retelling to determine presence of main ideas and significant supporting details.

To a certain extent, teachers need to keep open minds when analyzing retellings. Since comprehension depends heavily on the listener's or reader's prior knowledge, the teacher's notion of what's important may not always correspond to the adult's. Nonetheless, analyzing retellings for fluency, sequence, and breadth can be helpful in understanding an adult beginning reader.

Exploring Knowledge of Words

Dictation by the student (Davidson, Padak, & Padak, 1989; Stauffer 1980) is an excellent diagnostic tool for exploring the beginning reader's abilities as a reader, including his or her knowledge of words. The advantages of dictation over other means of diagnosis, such as word lists or standardized tests, are many. Understanding is ensured, and meaning is inherent in the learner's dictated accounts of experiences or ideas. Moreover, since dictations are recorded verbatim, vocabulary and language patterns will also be familiar to the adult. Finally, the diagnosis should be conducted in a supportive atmosphere, and working with dictations creates a supportive atmosphere.

The first step in taking dictation is to facilitate discussion about a topic. Discussing responses to interview questions during the intake session, for example, could easily form the basis for dictation. Next, the teacher asks the adult to summarize by providing information to be recorded on paper. Each statement should be recorded exactly as spoken, although standard spelling, capitalization, and punctuation should be used. Here is Will's dictation, taken during his first session in an ABE program:

> I'm pretty nervous about coming back to school. It been a long time, and I wasn't so good at it before. I didn't have no luck in school. I figured I was pretty dumb, but now I'm not so sure. Well, I can give it a try.

After the dictation is complete, the adult is asked to read it aloud. The teacher looks for ease and fluency and notes the words read successfully. After the adult has read his or her dictation, the teacher directs attention to words correctly identified and asks the adult to say each word. Words identified quickly and accurately are sight words. Later in the initial session, or at the next session, the adult is asked to read the dictation again, this time silently, and to underline all the words he or she knows. This process is completed twice. Finally, the teacher asks the adult to say each underlined word. An indication of the adult's ability to learn new words is given by comparing these responses with initial responses. This procedure can help teachers determine the extent of an adult beginning reader's sight vocabulary and his or her ability to learn new sight words in the context of familiar material. Of course, it's unlikely that working with one dictation will tell the whole story. If additional information is needed before instruction begins, the entire process can be repeated with another dictation.

It's fairly easy to form hypotheses about possible word identification strategies during work with a dictation. Making note of the adult's reaction to problems is probably the best way to do this. Does he or she seek help? Try again? How? Does the adult try to use context? Phonics? Sometimes the reader realizes that there's a problem, but doesn't know what to do about it. If so, a quizzical look or a comment ("That's not right") may be the clue to understanding. In cases like this, it's usually helpful to seek additional information: "You look puzzled. What's the matter?" Observing reading behavior, with particular attention to attempts to solve problems, can help teachers form hypotheses about the adult's reading ability and repertoire of reading strategies.

Making Instructional Decisions

Diagnosis involves asking questions and looking for answers. As questions are answered, a picture of the adult as a reader begins to emerge. Data and anecdotal information collected from all sources need to be consolidated in order to clearly see the picture. What is now evident about the adult's reading performance and what is not evident?

Holistic Reading and Writing Assessment for Adults (Davidson, 1990) contains sets of continuums in the following areas to think about in making instructional decisions: reading for meaning, using functional strategies for word identification, vocabulary-concept development, fluency, self-esteem related to reading, values related to reading.

Information collected about an adult's overall reading performance is recorded on appropriate continuums, thus allowing for progress to be plotted, over a period of time, on the assessment sheet. Instructional decisions and information about progress can

then be easily plotted, shared, and discussed with the adult learner. As teacher-tutor and adult learner gain additional insights about the adult as a reader, these insights can be recorded and dated, thus providing an ongoing means of justification for instructional decisions and activities.

All instructional activities need to be both meaning based and learner based. The most effective activities are those based on learners' strengths and needs that represent a high degree of authenticity. Adult learners must be actively involved in highly personalized literacy instructional programs. They must have critical roles in the instructional decision-making process and in recording progress toward their own goals. After all, they have a lifetime of literacy ahead of them.

References

Burke, C.L. (1980). The reading interview. In B.P. Farr & D.J. Strickler (Eds.), *Reading comprehension: Resource guide*. Bloomington, IN: Indiana University Language Education Department.

Davidson, J.L. (1990). *Holistic reading and writing assessment for adults*. Monroe, NY: Trillium Press.

Davidson, J.L., Padak, N.D., & Padak, G.M. (1989). *Reading, writing, thinking for life*, teacher's manual (Level I, Set 1). Monroe, NY: Trillium Press.

Padak, N.D. (1987). *Reading placement and diagnosis: A guide for elementary teachers*. Springfield, IL: Illinois State Board of Education.

Stauffer, R.G. (1980). *The language-experience approach to teaching reading* (2nd ed.). New York: Harper & Row.

Wixson, K.K., Bosky, A.B., Yochum, M.N., & Alvermann, D.E. (1984). An interview for assessing students' perceptions of classroom reading tasks. *The Reading Teacher, 37*, 346–352.

Measuring "Success" in Reading in Adult Basic Education: A United Kingdom Perspective

ANN FINLAY
COLIN HARRISON
NOVEMBER 1992

Which of these quotations gives the most accurate picture of the degree of success of adult literacy tuition? Or are both true?

The majority of adult literacy participants do not accomplish meaningful, practically significant reading improvements and leave training without having achieved *functional literacy.* (Diekhoff, 1988, p. 625)

The finding that the majority of learners enrolled in literacy schemes in the period in question were evidently making progress in their acquisition of skills related to reading and writing, and that the majority of tutors and learners were satisfied with the rate of progress being made, appears to provide further evidence of the beneficial effects of the initiatives that have been taken in recent years to extend and improve the provisions made for the teaching of literacy skills to adult students. (Gorman, 1981, p. 198)

An examination from a United Kingdom perspective of the background and nature of provision and curricula, as well as consideration of what is meant by *success* and the means of assessing it, may help us decide. Are there research results which confirm whether or not Adult Basic Education (ABE) tuition in reading is successful? Who judges success—students, tutors, or others? How is success currently being assessed? What is being assessed under the broad heading of *reading,* and are current methods appropriate?

Background

The first major impetus in the United Kingdom for adult literacy, as ABE was then called, did not occur until 1975 with the establishment of the Adult Literacy Resource Agency, now superseded by the Adult Literacy and Basic Skills Unit (ALBSU). With so brief a history it is not surprising that assessment philosophy and assessment techniques specific to ABE are still in their infancy when compared to other areas of education.

During ABE's brief existence, changes have occurred which affect the nature of provision and curricula—concerning what is offered and the way it is delivered. Two of the more significant changes are the move away from predominantly individual tuition to group tuition and the inclusion of numeracy with the traditional reading, writing, and spelling originally offered, At first most tuition was carried out one-to-one with volunteer tutors (as a result of which the term *tutor* rather than *teacher* is common in ABE). As the movement gained strength and more paid staff were recruited, an increasing number of students were directed to group tuition in ABE classes instead of being offered tuition in either their own or the volunteers' homes. Volunteers are still encouraged in many classes, and individual help is usually available when necessary.

Changes in curriculum, together with a move to using more paid staff instead of relying so heavily on volunteers, may have delayed the development of an established assessment code of practice in ABE. The lack of statutory minimum training or qualification requirements for paid staff may also have implications for the assessment issue.

In the past 10 years, various government initiatives from the Department of Employment in the United Kingdom have had an impact on the provision of ABE classes, which have become associated with Employment Training, the Youth Training Schemes, and the Training and Enterprise Councils. This adds further complexity to the great variety of provision available, which is generally based around projects and classes funded by local government, and taught in schools or further education colleges (which are similar to U.S. junior colleges). In addition, there are other specialized areas such as English as a Second Language and centers for those with learning difficulties, and special provision offered in prisons and the armed forces. Owing to the potentially conflicting criteria of success among these very different reference groups, discussion of success within this article will be limited to the most common type of provision; for example, that provided by the Berridge Centre (1990):

> Nottinghamshire Education Authority provides a comprehensive service for adults who need to improve their skills in reading, writing, spelling, math, and English for speakers of other languages. It caters for people at the beginning stages to those who wish to brush up their skills to pre-GCSE [an examination taken at the end of compulsory education in England] level for work, study or personal interest. (p. 1)

Assessment

Although this article is about success, assessment forms a large part of the content, as without it, how can success be demonstrated? It is needed so that progress may be monitored and the achievement of goals—the essence of success—recognized. It is in the interest of all involved parties, students, tutors, funders, and so forth. Any method of assessment incorporates assumptions about success, and as different parties in the success debate will have different criteria of success, one would expect any assessment method to reflect the criteria of the person making the choice.

If it were simply a matter of transferring the criteria used to judge the success of children's reading to adults' reading, there would be less of a problem in defining success and in agreeing on ways of assessing it. Charnley and Jones (1986) maintain that many tutors and ABE organizers are former primary school teachers who to some extent assess and judge success by virtue of their capability to remember approximate measures of reading age and to apply them to their adult students. But early on in the success debate there was a general feeling that this was an inappropriate way to test adults, particularly as students had by definition already failed at school and were not inclined to view testing favorably.

Furthermore, no widely used adult reading tests were in existence in England, although individual organizations sometimes produced their own schemes. For example, the Warwickshire Literacy Placement Guide (Mowat & Nicholls, 1976) was intended to help in forming an initial assessment only. The result of the absence of a nationally recognized test, together with a dislike of formal testing, led to the view that subjective judgments by tutors and students, rather than formal tests, were the acceptable face of assessment.

Charnley and Jones (1986) give an account, based on a survey of tutors' and students' observations, of typical tutor and student perceptions of success couched in these terms. Their exploration of the concept of success for ABE students not only rejected formal tests in favor of subjective judgments, but introduced affective and enactive criteria as well as the more usual cognitive ones associated with standardized testing. They were not the first to suggest informal methods with this group of students. Kohl (1974) had already advocated using this approach and had drawn up sample assessment forms to aid tutors and students come to joint agreements on initial and ongoing assessment.

Unlike Kohl, Charnley and Jones do not provide an assessment method. Their contribution lies in their analysis of the collection of responses made by ABE participants during their research. The resulting classification of responses into cognitive, affective, and enactive categories attempts to show that achievements in the affective domain are more valued by students than any other kind. Their findings have been influential in giving acceptability to the school of thought which uses affective achievements as a major marker of success.

The strengths of the above approach do not mean that it can be uncritically accepted. A range of assessment methods might have varying degrees of formality. One may think of the assessment situation as a continuum with standardized objective testing at one end and informal subjective assessment at the other. A variety of opinions may be found in relation to different positions on the continuum. It would also be interesting to investigate whether the degree of success claimed for ABE teaching correlates with the writer's pre-ferred type of assessment on the formal-informal continuum.

Standardized Assessment As a Measure of Success

A key assumption behind standardized testing is that success in reading can be reflected in test performance. Success is thus judged on cognitive rather than affective or enactive grounds. The assumption as far as enactive achievement is concerned is that cognitive gains will be transferable to enactive situations with the concomitant implications for "functional literacy" that this assumption makes. For the reasons given above, standardized testing of reading has been little used in ABE in the United Kingdom, but in the United States a different attitude prevails. It is worth considering U.S. testing methods and contrasting these with those used in the United Kingdom.

Current U.S. attitudes and tests in use in ABE programs are described by Sticht (1990). In his report, which also covers testing and assessment methodology, Sticht quotes the Adult Education Act which requires U.S. adult education agencies to collect standardized test data as part of their evaluation activities. Some freedom of choice is allowed in that the tests chosen may be norm referenced, criterion referenced, or competency based, but whichever type is used, it must be based on a systematic sampling of behavior, have data on validity and reliability, be administered and scored according to specific instructions, and be widely used. No such requirements exist in the United Kingdom although in a recent paper ALBSU (undated) is explicit about the importance of monitoring progress in evaluating effectiveness. However, this advisory document lays down no guidelines as to how success in reading should be measured or defined other than to say that it should be recorded on a regular and systematic basis.

In Sticht's report (1990), four ABE tests in the United States suitable for both initial and ongoing assessment are reviewed by G. Jackson. He selected ABLE (Adult Basic Learning Examination, 1967–86, The Psychological Corporation, Order Service Center, PO Box 839954, San Antonio, TX 78283-3954, USA) and TABE (Tests of Adult Basic Education, Forms 5 and 6, 1957–87, Publisher's Test Service, CTB/McGraw-Hill, 2500 Garden Road, Monterey, CA 93940, USA) because they are the most widely used, group administered, norm referenced tests of adult basic skills; CASAS (CASAS Adult Life Skills–Reading, 1984–89, CASAS, San Diego, CA, USA) as an example of a group administered competency-based test and READ (Reading Evaluation Adult Diagnosis [Revised], 1972–82, Literacy Volunteers of America, 5795 Widewaters Parkway, Syracuse, NY 13214, USA) because it is used by volunteer adult literacy groups for individual testing in one-to-one teaching situations.

ABLE and TABE receive some criticisms from Jackson; for example, the reading comprehension subtest in ABLE is criticized on the grounds that it demands inappropriate background knowledge and the TABE on the grounds that the lowest level of the test will be daunting for students with less than Grade 3.0 skills. The background knowledge issue is arguably a particularly important one for disadvantaged readers, since their lack of familiarity with print makes it likely that they have missed out on the sheer quantity of knowledge fluent readers have access to.

The situation is analogous to the Matthew effect (Stanovich, 1986) as regards the differences in volume of material processed by skilled and less skilled readers. The criticism of the TABE regarding its only assessing a minimum achievement level of third grade is equally significant, considering that ABE classes cater to beginner readers and upwards. It is these beginner and struggling readers, rather than those students who attend to brush up their English skills, with whom tutors tend to be most concerned.

CASAS is reviewed less positively than either ABLE or TABE, as, although the test is adult in tone, the specified competencies are measured by an insufficient number of items. For example, the competency "identify months of the year and days of the week" is assessed by only two items. This makes it unsuited to specific competencies. How much this is a drawback depends on how one interprets "functional literacy." Does one take a general or specific view of competency-based teaching? This is an issue to which we shall return.

Some American ABE schemes, like British ones, use volunteers as tutors, instead of professional staff. The READ procedure, which was developed for use by volunteers, might appear to be particularly suited to the United Kingdom, which still relies on volunteers to some extent. However, criticisms made by Jackson (in Sticht, 1990) and Fox and Fingeret (1984) cast doubt on its reliability and validity. The procedure is also described as awkward to administer.

Are these U.S. tests indeed capable of demonstrating success in North American ABE programs? The ideal way to show this, either by pre- and posttests or by observing progress at intervals, is made difficult by the attrition rate within programs. Darkenwald and Valentine (1985) report that a number of follow-up studies have been unable to secure response rates equalling 40% or more of the original sample. This makes it difficult to assess programs' effectiveness.

Where follow-up studies have been carried

out, they typically report increases of approximately 1.5 reading grade levels per year (Diekhoff, 1988). This may seem a respectable rate of progress when one considers that this is a faster than average rate of increase for school children in full time education. If this rate of increase were to be kept up, considerable gains would be made, but as most students only remain in programs for less than 18 months (Darkenwald & Valentine, 1985), total gains are not great. If improvements in reading grade levels alone are the criteria of success, then according to Diekhoff (1988) ABE is not being very successful.

Reasons for Accepting or Rejecting Standardized Tests

The existence and widespread use in the United States of these tests show that it is possible to both devise and administer standardized tests in spite of the difficulties. Criticisms made of them above have not prevented their use. This does not necessarily mean that they are desirable, and practitioners' criticisms of them find growing support in the literature. Designers may fail to take account of subjects' feelings about tests and the effect of this on results. No matter how well designed from a cognitive perspective a test is, it will fail to give an accurate picture if the human subject isn't in a fit state to take it. Sticht (1990) points out what many tutors have experienced, namely, that new students are often nervous at a first meeting. This anxiety, which may be severe, may be aggravated by their unpreparedness for test-taking strategies. As a result they may underachieve on a pretest. When posttested their gains may appear greater than they really are because familiarity and associated relaxation have contributed to improved performance.

To further cloud the issue, Sticht says that 10–20% of ABE students score better on the pretest than the posttest. He attributes this "negative gain" to various causes including guessing, regression to the mean, and change in test performance strategy, which ironically may lead to the use of a poorer strategy.

Another consideration is the question of the way information from tests is presented as reading ages or grade levels, with the assumption that one can generalize from performance on a test to performance in a real-life situation. Ehringhaus (1990) points out the importance of ecological validity and its relevance for functional literacy assessment. Unless testing takes this into account, how can one be sure that the adult will perform in real life in the same way that she or he performs during a test? When the effects of confidence on performance are also taken into account, it seems possible that significantly improved performance on tasks that matter to the student may occur and so the relatively small gains made in grade level might mask larger gains in real terms.

This might lead to the view that despite the lack of evidence from test data, ABE programs are in reality successful. Kilbey (1985), in a U.K. study, showed that the increase in reading age that occurred over 1 year was accompanied by an increase in confidence. It is interesting that he used a British test designed for children (Neale Analysis of Reading Ability) and found a similar increase in reading age (1.43 years) to that made in U.S. studies using tests for adults.

More theoretical support for the antitest lobby stems from the claim that standardized test-design philosophy assumes an inappropriate model of text on which to base tests. Also, tests may not be testing what is actually taught but rather what is in theory taught. Such drawbacks call into question the claims of testers that they are able to accurately demonstrate the success or failure of tuition in reading by testing.

Support for the suggestion that tests used on adults are based upon an inappropriate model of text theory comes from evidence assembled by Street (1984) who proposes that Western civilization has traditionally viewed text as *autonomous*. By this he means that text itself, unlike speech, is viewed as independent of the situation in which it is produced. It is as if the text producer had a single, model reader in mind who represented all possible types of reader. One could infer from this theory that the model views any one text as a product of a writing system in which symbols are related to units of language and not to concepts or ideas. Furthermore, correct reading is not distinguished from comprehension in that the model implies that the surface structure and deep structure are identical.

In contrast to the autonomous model, Street proposes an ideological model in which more than one valid interpretation of a text may be made according to the context in which the text is read or according to the background knowledge of the reader. Some texts by their nature lend themselves more to an autonomous interpretation while others are better viewed as ideological. The assumptions of the autonomous model are that every reader will interpret the text in an identical way if she or he is reading it correctly and that all readers will be using the same strategy.

All four tests reviewed by Jackson (in Sticht, 1990) relied on reading comprehension passages for part of the test material and all could therefore be described as assuming that the autonomous model applies to their material and that the background knowledge of the reader, situation, etc., would have no effect on text understanding.

Hill and Parry (1988) have used Street's theory to support their view that standardized testing is unsuitable for ABE students. The TABE in particular is singled out by them as an unsuitable test for assessing adult reading progress, and they maintain that an alternative to standardized tests is a necessity. One weakness of using Street's argument as a reason for abandoning certain types of tests is that although it could be used to justify rejecting reading comprehension tests in which only one right answer is acceptable, it could be used as an argument for replacing them with word recognition tests, and not testing comprehension at all. The issue here is partly one of generalizability: It seems that for a number of reasons it is more difficult to establish the construct validity and generalizability of tests in the ABE population. One reason for this may be the very great range of educational and cognitive backgrounds of the clients within the population, which is certainly greater than is the case with school students, for whom the majority of reading tests were written.

Related to this issue is the question of the literacy needs of each student. The prevailing philosophy in the United Kingdom is that each student negotiates a personal syllabus and a personal assessment program. How one defines and estimates success will depend on the nature of the student's specific instruction, and whether one is assessing a student by external criteria or estimating how well a student has met his or her own criteria of success. Crucial to this is the issue of functional literacy and competency-based assessment.

Functional Literacy and Competency-Based Assessment

In theory each ABE student negotiates with a tutor to produce an individual syllabus tailored to specific needs, so that a student asking for help with reading is provided as far as possible with customized reading materials. Few ABE students are complete beginner readers. Most have some reading expertise, but it is insufficient to meet the demands made on them, hence Charnley and Jones's definition of the adult illiterate as "an illiterate adult is an adult who thinks he has a reading or writing problem" (1986, p. 171). For example, a gardener might ask for help in reading horticultural vocabulary in order to cope better with his work even though he already has some reading ability.

If all students were beginner readers when first enrolling, initial and subsequent assessment would be a different matter. But the differing degrees of competence of new students combined with their differing needs makes a functional approach the ideal, and it may therefore be helpful to consider success in functional terms, specified uniquely for individual students. If tutors claim they are offering functional literacy tuition but in practice are offering a more general syllabus, there may be a mismatch between what is said to be offered and what in fact takes place. In such a case the assessment procedure may not assess what was taught or may assess what has been taught but not what has been wanted. This confusion over definitions of functional literacy is described by Valentine (1986) who distinguishes between the requirements of functional literacy based on the needs of the community and functional literacy based on the needs of the individual. He argues that teachers confuse the two and are usually concentrating on the former and not the latter.

Teachers intend to teach functional literacy but they often assume that this means presenting a package of identical material to all students, based, for example, on road signs, medicine labels, etc. But any one student's functional literacy needs may be quite different from those assumed in the production of the common functional literacy package. If a common package is in use, then it is possible to produce a standardized test such as CASAS or Wordpower (City and Guilds, Foundation Level, 1990) to measure progress in acquiring what is taught, but if each student is pursuing his or her own syllabus, such standardized methods will be invalid. Instead, customized tests to match customized tuition are needed.

Can such customized learning and assessment work in practice? Hayes and Valentine (1989), in a comparison of the self-reported needs and self-reported learning gains for functional literacy tasks, indirectly answer the question of how closely student needs correlate with the offered tuition. They took 20 items typical of functional literacy tasks, for example, reading mail, or reading and using road maps, and asked students how much they needed to know about each, using 4-point, Likert-type items to format the tasks. From this data, mean item scores were calculated for each functional literacy task and the tasks were ranked in terms of sample means.

After 6 months' tuition, individual items were ranked again, using the same methods as previously, according to gains made in functional competence. When the two ranks were compared, the study did not demonstrate the agreement which one would expect if tutors had successfully provided instruction in accordance with students' needs. For example, the three self-reported needs tasks ranked 1, 2, and 3 are ranked 19, 15, and 8, respectively, in terms of self-reported gains.

One could argue that some items are easier to improve than others, but the discrepancies between the needs ranking and gains ranking are so great that it seems reasonable to conclude that tutors were not successful in teaching the students what they needed. If success in such cases is to be measured by performance on a standardized test for general literacy, such as the TABE, or on a measure of common functional literacy, for example the competency-based CASAS, then such a ranking may not be important, but if success is defined in terms of meeting the students' needs, then the Hayes and Valentine study shows how a program may be failing to provide the students with opportunities to become successful in areas important to them.

One may conclude that increase in competence in carrying out functional literacy tasks, however defined, is a goal of instruction, and achievement of competency in carrying out such tasks is one measure of success. In the absence of standardized tests of functional competence, the introduction of a nationally recognized certificate requiring only a low level of literacy is seen by some as a means of giving the possibility of success to students, as well as providing information for employers, who would otherwise have only their own and their tutors' informal assessments on record.

This is the belief underlying the competency-based Wordpower, the Certificate in Communication Skills awarded jointly by the City and Guilds of London Institute and ALBSU and first introduced in 1989. It is currently being offered at ABE classes in England with varying degrees of enthusiasm. Although the higher stages require one to be a competent reader, for example, able to read a newspaper, at Foundation level the student is required to cope only with simple text. For the first four tasks the tutor is instructed to provide texts which are "no more than one paragraph, comprising short, simple phrases or sentences."

Success on Wordpower depends on completing the tasks and acquiring the certificate, not necessarily in making progress. It provides the opportunity for some students who would not otherwise be able to do so to obtain a qualification, but it is not a measure of progress in reading ability. It is geared towards common functional needs, not specific ones, although there is some leeway for tutors to orient material towards students' areas of interest.

In the United Kingdom, those students not working towards a qualification have generally been assessed by the combined subjective judgments of tutor and student, a procedure which has obvious weaknesses. Holland (1989) reports that the combination of ABE practitioners' expressed needs for a model of assessment and the assessment and accountability ethos of the 1980s provided the motive for the development by ALBSU of its "Progress Profile" which seeks to provide a structure for informal testing. This profile incorporates initial and ongoing assessment together with a strategy for planning and implementing a student-negotiated syllabus. It allows for specific functional literacy to be taught and assessed.

An objective element is to some extent included, in that the student and tutor may set specific goals. The student then acts as the arbiter of success by deciding at regular intervals whereabouts she or he is on a continuum ranging from "I've started" to "I'm confident about this now." Support to justify the priority given to specific functional literacy tuition, exemplified in the Progress Profile approach, over general literacy comes from Sticht (1985, p. 336): "the transfer from specific literacy training to general literacy ability is greater than the transfer from general literacy training to specific literacy skills."

Conclusion

There is no simple answer to the problem of defining success in ABE. Two groups of issues stand out. First, does one take a formal cognitive stance and interpret success purely in terms of an increase in reading tests scores, or is an informal affective approach acceptable, with the students' feelings of increased confidence a sufficient marker? Second, how should assessment in ABE take account of the functional or general content of the curriculum and the resulting implications for relating assessment to what has been taught? These issues have had their effect on practice in the United Kingdom to such an extent that the current situation is a confused one, with tutors and organizers having a great degree of freedom in choosing for themselves, with the only regular guideline given them being that record keeping and assessment are in principle desirable.

References

Adult Literacy and Basic Skills Unit. (Undated). *Evaluating effectiveness in adult literacy and basic skills.* An ALBSU Good Practice Document. London: Author.

Berridge Centre. (1990). *Adult basic education in Nottinghamshire.* Unpublished pamphlet. Nottingham: Author.

Charnley, A.H., & Jones, H.A. (1986). *The concept of success in adult literacy.* London: ALBSU.

Darkenwald, G.G., & Valentine, T. (1985). Outcomes of participation in adult basic skills education. *Lifelong Learning, 8*(5), 17–22, 31.

Diekhoff, G.M. (1988). An appraisal of adult literacy programs: Reading between the lines. *Journal of Reading, 31*(7), 624–630.

Ehringhaus, C.C. (1990). Functional literacy assessment: Issues of interpretation. *Adult Education Quarterly, 40*(4), 187–196.

Fox, B.J., & Fingeret, A. (1984). Reading evaluation adult diagnosis (revised). *Journal of Reading, 28*(3), 258–261.

Gorman, T.P. (1981). A survey of attainment and progress of learners in adult literacy schemes. *Educational Research, 23*(3), 190–198.

Hayes, R., & Valentine, T. (1989). The functional needs of low-literate adult basic education students. *Adult Education Quarterly, 40*(1), 1–14.

Hill, C., & Parry, K. (1988). *Reading assessment: Autonomous and pragmatic models of literacy* (LC Report 88–2). New York: Columbia University, Literacy Center, Teachers College.

Holland, D. (1989). *The progress profile. Assessment of student progress in adult literacy* (Final Report). Nottingham: University of Nottingham. Department of Adult Education.

Kilbey, K. (1985). *A prediction of outcomes? A psychological investigation into cognitive and affective development within the framework of adult literacy provision.* Unpublished doctoral dissertation, University of Aston, Birmingham, U.K.

Kohl, H. (1974). *Reading: How to.* London: Penguin.

Stanovich, K.E. (1986). Matthew effects in reading: Some consequences of individual differences in the acquisition of literacy. *Reading Research Quarterly, 21*(4), 360–406.

Sticht, T. (1985). Understanding readers and their uses of texts. In T.M. Duffy & R. Waller (Eds.), *Designing usable texts* (pp. 315–340). San Diego, CA: Academic Press.

Sticht, T.G. (1990). *Testing and assessment in adult basic education and English as a second language programs.* San Diego, CA: Applied Behavioral & Cognitive Sciences. (ED 317 867)

Street, B. (1984). *Literacy in theory and practice.* Cambridge: Cambridge University Press.

Valentine, T. (1986). Adult functional literacy as a goal of instruction. *Adult Education Quarterly, 36*(2), 108–113.

Learning from Researching: Literacy Practitioners and Assessment of Adults' Reading Progress

JEAN E. FARGO
MARILYN COLLINS
NOVEMBER 1989

Enthusiasm about teacher or classroom-based research has been in the air for well over a decade now. More and more educators are systematically exploring questions that have evolved from their own teaching and learning situations (Queenan, 1987), and discussion has emerged about the ways teachers best fit into the research process. Many in the field (for example, Patterson & Stansell, 1987, and Goswami & Stillman, 1987) are strong advocates of the teacher-researcher role. Others (for example, Applebee, 1987) view teachers as valuable partners in research but question how far that role should extend.

Unaware of these differences of opinion about the teacher-researcher role, we carried out a small research project at Literacy Volunteers of New York City. We were inspired by reading about classroom-based research and were spurred by the need to solve a practical problem in our adult literacy organization. We focused on the problem of how to effectively evaluate the progress of the adult beginning readers with whom we work.

We undertook the project to get information for dealing with this specific issue. However, it turned out to be a rich learning experience in many ways, by (1) giving us insights into designing and carrying out research in general, (2) broadening our understanding of the way students learn about the learning process, (3) enriching our everyday teaching and interaction with students, and (4) helping us view research by others in a new light.

Identifying the Research Problem

The development of effective assessment procedures has concerned our staff for a number of years. We had worked on procedures to supplement standardized tests, but either they proved inadequate or were never fully developed. This time, rather than exploring such ideas piecemeal, we set out as a team, in a carefully organized way, to develop and test a comprehensive assessment tool. Basic to the educational philosophy of Literacy Volunteers of New York City is the view that students should take charge of their own learning. Along with this, some of us had become concerned more and more with ways students' learning is affected by their perceptions of the learning process and the ways they think reading and writing should be taught. Our current assessment procedures, however, have not reflected these concerns and values; rather, they have been shaped by state requirements for standardized test scores and by limited staff resources. These evaluations, which are carried out after every 50 hours of tutoring, consist of administering standardized silent reading tests and having brief conferences with students and tutors to discuss these tests and other ways in which students feel they are progressing.

Our first task was to reconfirm the goals of the assessment tool. It would need to look at the ways students viewed the reading process, probe the strategies they were using and the ways these were changing, and actively involve the students in the evaluation process. Once we had the broad view of the assessment goals, we zeroed in on the specifics of the tool itself. We knew we wanted the major evaluation tool to be an interview, with discussion between a student and a staff member using a consistent set of questions. At this point our main concern became: What questions should we be asking in the interview to get the information we wanted about each student? We decided to fieldtest a set of interview questions and see where that led us. We would: (1) develop the questions, (2) ask them of a representative sample of students, (3) record the responses verbatim, (4) review and categorize the responses, and then (5) generalize about what kinds of responses were elicited by a specific question. Those questions that proved to elicit information that would help in accomplishing the assessment goals would become the basis of a regular assessment interview-discussion.

The interview we developed contained 30 questions grouped into categories such as "Other-than-school knowledge," "School experiences," "Perceptions of self as a reader," and "Perceptions of ways adults should be taught to read." We viewed it as a first draft of the interview we would eventually carry out regularly. The fieldtest involved interviewing 16 students, who represented a cross-section of our student population. The interviews averaged 1–1½ hours each.

Looking at the Data

The purpose of our project was not to test any particular hypothesis or to make a comparison with other data. We would examine the content of each student's response in order to discover: "What was the response to this question mostly about?" and "Were the responses to this particular question useful?"

We worked on this separately and then compared our results. Having two people working on this task turned out to be especially helpful in providing a good system of checks and balances. Working alone gave us the space to think out our own conclusions. Coming together to compare and revise our work helped us to step back and be more objective. An interesting phenomenon complicated this process, however. We found we had already begun the process of assessing the responses as we listened to the students during the interviews. We had begun to make immediate, impressionistic judgments that sometimes got in the way of our later work.

As practitioners who are usually immersed in responding directly to our students' learning needs, we were drawn toward thinking about ways to handle the issues raised in the student responses. The structured process of having to classify responses according to their content helped to move us into another mode of thinking. We had to step back from a more immediately responsive and intuitive "teacher style," to a more removed and analytical "researcher style." The process of identifying the content of each response was interesting in another way. The original categories into which the questions were grouped helped us identify the main thrust of a student's comments, but at the same time these categories would also bias us as to their actual content.

For example, one of our main concerns was to discover which interview questions would help us learn if a student's view of reading was based more on seeking meaning or more on reading words correctly. The questions that we felt would give us this information were those we grouped under the headings "Students' perceptions of the reading process" and "Ways students think adults should be taught to read." We examined the responses to these questions most closely for this information. It was not until we decided to examine all the questions for information on meaning-based models of reading that we found that nearly all the advanced students brought up the issue of meaning when they answered one of the questions in the category "Perceptions of progress," specifically "How will you be able to tell that you are a good reader?"

Further, in reviewing the data, we found that we had been somewhat inconsistent in asking the questions precisely as written. This, of course, affected the reliability of our findings. It brought up an important issue, however: that practitioners will not always ask questions as formulated, particularly if they do not seem appropriate for a specific situation. This would always be a concern, whether we were doing individual student assessments or trying to compare responses among a group of students. The variations in data resulting from the personality and style of interviewers is a problem that may not be solvable, but we may be able to find ways to minimize or identify these variations.

Learning about Students

The goal of this research project was to determine the usefulness of a particular set of interview questions. As we reviewed the responses, however, we could not help thinking beyond the content to how the students came to answer in the ways they did. What we began to look at were the different ways students described their reading process and learning process. Following are the responses of five different students to two different questions. They show a range in perceptions of and ability to discuss these processes.

Can you describe what you do as you read?

Carl (below Grade 1 reading level): I got to go over it about ten times before I know what the page means.

Dwayne (below Grade 1 level): I take the whole word apart piece by piece, letter by letter. Then I piece each letter together. Then sound each letter out and put it back together. And sometimes I can figure it out.

Geraldine (Grade 1 level): If I don't have a lot on my mind, I read better. If the teacher is here every time, I read better too. I can spell now. I couldn't before.

Peter (Grade 2 level): I try to read my lesson. Make out the words. Break them down.

Robert (Grade 3 level): I read the story. I underline words I don't know. I look up the words in the dictionary. I reread the sentence. I break the words down. I use the letters to help me. If I can't get it, I ask someone.

What would you do in a lesson if you were teaching a beginner how to read?

Carl: First teach ABCs. Then get a book like an ABC book. A for apple, B for boy. Teach them how to spell, like *car, cat.*

Dwayne: Start from scratch. Start with ABCs and spelling words. It would be like a format.

Geraldine: I would teach them to read one page till they got it good. I would give them homework. Give them a word and have them spell it and write it down. I would see if they could write things out of their head and spell things about that subject. I would not have them jump from page to page. The student should read a lot. The tutor should be there often.

Peter: I would do the same things [as my teacher]. The way my teacher is helping me. Breaking down words, syllables, in different ways.

Robert: I would give them easy books. I would read it to them. I would help them read it and help them with the hard words. I would have them listen to it on tape. I've been through the process. I think I could teach someone.

One reason for these differences could be the student's general articulateness and ability to describe what he or she does. Beyond this, however, it seemed to us that such differences also likely reflected the opportunities these adult beginning readers had had to discuss their learning process and to learn the language that describes reading and writing. In many cases, students may not have even considered that they should have a role in looking at the ways they learn.

Revision during Researching

As we carried out the research itself, questions emerged about the timing and integration of assessment into the educational program and about ways to facilitate students' taking a directive role in the assessment process. During the early stages, we took for granted that the new interview and discussion would simply be integrated into our current procedure of regular 50-hour tests and conferences. Further, we assumed that asking students about their reading process, in itself, would cause them to assume an evaluative role.

The amount of time involved in interviewing became a major concern. Lengthy interviews would not be practical for busy practitioners. The question was: how could we organize the interviews so they would be manageable timewise and also fit into the rhythm of the educational program? This led to our first major revision in the assessment procedure resulting from this research—a restructuring of the interview process.

Rather than one long interview every 50 hours, we decided on a series of short ones. They would take place: (1) when a student entered the program, (2) after the student's first few weeks, (3) when specific student-related issues emerged (such as attendance problems or difficulties in getting along with other students or staff), and (4) during periodic evaluations (every 50 hours of tutoring). These interviews would have different focuses, based on student and staff concerns most relevant at that time.

Observations about students' limitations in describing their learning process led to a second major change in the assessment procedure, which coincided with the first. Along with revising the timing and focus of the interviews, we reorganized the original questions and added new ones to help students look more closely at their own learning and give them greater responsibility for evaluating it. For example, in the interview that would take place after a student had been in the program a few weeks, we decided to include such questions as: "How will you be able to tell that you are a good reader?" "When you come to a difficult word how do you figure it out?" "What are some things you can do to help yourself in learning to read?" "What do you hope to accomplish in the next few months?" After 50 hours of instruction, we would follow up with such questions as: "In what ways do you think your reading has changed since you took your last test?" "When you come to a difficult word when you are reading, what do you do to figure it out?" "What are you doing now to help yourself learn to read? "What have you accomplished in the last few months? How do you feel about that?"

We also made another revision to the procedure. We developed a set of questions to use during ongoing teaching. Here our goal was to help students look at learning as it was taking place, rather than doing this only every 6 months or so and separately from the reading and writing experience. These included such questions as: "What do you think about what we are doing? What is the most helpful or interesting or difficult?" "What are some questions you have about what we have been doing?" "Do you have any ideas about what we should do next?"

Bringing Research to Our Teaching

Because we were literacy practitioners, elements of the research experience spilled over into our teaching in a very immediate way. Some of this was by design, some was anticipated.

Jean Fargo's experience

In the midst of our researching students' perception of their reading process, I initiated a spelling class with a small group of adult beginning readers. Being immersed in thinking out the evaluation process and the ways to draw students into that process, I thought it only natural to try it in a real teaching situation.

My plan was, at the first class session, to ask students a few questions about how they thought spelling should be taught, and after several months to ask these same questions again. The assessment research project provided a source of ideas for possible questions. The questions I asked were: "Have you tried to learn to spell in the past? What happened?" and "If you were me [the teacher] how would you teach a spelling class?" The adults' re-

sponses to the preclass questions provided quite general information. One student wrote: "I never been in a school. I didn't have a chance to go to school...." Another: "I look at the word and say the word." And another: "I would try to give you the sound of the word and the pronunciation of the word." [Original spelling corrected.]

I was rediscovering what we found in the original research project—that adult beginning readers often know very little about the ways reading and writing are learned and thus have difficulty discussing their learning in ways that are immediately helpful to a teacher. Well, I thought, it will be interesting to see how each student's ability to discuss such questions changes. The responses also made me wonder whether or not these were the best questions. Did I need to be more specific?

In the first few weeks of the class, I taught the students two different spelling strategies: one emphasized hearing sounds; the other focused on visual memory. During the next stage I planned to have students identify patterns of errors in their own spelling and work on their particular needs. Before we went on to this step, I decided to ask another set of assessment questions. This seemed a natural time for an evaluation, and I was curious to see how the students had integrated the strategies into their thinking about spelling. They were asked to write about what they had learned and ways their ideas about spelling had changed since we began.

My expectation was that they would describe ways they were successfully using the strategies we had worked on together. Instead, even before writing, Amelia began to talk about her constant spelling preoccupation—"I still can't hear the sounds." Dora defended her tutor's insistence on interrupting reading to look up words in the dictionary, "I fiend that I s[till] look up w[ords] in the d[ictionar]a. That hope me." More relevant was Ajka's response. She wrote describing that she had begun to think about spelling during her reading: "Wen I reding, I se the wort so meni tiem and I luk at [them alot]. This wey I thenk I go to remember it." I was disappointed. Struggling to find a positive response, I pulled back a bit. Then, without consciously deciding to do so, I found myself beginning to create a mental chart for categorizing each student's responses.

Later I went over their answers carefully, having learned that first impressions are often inaccurate. I found that Amelia did mention the visual memory strategy and that Dora did note hearing sounds at the beginning, middle, and ends of words. But most important, they were discussing spelling in an informed and focused way.

While I certainly espouse that teachers should always look at the *process* of their students' learning rather than the *product,* and try to practice this, the student research experience was providing me with additional tools to do so.

Marilyn Collins's experience

This research project gave me a new view of the ways questions can be liberating. There's so much students have to tell us about how they learn, how they feel about how learning is going for them, and what works for them—if we only give them the chance. This was demonstrated to me by a new student at the time I was involved in the research. Students often ask me to give them my opinion on their progress. This time it was Dawn who approached me with "How do you think I am doing?" Because I had not yet had a chance to observe one of her lessons (she is taught by a volunteer tutor I supervise), I told her I didn't really have enough information to give her a good assessment. Instead, I asked

her how she thought she was doing. "I'm learning a lot, a real lot," was her reply. Instead of patting her on the back and leaving it at that, as I might have, my experience with the research project prompted me to ask, "What do you mean?" She then told me, "Well, now I write stories I never wrote before. And now I read books. I hadn't picked up a book in years. And sometimes I read to my son. And I'm going for help now for my stress, so I can concentrate better on my learning."

This experience helped me realize that the type of questions we had been developing in our research took the power out of the questioner's hands and gave it to the student. We were asking questions that would help them think through and gain insights into themselves as learners. It's likely that Dawn, herself, hadn't realized the breadth of the changes caused by her new reading experiences until she was given an opportunity to articulate them.

Now, rather than asking, "Did you do your homework?" I ask, "How do you figure out words when you're working at home? What kind of homework really helps you learn? What can we show you that will make homework easier?"

This process was gratifying because I saw how this style of questioning was becoming a part of my ongoing work with students. I have found that students enjoy answering questions about learning—it brings to light for them things they have never realized before.

Ways research strategies can aid teaching

Practitioners traditionally see the purpose of research as providing a body of new data that helps answer a particular question. But, when the researcher is also a teacher, the research experience can make another valuable contribution—providing a framework that affects one's behavior during teaching.

As described earlier, we found that this:

- Creates an environment that fosters keener observation of our own teaching.
- Trains us to have carefully thought out questions in our heads as we teach, helping us to better catch key information.
- Provides a strategy for revising our practice in an informed way, using an orderly, analytical, methodical eye for gathering data, and standing back to organize and finally analyze it.
- Infuses our everyday work with new energy through the joy of discovery.

Learning from the Research Community

Once we had become immersed in the research experience, we found that we read research reports by others in a new light. The distance between ourselves and these authors diminished. Their work became less theoretical and abstract, we found more ways to make use of their ideas, and we began to feel part of a larger research community.

The ideas of Odell (1987) and Applebee, especially, immediately touched our experience, Odell because his work supports and illuminates the discoveries we made about our research process, and Applebee because he raises questions about the kind of role we took on in our research project.

Learning from Odell

Odell's article "Planning Classroom Research" helps us see our own experiences more clearly. His description of developing the research question (p. 130) is especially relevant:

> No one can predict exactly when or how we will arrive at the final version of a research question…. Research questions usually arise from a complex reciprocal process in which the collection and analysis of data may lead to a

revised question, and that question may lead to more data gathering, which in turn may require further revision of the question.

In our case, our first question "What information does a particular question elicit?" kept being transformed from "Which questions should be used?" to "When should we ask this question?" to "How can this question change the student's role in the evaluation and learning process?"

As the research proceeded, that is, as we learned from it, a new vision of our needs emerged. This led to taking action through revising our practice. We decided that student centered, process oriented assessment needed to be integrated into everyday teaching. It also raised the need for more research to determine if these revisions were indeed taking us in the direction we wanted. Odell puts it this way (p. 158):

> As we continue to do research, we continue to grow. We continue to learn. Our work cannot become stale, because we are continually redefining it. And this process of continual redefinition and renewal helps us retain the enthusiasm and commitment that brought us into this profession in the first place.

Learning from Applebee

Applebee has important questions about the role of teachers in research projects. He points out (p. 6) that:

> Though the knowledge that teachers bring to educational research is different from that brought by researchers trained in the various academic disciplines, we often treat it as though it *should* (author's emphasis) be the same…. Rather than encouraging systematic reflection on the special expertise that teachers have, this puts the focus instead on the methodological and disciplinary skills they don't have, and don't need to have in order to be excellent teachers. Instead of a powerful model in which the research is enriched by the differing exper-

tise of the participants, we have a weakened model that inadvertently undercuts the contribution that teachers can make.

We agree with Applebee that we must be concerned with the roles and expertise of teachers who carry out research. We felt we could have benefitted from more knowledge of experimental research. We especialy needed information about scientifically sound strategies for determining a research sample, improving reliability among researchers collecting data, and creating research designs that allow for replication and for comparison across studies.

Further, we should be scrupulous in acknowledging what we are capable of. Rather than try to imitate experimental research, and do it poorly, we should find out what we can do well because of our particular position, immersed daily in the learning-teaching situation.

We discovered that because we were teachers—the agents of change—we were able to:

- Carry out a research project that could meet current needs, without spending precious time waiting for funding or searching for outside researchers.

- Redesign aspects of the research while it was in progress, shaping it to our emerging knowledge and re-vision of the issue.

- View the problems and new issues that emerged during the research as challenges to take on and solve, rather than as shortcomings of the research that might detract from its value.

- Apply our findings immediately to our educational program.

We found this teacher-researcher project complex and rewarding. We learned more about research, about our students, and about our teaching, as well as about ways to carry out assessment. In describing our research experiences, we have tried to discuss some of the advantages and limitations of this approach. Literacy practitioners come smack up against tough problems each day and are eager to solve them. We discovered that a modest teacher-researcher project can be an effective approach to finding answers.

References

Applebee, A.N. (1987). Musings...Teachers and the process of research. *Research in the Teaching of English, 21*, 5–7.

Goswami, D., & Stillman, P.R. (Eds.). (1987). *Reclaiming the classroom*. Portsmouth, NH: Heinemann.

Odell, L. (1987). Planning classroom research. In D. Goswami & P.R. Stillman (Eds.), *Reclaiming the classroom*. Portsmouth, NH: Heinemann.

Patterson, L., & Stansell, J.C. (1987). Teachers and researchers: A new mutualism. *Language Arts, 64*, 717–720.

Queenan, M. (1987). Teachers as researchers? *English Journal, 76*, 88–90.

Reading Difficulty of Tests for Job Placement

PHILIP ASH
APRIL 1992

Evaluation of the reading difficulty of tests—including cognitive tests with high verbal loadings, personality and attitude inventories, and similar questionnaires—although not much attended to, is an important aspect of test validity. In both employment selection and educational placement, a significant discrepancy between the reading level required to succeed on the job or in the educational program and the reading demands imposed by testing instruments can result in misplacing or screening out otherwise qualified students or job applicants, and might also lead to charges of discrimination against minorities.

Colleagues and I, during the course of a 6-year project to evaluate the tests used in a major statewide merit system in the United States, evaluated about 200 of the system's tests. We found that many of the tests then used had reading (educational attainment) levels appropriate for high school or high school graduation, while the positions for which they were used to evaluate applicants

had reading grade requirements that were nominal (for example, sixth grade or below), especially for service (for example, animal care) and low-level maintenance jobs.

In fact, a major reason for undertaking the project was the perceived danger of adverse impact by the tests. The reading level of employment selection tests should be a bit lower than the job's educational requirements so that the applicant can concentrate upon the test's content.

Readability is an important factor in any written test, because of its effect on test reliability, but measurement of the reading difficulty of merit system tests may be affected by the use of jargon (usually common words used in bureaucracies, trades, and professions with special meanings). Jargon increases reading difficulty, especially in fields in which common words have been redefined for special purposes. In computereze, the meanings of such words as *bug, mouse, virus,* and *bit,* to name a few, have little relation to their everyday meanings.

Checking on the reading difficulty of tests and inventories that purport to assess the individual's qualifications is important. We must ensure that the measurement instrument imposes a reading requirement upon the examinee that is commensurate with the reading requirements of the tasks or assignments that individual will later face on the job.

[Information about the 6-year project mentioned here can be found in Philip Ash, "The Reading Difficulty of Merit System Tests," *Proceedings of the 1973 American Psychological Association Convention*, Washington, DC: American Psychological Association, 1974; and Philip Ash, N. Taylor, and L. Hoel, "The UCSSI: Update a Merit System," *College and University Personnel Association Journal, 23*(4), 1972, pp. 21–35.]

Rapid Estimate of Adult Literacy in Medicine (REALM): A Quick Reading Test for Patients

PEGGY W. MURPHY
TERRY C. DAVIS
SANDRA W. LONG
ROBERT H. JACKSON
BARBARA C. DECKER
OCTOBER 1993

Professionals in health care settings often assume that patients are able to read the usual educational brochures, written instructions, consent forms, prescription labels, and health questionnaires. However, adult patients with low literacy skills often try to hide their reading deficiencies, so potential problems with patient understanding are not recognized (Davis, Crouch, Wills, Miller, & Abdehou, 1990; Doak, Doak, & Root, 1985). The discrepancy between patient reading ability and readability of medical information can be a crucial factor in patient health care compliance, participation in preventive care, and clinical research.

Data from the English Language Proficiency Study (U.S. Department of Commerce, Bureau of the Census, 1982) and the 1980 U.S. census suggest that a high percentage of patients cared for in public health clinics are not fully literate. Previous studies by one of the authors, Terry Davis, revealed low reading levels of patients in several public clinics in Louisiana (Davis et al., 1990). These studies confirm and extend previous findings (Doak et al., 1985; Powers, 1988; Zion & Aiman, 1989) that patient education brochures, health questionnaires, and consent forms commonly used in public clinics are written on a level far above the average reading ability of public clinic patients. These studies also confirmed previous findings that patient educational status is not a valid indicator of reading ability (Davis et al., 1991; Doak et al., 1985; Jackson, Davis, Bairnsfather, & Gault, 1991). Patients in these studies read four to five grade levels below the grade they last attended.

Direct testing is the most reliable way for health care providers to identify patients with limited reading skills (Doak et al., 1985). Public health care providers are realizing the importance of screening patients for low reading levels so that education materials and prevention programs can be redesigned to meet their needs. In addition, investigators receiving support from the National Institutes of Health for community prevention projects are being asked to screen subjects for reading ability (Dr. Nancy Santanello, National Heart, Lung & Blood Institute, National Institutes of Health, personal communication, September 27, 1990).

Health care professionals have looked to the field of education for instruments to screen patient reading ability. However, the common standardized decoding and comprehension reading tests are not practical for use in busy primary care and public health settings. These tests are either too lengthy or not applicable for medical settings.

For example, previous research by the authors (Davis et al., 1993) found patients were not receptive to taking the Slosson Oral Reading Test–Revised (SORT–R) or the Wide Range Achievement Test–Revised (WRAT–R). Patients felt uneasy about having to read so many words on the SORT–R, and older patients found the print size too difficult to read. Readers with limited skills became rapidly frustrated with the difficulty of the initial items on the WRAT–R and often failed to complete the test.

These findings suggest that the WRAT–R and the SORT–R are not appropriate tests for adult patients whose reading levels are below ninth grade. The Peabody Individual Achievement Test–Revised (PIAT–R) was well received by the patients, but its length and high cost limit its use in busy public clinics. Looking for alternatives, we found that Doak et al. (1985) recommend the cloze technique to measure comprehension. The cloze procedure measures the reader's ability to replace words missing in a passage. One limitation is that its strict construction (every fifth word is omitted) may not allow health care providers to measure patient understanding of specific information.

We went on to develop a brief instrument called the REALM (Davis et al., 1991) to screen patients for low reading levels. The original REALM, which consisted of 125 words, correlated well with the SORT–R, WRAT–R, and PIAT–R (Davis et al., 1991). Then, in response to requests from researchers and clinicians, the REALM was revised and shortened to 66 words (Davis et al., 1993). This article is intended to establish the shortened REALM's utility and to inform the educational community of its existence. It is one more option

available, should health care professionals call on readers of this journal for advice.

Description of the REALM

The REALM is a reading recognition test that measures patient ability to pronounce common medical words and lay terms for body parts and illnesses. The revised test contains 66 words arranged in three columns in ascending order of number of syllables and increasing difficulty (Figure 1). The test is printed on purple paper and has large type set in widely spaced columns. These features give the REALM a friendly, nonthreatening appearance. The back of the examiner's copy contains a description of the test, standardized directions for administering and scoring it, and a chart converting raw scores to grade range estimates.

A linear regression analysis, using REALM raw scores to predict the raw scores from the SORT–R, was conducted to establish the grade range estimates of the REALM (Figure 2). Grade equivalents reported for the SORT–R were used as a guide to determine the REALM grade range estimates. The SORT–R was selected as a standard of comparison for the REALM because it is a widely used, nationally (U.S.) standardized test. Both the REALM and the SORT–R have a high concentration of words at low reading levels.

Please note that patient scores are interpreted as estimates of literacy, not grade equivalents. Clinicians and researchers use these levels to identify patients who have trouble reading words in medical settings. The REALM can also identify a nonreader so medical personnel may use repeated oral instructions or appropriate illustrations and models. If for any reason health care providers want a more complete assessment of reading skills, a more extensive instrument can be administered.

Figure 1
Rapid Estimate of Adult Literacy in Medicine (REALM)*

Reading level _____
Patient name/subject # _____ Date of birth _____ Grade completed_____
Date _____ Clinic _____ Examiner _____

List 1		List 2		List 3	
fat	_____	fatigue	_____	allergic	_____
flu	_____	pelvic	_____	menstrual	_____
pill	_____	jaundice	_____	testicle	_____
dose	_____	infection	_____	colitis	_____
eye	_____	exercise	_____	emergency	_____
stress	_____	behavior	_____	medication	_____
smear	_____	prescription	_____	occupation	_____
nerves	_____	notify	_____	sexually	_____
germs	_____	gallbladder	_____	alcoholism	_____
meals	_____	calories	_____	irritation	_____
disease	_____	depression	_____	constipation	_____
cancer	_____	miscarriage	_____	gonorrhea	_____
caffeine	_____	pregnancy	_____	inflammatory	_____
attack	_____	arthritis	_____	diabetes	_____
kidney	_____	nutrition	_____	hepatitis	_____
hormones	_____	menopause	_____	antibiotics	_____
herpes	_____	appendix	_____	diagnosis	_____
seizure	_____	abnormal	_____	potassium	_____
bowel	_____	syphilis	_____	anemia	_____
asthma	_____	hemorrhoids	_____	obesity	_____
rectal	_____	nausea	_____	osteoporosis	_____
incest	_____	directed	_____	impetigo	_____

Score
List 1 _____
List 2 _____
List 3 _____
Raw
score _____

* While the set of words used in REALM is copyrighted, its authors are placing the test in the public domain
  to encourage its use by physicians and reading specialists. Plastic laminated copies of the word list and
  examiner copies with instructions are available from Peggy Murphy, Department of Internal Medicine,
  LSUMC-S, PO Box 33932, Shreveport, LA 71130-3932, USA. Telephone: (318) 674-5813.

Figure 2
REALM vs. SORT–R: Scatter Plot with Regression Line

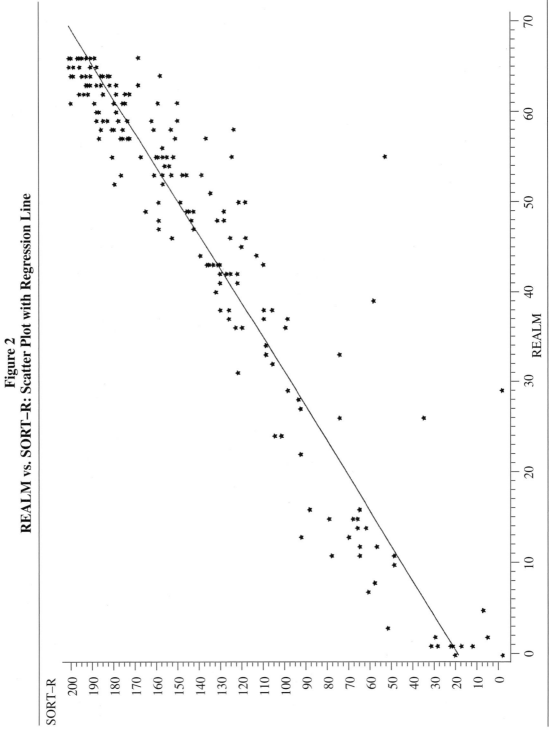

Figure 3

Figure 3
Correlation Analysis of REALM with Longer Reading Tests

3 'WITH'	Variables:	SORT–R	WRAT–R	PIAT–R
1 'VAR'	Variables:	REALM		

Simple statistics

Variable	N	M	SD	Sum
SORT–R	203	132.91133	56.05030	26981
WRAT–R	203	41.48276	17.23206	8421
PIAT–R	203	66.82266	24.87311	13565
REALM	203	44.26601	20.65603	8986

Simple statistics

Variable	Minimum	Maximum
SORT–R	0	199.00000
WRAT–R	0	87.00000
PIAT–R	0	98.00000
REALM	0	66.00000

Pearson correlation coefficients/Prob > |R| under Ho: $Rho = 0$ / N = 203

	REALM
SORT–R	0.94788
	0.0001
WRAT–R	0.88401
	0.0001
PIAT–R	0.95606
	0.0001

Note: All subjects were adult patients at a university medical clinic in the United States.

Decoding tests like the REALM, in which subjects read words aloud in isolation, are acknowledged as useful predictors of adult reading ability. Such reading recognition tests do not measure its comprehension, but they do alert health care providers to patients who have limited reading skills. Physicians need to be aware that patients who have trouble pronouncing words below a ninth-grade level will probably have difficulty comprehending most patient education materials.

Content validity was built into the REALM by selecting words from education materials and forms used in the Louisiana State University hospital clinics. Criterion validity was evidenced by high correlations between the REALM and the SORT–R (.96, $p < .0001$), the PIAT–R (.97, $p < .0001$), and the WRAT–R (.88, $p < .0001$). (See Figure 3.)

The REALM also appears to have good face validity, as evaluated by physician, staff, and patient receptivity to the test and its applicability to medical settings (Anastasi, 1988). Health care providers perceive the test words to be related to health care.

Administration and Scoring

The patient is asked to read orally from a laminated copy of the REALM, while the examiner records responses on an individual test form. Patients begin by reading the first words on List 1 and continuing until all lists are completed. Five seconds are allowed for pronunciation of each word before the patient is asked to go to the next. After reaching a point where no additional words can be read, patients are asked to look over the words remaining on the lists to see whether they recognize any of them. Testing is stopped when the patient is unable to pronounce any additional words correctly.

The test is scored by placing a plus by each correct response, a check by an incorrect response, and a minus by any word not attempted. The REALM scoring uses a dictionary pronunciation guide (Gove, 1981). Raw scores are determined by adding the number of correctly pronounced words. These can then be converted to grade range estimates: third grade and below, fourth to sixth grade, seventh to eighth grade, and high school (Figure 4).

Figure 4
REALM Grade Estimate

Raw score	Estimated grade range and practical meaning
0–18	**Third grade and below** These patients may not be able to read most educational materials and probably cannot even understand simple prescription labels. Repeated oral instructions will be needed to enhance compliance: the doctor cannot simply write a prescription or give standard levels of instruction and expect compliance. Materials, including simple video and audio tapes, may be helpful if a health care worker is present during their use and is available to answer questions. Repeated oral instructions will be the key to establishing long-term compliance.
19–44	**Fourth to sixth grade** Tremendous potential for improvement exists in this group They should respond well to direct instruction by health care providers and should be able to read and comprehend materials written on elementary school levels. Appropriately written materials may still require one-on-one counseling for adequate understanding.
45–60	**Seventh to eighth grade** These patients will certainly benefit from appropriately written materials, but material (both oral and written) should not be too simple (for example, first grade) or too complex. Material written for a fourth- to sixth-grade level may be appropriate.
61–66	**Ninth grade and above** These readers can understand much high school level material presented to them; therefore, current educational brochures may be effective. These individuals should also be able to converse with their physicians about matters of lifestyle.

Practical Application

The REALM is a practical tool for busy public health clinics. All patients can be given this screening instrument during the standard intake procedure. The REALM takes about 2 to 3 minutes to administer and score. Physicians, nurses, social workers, research assistants, office personnel, and other health care professionals can be trained to administer and score the test. It can then be placed in the patient's chart to alert medical personnel to adjust communication with the patient to a level commensurate with his or her reading ability. When physicians have estimates of patient reading grade ranges, they can adjust their patient interaction language to appropriate levels. They can also select or design more appropriate written patient education materials.

Currently, the REALM is being used routinely with more than 1,000 patients per year in a preventive medicine clinic at Louisiana State University Medical Center in Shreveport. Information thus obtained on patient reading levels is proving useful in directing patient-physician communications and appears to reduce errors due to physician assumptions that patients understand commonly used oral and written medical information.

Conclusion

Experience with the REALM (Davis et al., 1991; Davis et al., 1993; Jackson et al., 1991) suggests several conclusions. (1) The REALM is useful in medical settings as a quick identifier of patients who have less than high school level reading abilities (Davis et al., 1991). (2) The REALM has identified more than the expected number of patients who may have difficulty with all forms of patient-physician interaction because of their limited reading ability. (3) Patients who read above the 9th-grade level probably can use standard written medical information (most are written on the 11th- to 12th-grade level, as assessed by the FOG readability formula). Patients who read below the 9th-grade level will need materials adjusted to meet their needs. For example, patients reading at the 3rd-grade level or below will need simplified written instructions in large print, with liberal use of culturally sensitive pictures and, if possible, audiovisual tapes. (4) After individual patient reading ability is determined, appropriate educational programs can be developed for identified groups of low level readers.

Implications

Traditionally, nurses have been responsible for patient instruction, but the medical community now recognizes the need for educators to work with medical personnel to provide knowledge about reading and assessment methods. Educators have skills needed to improve the health education of patients with limited literacy skills. Educators may be asked to help develop patient education programs, including composing health instructions, brochures, and questionnaires. Collaboration between educators and health care professionals may enhance communication between patients and health care providers, improve overall health care, reduce the occurrence of acute but preventable disease, and ultimately lower the cost of health care.

References

Anastasi, A. (1988). *Psychological testing*. New York: Macmillan.

Davis, T.C., Crouch, M.A., Wills, G., Miller, S., & Abdehou, D.M. (1990). The gap between patient reading comprehension and the readability of patient education materials. *Journal of Family Practice, 31*, 533–538.

Davis, T.C., Crouch, M.A., Long, S.W., Jackson, R.H., Bates, P., & George, R.B. (1991). Rapid assessment of literacy levels of adult primary care patients. *Family Medicine, 23*(6), 433–435.

Davis, T.C., Long, S.W., Jackson, R.H., Mayeaux, E.J., George, R.B., Murphy, P.W., & Crouch, M.A. (1993). Rapid estimate of adult literacy in medicine: A shortened screening instrument. *Family Medicine, 25*, 391–395.

Doak, C.C., Doak, L.G., & Root, J.H. (1985). Teaching patients with low literacy skills. Philadelphia, PA: Lippincott.

Gove, P.B. (Ed.). (1981). *Webster's third new international dictionary of the English language unabridged.* Springfield, MA: Merriam-Webster.

Jackson, R.H., Davis, T.C., Bairnsfather, L.E., & Gault, H. (1991). Patient reading ability: An overlooked problem in health care. *Southern Medical Journal, 84*(10), 1172–1175.

Powers, R.D. (1988). Emergency department patient literacy and the readability of patient directed materials. *Annals of Emergency Medicine, 17*, 124–126.

U.S. Department of Commerce, Bureau of the Census. (1982). *English language proficiency study* (ELPS-43-15-82 559-010/55). Washington, DC: U.S. Government Printing Office.

Zion, A.B., & Aiman, J. (1989). After office hours. Level of reading difficulty in the American College of Obstetrics and Gynecologists patient education pamphlets. *Obstetrics and Gynecology, 74*(6), 955–959.

What Works: Adult Literacy Program Evaluation

NANCY D. PADAK
GARY M. PADAK
FEBRUARY 1991

Evaluation appears to be a particularly problematic aspect of adult literacy programs and services. Three recent statewide surveys in the U.S. have concluded that evaluations are either seldom undertaken or are reported in ways that make meaningful interpretation difficult (Bear, Ferry, & Templeton, 1987; Knudson-Fields, 1989; Steele, 1989). The haphazard state of program evaluation has led to a "misinterpretation that 'everything is fine' in adult literacy" (Diekhoff, 1988, p. 629).

Certain evaluation difficulties may be a function of the design of adult literacy programs. For example, many programs adopt open-entry policies or employ volunteer tutors to accommodate as many learners as possible. Open-entry policies may exacerbate evaluation problems, however, because several aspects of a program must be evaluated. Attempting to account for attendance differences when reporting achievement data, for example, requires sophisticated statistical procedures. These may not be easy to apply nor appropriate when qualitative or holistic measures of growth are being used.

Open-exit poses a related evaluation problem: Are achievement data about "persisters" a true picture of a program's effectiveness? Differences in volunteers' understanding of instructional principles and practices also may cause difficulties in evaluating a program's success. Finally, when evaluations are tied to requests for funding, natural tendencies to highlight the positive and downplay the negative may overstate successes and obscure the program's weaker aspects.

Despite these difficulties, evaluation serves at least two critical purposes. At the individual program level, future planning can be based on a careful evaluation of present practices. Moreover, if we seek to improve practice, we need to know what works so as to "identify and eliminate the barriers to effective programs" (Diekhoff, 1988, p. 630). Both researchers and practitioners in adult literacy education could therefore benefit from increased attention to program evaluation. A first step in this endeavor is to determine and evaluate criteria typically used to demonstrate program effectiveness. This article presents results of a research review designed to fulfill this purpose.

We searched for program evaluations or research reports referenced in three major data bases (ERIC, *Psychological Abstracts*, and *Dissertation Abstracts*) and in IRA's *Annual Summary of Investigations Relating to Reading* (1980 to 1988), seeking information about criteria. The search yielded 65 citations, which were then read to determine their pertinence for our purposes. In all, 19 program descriptions or research reports provided data for the study. Eight of these reported on more than one program (Balmuth, 1986; Borei & Shively, 1981; Clark, 1986; Delker, 1981;

Fields, Hull, & Sechler, 1987; Gadsden, 1989; Royce, 1981; Samuelson & Faddis, 1986).

Categories of Program Effectiveness

A list of evaluative criteria used to determine program effectiveness was created from an analysis of the 19 program descriptions and research reports. We then grouped individual items into broader categories that captured typical aspects of program effectiveness. Three broad categories (each with subcategories) emerged: personal factors, programmatic factors, and external factors. Figure 1 shows the sources for each category and subcategories.

The personal category included measures of effectiveness directly related to adult learners. One subcategory addressed adults' growth as readers in academic terms. Here the most common form of achievement data was learners' gain on standardized tests or success rates with the General Educational Development test (GED), although Borei and Shively (1981) noted that a significant number (45%) of the 523 programs they surveyed employed informal assessment of learners' academic progress as well.

Another personal subcategory focused on changes in the quality of learners' lives. Learners reported changes in self-esteem, in relationships with others, and in literacy-related or general self-confidence, and in some cases these factors were used as indicators of program effectiveness. Learners' perceptions of their own growth as readers and writers or of progress toward their own goals were considered occasionally to assess the strengths of a program.

The second broad category of evaluation criteria was related to program structure or content. Such factors as success in recruitment and the number of adults who enrolled and regularly attended programs were cited

Figure 1
Categories for Determining Program Effectiveness

Categories	Sources
Personal factors	
Academic achievement	Borei & Shively, 1981; Clark, 1986; Delker, 1981; Fields, Hull, & Sechler, 1987; Gold & Johnson, 1982; Lafayette Parish, 1987; Royce, 1981
Quality of life	Borei & Shively, 1981; Delker, 1981; Diem, 1986; Jones & Charnley, 1977; Lafayette Parish, 1987; Royce, 1981; Topping, 1985, 1986
Programmatic factors	
Program structure	Balmuth, 1986; Jones & Charnley, 1977; Lafayette Parish, 1987; Meyer & Keefe, 1988; Pasch & Oakley, 1985; Samuelson & Faddis, 1986
Program content	Balmuth, 1986; Gadsden, 1989; Gold & Johnson, 1982; Hutchinson, 1978; Jones & Charnley, 1977; Manning, 1978; Meyer & Keefe, 1988; Pasch & Oakley, 1985
External factors	
Context-based	Clark, 1986; Fields, Hull, & Sechler, 1987
Financial	Fields, Hull, & Sechler, 1987; Royce, 1981

as support for effectiveness. Program content factors clustered around instructional methods, staff quality, and the availability of staff-development activities.

Finally, some programs relied upon external indicators of success. The subcategory of context-based external factors involved assessment of changes in learners' behavior or attitudes by persons who were not associated with the literacy programs. For example, prison guards might assess changes in learners' trust in or respect for others (Clark, 1986); job supervisors might assess changes in learners' interactions on the job or their performance of job duties (Fields, Hull, & Sechler, 1987).

Financial factors were occasionally used to determine program effectiveness as well. An industry-based program was evaluated by comparing learners' earnings to those of other employees (Fields, Hull, & Sechler, 1987). Another report included an assessment of financial savings to the community, with data about program costs and estimated savings from, for example, persons no longer needing public assistance (Royce, 1981).

With rare exceptions, program evaluations were based on more than one criterion, often from more than one category, but a great deal of variation was evident within categories and across programs. Some of this variation may be a function of differences in program missions or goals. That is, one expects an evaluation of an industry-based program to differ from that of a community program.

Still, our results tend to support the charge that American adult literacy program evaluation is haphazard. Fortunately, the results can also form the foundation for developing more systematic approaches.

Guidelines for Program Evaluation

Adult literacy program evaluation can be improved by following several important guidelines (highlighted in Figure 2).

The most important is that evaluation must focus on the extent to which program goals have been met. In other words, evaluation guidelines should be established when programs are planned, and the program's goals should direct the nature of evaluation. Such an approach also assures that the evaluation will be comprehensive, which is another important guideline, and it facilitates the later use of data to identify aspects of the program that need to be strengthened.

These notions lead to another important guideline: Program evaluations should be systematic. Anecdotal information, while often interesting, rarely provides the kind of evidence needed to determine if goals have been met or to direct program improvement (Bear, Ferry, & Templeton, 1987). Evaluation data may take a variety of forms—formal or informal test results, results of interviews with learners or staff, information gleaned from observations—but whatever the source of information, it should be gathered and reported in a systematic manner.

Diversity in the focus of evaluation is to be expected, due to differences in program goals. However, as most programs' goals revolve around aspects of the three categories presented in Figure 1, evaluations should as well. Questions related to these categories, then, can provide the framework for comprehensive, systematic program evaluation.

Personal Growth

Evidence of learners' growth in literacy must be a part of program evaluation. As Diekhoff (1988, p. 627) has noted, "Any evaluation that fails to document reading improvement has failed to document pro-

Figure 2
Guidelines for Adult Literacy Program Evaluation

1. Base evaluation on the program's stated goals.
2. Make the evaluation comprehensive.
3. Make the evaluation systematic (not anecdotal).
4. Use a variety of assessment forms, both qualitative and quantitative.
5. Review the evaluation results in terms of the three categories of program effectiveness: personal factors, programmatic factors, external factors.
6. Use evaluation data to identify parts of the program that need strengthening.

gram effectiveness." Although the research literature indicates that many programs conceive of literacy learning as "reading only," documentation of writing growth is equally important.

Documentation should take several forms. Most programs evaluate academic achievement by reporting results from standardized measures. Growth of 1.3 to 1.5 grade equivalents after several months of instruction is typical and might be used as a benchmark against which to evaluate programs (Diekhoff, 1988).

However these data cannot stand alone to evaluate learners' literacy achievements. Standardized test results, for example, provide no evidence of increased fluency, of ability to solve problems encountered during reading or writing, or of the functional use of reading and writing. Thus, program evaluations based solely on results of standardized tests may underestimate program effectiveness.

Informal measures of literacy achievements, coupled with interview data from learners and teachers, can complement standardized test data to provide a more complete view. Topping (1985, 1986), for example, asks learners to select a book, read a page or two aloud, and retell after reading. Miscues are noted (and later analyzed) and fluency and the retellings are evaluated qualitatively. Likewise, informal evaluation of learners' growth in writing can be done through holistic evaluation of writing samples. These procedures, which can be conducted at the beginning and end of each program cycle, provide information about reading and writing abilities that cannot be measured through standardized tests. An additional benefit is that each yields useful diagnostic information for establishing goals for individual learners.

Interviews, too, with learners and staff members can provide evaluative data. Learners should be asked to evaluate their own progress. As Jones and Charnley (1977) note, growth that seems minimal when measured by a standardized test may seem remarkable from the learner's perspective. Moreover, routine self-evaluations encourage ownership in literacy learning and metacognitive analysis of reading and writing. Teachers or tutors might be asked to share their perceptions of learners' academic growth as well.

Although academic achievements are an important indication of effectiveness, program impact on other personal factors should also be evaluated. Participants' evaluations of progress toward their own goals, for example, may yield perceptions and opinions beyond their growth as readers and writers (Delker, 1981). Changes in self-confidence or self-esteem or perceptions of improved relationships with others are logical quality-of-life factors that might be evaluated through interviews or conversations with adult learners. Learners' comfort with and confidence in

their own reading and writing abilities might also be probed.

Royce (1981, p. 151) has suggested that a program is effective to the extent that it makes "a contribution to the lives of its students." Evaluations should address the extent to which these contributions go beyond academics.

Program Evaluation

Evaluations of program structure currently include demographic information about adults served, numbers and qualifications of staff members, and typical instructional blocks (for example, times and lengths of sessions). This sort of information adequately describes the structure of a program but offers little about its worth. Is the structure of Program A more effective than the structure of Program B because Program A served more adults? It seems clear that descriptive information that also allows evaluative judgments might provide preferable data.

Advice abounds about the program structure that best supports adult learners' growth. Instructional atmospheres described as secure, comfortable, convenient, and informal are said to be related to program effectiveness (see, for example, Fields, Hull, & Sechler, 1981; Mikulecky, 1986; Royce, 1981; Topping, 1985, 1986). If programs aim to achieve this sort of environment, one goal for evaluation should be to determine the extent to which the aim was met. Interviews with adult learners and staff members can yield information, as can observations of instructional sessions.

The qualifications of program personnel may also be reported in program evaluations. Key indicators of staff qualifications might include educational experience generally and training and experience in adult education specifically. Adult learners' perceptions of

Figure 3
Questions to Guide Program Evaluation

Personal:

• **Academic achievement**

To what extent have learners grown as readers and writers?
To what extent have learners achieved greater fluency in their literacy?
To what extent do learners and teachers feel that progress has been made toward academic goals?

• **Quality of life**

To what extent has learners' self-confidence as readers and writers increased?
To what extent have learners achieved their own goals?
To what extent has learner self-esteem increased?

Programmatic:

• **Program structure**

What are the qualifications of program personnel?
What is the quality of recruitment and retention practices?
To what extent does the program structure meet learners' needs?
To what extent does the program show evidence of coordination or collaboration with outside agencies and constituencies?

• **Program content**

What theoretical principles about reading, writing, and learning underlie program content?
To what extent does the program content meet learners' functional and academic needs and interests?
To what extent do learners participate in establishing instructional goals and evaluating progress toward them?
What is the quality of the social context for instruction (interactions between and among learners and teachers)?
What are teacher perceptions of program effectiveness?

External:

• **Context-based**

What is the rate of participation?
To what extent does the program meet needs identified by external groups (such as the community or job supervisors)?

• **Financial**

To what extent has learners' earning power increased?
To what extent does the program show a return on investment (savings to industry, persons off public assistance)?

---

their teachers' strengths and weaknesses should also be sought. Further, comprehensive and systematic staff development programs are offered in the most exemplary programs (Samuelson & Faddis, 1986), so program evaluations should include data regarding staff perceptions of inservice offerings and any other indicators of effective staff development (for example, observed changes in instruction).

Program content is a critical focus for evaluation. Above all, literacy instruction should be grounded in current theories about the reading and writing process (Gold & Johnson, 1982; Meyer & Keefe, 1988). Programs that are atheoretical or rooted only in traditional wisdom will have limited potential for effectiveness. They will also be difficult to evaluate.

Evidence that learners and teachers collaborate in establishing and assessing progress toward instructional goals provides a strong indication of program effectiveness (Borei & Shively, 1981; Royce, 1981; Samuelson & Faddis, 1986). Curricula developed to meet learners' interests and functional literacy needs are further indicators of the likelihood of program effectiveness (Fields, Hull, & Sechler, 1987; Jones & Charnley, 1977; Samuelson & Faddis, 1986). Teaching techniques, as well as program content, must be designed to meet learners' needs (Gold & Johnson, 1982; Mikulecky, 1986).

Data about these aspects of the program can be obtained through interviews with teachers and learners, by analyzing instructional documents, by observing class sessions, and by reviewing professional literature. Interviews with learners might focus on their own needs and goals, as well as their interest in sessions and their sense of progress toward goals. Instructional materials, lesson plans, or student-generated products can be examined to learn about the nature of instruction.

Finally, program goals and procedures can be compared to advice provided in the professional literature and to published descriptions of the reading, writing, and learning processes. Such a comparison can be used to evaluate the validity of program content.

Evidence of the program's impact in a broader context may indicate its effectiveness. Links with public schools or other community agencies and services suggest effective programs (Royce, 1981; Samuelson & Faddis, 1986; Villa, 1986). Documented efforts at coordination with outside agencies can be included along with other indicators of increased community involvement (for example, students obtaining citizenship or registering to vote).

Members of the community might provide their assessments of a program's impact by writing letters or consenting to interviews (Royce, 1981). In addition, members of the local literacy council might be asked to observe and evaluate the instructional environment.

Finally, some have suggested that effective programs should be able to show clear financial return on investment (Fields, Hull, & Sechler, 1987). Such data as change in learners' employment, earnings, or need for public assistance may not be directly attributable to literacy programs, but they can offer some evidence of a program's financial effects.

The Need for Evaluation

Program evaluation data should strike a balance between quantitative measures and qualitative assessments of program impact. Numbers alone, whether counts and demographics about adults served or results of tests, cannot reveal the depth and breadth of program effectiveness. Moreover, since the literacy learning that takes place is intended to have practical applications for adult learners, some effort to evaluate this external impact is also warranted.

"An effective evaluation will assist in future planning,...will help to improve program offerings for students, and will insure the accountability of expenditure of federal, state, and local dollars" (Willing, 1989, p. 4). Questions to guide effective evaluations are provided in Figure 3. Systematic, comprehensive evaluations based on program goals can provide information with which to judge individual program effectiveness. Such an approach to evaluation can also help the adult literacy community answer the broader question "What works?"

References

Balmuth, M. (1986). *Essential characteristics of effective adult literacy programs: A review and analysis of the research.* (ED 273 823)

Bear, D.R., Ferry, C., & Templeton, S. (1987). *Project TACL: A team approach to community literacy, needs assessment.* (ED 291 057)

Borei, S.H.E., & Shively, J.E. (1981). *Appalachian adult literacy programs survey (ALPS). Final Report.* (ED 211 671)

Clark, C. (Ed.). (1986). *LSCA final reports: Third series.* (ED 277 378)

Delker, P.V. (1981, January). *State of the art in adult basic education.* Paper presented at the National Adult Literacy Conference, Washington, DC. (ED 241 698)

Diekhoff, G.M. (1988). An appraisal of adult literacy programs: Reading between the lines. *Journal of Reading, 31*, 624–630.

Diem, R.A. (1986). Microcomputer technology in educational environments: Three case studies. *Journal of Educational Research, 80*, 93–98.

Fields, E.L., Hull, W.L., & Sechler, J.A. (1987). *Adult literacy: Industry-based training programs.* Columbus, OH: National Center for Research in Vocational Education, The Ohio State University. (ED 284 981)

Gadsden, V. (1989). Adult literacy learning and instruction. *Dissertation Abstracts International, 49*, 12.

Gold, P.C., & Johnson, J.A. (1982). Predictors of achievement in reading, self-esteem, auding, and verbal language by adult illiterates in a psychoeducational tutorial program. *Journal of Clinical Psychology, 38*, 513–522.

Hutchinson, L.P. (1978). The relationship between expressed interests and reading achievement in functionally illiterate adults. *Reading Improvement, 15*, 203–207.

Jones, H.A., & Charnley, A.H. (1977). *Adult literacy: A study of its impact.* (ED 199 473)

Knudson-Fields, B. (1989). A study of adult literacy service providers in the state of Idaho. *Dissertation Abstracts International, 49*, 10.

Lafayette Parish School Board. (1987). *Lafayette Parish cooperative jail project—LPCJP.* (ED 290 877)

Manning, D.T. (1978). Everyday materials improve adults' reading. *Journal of Reading, 21*, 721–724.

Meyer, V., & Keefe, D. (1988). *The Laubach way to reading: A review. Lifelong Learning, 12*, 8–10.

Mikulecky, L. (1986, December). *The status of literacy in our society.* Paper presented at the meeting of the National Reading Conference, Austin, TX. (ED 281 182)

Pasch, M., & Oakley, N. (1985, April). *An evaluation study of project LEARN.* Paper presented at the meeting of the American Educational Research Association, Chicago, IL. (ED 255 759)

Royce, S. (1981). *Adult educator exchange program, PA 310 project, final report.* (ED 215 226)

Samuelson, J.A., & Faddis, C.R. (1986). *The Indiana adult literacy initiative replication guide.* (ED 268 225)

Steele, H. (1989). Illiteracy then and now: North Carolina and Wake County, 1900-1980. *Dissertation Abstracts International, 49*, 7.

Topping, K. (Ed.). (1985). *National paired reading conference proceedings* (2nd). (ED 285 125)

Topping, K. (Ed.). (1986). *National paired reading conference proceedings* (3rd). (ED 285 126)

Villa, N. (1986). Statewide assessment of ABE in South Dakota. *Dissertation Abstracts International, 47*, 5.

Willing, D.C. (1989). Program evaluation as a strategy for program improvement in adult basic education. *Lifelong Learning, 12*, 4–9, 23.

General Teaching Methodology

> " *In the last analysis, what Eugene O'Neill designates 'the human equation' will count for them more than any element in their learning the skills we need to teach them.* "
>
> – SHUMAN, 1989, P. 353

*T*his section provides a variety of methods for use with the adult learner, most of which are grounded in "the human equation" referred to above. Keefe and Meyer provide instructional suggestions specific to adults at different levels of literacy. Following pieces are Biggs on bridging the literacy gap for African Americans; Mocker on cooperative learning; Austin-Anglea on word banks; Danielson on picture books; Ford on storytelling; Hill and Rabideau on high interest–low readability books; Kazemek and Rigg on the reading of poetry, followed by Conniff, Bortle, and Joseph on writing in this genre; Rosow on consumer advocacy; and Schierloh on classic novels. Several pieces focus on writing: Pates and Evans on writing workshops; Stasz, Schwartz, and Weeden on oral history; Solé on student journals in the workplace ESL classroom; D'Annunzio with language experience for ESL students guided by nonprofessional tutors; and Best with tips for correcting adult students' writing errors. Interestingly, two of the pieces—those by Conniff and Stasz and their respective coauthors—focus on writing with women.

The use of cooperative learning and other group work described in many of these articles represents a departure from perceptions that the adult student prefers to hide his or her literacy difficulties and to work alone. Meloth (1991) warns us that cooperative tasks are, by their very nature, high in ambiguity and risk. For example, concrete products of discussions may not be easily identifiable. If goals and strategies are obvious, students may be able to easily accomplish a task independently, but if the tasks are overly complex, it may be difficult for the group to recognize what they must do. As such times, the likelihood that students will simplify the task increases. Some group members may be uncomfortable with any ambiguity and may orient the group's discussion to a comfortable level. Thus, effective cooperative tasks are constantly in danger of being transformed into low-level procedural ones that may not help students improve their reading.

With this in mind, it is interesting to reflect on why the cooperative projects in these pieces were successful. Descriptions of the "trust engendered through equal participation of all" described in Pates and Evans' writing workshops, the creative freedom in the painting studio atmosphere described by Stasz and colleagues, and the comfort for ESL students in working with bilingual nonprofessional tutors in the D'Annunzio program support a sociocognitive rationale for the projects' success. In such a view, attention is paid to the social purposes to which the literacy skills are being put (Langer, 1991).

The varied methodology described in this section's articles provides a wealth of solid options from which educators can choose in weaving together a program appropriate for their own situation.

References

Langer, J.A. (1991). In E.H. Hiebert (Ed.), Literacy for a diverse society (pp. 9–27). New York: Teachers College Press.

Meloth, M. (1991). Enhancing literacy through cooperative learning. In E.H. Hiebert (Ed.), Literacy for a diverse society (pp. 172–183) New York: Teachers College Press.

Shuman, R.B. (1989). Some assumptions about adult reading instruction. Journal of Reading, 32, 348–354.

G e n e r a l T e a c h i n g M e t h o d o l o g y

Profiles of and Instructional Strategies for Adult Disabled Readers

DONALD KEEFE
VALERIE MEYER
APRIL 1988

An adult literacy tutor asks: I've been working with Marty for 8 months now. He tries really hard, remembers to bring his books, and is faithful about meeting me at the library for our weekly sessions. I keep wondering though, it's like I'm not sure if he's making that much progress.... He rubs his eyes a bit, and sometimes I have to repeat directions.... I thought Marty would be doing much better by now, maybe even reading the newspaper. What can I do to really see where Marty is and where he can go?

This type of question is common for us; we've been working very closely with adult literacy volunteers for the last few years (Meyer, Keefe, & Bauer, 1986). We suspect the question is not an unusual one, perhaps asked by hundreds of volunteer tutors across America who have responded to state and local appeals to assist adult new readers in learning to read.

This article describes findings for a project called "The Literacy Prescription," which has been funded since 1986 by the Office of the Secretary of State and Illinois State Library. The project grew out of earlier research by the authors on adult illiteracy (Keefe & Meyer, 1980). As project directors, we wanted to provide a unique support system for volunteer tutors and adult basic education (ABE) instructors. The Literacy Prescription provides individualized diagnostic testing and offers instructional suggestions. Our diagnosticians included current and former graduate students who majored in reading. In addition to expertise in reading, many of these diagnosticians had undergraduate teaching majors in fields such as speech and hearing, special education, and educational psychology.

The diagnostic tests varied, but generally they included the Keystone School Vision Screening Test (1972), the Wepman Auditory Discrimination Test (1986), the Basic Reading Inventory (Johns, 1985), the Burke Reading Interview, and the Slosson Intelligence Test (1984). (The Slosson was used to determine general strengths and weaknesses in academic areas rather than as an IQ measure.) A series of screening tests based on Jordan's *Dyslexia in the Classroom* (1977) was administered as appropriate.

Prescriptive instructional suggestions came from a computer data base of 126 strategies developed by the authors. About one-third of the strategies in the data base are traditional approaches such as the language experience approach, VAKT, and Anthony Manzo's ReQuest procedure (Harris & Sipay, 1985). The remaining two-thirds are original

strategies for which we have been provided feedback about effectiveness by adult literacy volunteers, ABE instructors, and the students.

To date, the Literacy Prescription has provided complete diagnostic reports for 106 clients. An analysis of the data from the reports established five separately identifiable groups of adult disabled readers. The remainder of this article outlines these five emergent groups and describes what we consider to be optional instructional techniques for each.

To organize our data, we simply labeled our adults as Groups 0, 1, 2, 3, and 4. A summary of our project findings appears in the figure.

Group 0

This is the lowest reading ability group and constitutes slightly less than 10% of the population we tested. Adults in Group 0 cannot read the simplest preprimer text and at most can read only a few words, such as their names. When text is read to them, they can understand up to the 1st or 2nd grade level. Without exception, this group had extremely limited general knowledge and were unable to repeat short sentences, could not add single digit numbers, and had difficulty copying short paragraphs. Approximately 78% of this group have language disabilities, 89% have vision problems, and 78% have auditory discrimination problems.

Literacy coordinators and ABE instructors should be cautious about assigning volunteer tutors to work with such persons. The volunteer tutors or ABE instructors who had worked with learners from this group often worked for two or more years and saw very little progress for their efforts. Limited experiences (possible borderline mental retardation), multiple physical disabilities, and severe language disabilities made these clients difficult if not impossible to teach.

Overview of Adults Tested*

	Group 0 n = 9	Group 1 n = 14	Group 2 n = 31	Group 3 n = 20	Group 4 n = 32
Reading levels					
Independent	0	1.0	1.6	1.7	5.2
Instruction	0	1.2	1.7	3.0	7.0
Frustrational	0	2.1	2.1	4.2	8.1
Listening	1.5	2.6	5.6	6.2	9.5
Have vision problems**	89%	78%	68%	65%	53%
Have auditory discrimination problems	78%	57%	45%	40%	31%
Views reading					
As "sounds"	22%	71%	58%	55%	50%
As "words"	22%	14%	26%	25%	22%
As "meaning"	0	0	3%	20%	25%
Have a specific language disability	78%	50%	55%	30%	31%
Last grade completed	6.7	8.5	7.0	9.1	10.6
Age	40	36	38	36	32
Sex					
Male	56%	21%	68%	60%	47%
Female	44%	79%	32%	40%	53%

*Data do not include a category called "Other" (n = 5) and do not include adults tested for vision or hearing only.
**All adults who owned glasses wore them during testing.

If Group 0 clients are assigned a tutor, we recommend the following strategies:

1. Make a book using a photo album in which you place environmental print words your student can read. Cut the advertisements out of magazines and newspapers with words such as Coca Cola and McDonald's. Place these pictures on one side of a page. On the other side of the page, print in large letters the words taken from the logo or ad. These words are often a part of most adults' sight vocabulary, even if the learner is not aware that this is "reading." Stress that, indeed, your student can read something.

2. Find highly predictable stories with patterns that lead the reader to "read" the text.

3. Write sentence stems such as "I can _____" or "I like _____." I can walk, I can talk, etc., or I like candy, I like apples, etc. Invite the student to complete the stems, using his or her own words.

Group 1

Group 1 adults had more capacity, fewer physical and language disabilities than Group 0, and could read "just a little." Their estimated capacity to read was suggested by their listening capacity score on the Basic Reading Inventory (see figure) and was somewhat better than the very low range of Group 0. This group could answer questions relating to their age and birthdate, name the days of the week, and perform simple computation. In all probability, Group 1 adults should be able to read simple texts with individualized help.

We recommend the following types of

strategies for Group 1 students. Strategies from the previous groups should be used if the learner is virtually a non-reader.

1. Language experience stories are appropriate. Student talk about meaningful events in their lives should be written down exactly as said, read, and re-read to them, and then read by them. These stories then should be taped so the learners can listen to and read them at home.

2. Since more than 70% of the clients in this group stated they thought reading was sounding out words rather than "making meaning," we feel tutors should stress the "meaning making" nature of reading. Learners should be encouraged to skip unknown words and continue reading to gain meaning and self-correct miscues. If no self-correction takes place, and the miscue is significant, work with the learners to figure out the word rather than correcting the "error" during first reading. The latter assistance may include "sounding it out."

3. Encourage learners to take risks and make guesses. Group 1 adults are low risk takers with debilitating reading experiences from their earlier lives. They worry about making errors and usually have "their brains tied up in knots." Encourage them to guess and think. For example, give them a popular advertisement torn into five or six pieces. Encourage them to guess what the ad is. Stress that they can figure out a lot if they try.

Group 2

Group 2 adults had a significantly higher reading capacity as determined by the listening score on the Basic Reading Inventory than the Group 1 learners, even though they could not read much better at initial testing. A high percentage of them had language and physical disabilities which may have accounted for their low reading level. With a tutor's help, adults in Group 2 can read the newspaper.

Recommended sample strategies for Group 2 include previously mentioned strategies, if appropriate, as well as the following:

1. Readers often will read a sentence with no idea what it means. They are processing sounds and words but not meaning. We recommend Silly Sentences. Make up a sentence in which one word is silly and does not make sense; for example, "I smell with my knees." Ask the learners to figure out which word is silly, forcing them to look at meaning rather than sounds.

2. Written conversation is an enjoyable reading–writing activity for this group. Instead of talking "out loud" about something, the conversation is written. Write about a specific event, your feelings about home, children, etc. The conversation is started by the tutor, who briefly writes down what she or he wants to say. The conversation continues, always in writing. Go back and forth and keep it simple, without concern for spelling or grammar.

3. Flash card directions force word callers to read more than one word at a time. Place a few words of direction, such as "Put your hands on the table," on a card. Flash each card, asking the learner to do what the card says. Often the learners will read only the first word. Encourage "chunking" all the words in one glance. Flash the cards again. Explain that they must read all the words in one quick glance. It may take four or five flashes for the learners to understand and do what is directed on the card. Explain that good readers see words in meaningful "chunks" rather than individually. After the learners have mastered the one-direction flash card, use cards with two or more related directions.

Group 3

Group 3 adults were characterized by a higher instructional, frustrational (2.0 vs. 4.0), and listening capacity level than Group 2. Like Group 2 adults, they viewed reading as a "sounding out" or "word calling" activity, and tutors must work continuously to dispel this "misnotion." Group 3 had considerably fewer language disabilities than Group 2 and progressed more rapidly in learning to read. These learners worked well with beginning tutors.

Group 2 strategies might be used with this group if appropriate. The following also are suggested:

1. To dispel their misnotion of reading, talk about the characteristics of a good reader (Cooper & Petrosky, 1976):

- Good readers bring what they know about the topic to the print on the page. They are active readers.
- Good readers take chances; they risk being wrong.
- Good readers guess at or skip words they don't know and read on for help.
- Good readers expect the material to make sense.
- Good readers try not to read too slowly.

These five characteristics need to be discussed every session until they are demonstrated.

2. Instead of looking up unknown or difficult words in the dictionary or asking someone what they mean, we suggest these readers jot down difficult words on blank bookmarks titled "List It and Skip It." Upon completion of a passage, they can return to the bookmark list to see if the difficult words were solved through the use of context.

3. "Alternate model reading" requires learners to read faster. The tutor quickly reads a phrase or longer part of a sentence and stops. The students then read on, continuing the sentence. After the learners have read a phrase or part of a sentence, the tutor interrupts and quickly reads on again. Students are encouraged to keep up with their tutors, read faster, and model them. This technique forces learners to look at complete phrases and anticipate where their tutors are going to stop or interrupt.

Group 4

While Group 3 learners often were in Adult Basic Education programs, Group 4 adults were usually found in GED programs. They had a listening capacity which suggested that they might be able to read at the high school level, appeared to have average range intelligence, and expressed far fewer language and physical disabilities than the other groups. Group 4 learners had completed more schooling, usually 10 years, and 25% of them perceived reading as a "meaning making" process. They were strong candidates for GED diplomas and benefitted from work with volunteer tutors.

The following strategies are appropriate for Group 4 adults:

1. Key-word predicting activites are particularly powerful with this group. The tutor first selects a story, a chapter, or an article and notes 10 "key words" from the selection. These words are shared with the learners, who are asked to predict the piece's content. The learners must make "sense" of the 10 to 15 "key words." This predicting activity prepares readers for meaning. Next, they should read the piece to discover if predictions were right or wrong (confirm or disconfirm). Adults like this activity. Key-word predicting works well with Groups 2 and 3 if easier and highly predictable pieces are selected.

2. "GIST" making requires readers to reduce the first sentence of a passage to 3 or

4 words, then the first two sentences to 5 or 6 words, three sentences to 7 or 8 words, etc., until a paragraph is reduced to 15 or so words that reveal the "gist" of the paragraph. This activity requires readers to "make meaning" and determine their own "key words."

3. Prepare directions for playing a simple card game, leaving out a crucial instruction or explanation. Ask the readers to try to play the card game with these directions. Ask the learners to determine what missing direction or explanation is needed to play the game. This activity introduces the notion of critical reading.

Conclusion

This article has described five emergent groups of adult disabled readers. Patterns and problems are evident for those involved in literacy projects.

- Of the 111 adults tested, 42% had hearing problems (most often auditory discrimination) and 66% had vision problems. Of the 66% who had vision problems, 63% had near point vision problems. The need for vision and hearing screening in adult literacy projects is evident.

- Almost half the adults in Group 1 and more than three-fourths of the learners in Group 0 were referred by literacy volunteer projects. Adults who appeared to have the most disabilities were tutored an average of only 1½ hours per week.

- Almost all activities suggested for our five groups center on the notion that the brain must be activated in a search for meaning. We favor activities which force disabled readers to use intuitive knowledge of language and the world instead of emphasizing phonics, word attack, and isolated comprehension drills.

References

Auditory Discrimination Test (2nd ed.). (1986). Los Angeles, CA: Western Psychological Services.

Basic Reading Inventory (3rd ed.). (1985). Dubuque, IA: Kendall/Hunt.

Cooper, C.R., & Petrosky, A.R. (1976, December). A psycholinguistic view of the fluent reading process. *Journal of Reading, 20*, 184–207.

Harris, A.J., & Sipay, E.R. (1985). *How to increase reading ability* (8th ed.). White Plains, NY: Longman.

Jordan, D.R. (1977). *Dyslexia in the classroom* (2nd ed). Columbus, OH: Merrill.

Keefe, D., & Meyer, V. (1980, Summer). Adult disabled readers: Their perceived models of the reading process. *Adult Literacy and Basic Education, 2*, 120–124.

Keystone School Vision Screening (1972). Davenport, IA: Mast/Keystone.

Meyer, V., Keefe, D., & Bauer, G. (1986, March). Some basic principles of the reading process required of literacy volunteers. *Journal of Reading, 29*, 544–548.

Slosson Intelligence Test (1984). East Aurora, NY: Slosson Educational Publications.

Building on Strengths: Closing the Literacy Gap for African Americans

SHIRLEY A. BIGGS
MAY 1992

To understand and ultimately address the problems of the literacy gap between African American and European American adults, it is necessary to examine the context in which it occurs. That context shapes our perceptions about the gap and affects the manner in which we use our energies to address it.

One aspect of the context is the data that is available about literacy achievement, much of which is "unreliable, unrepresentative, or noncomparable over time" (Stedman & Kaestle, 1987, p. 10). The data must be interpreted with its flaws in mind. Literacy achievement must also be seen in its historical context—while most groups in America have made remarkable progress in achieving productive levels of literacy over the years, African Americans achieved in the face of unrelenting social, economic, and political barriers (Biggs, 1992).

The Gap

When Cook (1977) traced the decline of illiteracy in the United States from the late 1800s to 1970, she noted that while the available figures can be misleading, literacy rates improved over the years for both white and non-white populations. She also noted that when literacy was defined as the ability to read and write, illiteracy rates for whites dropped from 12% to 2% between 1870 and 1959, for non-whites from 80% to 8%.

When literacy is defined on the basis of the number of school years completed, the gap continues to be evident. Earlier in this century, fewer years of schooling defined what it meant to be literate—completion of fourth grade, later eighth grade, later still high school graduation. Recent census figures describing high school graduation rates show the percentage of whites aged 25 years and older completing high school to be 70.5% in 1980 and 77.7% in 1988; completion percentages for blacks of comparable ages were 51.2% in 1980 and 63.3% in 1988. Despite the fact that both groups made significant progress in this area, the gap is evident (U.S. Bureau of the Census, 1989).

National Assessment of Educational Progress data reveal a similar gap among each of its age cohorts which includes young adults (NAEP, 1981, 1985). However, in each of the examples cited here, the gap appears to be closing, with blacks showing the largest degree of positive change. Still, the challenge of the 1990s and beyond makes it increasingly important to eliminate the gap for blacks and other minorities at risk and to aim for higher, more complex literacy achievement for all groups.

Closing the Gap

If those of us who are responsible for literacy education are to close the gap, we must act quickly to begin to reclaim the losses that accrue when any group is kept from functioning at its best. An important first step is to rethink our literacy improvement efforts by raising and thoughtfully answering questions like the following:

What kind of assumptions do we make about African Americans and their ability to learn and become more literate? Where have we invested our research, instructional, and support efforts? Do minorities play significant roles in these efforts? To what extent do we use what has been learned to make a positive difference in closing the literacy gap?

One assumption made by the uninformed to explain the gap has been that African Americans place little value on literacy and on education in general. Statistics are cited that indicate that, even though more young blacks than ever are attending and completing high school, fewer are attending college. Also fewer are completing General Equivalency Diploma (GED) requirements (Baldwin, 1990). Since these trends are reflected in the general population (U.S. Bureau of the Census, 1990), they may be more a result of limited finances than lack of interest. Further, there is historical and research evidence suggesting that African Americans have and continue to place a high value on literacy and learning (Engs, 1987; Smith, 1989). For example, Engs argues that:

> Beginning around the turn of the century and continuing to this day, blacks began to pursue an unarticulated but discernible strategy that included two primary thrusts. First, blacks left the South in huge numbers in search of better opportunity in both employment and education. Second, they attacked inadequate and discriminatory education for blacks wherever it existed (p. 16).

Another assumption that undermines literacy efforts for minority and other learners is the belief held by some that illiterates are necessarily unintelligent or unwilling to invest their time and energy in learning. Fingeret (1990) reasoned that: "Like members of all oppressed groups, adults with low print literacy skills have had to invest far more energy in understanding the ways of mainstream culture than is true in the reverse.... They must and do participate in a wide range of literacy practices on their jobs and in their communities" (p. 27).

We have long been concerned about literacy. However, we have tended to focus our efforts on variables that are difficult if not impossible to change. This tendency to dwell on those things not likely to produce positive change has led to another assumption—that little progress can be made even when great effort is exerted. Pollard (1989) suggests that there are variables amenable to change that could positively affect achievement in individuals from the group she describes as the underclass.

Pollard studied those who achieved academically and identified seven areas of promise that those responsible for literacy instruction for African Americans may find productive. The areas include:

1. Social Attitudes—about education, race, and individual success

2. Self-Perceptions of Ability—including self-concept of ability and perceptions of school performance

3. General Social Support—encouragement from others

4. Teacher Support—encouragement...and help from teachers

5. Parental Influences—including parental support and parental educational aspirations for their children

6. School Involvement—involvement with peers and in activities in school

7. Active Problem-solving—the degree to which the child sought help from others for problem-solving and the child's perception of the effort used to solve problems. (pp. 304–305)

Taking Action

Individuals responsible for teaching, establishing curricula, and general program development may find opportunities to implement activities based on Pollard's seven variables. Following are examples of action that can be taken using just three of the variables.

One alterable variable is social beliefs. A growing number of social scientists (for example, Christmon, 1989; Fordham & Ogbu, 1988; Howard and Hammond, 1985) suggest that the issues of social attitudes and self-perception of ability are intricately related. They propose that the perpetuation of unexamined or distorted beliefs about African American ability led the general public, educators, and African American learners themselves to accept the stereotypes as reflections of reality. The achievement gap reinforced those beliefs.

Educators were affected by the beliefs and responded with lowered learning expectations as additional proof that they lacked ability and responded to efforts to teach them by giving up at the first sign of difficulty. The preceding scenario reflects the importance of addressing a combination of two alterable variables if academic success is to be achieved—(a) attitudes about learning, race, and success; and (b) self-perceptions of ability.

What can be altered is the knowledge that academic achievement is possible. African Americans have achieved in the past against great odds. They continue to achieve with determined effort. When adults first realize that they can control their learning through their own efforts, their attitude can be altered. When educators, particularly teachers, realize that the stereotypes do not reflect the reality and that their level of expectation plays as much a role in their students' achievement as their knowledge of strategies for teaching reading and writing, attitudes can then be altered.

One approach is the use of teacher anecdotes that reflect a positive African American presence in the society. As analogies are drawn to illustrate points in the text to be read, positive experiences can be shared—kindnesses shown by African American neighbors, intelligence evident in a black TV character, resourcefulness reflected in the manner in which a local hero has solved a practical problem.

A second approach is to use literature written by or about blacks that reflects not only the contributions that they make but the diversity in the nature of those contributions. The literature also demonstrates that African Americans can and do achieve. Brooks (1985) and Pugh and Garcia (1990) provide examples of such literature and offer suggestions for using it.

Another alterable variable is support for students. Researchers have concluded that throughout the school experience, African American students—particularly males—receive less attention and more nonconstructive criticism than other students (Bridges, 1989; Calvin, 1988; Cazden, 1982; Rowan, 1989). Teachers can alter such negative behavior and express support in a variety of ways.

Examples of productive teacher behaviors include making comments that acknowledge students' productive efforts, providing opportunities for students to demonstrate newly acquired skill and knowledge, and assisting students when they experience difficulty as they struggle to learn.

A third variable that can be effectively addressed for African American students is that of providing instruction that addresses the importance of problem-solving in learning. Studies describing classroom instruction and achievement reveal that instruction for students perceived as less able differs in character and quality from instruction for those perceived as more able (Allington, 1983; Applebee, Langer, & Mullis, 1988). Further instruction for less able readers is often focused on a series of unrelated exercises that purport to build skills of questionable value. Little attention is given to the application of school-based learning to the life of the adult.

African American adult literacy students are likely to have experienced a great deal of frustration as school children. Since few strategies were offered to them in their early attempts to become literate, they come to literacy courses reluctantly—fearing repeated failure in what they may feel is their last opportunity to become productively literate. Without guidance in the use of problem-solving and critical thinking skills, they may give up before they have allowed themselves a chance to learn, practice, and apply literacy skills.

Teachers of African American adult literacy students may benefit from the results of research indicating that instruction in problem-solving and critical thinking is likely to make the study of other school subjects more successful (Howard & Hammond, 1985; Ross & Ross, 1989).

Finally, two major strategies can help close the gap—authentic assessment and pragmatic instruction. First, standardized tests used to assess adults are designed to generate scores that compare a specific reader or test taker with other test takers for program accountability purposes. While test manuals often suggest that the tests can be used diagnostically, to help the teacher make instructional decisions, many teachers do not in fact have access to such information. Even if they did, the information may not reflect the test taker's actual reading ability and use of underlying strategies (Sternberg, 1991).

A better approach, authentic testing (Wiggins, 1989), differs in terms of structure, design, grading and scoring standards, fairness, and equity. The information gained can be applied directly to instruction. The test taker reads more realistic, challenging, contextualized materials. The reading may take place over several sessions so that patterns of what the student does well and not so well can be determined. The student is also asked to participate in interpreting his or her own reading and writing behavior. During the process, the student is informed about strengths as well as problems to be solved through instruction.

African Americans have been ill-served by the negative comparisons that grow out of normative testing. Such testing has failed to reflect the context of the performance and the strengths that could be used as the basis for instruction. Thus, while it may be important to document a certain type of achievement with norm-referenced tests for accountability purposes, it is also critical to provide assessment that informs and enhances instruction.

Second, literacy instruction for African American and other minority adults needs to be pragmatic in that it assists them in meeting both personal and societal goals (Park, 1987). For example, a large part of the comprehension instruction offered to adult literacy students requires that they read and identify main ideas in written material. A common format for response is multiple choice.

While skill in responding to multiple choice items is useful in school and standardized test environments, it has little use in day-to-day life where people read to get the gist and communicate that they got it in a way appropriate to the context. Such a skill has real-life value—it allows an adult to understand the joke told in a social gathering, to explain a concept to one's child from a newspaper or TV report, to provide bottom-line information to colleagues at work, and to share important events with a loved one in a letter.

Thus, the role of instruction is to provide learning, practice, and application opportunities. Pragmatic instruction goes beyond achieving traditional classroom goals; it must address the adult student's work, social, and family goals.

On the basis of a careful review of successful adult literacy programs, Padak and Padak (1991) recommend guidelines and related questions to be used in program evaluation. Those listed below reflect the alterable variables discussed above and are particularly important if authentic assessment and pragmatic instruction are to be provided for African American learners. Effective programs address (p. 378):

1. Academic achievement—To what extent do learners and teachers feel that progress has been made toward academic goals?

2. Quality of life—To what extent have learners achieved their own goals? To what extent has learner self-esteem increased?

3. Program structure—To what extent does the program show evidence of coordination or collaboration with outside agencies and constituencies?

4. Program content—To what extent does the program content meet learners' functional and academic needs and interests? What is the quality of the social context for instruc-

tion (interactions between and among learners and teachers)?

5. Real-life context—To what extent does the program meet needs identified by external groups (such as the community or job supervisors)?

If we are to close the gap in school achievement between African Americans and European Americans, we must rethink our assumptions and set about making sure that they have merit, are supportable, and contribute to solving literacy problems for all who need assistance.

Further, we need to look to the manner in which we apply our efforts and resources to make positive change in literacy. We must ask ourselves to what extent we are working on areas less likely to be productive. Attitudes about African Americans' ability to learn, instructional encouragement and support, and the inclusion of problem-solving and critical thinking curricula are variables that can be changed to assist student achievement. In addition, inviting participation in the form of planning and evaluating from those who are served in the programs is likely to enhance the chance for closing the gap. Finally, rethinking the nature of classroom assessment and instruction and implementing authentic testing and pragmatic teaching can go a long way in achieving this goal.

References

Allington, R.L. (1983). The reading instruction provided readers of differing abilities. *Elementary School Journal, 83*(5), 548–569.

Applebee, A.N., Langer, J.A., & Mullis, I.V.S. (1988). *Who reads best? Factors related to reading achievement in grades 3, 7, and 11* (Report No. 17-R-01). Princeton, NJ: Educational Testing Service.

Baldwin, J. (1990, September). GED *profiles: Adults in transition.* GED Testing Service of the American Council on Education.

Biggs, S.A. (1992). African American adult reading performance: Progress in the face of problems.

In A.M. Scales & J.E. Burley (Eds.), *Perspectives from adult literacy to continuing education*. Dubuque, IA: Brown.

Bridges, R.E. (1989). *Black male development: A broken model*. Paper presented at the annual conference of the National Black Child Development Institute, Miami, FL.

Brooks, C.K. (Ed.). (1985). *Tapping potential: English and language arts for the black learner*. Black Caucus of the National Council of Teachers of English. Urbana, IL: National Council of Teachers of English.

Calvin, S.B. (1988, April). *Creating effective learning environments for disadvantaged learners: Implications for the design of educational programs*. Paper presented at the annual meeting of the American Educational Research Association, New Orleans, LA.

Cazden, C.B. (1982). Contexts for literacy: In the mind and in the classroom. *Journal of Reading Behavior, 14*(4), 413–427.

Christmon, M. (1989). *Black students: Self-esteem and achievement*. New York: ERIC Clearing House on Urban Education. (ED 314 511)

Cook, W.D. (1977). *Adult literacy education in the United States*. Newark, DE: International Reading Association.

Engs, R.F. (1987). Historical perspectives on the problem of black literacy. *Educational Horizons, 66*(1), 13–17.

Fingeret, H.A. (1990). Who are illiterate adults? *Adult Learning, 1*(6), 27.

Fordham, S., & Ogbu, J.U. (1986). Black students' school success: Coping with the "burden of acting white." *Urban Review, 18*(3), 176–206.

Howard, J., & Hammond, R. (1985, September). Rumors of inferiority. *New Republic, 192*, 17–21.

National Assessment of Educational Progress. (1981). *Three national assessments of reading: Changes in performance, 1970-1980* (Report No. 11-R-01). Denver, CO: Education Commission of the States.

National Assessment of Educational Progress (1985). *The reading report card, progress toward excellence in our schools: Trends in reading over four national assessments, 1971-1984* (Report No. 15-R-01). Princeton, NJ: Educational Testing Service.

Padak, N.D., & Padak, G.M. (1991). What works: Adult literacy program evaluation. *Journal of Reading, 34*(5), 374–379.

Park, R.J. (1987). Three approaches to improving literacy levels. *Educational Horizons, 66*(1), 38–41.

Pollard, D.S. (1989). Against the odds: A profile of academic achievers from the urban underclass. *Journal of Negro Education, 58*(3), 416–429.

Pugh, S.L., & Garcia, J.G. (1990). Portraits in black: Establishing African American identity through nonfiction books. *Journal of Reading, 34*(1), 20–25.

Ross, R.R., & Ross, B.D. (1989). Delinquency prevention through cognitive training. *Educational Horizons, 67*(4), 124–130.

Rowan, J.L. (1989). *The effect of gender on the non-promotion of black males*. New York: ERIC Clearing House on Urban Education. (ED 313 456)

Smith, A.W. (1989). Educational attainment as a determinant of social class among black Americans. *Journal of Negro Education, 58*(3), 416–429.

Stedman, L.C., & Kaestle, C.F. (1987). Literacy and reading performance in the United States, from 1880 to the present. *Reading Research Quarterly, 22*(1), 8–46.

Sternberg, R.J. (1991). Are we reading too much into reading comprehension tests? *Journal of Reading, 34*(7), 540–545.

Wiggins, G. (1989). Teaching to the (authentic) test. *Educational Leadership, 46*(7), 41–47.

U.S. Bureau of the Census. (1989). *The black population in the United States: March 1989* (Current Population Reports, Series P-20, No. 442). Washington, DC: U.S. Department of Commerce.

U.S. Bureau of the Census. (1990). *United States population estimates, by age, sex, race, and Hispanic origin: 1980 to 1988* (Current Population Reports, Series P-25, No. 1045). Washington, DC: U.S. Department of Commerce.

G e n e r a l
T e a c h i n g
M e t h o d o l o g y

Cooperative Learning Process: Shared Learning Experience in Teaching Adults to Read

DONALD W. MOCKER
MARCH 1975

Most educators involved in teaching reading to adults realize that procedures used in teaching children, although frequently used with adults, do not serve the best interest of the adult student. If the methods, materials, and approaches used in instruction reflect the characteristics and needs that make the adult different, adults will not only learn more but will also realize greater satisfaction in learning.

The Commission of Professors of Adult Education (1961) indicated two significant differences between children and adults as learners: (1) they (adults) enter an educational activity with a greater amount of experience from which they can relate new experiences and (2) they enter with more specific and immediate plans for applying newly acquired knowledge.

Knowles (1970) extended this idea when he identified the assumptions on which adult education is based: (a) his (adult) self-concept moves from one of being a dependent personality toward one of being a self-directing human being; (b) he accumulates a growing reservoir of experience that becomes an increasing resource for learning; (c) his readiness to learn becomes oriented increasingly to the developmental tasks of his social roles; and (d) his time perspective changes from one of postponed application of knowledge to immediacy of application, and accordingly his orientation toward learning shifts from one of subject-centeredness.

Because adult education is based on a different set of assumptions than education of children, writers in the field have suggested that teachers of adults should acquire special knowledge, behavior, and attitudes. This position is summed up in Fay's (1966) statement: "Once we recognize the major psychological characteristics of adults, it is not difficult to adjust teaching methods and approaches to the learning situation so that they are effective with adults."

Directed reading activity is a standard format for teaching reading to children. Classroom procedures and the use of basal reading series all reflect the teacher's commitment to this approach. Emmett Betts (1946) outlined the format:

> The authors of basal readers are in general agreement on these basic principles and assumptions regarding directed reading activities. First, the group should be prepared, oriented, or made ready, for the reading of a story or selection. Second, the first reading should be guided silent reading. Third, word recognition skills

and comprehension should be developed during the silent reading. Fourth, the reading—silent or oral—depending upon the needs of the pupil should be done for purposes different from those served by the first, or silent reading. Fifth, the follow-up on the "reading lesson" should be differentiated in terms of pupil needs.

This approach does an excellent job of establishing a student-teacher and teacher-student line of communication, but, in its application by teachers and through basal readers, fails to deal with the following aspects of adult learning: (a) establishing a student-student line of communication, thus not recognizing the experience and knowledge which each student brings to class; (b) placing responsibility for learning on the student, thus not helping the adult to become more independent, and (c) teacher acting as a co-learner, thus giving the student the idea that the teacher has all the answers. The very name, directed reading activity, implies teacher direction.

The directed reading activity has been extended in recent years by Stauffer (1969) with his modification, "the directed reading-thinking activity." Stauffer sees pupils setting their own purpose and places major emphasis on the thinking process. He suggests that purposeful reading, like problem solving, has three phases: (1) confrontation by a problem, (2) reading to find a solution, and (3) finding the solution or failing to find it. These phases are translated in the three major steps in the directed reading-thinking activity; (1) declaring purpose; (2) reasoning while reading; and (3) judging.

Although this approach does emphasize the problem solving and critical thinking aspects, it falls short in meeting two of the special requirements of the adult student. First, this approach fails to recognize the student's right and responsibility for learning by failing to allow the student to select what is to be read. In addition, this approach is highly teacher directive in nature.

The cooperative learning process borrows from both of these approaches but is more than a modification. In addition to the student playing a new role by virtue of sharing responsibility for learning, the pathways of interaction between the teacher and student are greatly altered, and the approach defines a new role for the teacher. In this role the teacher no longer functions as the "all knower," or what Freire (1972) calls "bankers," but functions as a guider or planner.

Cooperative Learning Process

The first item in cooperative learning is to have the students select the material which they want to learn how to read. That is, have the students select a problem which is of concern to them. This relates to Knowles' fourth assumption, since a teacher can have unlimited resources, modern facilities, audiovisual equipment and the latest material, but without the adult being motivated, little will happen. Weinstein (1970) identified the source of motivation: "Concerns, wants, interests, fears, anxieties, joys, and other emotions and reactions to the world contain the seeds of 'motivation'." This is the first attempt at getting the students to interact with each other and to place a portion of the responsibility for learning on the adult. Bergevin (1965) made this point when he stated: "We do not learn to be responsible participants by merely hearing our responsibilities described. After we know what responsibilities are involved, we really learn by practicing over a long period of time."

Selection of material is the student's right and responsibility. The discussion can be initiated by such questions as "Select your main problem." "What could you learn which you could use to help your child in school?" or "What problem did you have today?" One caution—a student's ability to verbalize is often closely related to his ability to read. Therefore, other methods may have to be developed to elicit this response. Students can be encouraged to bring into class the "thing" which they would like to learn to read. Creative programs (Freire, 1972) use pictures of the "things" which are pressing community problems to stimulate language development.

In addition to being involved in the selection of the material, the learner must also be involved in deciding the purpose for reading the material. It is here that the teacher as a "guider" can help adults "...recognize that as men they have the right to have a voice" (Freire, 1970).

Since the adult has helped set the purpose for the reading lesson, it is not necessary to restate the purpose prior to beginning the lesson. However, it is important to begin the lesson with the adults verbalizing why this lesson (content) is important and what it will mean to each one of them so learning will be personal. During this part of the lesson, the adult, through interaction with other students, will gain insight into her or his own behavior and feelings. It is at this point that the student will learn to move from reading to action. The teacher can begin the discussion with "How will you be able to use this information?" or "How can this information make a change in your life?"

Guided silent reading should be used first to get the "total picture" of the story, to stimulate interest, and to develop the practice of reading for a purpose. As in the traditional approach, careful attention to reading problems must be observed. Watch for subvocalization, finger pointing, and showing signs of general physical discomfort.

Next, concentrate on developing comprehension and interpretation. Here the teacher again has the opportunity to establish student-student interaction. Rather than asking a comprehension question per se, the questions can be structured in the form of a problem which the adults must solve. An example of this process would be for the teacher to ask the class, not any single individual, to list on the board possible alternatives for the outcome of the story. As the class begins to identify these alternatives, the teacher lists them on the board. After the class is satisfied that the list is exhaustive, then the teacher can respond with another question such as "What are the possible consequences of these alternatives?" Again, the teacher records the responses as the students interact. The teacher may then want the class to rank the alternatives in the order which they think is most plausible.

Through this approach, adults are encouraged to process concepts which are not dealt with in their everyday life. The process of languaging continues.

Little change can be made from the traditional format of teaching word skills except to point out that we are now teaching them in the context of a problem which has been identified by the adult student. The teacher is using the material which the adult has selected as the basis of his instructional program. Again, the notion of the learner's responsibility is reinforced.

During oral or silent rereading, techniques such as role playing and simulation can be used to encourage interaction among students. The teacher can pose a question to the students. The students can create a role playing situation where they begin by reading the points of the story which they feel are important to the question. They then role play to the conclusion of the question. Again, we have returned to a problem solving situation with the responsibility for solution on the part of the student.

Mastery of skill is not the product of follow-up activities per se. Rather one should attempt to create a means for the adult to transfer the classroom skill into a life skill. It is one thing to teach the skill of reading, and quite another to get a person to read. In elementary education, when a skill is taught, the pupil is forced to use that skill because he is a child and in school. Failure of this process usually results in poor readers. However, an adult who is illiterate, by definition, does not have to follow this process, and does not have built-in reinforcement. Special attention must be given to the adult who wants to "practice" a newly acquired skill.

Classroom Format

Joyce (1966) conceived of school curriculum as having three levels, or what he referred to as "tiers or modes." The first level is made up of those skills which are generally accepted as the essential building blocks of intellectual development: reading, writing and arithmetic. The second level consists of developing latent talents and abilities of the learner. The third level is what he calls "group-inquiry" curriculum, and is organized around social issues and problems which concern the individual. It is in the context of Joyce's third level that the cooperative learning process is most appropriate.

Beginning readers (0-3), because of their special needs in language development, should be taught as a separate group. No change in procedure is required except that rather than using a "pre-written" story or article, the teacher should develop a story using the language experience approach (Hall, 1972).

Advanced readers (4-8) can work as a single group using the same instructional materi-al. The general reading level of the material should be low enough so it can be easily read by all students. The issue here is not one of readability, but one of relevance and what the teacher and students do with the material.

If many problems are identified as material students want to learn, it will be necessary to establish priorities. Responsibility for learning is again placed on the learner.

As we begin to involve the adult in the selection of what is to be learned and why it is to be learned, and as we reinforce student-student interaction throughout the reading lesson, concluding by helping the adult to see the application to his life, then the cooperative reading process can be a potent technique in adult basic education.

Maintaining the integrity of a systematic approach but accommodating for adult learners' characteristics will improve the reading lesson format so that it will create a more powerful impact on the life of the learner.

References

Bergevin, Paul, & McKinley, John. (1965). *Participation training for adult education.* St. Louis, MO: Bethany Press.

Betts, Emmett. (1946). *Foundations of reading instruction.* New York: American Book Company.

Commission of Professors of Adult Education. (1961). *Adult education: A new imperative for our times.* Washington, DC: The Adult Education Association of the U.S.A.

Fay, Jean B. (1966). Psychological characteristics affecting adult learning. In F.W. Lanning & W.A. Many (Eds.), *Basic education for the disadvantaged adult,* New York: Houghton Mifflin.

Freire, Paulo. (1970). The adult literacy process as cultural action for freedom. *Harvard Educational Review, 40,* pp. 205-225.

Freire, Paulo. (9172). *Pedagogy of the oppressed.* New York: Seabury Press.

Hall, Mary Anne. (1972). *The language experience approach for the culturally disadvantaged.* Newark, DE: International Reading Association.

Joyce, Bruce R. (1966). *Restructuring elementary education: A multiple learning systems approach.* New York: Teachers College.

Knowles, Malcolm. (1970). *The modern practice of adult education.* New York: Association Press.

Stauffer, Russell G. (1969). *Teaching reading as a thinking process.* New York: HarperCollins.

Weinstein, Gerald, & Fantini, Mario D. (1970). *Toward humanistic education: A curriculum of affect.* New York: Praeger.

Sample Word Bank for the Topic "Gardening"

plant	weeds	tree
tomato plant	dig	hole
shovel	rake	lawn mower
weeder	air blower	sweep
hose	fertilize	seeds
corn	clippers	pruner
carrrot	onion	tulips
lettuce	hoe	chives
rocks	grass	sod
rototiller	axe	renting
buying	dump	toolshed
plastic bags	equipment	goggles

General Teaching Methodology

Word Banks for Adult Literacy

Lynne Austin-Anglea
December 1990

A word bank, in the traditional sense, is a list of words that have been accumulated to build sight vocabulary. However, my adult new readers combine the word bank with the language experience approach to create a versatile tool for vocabulary learning.

Because it uses the student's own vocabulary, a word bank can become an endless resource for building vocabulary, practicing spelling, and developing critical thinking skills. In addition, it is an excellent warm-up activity before reading or writing, assessing and enriching the student's prior knowledge of a topic.

The procedure is simple and adaptable to both tutoring and classroom settings. Select a topic related to either a story to be read or an interest of the student (such as gardening). State "When I think of gardening I think of plants. What do you think of?" Record both your response and the student's response, and continue until your word bank includes 20–50 words, depending upon topic familiarity. (See sample word bank.)

Once the list is complete you have a supply of words to use in a variety of language lessons:

1. Build critical thinking skills by looking for clusters of words that belong together. My list contains clusters under the titles "Kinds of Seeds," "Gardening Tools," and "Gardening Jobs" and can easily take the form of a semantic map. (See sample map.)

2. Add prefixes and suffixes to words in the word bank. Build upon *seed* to create *seedling, seeded,* and *seeding.* Build upon

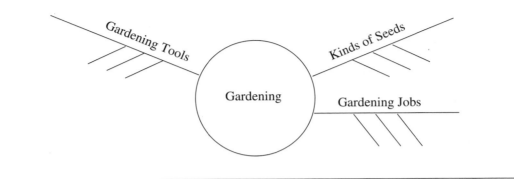

fertilize and create *fertile, infertile, fertilizer, over-fertilize, fertilization, fertilizing,* etc. Discuss how changing the form can change the meaning of a word.

3. Focus on spelling by calling attention to the root words and affixes like those used above. Practice syllabication, and your student will be amazed at how well she or he can spell lengthy words like fertilization and transplanting.

4. Plan a writing exercise using ideas from the word bank. Determine a pattern of organization according to the purpose of the writing, whether it's a how-to (chronology), a personal experience (narrative), or a description (topic characteristics).

5. Use the word bank as a prereading exercise to anticipate what a story will be about. Prediction increases the interaction between reader and text and improves reading comprehension.

6. Add new vocabulary words to the word bank as they are discovered through reading and conversation.

7. Keep a collection of word bank pages to illustrate your student's growing vocabulary on a variety of topics.

General Teaching Methodology

Picture Books to Use with Older Students

KATHY EVERTS DANIELSON
MAY 1992

Picture books, in the hands of a skilled language arts teacher are a medium for all ages. Some quite recent picture books have special uses for a middle school or junior high or high school teacher working with developmental readers and with linguistically and culturally diverse students.

Teachers willing to try using picture books with older learners should know that the practice has been documented as successful. Picture books are often motivators, since they are both beautiful and charming while they present human experiences in microcosm. They have been used to enhance fifth graders' visual literacy and the critical thinking of junior high students. They give opportunities for integrating reading and writing and for developing even high school students' vocabularies. They often fit well into a social studies course, bringing variety to a topic.

Here are several recent picture books that I would recommend, grouped under headings suggesting potential special uses, with extra activities noted. All the books are visually attractive.

Dialect and Character Development

Mirandy and Brother Wind (McKissack, 1988)—American southern black

Hanna's Hog (Aylesworth, 1990)—rural American

Iva Dunnit and the Big Wind (Purdy, 1985)—American old west slang

The Tale of Meshka the Kvetch (Chapman, 1980)—Yiddish dialect

Charlie Drives the Stage (Kimmel, 1989)—American old west slang

Jargon and Lingo

Frank and Ernest (Day, 1988)—lunch counter lingo

Frank and Ernest Play Ball (Day, 1990)—baseball terminology

Extra activities: Students collect other jargon or lingo (interview a coach or player, read the sports page). Students add to class charts about slang or dialect, or listen to note linguistic differences in everyday language.

As they write stories that have characters from different areas, they can add dialect or slang to enhance characterizations and setting.

Parts of Speech

A Cache of Jewels (Heller, 1987)—Collective nouns (in rhyme)

Merry-Go-Round (Heller, 1990)—All kinds of nouns (in rhyme)

Many Luscious Lollipops (Heller, 1989)—Adjectives (in rhyme)

Kites Sail High (Heller, 1988)—Verbs—tenses, irregular forms, moods (in rhyme)

Extra activities: Students keep notebooks or add to charts interesting or descriptive nouns, verbs, or adjectives. They use these charts when revising their own writing.

Writing

Faithful Elephants (Tsuchiya, 1988)—Write a journal entry from the zoo keeper's or the elephant's point of view.

Alligator Arrived with Apples (Dragonwagon, 1987), *Animalia* (Base, 1986), *Alison's Zinnia* (Lobel, 1990), *Elfabet* (Yolen, 1990), *The Z Was Zapped* (Van Allsburg, 1987)—Students can do their own alphabet book after reading these alliterative versions of alphabet books.

Step into the Night (Ryder, 1988), *Mockingbird Morning* (Ryder, 1989), *Under Your Feet* (Ryder, 1990), *Apple Tree* (Parnall, 1988), *Winter Barn* (Parnall, 1986), *The Rock* (Parnall, 1991), *Woodpile* (Parnall, 1990)—Examine the ordinary to find the extraordinary.

Extra activities: Students write about something seemingly common and notice the details surrounding it.

Students keep learning logs of plants, rocks, or trees that they see every day to enhance their observational and descriptive writing skills.

The Frog Prince Continued (Scieszka, 1991), *'Twas the Night Before Thanksgiving* (Pilkey, 1990), *The Completed Hickory Dickory Dock* (Aylesworth, 1990)—Parody

Extra activities: The format of other traditional poems could be used to get students to write their own parodies.

Some Suggested Picture Books

Aylesworth, J. (1990). *The completed hickory dickory dock.* Ill. by Eileen Christelow. New York: Atheneum.

Aylesworth, J. (1988). *Hanna's hog.* Ill. by Glen Rounds. New York: Atheneum.

Base, G. (1986). *Animalia.* New Yor:, Abrams.

Blos, J.W. (1987). *Old Henry.* Ill. by Stephen Gammell. New York: Morrow.

Chapman, C. (1980). *The tale of Meshka the Kvetch.* Ill. by Arnold Lobel. New York: Dutton.

Day, A. (1988). *Frank and Ernest.* New York: Scholastic.

Day, A. (1990). *Frank and Ernest play ball.* New York: Scholastic.

Dragonwagon, C. (1987). *Alligator arrived with apples.* Ill. by Jose Aruego & Ariane Dewey. New York: Macmillan.

Gerrard, R. (1990). *Mik's mammoth.* New York: Farrar, Straus, & Giroux.

Heller, R. (1987). *A cache of jewels and other collective nouns.* New York: Grosset & Dunlap.

Heller, R. (1988). *Kites sail high.* New York: Grosset & Dunlap.

Heller, R. (1989). *Many luscious lollipops.* New York: Grosset & Dunlap.

Heller, R. (1990). *Merry-go-round.* New York: Grosset & Dunlap.

Kimmel, E.A. (1989). *Charlie drives the stage.* Ill. by Glen Rounds. New York: Holiday House.

King, L.L. (1988). *Because of Lozo Brown.* Ill. by Amy Schwartz. New York: Viking.

Lindbergh, R. (1990). *Johnny Appleseed.* Ill. by Kathy Jakobson. Boston, MA: Little, Brown.

Lobel, A. (1990). *Alison's zinnia.* New York: Greenwillow.

McKissack, P. (1988). *Mirandy and brother wind.* Ill. by Jerry Pinkney. New York: Knopf.

Parnall, P. (1988). *Apple tree.* New York: Macmillan.

Parnall, P. (1991). *The rock.* New York: Macmillan.

Parnall, P. (1986). *Winter barn.* New York: Macmillan.

Parnall, P. (1990). *Woodpile.* New York: Macmillan.

Pilkey, D. (1990). *'Twas the night before Thanksgiving.* New York: Orchard.

Provenson, A. (1990). *The buck stops here.* New York: Harper & Row.

Purdy, C. (1985). *Iva Dunnit and the big wind.* Ill. by Steven Kellogg. New York: Dial.

Ryder, J. (1989). *Mockingbird morning.* Ill. by Dennis Nolan. New York: Four Winds.

Ryder, J. (1988). *Step into the night.* Ill. by Dennis Nolan. New York: Four Winds.

Ryder, J. (1990). *Under your feet.* Ill. by Dennis Nolan. New York: Macmillan.

Scieszka, J. (1991). *The frog prince continued.* Ill. by Steve Johnson. New York: Viking.

Scieszka, J. (1989). *The true story of the three little pigs.* Ill. by Lane Smith. New York: Viking.

Tsuchiya, Y. (1988). *Faithful elephants.* Translated by Tomoko Tsuchiya Dykes. Ill. by Ted Lewin. Boston: Houghton Mifflin.

Van Allsburg, C. (1988). *Two bad ants.* Boston, MA: Houghton Mifflin.

Van Allsburg, C. (1987). *The z was zapped.* Boston, MA: Houghton Mifflin.

Wahl, J. (1990). *Dracula's cat & Frankenstein's dog.* Ill. by Kay Chorao. New York: Simon & Schuster.

Yolen, J. (1990). *Elfabet.* Ill. by Lauren Mills. Boston, MA: Little, Brown.

Books are illustrated by the author unless otherwise noted.

Sources of Activities Using Picture Books

Barton, B., & Booth, D. (1990). *Stories in the classroom: Storytelling, reading aloud, and roleplaying with children*. Portsmouth, NH: Heinemann.

Beckman, J., & Diamon, J. (1984). Picture books in the classroom: The secret weapon for the creative teacher. *English Journal, 73*, 102–104.

Flatley, J.K., & Rutland, A.D. (1986). Using wordless picture books to teach linguistically/culturally different students. *The Reading Teacher, 40*, 276–281.

Graves, D. (1989). *Discover your own literacy*. Portsmouth, NH: Heinemann.

Johnson-Weber, M. (1989). Picture books for junior high. *Journal of Reading, 33*, 219–220.

Polette, K. (1989). Using ABC books for vocabulary development in the secondary school. *English Journal, 78*, 78–80.

Rutland, A.D. (1987). Using wordless picture books in social studies. *History and Social Science Teacher, 22*, 193–196.

Stewig, J.W. (1990). Choosing the Caldecott winner: Fifth graders give their reasons. *Journal of Youth Services in Libraries, 3*, 128–133.

Because of Lozo Brown (King, 1988), Old Henry (Blos, 1987), *Mik's Mammoth* (Gerrard, 1990)—Complete plot told in rhyme.

Extra activities: Students write their own stories told in rhyme.

Johnny Appleseed (Lindbergh, 1990), *The Buck Stops Here* (Provensen, 1990)

Extra activities: Instead of a traditional report, a rhymed poem about a famous person.

True Story of the Three Little Pigs (Scieszka, 1989)—Wolf's point of view, *Dracula's Cat & Frankenstein's Dog* (Wahl, 1990), *Two Bad Ants* (Van Allsburg, 1988)

Extra activities: Students can write stories from different characters' points of view.

General Teaching Methodology

Storytelling for Adults

PEGGY FORD
MARCH 1992

Storytelling for adults? Whoever heard of such a thing! It will become a turn-off! It will be received with cries of protest! Nonsense is what I reply.

For me, storytelling has proven to be one of the most effective means to share the joys of reading with avid readers, to stimulate good but lazy readers, to encourage reluctant readers, and to introduce (or perhaps reintroduce) poor readers to the world of print.

Students in my reading classes range in age from 17–70, with reading levels from grades 3–20. I have students who have never finished middle school, students with master's degrees, students who are required to take the course, and those who elect to take the course. While the bulk of their semester's work is of the individual prescriptive type, when it comes to storytelling, the students become one big ear tuned into the Adult Story Hour.

When one-third to one-half of my students indicate that they not only do not like to read but also that they hate to read, I pull out my trusty file of paperback books and spend a classtime or two telling them stories. Because my major goal is to create in students the desire to read, the subject matter of my stories is as varied as my students.

For 1 hour and 20 minutes the students literally sit mesmerized visualizing characters. My listeners travel vicariously first to one country and then to another; out of one era and into another; visit with the poor and the rich alike; become acquainted with the famous and the infamous; experience joy or sorrow, delight or disdain.

The best part for me occurs when storytelling time is over, because then the spell is broken; the students come back to the reality of the classroom with an interest in reading a particular book, or they remember a book they have read, enjoyed, and want to share with the rest of us.

Questions come fast and furious. "What was the name of the book where such or so happened?" "Do we have that book upstairs in our library?" "Do you have a list of those books you talked about?" "Can we do this again next classtime?" Questions are followed by positive comments. Sixteen years of storytelling has yet to yield a negative reaction. Sometimes we teachers do have to prime the pump a little to receive the product—the product being students who want to read.

I keep a long list of books for my storytelling. I find that I run out of classtime long before I run out of subject matter. The main ingredient for a successful storytelling time is being an enthusiastic, well-read instructor. Enthusiasm is an extremely contagious condition, and it is one that is easily transmitted. The following list of titles is representative of books that I have successfully used during storytelling. Titles include those from chil-dren's, young adult, and adult literature. As the advertising slogan goes, "Try it, you'll like it!" And so will your students.

Books for Storytelling

Arnow, H.L. (1954). *The dollmaker*. New York: Avon.

Buck, P.S. (1931). *The good earth*. New York: Harper & Row.

DeBlasis, C. (1978). *The proud breed*. New York: Bantam.

Lewis, C.S. (1950). *The lion, the witch, and the wardrobe*. New York: Macmillan.

Marshall, C. (1967). *Christie*. New York: McGraw.

McCullough, C. (1977). *The thorn birds*. New York: Harper & Row.

Michener, J. (1959). *Hawaii*. New York: Random House.

Owens, J. (1976). *Jesse: The man who outran Hitler*. New York: Fawcett.

Peck, R.N. (1972). *A day no pigs would die*. New York: Knopf.

Rawls, W. (1961). *Where the red fern grows*. New York: Doubleday.

Schlissel, L. (1982). *Women's diaries of the westward journey*. New York: Schocken.

Speare, E.G. (1958). *The witch of Blackbird Pond*. Boston: Houghton Mifflin.

Specht, R. (1984). *Tisha: The story of a young teacher in the Alaska wilderness*. New York: Bantam.

Ten Boom, C., & Scherrill, J. (1984). *The hiding place*. New York: Bantam.

Thompson, T. (1976). *Blood and money*. New York: Doubleday.

Tolkien, J.R.R. (1966). *The hobbit*. New York: Ballantine.

Wilder, L.I. (1953). *Farmer boy*. New York: Harper & Row.

Wilder, L.I. (1953). *The long winter*. New York: Harper & Row.

G e n e r a l
T e a c h i n g
M e t h o d o l o g y

High Interest–Low Readability Books for Adults

SARA LOUISA HILL
DAN RABIDEAU
SEPTEMBER 1992

D uring the past 15 years, we have seen the development of a new genre of literature, high interest–low readability books for adult new readers in the United States and Canada. When people encounter these books for the first time, they are frequently surprised that high-low authors manage to write such engaging stories in such a few pages. (They don't call them "high interest" for nothing.) In addition, student writing is being commercially published, especially through publishing efforts based in literacy programs. These materials are especially engaging for adult literacy students.

It is worth mentioning that many English as a Second Language (ESL) teachers working with students at an intermediate level are finding that their students enjoy these books as well. Although the books are written for Adult Basic Education (ABE) students rather than ESL students, it's interesting to note that two of the series described below are books about immigrants. Many ESL teachers are looking at high-low books as another source of comprehensible input for their students.

People of all instructional philosophies agree that in order to become good readers, people need time to read. Books should be accessible—within the reading ability of the reader, well written, and engaging. The books need both to tap our students' experiences and interests and to describe the experiences of other people.

The following is a list of some series of books that we've found to be particularly good.

High Interest–Low Readability Series

An American Family. *Fearon Education (Fearon, Janus, Quercus, 500 Harbor Blvd., Belmont, CA 94002, USA; 800-877-4283). Reading level 4.5.*

Eight 80-page historical fiction books including stories from the settlement of the North American colonies through the post-World War I era. Some are quite good.

Lifetimes I and II. *Fearon Education. Reading level 2.0–3.0.*

Two wonderful series of 7 books each, with adult themes at a manageable reading level.

Hopes and Dreams. *Fearon Education. Reading level 2.0–3.0.*

Written by the same author as the Lifetimes series, these 10 books introduce adult beginning readers to U.S. history through fictionalized accounts of the experiences of various immigrant groups.

Kaleidoscope. *New Readers Press (Department 92, Box 888, Syracuse, NY 13210, USA; 800-448-8878). Reading level 1.0–2.0.*

An easy-to-read series of 16 books at two levels with interesting stories for beginning readers.

Fastback books. *Fearon Education. Reading level 4.5–5.0.*

Several series of high interest–low readability fiction. Series include romance, mystery, sports, spy, and horror.

Flashback Series. *Fearon Education. Reading level 4.0–5.0.*

Fictionalized characters in the backdrop of historic events, war, sports, and disasters. The disaster series describes historical events such as the sinking of the *Titanic,* an earthquake in Mexico, Mount Saint Helens volcano, etc.

Fitting In. *New Readers Press. Reading level 1.0–2.0.*

These 8 books are similar to the Hopes and Dreams series, because the stories describe the experiences of individuals from different immigrant groups as they settle in the United States. The stories deal with more recent immigrant groups such as South and Central Americans and Southeast Asians. Very well written stories.

Sundown Books. *New Readers Press. Reading level 3.0–3.6.*

The stories have a lot of human interest, and even more advanced students enjoy them.

Writers' Voices. *Literacy Volunteers of New York City (121 6th Avenue, New York, NY 10013, USA; 212-925-3001). Reading level 3.0–6.0.*

Each title includes an unedited selection from the original work as well as a summary of the book, a short biography of the author, and a list of thought-provoking questions about the material. The publisher tries to provide readers with enough background information to make the unedited text more readable.

Publications of Student Writing

Opening Doors Books, Series I. *Opening Doors Books (Box 379, Bristol, VT 05443, USA; 802-453-3459). Reading level approximately 3.0–5.0.*

A collection of 6 books written by adult literacy students in Vermont. Some very good stories with adult topics such as rape and child abuse.

New Writers' Voices. *Literacy Volunteers of New York City. Reading level 1.0–5.0.*

A collection of 12 books written by students at LVNYC. Some are anthologies around themes such as work and health; some are stories written by individual students.

Voices: New Writers for New Readers. *Lower Mainland Society (9260 104th Street, Surrey, British Columbia, V3R 2B4 Canada; available in the United States through Voices Magazine, Delta Systems Co., Inc., 570 Rock Road Drive, Unit H, Dundee, IL 60018-9922, USA; 708-551-9595).*

A Canadian periodical containing writings by students in ABE programs in Canada and the United States.

Anthologies for New Readers

More than a Job; Readings on Work and Society. *New Readers Press. Reading level 3.0–5.0.*

A collection of readings revolving around the theme of work. Includes chapters from novels by well known authors, poetry, and song lyrics.

Words on the Page. The World in Your Hands, Books I, II, and III. *Harper & Row (Perennial Library, 10 East 53rd Street, New York, NY 10022, USA).*

Rather than write abridged versions of texts at an elementary level, these editors have contacted contemporary authors for permission to print some of their works.

Other authors wrote pieces especially for this anthology. In the words of the editors, "Rather than 'writing down' to their readers, the distinguished authors in the Harper & Row Collections have written *to* them." The result is a three-book anthology.

*General
Teaching
Methodology*

Four Poets: Modern Poetry in the Adult Literacy Classroom

Francis E. Kazemek
Pat Rigg
December 1986

As teachers and tutors of adults who are becoming literate, we have been quite concerned with finding materials for these people. Most commercial materials focus on such "functional" literacy skills as reading want ads and filling out job applications (Rigg & Kazemek, 1985), which are restrictive in at least two senses: These materials narrow rather than enlarge a student's view of literacy; and the snippets of language they display are almost always bereft of verve or grace.

We think that poetry offers a gold mine of materials for adult literacy students. In this article we describe four poets whose work we have used with literacy students, and we report on the basic techniques of using poetry.

Why Poetry?

There are several reasons for using poetry with adult literacy students. First, it opens a world, or a view of the world, that has been closed for many of them. Our adult students tell us that the writing assignments they had in school were always what Britton (1982) calls *transactional*, that is, using language to get something done. Typical assignments were filling in blanks, underlining subjects and verbs, and drawing lines from words in a list to definitions in a parallel column. Sometimes they wrote book reports, and at least once a year a report on their summer vacations; but these assignments too were transactional.

The reading materials they typically handled were either content area textbooks, rewritten and simplified versions of literature, or short stories and texts written for the "reluctant reader." Because the adults that we work with had low grades in English classes, they were never assigned to the higher track nor given creative writing assignments and really good literature.

As a result, many of our students expect to use reading and writing to get better jobs or look better in their children's eyes when they help with homework assignments, but they don't see literature that they read or write as doing what Gardner says it can: "True art clarifies life, establishes models of human action, casts nets towards the future, carefully judges our right and our wrong directions, celebrates and mourns" (1978, p. 100).

Reading and writing poetry opens our students' eyes to what literacy can mean; it helps them see the difference between knowing *how* to read and *wanting* to read to understand themselves and their world better.

A second reason for using poetry with adults, and an obvious corollary to the first, is that the material intrinsically motivates reading, writing, and talking with others in and out of class. When adults use language in what Britton calls the *poetic* mode, they are able to "take it up as it were in the role of spectators" (1982, p. 37). They are able to observe and explore their own past lives, imagined futures, and to dream of impossible events. Poetry allows adults to participate through metaphor, dream, make believe, and symbolism skillfully used in that which makes human life an intellectual and imaginative adventure.

A third reason for using poetry with adults who are beginning to read and write is that, if carefully selected, poetry is easy to read and write, often easier than the practice job applications in the literacy textbook (Weibel, 1983). The ideas and images of poems are readily accessible to adults, or can be if the poetry is chosen to fit the students.

Characteristics to Look For

Poetry for adult beginning readers and writers is easier to read when it is predictable, both in ideas and form. Poetry which connects in some real way to the adult's life—poetry which, as Emily Dickinson said, makes one feel as though one's head will explode—will be much easier to read than poetry that does not. Poetry that deals with familiar themes or ideas, has clearly developed patterns and sequences, uses repeated words, phrases, or lines, and employs an identifiable rhythm or meter (not necessarily rhyme) is generally the easiest to read.

Poetry written in familiar language or in a vernacular is usually easier than poems in stilted or archaic "literary" language. Rhymed poetry is often the only kind that many adults consider to be real poetry. Yet rhyme is not necessarily an element of predictability; the use of a particular rhyme scheme often results in unusual diction or twisted, unnatural syntax. Any rhymed poetry therefore needs close examination before it is used in the literacy classroom.

Four Poets

Here we briefly discuss four poets, much of whose work can be used with adults at all levels of literacy development. Carl Sandburg, Lucille Clifton, William Carlos Williams, and Langston Hughes are all American and all contemporary. We have selected them as models because of their genius with language, their wide range of themes and ideas, and because their work is readily available, relatively inexpensive in paperback, and in most public libraries.

We hope, of course, that reading their poems leads to further exploration of other poets' work.

Carl Sandburg

Sandburg's poetry is rooted in the commonplace; he writes of everyday themes and everyday people. The colloquial language of his poems has a rhythmic vitality. Often they sound like the people who, Sandburg said, "sometimes talk poetry without writing it, but they don't know they are talking poetry" (1958, p. 14). Sandburg's humor, wit, and frequent irony all help to make his poetry especially appropriate for use with adults. The poem "Buffalo Dusk" from *Early Moon* (1958, p. 45), an inexpensive paperback selection of Sandburg's poetry. This elegiac poem captures the sense of irretrievable loss that comes with understanding that a particular creature and, indeed, an entire way of life are no more. Sandburg's use of simple but eloquent repetition heightens the underlying pathos of the poem. Every adult has longed for a time that is no more; this poem speaks to that longing.

The theme of "Buffalo Dusk" can elicit a wide range of response and discussion, from a political exploration of the past and present plight of Native Americans, to a consideration of some more personal loss. The language helps make this poem predictable, both in its vividness and in its repetition.

In another poem, "Soup," in the same collection (p. 97), Sandburg explores the nature of fame and power. The simple declarative language and syntax of "Soup" make it accessible to the beginning reader. The theme is sure to engender discussion of the lives of the rich and famous. Literacy teachers can use this poem as a catalyst for further exploration of power, fame, and everyday life.

Lucille Clifton

A quite different collection of poetry is *two-headed woman* (1980) by Lucille Clifton, poet and author of many children's books. In this particular collection, Clifton celebrates the joys, beauty, pain, and love of being a woman, a black woman in particular. She speaks as a mother, a daughter, a lover, and a person deeply concerned with spiritual and religious questions. While her poetry will appeal to most people, it speaks most directly to women because of its themes and celebrations of womanhood. In "homage to my hips" (p. 6), for example, Clifton sings of her big, powerful hips with a gusto that swings the poem off the page and readers off their feet.

> these hips are big hips.
> they need space to
> move around in.

> they don't fit into little
> petty places. these hips
> are free hips.
> they don't like to be held back.
> these hips have never been enslaved,
> they go where they want to go
> they do what they want to do.
> these hips are mighty hips.
> these hips are magic hips.
> i have known them
> to put a spell on a man and
> spin him like a top!

(Reprinted by permission of Curtis Brown, Ltd. from *two-headed woman*. ©1980 by the University of Massachusetts Press.)

The everyday language and the repetition help to make this poem appropriate for many adults, but it is primarily the theme that makes it one literacy students read with ease and eagerness. The sheer celebration of one's body and sexuality gives the poem an energy that moves the reader, and it is this feeling that we want adult beginning readers and writers to experience from the start of their literacy instruction. This poem helps them understand that "being literate is just more fun, more joyful, than being illiterate" (Delattre, 1983, p. 54).

Since writing must be an integral part of literacy instruction (Kazemek, 1984), poems which serve as models for students' own poetry can be especially useful. Clifton's "homage to my hips" can serve as a catalyst for a variety of adult "homages" to eyes, hands, hair, and so forth. In fact, Clifton seems to have been inspired to write a companion piece, "homage to my hair" (p. 5).

> homage to my hair
> when I feel her jump up and dance
> i hear the music! my God
> i'm talking about my nappy hair!
> she is a challenge to your hand
> Black man,
> she is as tasty on your tongue as
>   good greens

Black man,
she can touch your mind
with her electric fingers and
the grayer she do get, good God,
the Blacker she do be.

Clifton's poetry doesn't use standard punctuation or grammar. It can help adults appreciate the vitality of language well used and the vigor of dialects; it can also help adults begin to explore conventions of grammar, spelling, and punctuation in print. The rest of the poems in this collection are equally appropriate for use with adult literacy students.

William Carlos Williams

In his poetry William Carlos Williams tried to capture what he called the "American idiom"—the music and vitality of American speech. Accordingly, many of his poems read like prose that simply has been broken at certain points to give it the look of poetry. But that is only how they look: Those poems that most seem like prose move with a rhythm and a sharpness of image that enable the reader and listener to see and to feel the world differently, with more clarity and intensity.

Williams was a practicing medical doctor most of his life. Many of his poems are relatively short, like lines jotted between house calls or office visits. This brevity, together with the condensed American speech that Williams used and the everyday nature of his themes, make many of his poems appropriate for adults who are just beginning to see themselves as literate. In his well known "This is just to say," for example, we see how Williams is able to celebrate something as common as plums with a sharpness of imagery and a seeming simplicity of language (1966, p. 33).

I have eaten
the plums
that were in
the icebox

and which
you were probably
saving
for breakfast

Forgive me
they were delicious
so sweet
and so cold

We think this poem can be used to show adult literacy students that a famous American poet uses language that is not unlike theirs. It can help them to see the value of everyday language that they hear, use, and understand; it helps take the mystery out of what many adults fear as the most mysterious kind of language—poetry.

Several of Williams's "object" poems can also be used to help adults see how everyday langauge can help us focus closely and imaginatively on the most common things of life. The poems are demonstrations of using written language to see the world more clearly. "The Red Wheelbarrow" (1966, p. 21) not only makes us see the wheelbarrow but also requires us to consider its significance in the world.

so much depends
upon

a red wheel
barrow

glazed with rain
water

beside the white
chickens.

This kind of object poem lends itself to the exploration and composition of object poems written in class. Language experience strategies modified for adults can be used quite effectively with this sort of poem (Rigg & Taylor, 1979).

Finally, poems like "The Thing" (1966, p. 50) are appropriate for the kind of language play that we think is necessary for all beginning readers and writers, whatever their age.

Each time it rings
I think it is for
me but it is
not for me nor for

anyone it merely
rings and we
serve it bitterly
together, they and I

(From *Collected Earlier Poems*. ©1938 by William Carlos Williams. Reprinted by permission of New Directions Publishing Corporation.)

This kind of language play—using language for riddles, jokes, interesting juxtapositions, paradoxes, pleasing sound arrangements, and so forth—not only helps the beginning readers and writers feel at home with the language in its written form, but also helps them to better understand its almost infinite possibilities.

Langston Hughes

Langston Hughes was a prolific author and an articulate, impassioned spokesperson for black people. However, his poetry, stories, plays, and essays, whether they are written in black English vernacular or in standard English, have a universal character that make them meaningful and memorable to both black and white, to young and old.

We believe that Hughes' early poetry, especially the collection *The Dream Keeper and Other Poems* (1959), can be used effectively with most adults to help them appreciate the beauty of his poetry and his skillful use of language. Moreover, Hughes' poetry often inspires exploration and discussion of themes that are important to all of us, such as love, friendship, and ethnic pride. An example is "Poem" (1959, p. 12), one that we like and have used successfully with adults:

I loved my friend.
He went away from me.
There's nothing more to say.
The poem ends,
Soft as it began—
I loved my friend.

(From *The Dream Keeper and Other Poems* by Langston Hughes. ©1932 by Alfred A. Knopf, Inc.; renewed 1960 by Langston Hughes. Reprinted by permission of the publisher.)

The simple, declarative nature of this poem, the repetition of the line "I love my friend" and the almost haunting, largely unexplainable pathos that it evokes in most readers all serve to make this a poem that can be used over and over again with adult students. As one of ours remarked, "Yeah, that's just the way it is. That's what happened to me and one of my friends."

"Dreams" (1959, p. 7) appears in numerous anthologies and can be found in some basal readers, but we think that it is most appropriate for adults who have lost dreams.

Hold fast to dreams
For if dreams die
Life is a broken-winged bird
That cannot fly.

Hold fast to dreams
For when dreams go
Life is a barren field
Frozen with snow.

(From *The Dream Keeper and Other Poems* by Langston Hughes. ©1932 by Alfred A. Knopf, Inc.; renewed 1960 by Langston Hughes. Reprinted by permission of the publisher.)

The images are sharp: Life is a broken-winged bird; life is a barren, frozen field. The two ballad stanzas state the same cause-effect relationship, so that the repetition of structure and phrases contributes to its effectiveness and predictability. This poem leads into class writing, both individual and group collaborative poems.

Hughes is widely known for his prose stories and his narrative poetry, often written in black English vernacular. His use of this dialect shows how important to Hughes is each individual (because he lets each individual speak with his or her own voice) and the individual's life, stories, hopes, and dreams. "Aunt Sue's Stories" (1959, p. 65) begins:

Aunt Sue has a head full of stories.
Aunt Sue has a whole heart full of stories.
Summer nights on the front porch
Aunt Sue cuddles a brown-faced child to
   her bosom
And tells him stories....

(From *Selected Poems* by Langston Hughes. ©1926 by Alfred A. Knopf, Inc.; renewed 1954 by Langston Hughes. Reprinted by permission of the publisher.)

Aunt Sue goes on to tell stories of slavery and stories "right out of her own life."

All of us have stories that come right out of our own lives. Most of us never get those stories, those lives, on paper and something important in the world is lost. Adults with a history of failure in school and with reading and writing almost certainly have not even begun to put their stories, their lives, on paper. We believe that poetry like "Aunt Sue's Stories" can get adults to talk, write, and read about their own lives. The oral history and interview techniques demonstrated in *The Foxfire Book* (Wigginton, 1972) and discussed by Rigg (1985) offer the means to get these stories down on paper.

Techniques for Using Poetry

We have referred throughout this article to poetry writing and have mentioned a few techniques: language experience, oral history, group collaboration. Because we focus on the work of four American poets and how that work is appropriate for adults who are beginning to see themselves as literate people, we will not go into specifics of writing instruction in the literacy setting (see Kazemek, 1984, for suggestions). Three techniques that help adult literacy students read poetry are reading aloud, rereading, and discussing.

Reading aloud. If you introduce a poem to your students by reading it aloud yourself, you are doing three things.

1. You are giving the poetry some of its life that is often hidden when the poem lies flat on its page.

2. You are making it easy for your students to read the poem when they see the printed copy.

3. You are spinning a thread between yourself and your students, making a bond. Item three is as important as one and two.

We talked earlier about how poetry can help us know ourselves, but it can also help us know each other. When we read "homage to my hips" to our students, we let our enjoyment show; when we read Hughes's "Poem" we give it the thoughtful silence afterwards that it deserves. Our students see and hear by the way we read them aloud that the poems speak to us, and that we delight in sharing with our students something that we feel is terribly important and something that we love.

Rereading. We read the poem again, this time while our students have copies in front of them. Why again? Most poetry is tightly packed expression; unlike reading a newspaper report, we don't get the best of a poem by skimming and scanning. We don't mean that our students plod through line by line. That destroys both the poem and any interest in it that we or our students had.

But rereading a poem that we enjoy two or three times gives us and our students more than one chance for the poem to live for all of us. It's a little like making a friend: If you give a poem the sort of glance that you give strangers on the street, the poem will stay a stranger, and you won't even remember its face. Rereading also makes the poem more readable for the adults who are just beginning to see themselves as literate people.

Discussion is the third technique we use constantly. After rereading, we often invite comments. We don't try to tell our students what any poem means, since it will mean something different to each person. We have had quite interesting discussions about the poems we've brought to our students that were as intense and intellectually stimulating as any we've sat through in graduate English literature seminars. These discussions came about through our listening to the students' comments and directing their questions to each other and the group as whole, rather than trying to answer those questions ourselves.

More Readable and More Fun

The work of Sandburg, Clifton, Williams, and Hughes contains many poems that we believe can be used with adults at all levels of literacy development. (See the accompanying list of other collections by these four poets.)

There is a common assumption that poetry is only for those who have already demonstrated their literacy competency in some way; we believe that this is a misconception. We have used the poems we've mentioned here and many, many others with adults who swore they could not read a single word.

The result of our experience is that we strongly believe that this sort of poetry is not only readable by adult beginning students of reading and writing, but is more readable than many of the commercial materials available. And it's much more fun.

Good Collections of Poetry for Adult Literacy Students

Clifton, Lucille. (1972). *Good news about the earth*. New York: Random House.

Clifton, Lucille. (1980). *two-headed woman*. Amherst, MA: University of Massachusetts Press.

Hughes, Langston. (1959). *The dream keeper and other poems*. New York: Alfred A. Knopf.

Sandburg, Carl. (1958). *Early moon*. New York: Harcourt Brace Jovanovich.

Sandburg, Carl. (1960). *Harvest poems 1910-1960*. New York: Harcourt Brace.

Williams, William Carlos. (1966). *The William Carlos Williams reader*, edited by M.L. Rosenthal. New York: New Directions.

Williams, William Carlos. (1962). *Pictures from Brueghel and other poems*. New York: New Directions.

References

Britton, J. (1982). *Prospect and retrospect: Selected essays of James Britton* (G.M. Pradl, Ed.). Montclair, NJ: Boynton Cook.

Delattre, E.J. (1983). The insiders. In R.W. Bailey & R.M. Fosheim (Eds.), *Literacy for life: The demands for reading and writing*. New York: Modern Language Association.

Gardner, J. (1978). *On moral fiction*. New York: Basic.

Kazemek, F.E. (1984, April). I wauted to be a Tenera to help penp to I _____: Writing for adult beginning learners. *Journal of Reading, 27*, 614–819.

Rigg, P. (1985, February). *Desert wind:* A fresh breeze in Indian education. *Journal of Reading, 28*, 393–397.

Rigg, P., & Kazemek, F.E. (1985, May). For adults only: Reading materials for adult literacy students. *Journal of Reading, 28*, 726–731.

Rigg, P., & Taylor, L. (1979, March). A 21-year-old learns to read. *English Journal, 68*, 52–56.

Weibel, M.C. (1983, October). Use the public library with adult literacy students. *Journal of Reading, 27*, 62–65.

Wigginton, E. (Ed.). (1972). *The foxfire book.* Garden City, NY: Anchor.

G e n e r a l
T e a c h i n g
M e t h o d o l o g y

Poetry in the Adult Literacy Class

BRIAN CONNIFF
CHAD BORTLE
MATTHEW F. JOSEPH
DECEMBER 1993–JANUARY 1994

In a recent review of new books on literacy, Patricia Bizzell (1991) writes that many faculty in American university English departments are currently "talking about literacy because we are having a collective identity crisis about being English teachers" (p. 316). Faced in recent years with a series of budget cuts and a wide range of attacks from within (Bloom, 1987; Kimball, 1990) and without (Bennett, 1984; Cheney, 1990), many English departments have found themselves explaining their missions in terms that are increasingly sensitive to the interests of the public at large. In the words of Gerald Graff (1992), the leading historian of the profession, the departments are clearly feeling "an obligation to do better than we have in clarifying the implications of our work to students and other lay audiences" (p. 356).

In the Dayton (Ohio) Literacy Project, we have been developing strategies to fulfill this obligation by applying the resources of the University of Dayton, especially the various skills of faculty and students in the Department of English, to improve literacy in the local community. At the same time, and even more fundamentally, we have tried to demonstrate that the most traditional of English departments can redefine itself, and restructure its curriculum, in terms of community needs. In the process, we have learned that even those skills that are usually assumed to be especially esoteric—like the reading and teaching of "great poetry"—can, in fact, be used to address the most urgent literacy issues.

Our program began in the fall of 1992, with the aid of a University of Dayton Urban Fellowship received by Brian Conniff and Betty Youngkin for the purpose of integrating direct literacy work with more conventional coursework. During one meeting each week, lasting 2 hours and 45 minutes, University of Dayton undergraduates act as literacy mentors for women who are enrolled in Adult Basic Education (ABE) classes in the city of Dayton and receiving Aid to Families with Dependent Children.

All of the participants—ABE women, undergraduates, and faculty—take part in a variety of activities involving the reading and writing of different literary genres, including poetry, short stories, horror stories, autobiography, children's literature, and group stories. The activities are designed to introduce the

ABE women to a great variety of literary genres, so they can begin to reconceive literacy in the broadest possible terms, and to provide them with frequent opportunities to expand their own writing skills. At some point in each exercise, the undergraduates provide individual tutoring.

At a separate session each week, the undergraduates and faculty meet to discuss the week's literacy work, as well as assigned readings on literacy and related issues. Our first semester's assignments included *Lives on the Boundary* by Mike Rose (1989), *Illiterate America* by Jonathan Kozol (1985), *Orality and Literacy* by Walter Ong (1991), and *Women's Ways of Knowing* by Mary Belenky and her associates (1986). The class discussions are wide ranging but always attempt to relate academic readings to the students' direct work as literacy mentors. In addition, undergraduates and faculty collaborate on research projects directly relevant to the ongoing literacy work.

The overall goals of the program are to build the ABE women's self-esteem, especially with regard to reading and writing; to help them develop strategies for coping with real-life literacy problems like taking the General Equivalency Diploma (GED) exam and passing a driver's test; and to introduce them to the world of literature.

Eleanor

One ABE student who demonstrated a significant level of improvement in her writing skills over the initial 12-week period of our literacy program was Eleanor Simpson (not her real name). After interviewing Eleanor and reading the life story she wrote during the second week of our program, we were able to assemble a brief biography that provides a sense of the difficulties and motivations that brought her to us.

Eleanor was born on March 25, 1941, in Natasulga, Alabama to a sharecropper, Robert, and his wife, Addie. She was the sixth of seven children in a poor but loving family, and she was usually the one who kept the peace between her siblings. One of her older sisters taught her how to read and write.

When Eleanor was 16, her parents separated, and she went to live with her mother. Before long, however, her mother had problems making ends meet and sent her to live with her older sister in Dayton, Ohio. It was at this time that Eleanor stopped going to school in order to watch her sister's babies while her sister was working.

By 1959, at age 18, Eleanor was married, working, and raising a son of her own. In 1964, her marriage ended in divorce, and she retained custody of her son. She was laid off in 1982 and has been dependent on welfare ever since.

Today, Eleanor is a single mother with a second child, a 14-year-old daughter, living at home. She is active in her church and is finally getting a chance to continue her education. She has high goals for the future: She would like to marry again, raise a family, earn her GED, go to college, and get a job that will allow her to support herself and her daughter.

In Eleanor's first written exercise, a life story composed during the first 2 weeks of our program, her writing was full of organizational and grammatical problems. She demonstrated little ability to organize her writing in any way other than chronological sequence, and even within this basic narrative framework, she seemed to have no clear sense of developing conflict or resolution. Her paragraphs typically consisted of two or three sentences, with little command of the sentence as a unit of thought:

> I got married and got a job at 19 years of age had a baby boy name James. I stayed married

for 5 years got a divorce and I've been single since 1964. In 1978 I got Pregnant with my daughter, my son 21 year older than she is.
I got laid off from work 1982 that when I got welfare and still there but I know some day I will a job to be self sufficient.

Her difficulties distinguishing compound words—laidoff and some day—suggested that she was composing from remembered speech rather than reading. When the separation of words could not be determined by sound—that is, when two words had been heard together so often that they seemed to be one—she would write them as one. A single word that was likely to be spoken more slowly, or with some separation for emphasis, would probably be written as two.

Even though our prewriting exercises—constructing collages from magazine clippings—invited each ABE student to envision his or her life "as it is now" and "as you see it in the future," Eleanor's narrative focused exclusively on her past. When her story reached the present, it came to an abrupt end, though not without a closing declaration of faith in her eventual triumph: "I know one day I will have victory in the things I want out of Life a family a home, a car and Love this is my Life."

Regardless of all its departures from standard written English, Eleanor's story was in other respects highly sophisticated. Throughout, it involved a high degree of moral reflection. Early on, she told how as a child she was the peacemaker in a troubled family, and near the end she explained that she views her religious faith as a call to share the one thing she always has, "not a lot of money but *myself*!" At times, Eleanor also demonstrated a striking ability to control the tone of her writing with wit: "My marriage didnt go very well but the next time I get married I will know how to treat a husband they do not come with instructions."

Despite all her writing's surface errors, and no matter how difficult the events she described might seem to have been, her life story never lapsed into remorse or resignation. In this sense, she was able to exert a high degree of control over her story; her problem as a writer was that this control was not often exerted at the level of conventional grammar or academic rhetoric.

Working with Poetry

The actual complexity of Eleanor's language became more apparent—and her ability to use her writing as an instrument of reflection reached a new stage—the first time we worked with poetry. During the fifth week of our program, we read aloud Wallace Stevens's "Thirteen Ways of Looking at a Blackbird" and examined a few of the ways in which Stevens suggests it is possible to look at a blackbird: as "the only moving thing" amidst "twenty snowy mountains," as a metaphor for a state of mind, as the moving edge of "one of many circles," as the source of musical "inflections" and "innuendoes," and so on (Stevens, 1982, pp. 92–94).

Next, we exercised our own abilities to view an object from many perspectives. We placed an abstract metal sculpture—a collection of mostly triangular shapes, bent in many directions and playfully painted—in the middle of the room. Orally, we practiced "ways of looking at a work of art." The ABE students were immediately engaged: They saw the sculpture as a group of whales diving into the ocean, a tropical island with palm trees, a tidal wave, a pile of junk from the city streets.

Finally, each of us wrote an imitation of Stevens's poem, using the method for teaching "great poetry" to children described by Kenneth Koch in *Rose, Where Did You Get*

That Red? (1974). We began with a "poetry idea," the kind of suggestion Koch used to encourage his students to write "poems of their own in some way like the poems they were studying" (pp. 3–4). For "Thirteen Ways," we took our poetry idea directly from Koch's book: "Write a poem in which you look at the same thing in a number of different ways" (p. 116). We placed no limit on the choice of subjects; we merely provided as a starting point a fill-in-the-blanks formula: "_____ Ways of Looking at a _____."

Eleanor entitled her first draft "5 Ways of looking at a Piece of Art." She finished only the first two ways:

1) On the edge of the water front I saw two whale tails one small a one large

2) I saw the spinning top on the other side

The "whale tails," like the "Piece of Art" in her title, were taken directly from the class discussion. Below this initial sketch, she made a brief try at a third way—"I was in 3"—which she then crossed out. Next, she tried revising her first way, apparently for more poetic phrasing: "On the water front looking into the water/ I saw two whale." Before long, however, she blackened out both the beginning and the end of her title, "5 Ways" and "Piece of Art." In effect, she managed to revise her way back to the start: All she had left was "of looking at."

Then Eleanor turned to a new page to begin a new poem. This time, all she managed was a title: "4 ways of looking a life." Again, she turned the page.

On her third try, Eleanor finally arrived at the topic that would result in a complete poem:

"Three ways of looking at the Autumn."

The moon is Orange and bright.
I wonder where you are tonight.
that's how I feel under the harvest moon.

The flower shows its last

scene. All color has unfolded and
its time to go and rest. We
all need a rest from our labor.

The trees are so different in the
fall, the wind blowing leaves
on the ground, Oh what
Beautiful colors all around.

Her finished poem shows remarkably little evidence of revision, only a couple of corrections of subject and verb agreement and a correction of *or* to *our* in the middle stanza—and these minor changes were the only stages in her composition in which she seems to have received any help from the college students. The first and third stanzas were written in a single draft, with no revision.

The various poetic techniques—rhyme, stanza, repetition, parallel construction, exclamation—had no sources in "Thirteen Ways of Looking at a Blackbird" or in our group discussion. They were Eleanor's own attempts to make her writing "poetic." Most impressive, perhaps, was her use of stanzas to move from the first person singular, focusing on personal longing; to the first person plural, suggesting an identification with the flower and a universal need for rest; and finally to the apparent third person speaker of the last stanza, helping to create a sense of losing the self, and the burdens of labor, in the beauty of nature.

In a more conventional basic education setting, this shifting focus might be viewed— and, if it were written in prose, it certainly would be viewed—as grammatical inconsistency, or as a lack of coherence. But within the stanzaic structure of Eleanor's poem, it is clearly something more important. More than anything else, the achievement of a universal voice, "we all need a rest from our labor," is the beginning of an attempt, on the one hand, to remove herself from the tyranny of the past—the past she never really escaped in her life story—and, on the other hand, to see her struggles as very much like those of everybody else.

All of Us Are Writers

Eleanor's variation on a "great" poem, like so much of our work with ABE women, has confirmed many of our hopes for our program. At no time was this confirmation more clear than in the third week of our program, when Toni Cade Bambara came to the university as guest writer for our Scholars program. The week before her arrival we read and discussed the short story "My Man Bovanne" from her early collection *Gorilla, My Love* (1981). Then, we arranged for Bambara to visit our literacy project in the spare hour between the arrival of her plane and her scheduled dinner.

For their writing assignment that week, with the help of the college students, the ABE women had prepared a list of questions to ask the "real live author" when she arrived. Eleanor's questions were typical. Mostly, they focused on the process of becoming a writer: How old were you when you started writing? How much of you is in your stories? Who has inspired you to put your experiences into writing?

When she arrived, Bambara told our group about the first "real writers" she had met as a child in Harlem: her neighbor Langston Hughes, who would sit in the children's section at the public library and talk with the local kids, and Gwendolyn Brooks, who came one day to read at the YMCA. Then she told us that we, too, all of us, are writers; in our spare moments, at least, we all compose stories of people we see riding the bus, doing laundry, walking down the street.

Eleanor never did ask her questions, though several of the other ABE students asked similar ones. But the next week, when one of our assignments was to write a letter to

Toni Cade Bambara herself, Eleanor's was particularly revealing. She thanked Bambara for coming, added that she had told her children about the visit, and mentioned that the questions asked by the students "didn't seem to come out just right."

But far more importantly, she wrote, "We didn't know we were writers until you told us (smile)."

Perhaps that is the best explanation for how poetry has worked in our literacy program—and how it should be able to work in many others. ABE instructors and other literacy volunteers should not give in to the traditional belief, held most of all in the university, that poetry is a particularly elevated literary genre, above and beyond the comprehension of ABE students. Eleanor's poem demonstrates that poetry can enhance the reading and writing skills of lower level readers, at the same time that it helps them develop the confidence with language necessary to become better readers and writers.

Poetry can provide a rare opportunity for a student like Eleanor to *act* like a writer. When she wrote a poem of her own, she put in rhymes and stanzas, not because they were in the model we provided, and not because she was instructed to do so, but because that is how she imagined a poet is supposed to work. And so she assumed a control over her language that could no longer be considered remedial. At least for a while, she allowed herself to be a poet.

References
Bambara, T.C. (1981). *Gorilla, my love.* New York: Random House.

Belenky, M., Clinchy, B., Goldberger, N., & Tarule, J. (1986). *Women's ways of knowing.* New York: Basic.

Bennett, W.J. (1984). *To reclaim a legacy.* Washington, DC: National Endowment for the Humanities.

Bizzell, P. (1991). Professing literacy: A review essay. *Journal of Advanced Composition, 2*, 315–321.

Bloom, A. (1987). *The closing of the American mind.* New York: Simon.

Cheney, L.V. (1990). Tyrannical machines. Washington, DC: National Endowment for the Humanities.

Graff, G. (1992). The scholar in society. In J. Garibaldi (Ed.), *Introduction to scholarship in modern languages and literatures* (pp. 343–367). New York: Modern Language Association.

Kimball, R. (1990). *Tenured radicals.* New York: Harper.

Koch, K. (1974). *Rose, where did you get that red?: Teaching great poetry to children.* New York: Vintage.

Kozol, J. (1985). *Illiterate America.* New York: New American Library.

Ong, W. (1991). *Orality and literacy.* New York: Routledge.

Rose, M. (1989). *Lives on the boundary.* New York: Penguin.

Stevens, W. (1982). *The collected poems.* New York: Random House.

General Teaching Methodology

Consumer Advocacy, Empowerment, and Adult Literacy

LA VERGNE ROSOW
DECEMBER 1990–JANUARY 1991

"This woman used hairlong protein vitamin lotion. She used because she think her hair it is grow in just one week. For me it is falsehood so miny people buy this products theirs are think this produts it is good in my opion it not good."

As she critiqued a nationally distributed ad for a lotion that claims to give "lovelier, longer, fuller hair in just one week," Maria (proper names of all students have been changed), who aspires to beauty-shop ownership, was changing her outlook on how she should advertise some day. She looked critically at the content of an ad that called for US$6.95 to make a wish come true and began to identify a kind of victimization with which she wanted no future association.

By analyzing an ad she had selected, arriving at her own conclusions, and expressing them in her own words, Maria was gaining power through literacy that would not have been possible by means of a traditional, teacher-centered writing assignment. She was engaged in a series of exercises that employ the learner as critic.

Because the media tend to repeat conventional ideology (Brookfield, 1986) rather than raise questions about it, and because commercial promotions are designed more to convince than to inform, consumers like Maria need to learn how to ask their own questions. They must be given the power to analyze the information that influences each day they live in a literate society. Indeed, consumer education must be part of education for all citizens.

Maria was a student in my night class of multilingual, multicultural teens and adults, all at different levels in learning English. There was an official set of civics books assigned for use in class only, but it was being used by another teacher in another building. The students were free to buy their own copies but the shipment had not yet arrived at the bookstore. That left an expensive, skills-based English grammar workbook, owned by only a few students, as the sole possible class text.

Analysis of television programming seemed like a good way to promote critical thinking, so I signed up for the school's media services. Then I found that video equipment in operating order was not even available to instructors. The time-consuming process of trying to make poorly maintained machines run and tapes turn was frustrating for students and teacher.

In a desperate attempt at giving my students *something* to analyze, and as a way of awakening consumer advocacy, I began to introduce newspapers and junk mail promotions in class.

Rationale for Implementing the Program

The lack of teaching materials available to me led most directly to my decision to use ads and promotions to teach my students. But it seemed to me that in this case necessity generated an effective teaching device. Through the use of junk mail, I was able to instruct my students not only in English but also in the basics of consumer advocacy and American civics.

Upon reflection, I realized that teaching consumer advocacy fit in well with current thought on learning theory.

1. It addresses the affective domain by giving credit to the learner for all she or he brings to the fore.

2. It employs background information in the grounding of a new literacy activity.

3. It starts at the level of the learner, allowing for the assimilation of new information (Krashen, 1985a).

4. It is relevant and useful in content (Eskey, 1986; Krashen, 1988; Smith, 1986a & 1986b).

5. It gives meaningful, useful thinking strategies that will outlast any formal class (Eskey & Grabe, 1988; Freire, 1984).

6. It encourages the risk-taking that is essential to cognitive development (Goodman, 1986; Harste, Woodward, & Burke, 1984; Rosow, 1988 & 1989).

7. It allows learners to structure responses and to use words that express what is important to them. That's empowerment!

Teaching Consumer Literacy

My change of attitude from needy to endowed caused an undeniable change of luck. Free teaching aids suddenly began to arrive from all over the country. Among other things, I received a mailer telling me that I'd won a car and another terrific prize (though the fine print stated "one gift per vehicle"). All I had to do, according to the congratulatory letter, was go to a villa resort (3 hours from my home), hear a 90-minute sales pitch, take a tour of the resort with an authorized representative, "meet the conditions of eligibility listed on the enclosed," and then turn in my lucky number.

I called to verify that I'd won and recorded the conversation for my students to hear that night. I photocopied material, enlarging the fine print I'd discovered on a very small piece of paper that was tossed in the envelope.

It took a number of replays of the tape for my students to understand how, through carefully worded dialogue and skillfully mumbled phrases, I had not only been led to think I'd won the car but also US$5,000. Together we read and scrutinized the letter. Several times I was asked if it was real, if I really had won the car, if I might not lose my chance by telling what happened. Clearly, there was some doubt about my ability to read English! Through this process, I was able to introduce to the class the notion of consumer advocacy.

We discussed the natural trust many people put in a celebrity or other familiar person. We sidetracked into why incumbents win elections, regardless of record. We talked about consumer fraud, mail fraud, misrepresentation, rights, freedoms, and honesty. We looked up the words *free*, *winner*, *eligibility*, and *null and void*. We talked about what a time-share "investment" really means. (Time share was what was really being promoted in the mailing I received.)

Though math was not in my curriculum, we worked out the cost per week for a "minimal" investment. And, using the enlarged copies of the fine print, we were able to examine the odds of winning anything desirable. (The odds on the car were 1 in 100,000.)

Should I write my congressman, the Better Business Bureau, the Chamber of Commerce, or the police? I was prepared to follow the advice of my students.

The purpose was not to get even with the resort for wasting my time; it was to give my students an inside view of active, critical, empowered citizenship. They were not ready for action. They told me to throw the trash in the trashcan.

This exercise proved to be the start of an incubation period. A week later the class was given a variety of TV guides and grocery store tabloids from which to select and cut out ads to critique. The object was to empower—and at the same time to gain the language and skills that come from reading interesting materials.

This was no trick. Mahon (1986) suggests explaining theory to learners. At least once a week I explained the graphs in a Krashen study or discussed a Frank Smith quote. And my students were reminded regularly that high interest reading leads to painless learning of vocabulary, spelling, and punctuation (Krashen, 1985b).

Critiques and Changing Attitudes

As critic, the learner engages in a deliberate process of questioning text—not idly asking "What does it want me to think?" but rather "What do I think about it?" and "What is missing here?" This can provoke a shift of attitude and prompt action. (For discussions of literacy and power, see, for instance, Kozol, 1985; Luke, 1986; McLeod, 1986; Rist, 1970; and Rosow, 1989).

Ellie, a farm worker, selected a quarter-page ad, most of which was filled with a close-up photograph of a slim, trim, barely clad female rear end that ostensibly promoted a cellulite-reducing cream. "It's a fraud and lie," she reported. She knew someone who had spent hundreds of dollars on the US$10 a jar product.

The notion that consumers should actively respond to being cheated had sent her beyond the dictionary and into the thesaurus. I was unable to collect that assignment from her because she was still expressing her opinion when it was time to leave. Tired though she was every evening, she wanted to take this home for further work.

Lee, a meat cutter who hates his work, selected an ad for a psychic astrologer who promised to assist people with "money-health-love" problems. "I think this kind of ad: it is the last way to solve these problems and the most wrong way by telephone."

Weeks later he gave a more elaborate critique of a product: "I found something wrong for the consumer in this add if someone buys the cassette player. They warranty the money back in 15 days if no satisfied bat is it not the thru because we recibe back only a credit."

Miguel, a teenager with a troubled past of military activity, is eager to be part of a country in which the government does something to safeguard its citizenry. Of an ad that promised riches from the California lottery for just US$9.95 he wrote, "This add talk about how can be rich sending name, birthdate, and $9.95. Here in California there are many ads of that way like it mislead. The government of U.S. should take all mislead ads to not involved the citizen because no is right."

Another teenager, Joseph, was always the first to want to know more about court cases and legal definitions. Of an ad for an astrologer who takes payment via credit cards, Joseph wrote, "My opinion in this ad is: this people are trainig to get victim and mislead them."

George, a university-trained artist, eagerly awaits the photocopies of language acquisition articles I bring in for him each week. Though he believes the translation he does of them is teaching him English, I'm hoping the theoretical messages will begin to impress him. I believe that understanding the theory behind schoolwork encourages the student to take an active part in the learning process. This is not underhanded—I told him what my motivation was.

Of a lottery ad, he wrote, "When I read this anounces ofert this information I thing is posible what existing person credulity and superstition yet. I'm sceptic. I thing is imposible get money and happened playing lotto and other sistem aparently easy. Only working and learning we are happy."

Though these students are still struggling to learn English, they are not without the cognitive potential for analyzing text. What worked for them was finding authentic text—material that was familiar to them and held their interest. (No two students worked on the same ad.) Fortified with a notion of what critiquing was about and free to write as much or as little as was needed to express their opinions, they surprised themselves with their work.

A Different Exercise

Even though most of these adult students were usually very tired by the time they got to class, each was encouraged to identify a product or service she or he might try to sell some time in the future. The task was to write promotional materials that were both honest and productive. Those who were comfortable attempting full sentences were free to elaborate; those who wanted to fall back on simple phrases or single words could also complete ads. As always, they were free to refer to earlier lessons, ads, the dictionary, thesaurus, or any other reference source they could find.

Though these ads documented linguistic advancement, most of them lacked polish; they were dreadfully honest and flat. Still, these students were advancing on multiple fronts simultaneously. They were reading in English, interpreting not only the language but legal and ethical implications in ways they had never done before, and they were writing about new ideas, using new vocabulary.

Part of the moral here is that education takes time; when things don't develop on schedule, they may need more time (Krashen, 1982). And that applies to nearly every student nearly every term. Only by an occasional fluke do arbitrary timeframes fit individual learners.

Fortunately, in many adult education classes, the disempowering process of grading the students' products has been discarded. Obviously, grading products of the cognitive process teaches nothing, discourages risk-taking, and insults both the learner and the educational process. People want to learn as much as they can; no external motivators are necessary or even beneficial. Judging from the level of interest and the peer support that was developing for even the least vocal students in the class, I believe that 2 more weeks of analysis of good ads could have fostered a verbally and ethically strong corps of entrepreneurs.

As it was, the thinking had moved from buyer to seller, from passive to opinioned. The students now understood that they had unique and valuable perspectives on the world and began to view themselves as bringers of change, personally, and publicly.

Empowering Attitudes Outside the Classroom

I eventually had to fall back on the cheapest of texts: newsprint. When my students saw that I expected them to behave as thinking, literate adults who had important ideas to document, they participated actively. Text analysis provided an avenue for ongoing self-teaching that could be done long after the teacher and the school were out of the picture.

When one man, who was often absent because of his work and had to return to Mexico before the end of the term, came to say goodbye, he wanted me to know that he had begun to spend 10 minutes of his lunch each day reading the paper. Remembering that I regularly asked for input on what was working in class and what wasn't, he wanted me to be sure to keep reminding students to read 10 minutes a day. "It's good," he told me. "It's help me a lot. It's some mislead, but I thing it's good."

Empowerment Doesn't Just Happen

Empowering attitudes must be discovered and rediscovered. I'm not trying to peddle these particular activities; they were right, at this time, for these learners. It is up to each teacher to determine anew what will work in each situation, to the maximum benefit for each class.

Asking the question "Why am I using this particular lesson?" can help stave off inappropriate, restrictive programming. I had begun this term intending to use TV analysis as a method of instruction. I had to meet anew the truisms that again seem so clear: Much of what we do as educators is designed to fit stereotypical formats, rigid timeframes, familiar assignments, and limited, disempowering expectations. It took the serious notion of authentic text application to make me see a new level of potential in my students.

Of course, the experiment could have failed. It was risky to move away from safe, controllable, rote drills and contrived pattern practice into exercises in applied citizenship. But, viewing the classroom as an experimental station—a safe haven where people can think things through without getting hurt and can express opinions freely—fosters confidence in both teacher and student.

In the protected environment of the classroom, we can take risks in teaching that allow our students the latitude to take risks in thinking. When we share our own reasons and reservations, we allow our students to see that the solutions to problems are always tentative and that we must work cooperatively to succeed. The learner who assumed the job of critic also assumed the position of authority. We thereby give our students the power to develop independently by resisting the urge to control how much, how fast, and in what direction that development will go. Power is having the strength and ability to design questions from conventional givens and the courage to let the answers change over time.

Only educators who have power can give power. Those who are able to take risks and to challenge the obvious must define and redefine the line between caregiver and liberator. For those who are up to it, for those who discover how to give power away, there is a limitless supply. There is enough power for every student every day.

Postscript

Over the holidays, I was invited to the home of one of my students. When I arrived, a vacuum salesman was ending what must have been a very long pitch. A tower of merchandise was piled in the livingroom. Then my hostess was offered her choice of five sealed envelopes. Hers contained a coupon for an overnight bus tour to Las Vegas. In complicated language the fine print said participants had to restrict their holiday to the casinos assigned by the tour company.

After the salesman left, she explained to me "Is mislead. He say no sell nothing...he say no time...he mislead." After an extensive hard-sell demonstration that had taken place under the guise of winning a surprise trip, she had not bought the US$1,500 vacuum cleaner—and I don't think she plans to be on the bus tour to Las Vegas either.

References
Brookfield, S. (1986). Media power and the development of media literacy: An adult educational interpretation. *Harvard Educational Review, 56*(2), 151–170.

Eskey, D.E. (1986). Theoretical foundations. In F. Dubin, D.E. Eskey, & W. Grabe (Eds.), *Teaching second language reading for academic purposes*. Reading, MA: Addison-Wesley.

Eskey, D.E., & Grabe, W. (1988). Interactive models for second language reading: Perspectives on instruction. In P.L. Carrell, J. Devine, & E. Eskey (Eds.), *Interactive approaches to second language reading*. Cambridge, England: Cambridge University Press.

Freire, P. (1984). *Pedagogy of the oppressed*. New York: Continuum.

Goodman, K. (1986). *What's whole in whole language*. Portsmouth, NH: Heinemann Educational.

Harste, J.C., Woodward, V.C., & Burke, C. (1984). *Language stories and literacy lessons*. Portsmouth, NH: Heinemann Educational.

Kozol, J. (1985). *Illiterate America*. New York: New American Library.

Krashen, S. (1982). *Principles and practice in second language acquisition*. Oxford, England: Pergamon.

Krashen, S. (1985a). *The input hypothesis: Issues and implications*. White Plains, NY: Longman.

Krashen, S. (1985b). *Inquiries and insights*. Hayward, CA: Alemany.

Krashen, S. (1988, Fall). Notes from University of Southern California lectures.

Luke, A. (1986). Linguistic stereotypes, the divergent speaker and the teaching of literacy. *Journal of Curriculum Studies, 18*(4), 397–408.

Mahon, D. (1986). Intermediate skills: Focusing on reading rate development. In F. Dubin, D.E. Eskey, & W. Grabe (Eds.), *Teaching second language reading for academic purposes*. Reading, MA: Addison-Wesley.

McLeod, A. (1986). Critical literacy: Taking control of our own lives. *Language Arts, 63*(1).

Rist, R. (1970). Student social class and teacher

expectations: The self-fulfilling prophecy in ghetto education. *Harvard Educational Review, 40*(3).

Rosow, L. (1988). Adult illiterates offer unexpected cues into the reading process. *Journal of Reading, 32*(2), 120–124.

Rosow, L. (1989). Arthur: A tale of disempowerment. *Phi Delta Kappan, 71*(3), 194–199.

Smith, F. (1986a). *Insult to intelligence: The bureaucratic invasion of our classrooms.* New York: Arbor House.

Smith, F. (1986b). *Understanding reading.* Hillsdale, NJ: Erlbaum.

G e n e r a l   T e a c h i n g   M e t h o d o l o g y

Using Classic Novels with Adult New Readers

Jane McCabe Schierloh
May 1992

Whole language proponents argue that students with minimal literacy skills should be reading whole selections of well written literature, not "bits and pieces" (Goodman, 1986). However, most reading materials published for adult basic education (ABE) students *are* bits and pieces selected to teach specific reading skills such as finding the main idea, recognizing details, and understanding inference. ABE teachers who want their students to read whole books of fiction have a problem—not much is published for the mature adult reading at third-, fourth-, and fifth-grade levels. So what are ABE teachers to do?

Benefits of Reading Good Fiction

Of course some may ask, "Why *should* ABE students read fiction—good, bad, or indifferent? How will reading Charles Dickens's *Great Expectations*, for example, help students read medicine bottle labels, job training manuals, and tax forms?"

One answer to this legitimate question is to look at the reasons why adults enroll in ABE classes. In 325 face-to-face interviews with randomly selected ABE students across Iowa, Beder and Valentine (1990) identified 10 reasons why U.S. adults participate in federal adult basic education programs. The four factors ranked most highly were (1) *educational advancement* ("I want to prove to myself that I can finish school"), (2) *self-improvement* ("I want to feel better about myself," "be more intelligent"), (3) *literacy development* (reading, writing, and speaking skills), and (4) *community and church involvement* ("I want to be able to read the Bible better").

The seventh ranked factor was *diversion,* which was rated most highly by older students. In Beder and Valentine's view "this factor...suggests that some learners participate in ABE, not for its instrumental value, but because it represents a constructive way to spend one's time."

The implications of this study are that ABE students have much broader educational goals than day-to-day survival or job readiness. Reading literature can benefit students who have diverse goals. It is essential for those who choose to finish school by passing the General Equivalency Diploma (GED) tests (indeed, one of the five subtests of the GED is called Interpreting Literature and the Arts). Reading literature also can help students feel better about themselves. Additionally, it develops their reading and writing skills, improves their ability to read the Bible, and most assuredly it provides diversion.

Most important, reading fiction is just plain fun, especially when the experience is shared with others. This is not a minor point. If reading is not enjoyable, students do not read (Allington, 1977). And if they do not read frequently, they do not become fluent, skillful readers.

Advocates of literature-based instruction point out other benefits of reading literature. It can teach critical thinking (Commeyras, 1989). It can be a natural springboard to writing (Atwell, 1987). It can help students develop background knowledge, particularly in the social studies (Brozo & Tomlinson, 1986).

And finally, as this article will show, mature adult students should read whole books of well written fiction because they have the capacity and experience needed to relate to the universal experiences captured in great classic literature. Although their literacy skills are limited, their life experiences are deep and sophisticated.

Problem > Idea

Like many instructional innovations, this one began in response to a problem—too many students reading at third- and fourth-grade levels were dropping out of ABE classes in our reading center.

The Downtown Adult Reading Center is a program of Project: LEARN, an adult literacy organization located in Cleveland, Ohio.

When the center was set up as an experimental ABE program in 1985 with startup funding from local foundations and the Cleveland Public Schools, one of its major goals was to offer ABE classes specially tailored to the needs of students who had completed a beginning adult literacy course called the Laubach Way to Reading (Laubach, Kirk, & Laubach, 1981). Those of us who designed and taught the classes saw our role as helping adult new readers make the transition from one-to-one tutoring to small group instruction, and from primarily controlled-vocabulary reading materials to uncontrolled-vocabulary pre-GED materials on fourth- to eighth-grade levels.

Naturally I became concerned when I noticed that a disproportionate number of students at lower reading levels were dropping out of classes. I suspected that the reading materials we were using were too difficult for adult new readers. My observations of their oral reading convinced me that they needed considerable practice reading materials at third- and fourth-grade levels with uncontrolled vocabularies in order to gain fluency, speed, and the confidence to take risks in predicting unknown words.

Unfortunately, we lacked a variety of well written materials appropriate to their needs and especially their mature interests, so I began a search. I found very few books of interest to adults. Most books were aimed primarily at adolescents. They featured fast cars and sports stars. But few of our students were young people. Most were in their 30s and 40s, and a sizeable number were retired men and women in their 60s and 70s who showed polite indifference to much of the fiction and nonfiction geared to young people.

After extensive searching I noticed some attractive adapted or abridged versions of classic novels. My first reaction was positive.

Some of these little books were interesting and readable. But my second reaction was negative. They came close to being simply plot summaries, the type high school and college students use who want to pass a test without reading the assigned novel. The characters were rather flat and one dimensional. Out of necessity, the writers had omitted some of the authors' themes in order to reduce the 400-page novels to 100 pages or less. Sadder yet, they had been forced to sacrifice much of the authors' rich, powerful language. For example, the passionate love scene in *Jane Eyre* by Charlotte Brontë that has stirred the hearts of millions of readers was reduced to "I love you, Jane. I love you—only you. And I shall love you forever."

Suddenly, it struck me that if I read aloud to students short excerpts from the original novels on which the adaptations were based, I could give students at least a taste of the reading experience in store for able readers. Excerpts could be chosen that would add the details necessary to make a character come alive, to introduce or develop a theme, or to illustrate the language of the writer and demonstrate its power to move the reader. "If reading aloud to children is so effective," I reasoned, "why not read aloud to adults?"

Classroom Experiences

My colleagues and I began the experiment using an adaptation of Robert Louis Stevenson's *Treasure Island* (1973) with three groups of 8 to 10 students each. At the close of the first class session, we asked students for their suggestions. They said that they preferred to have copies of the excerpts in front of them so that they could read along with the teacher's voice.

The second day we followed up on their suggestion. Our concern that they wouldn't be able to follow along proved groundless. As one student said, "Once in a while you lose me, but in a few seconds I find where you are."

We were encouraged by this development because when students listen to a teacher read aloud, they become actively involved in language at its best (Trelease, 1985). Furthermore, they see a skillful reader modeling fluency, phrasing, and dramatic expressiveness.

There were a number of scenes in *Treasure Island* (1947) that lent themselves well to oral reading. One that held us in the grip of excitement and fear was the scene in which Jim, the young boy who narrates this pirate tale, is attacked by Israel Hands, one of the pirates, and fights desperately for his life. The scene begins like this:

> Perhaps I had heard a creak, or seen his shadow moving with the tail of my eye; perhaps it was an instinct like a cat's, but sure enough, when I looked round, there was Hands, already halfway toward me, with the dirk in his right hand.

For a few minutes all of us were that defenseless young boy facing a pirate with a "bloodstained dirk" in his upraised hand. Only our wits could save us from a violent death.

> Seeing that I meant to dodge, he also paused; and a moment or two passed in feints on his part and corresponding movements upon mine. It was such a game as I often played at home about the rocks of Black Hill Cove; but never before, you may be sure, with such a wildly beating heart as now.

Students who tended to read a word at a time were pulled along by the teacher's voice and forced to read in rapid fluent phrases, and those who read in a flat monotone without attention to meaning learned how a good reader translates print into an exciting experience.

My other concern about asking students to read a 92-page novel was the problem of continuity. Because of our open enrollment policy, new students enter the class continually. Furthermore, because of illness, family problems, and financial needs, students are frequently absent. Would students lose track of the plot, become discouraged, drop out of class?

Quite the contrary: students became intrigued by the unfolding story. It was rather like watching the soap operas on television. One could miss an episode or two and still remain involved with the characters and plot.

And as with the soaps, one could become addicted. For instance, we noticed that some of our books were disappearing. One particular day students had to share copies of the book because five copies were missing. Pat T., a woman in her late 20s, came late to class, slipped into her seat, and sheepishly pulled a copy of *Treasure Island* out of her book bag. "I'm sorry," she said, "I just had to know how it came out."

To solve our continuity problem, we borrowed an idea from the soaps. We began each class with a brief review of the plot to date. This brought on board students who had been absent as well as students who were new to the program. It also refreshed the memory of those who were in class the previous session in a way reminiscent of the introductory synopses used in TV serials.

As the weeks went by, we slipped into a comfortable routine that accomplished some of our reading objectives: (a) quick review of the plot, (b) silent reading of a chapter, (c) discussion, (d) pronunciation of unfamiliar words, (e) oral reading and discussion, (f) reading of an excerpt from the original novel, (g) discussion of a writing question, and (h) writing.

Encouraged by students' positive reactions to *Treasure Island*, we decided to try an adaptation of *Jane Eyre* (1987). *Jane Eyre* was an even greater favorite. The abuse Jane endured as an unwanted child in her aunt's home touched their hearts. They were curious about the unfolding mystery of the screams in the attic, and they were moved by the passionate love story of Jane and Mr. Rochester. They got into a lively debate about whether Mr. Rochester should have concealed from Jane the fact that he was already married. The debate resulted in some interesting pieces of writing.

Our next choice was an adaptation of Charles Dickens's *Great Expectations*. Our students identified with Pip's desire to escape from the working class to become an educated gentleman in London. Several African-American women in their early 70s had spent most of their lives cleaning buildings at night and caring for their children during the day. These children, now grown, are teachers, lawyers, and business people. Other students in their 30s and 40s were trapped in dead-end jobs that required back-breaking labor. And some of our students could no longer work those back-breaking jobs because of back injuries, heart trouble, and high blood pressure. All of these students believed, like Pip, that education is the way out of poverty.

At the same time, however, they foresaw the hazards of this climb from one social class to another. "Money changes people," they said and shook their heads sadly when they read that Pip became ashamed of the good people back home who loved him for what he was, not for what he had. This major theme led to a discussion on the problems as well as the benefits of improving one's education and socio-economic status.

"Some people 'get theirs' and never look back," some said. "They think they're better than other people."

"But you can't blame them for wanting to get out of the ghetto," others countered.

One day we read the episode in which Pip's stepfather Joe explains to the boy why he never learned to read and write. We had to abandon the lesson plan that day because one student after another shared personal stories of why they hadn't learned to read when they were children, how they coped with their handicap, and why they were grateful for their literacy skills. Three African American women in their 60s and 70s recalled picking cotton on farms in Alabama. "We picked from sunup," said one, and "to sundown!" answered the other two in chorus. "There wasn't no time for school," they said.

A 35-year-old white man asked, "Why are people afraid to admit they can't read? It's not a shame to admit you can't read. I used to be shy to admit it. I was afraid they'd laugh at me and say, 'How did you graduate?' Now I tell them the truth and they tell me, 'That is the best thing you can do.' I'm very happy with myself, and now I can read a little better than before."

When we finished the last page of *Great Expectations*, one man in his late 30s breathed a deep sigh of satisfaction. "This is the first book I ever finished," he said. Most of the students in the group agreed that reading a book from cover to cover was a new experience for them.

Our plan had been to recycle the books with new groups of students every year or two. However, so many students stayed in our classes for 2, 3, and even 4 years that we found it necessary to offer additional titles such as an adaptation of H.G. Wells's science fiction classic *The Time Machine* (1980) and Robert Louis Stevenson's *Dr. Jekyll and Mr. Hyde* (1985). Not all adapted novels worked out well in the ABE classroom, however.

Guidelines for Selecting Adapted Novels

Over the past four years my colleagues and I learned some things about selecting successful adapted novels. We learned to reject some adaptations on the basis of a single reading. Some books force the reader to move too quickly through complex plots. In others, the characters are not developed enough to interest the reader, or the new characters are introduced so rapidly that the reader cannot remember them from one page to the next.

Here is a passage from a book called *King Arthur and His Knights* (1988) that introduces seven characters in the first two paragraphs of the book:

> Many years ago Uther fought to make himself king of all England. Two true friends helped him. One was wise Merlin, the famous magician. The other was a great knight and fighter named Ulfius. At last Uther beat his enemies and became king.
>
> Then Uther married Igraine, a widow. She had three daughters, Elaine, Margaret, and Morgan le Fay... Morgan le Fay could do more magic than anyone but Merlin. The girls soon married three kings who had made friends with Uther.

This is information overload for ABE teachers as well as ABE students.

We had to reject some adaptations because they appeared to have been written according to a formula for sentence length. Their short, choppy, monotonous sentences made comprehension difficult. The passage from *King Arthur and His Knights* above illustrates this problem.

Sentences do not have to be uniformly short to be accessible to an adult new reader. Notice the easy natural flow of the sentences in the opening paragraph from an adaptation of *King Solomon's Mines* by H. Rider Haggard (1976).

Some Classic Novels Used with Adult New Readers

Brontë, C. (1987). *Jane Eyre*. Adapted and abridged by S.E. Paces. Belmont, CA: David S. Lake.

Brontë, C. (1975). *Jane Eyre*. New York: Oxford.

Dickens, C. (1987). *Great Expectations*. Adapted and abridged by T.E. Bethancourt. Belmont, CA: David S. Lake.

Haggard, H.R. (1976). *King Solomon's Mines*. Retold by J. Oxley. New York: Oxford.

King Arthur and His Knights. (1988). Adapted by W. Kottmeyer. New York: Phoenix.

Stevenson, R.L. (1985). *Dr. Jekyll and Mr. Hyde*. Adapted and abridged by T.E. Bethancourt. Belmont, CA: David S. Lake.

Stevenson, R.L. (1988). *Kidnapped*. Adapted and abridged by W. Kottmeyer. New York: Phoenix.

Stevenson, R.L. (1947). *Treasure Island*. New York: Grosset & Dunlap.

Stevenson, R.L. (1973). *Treasure Island*. Adapted and abridged by J. Gray. Belmont, CA: David S. Lake.

Wells, H.G. (1986). *The Time Machine*. Adapted and abridged by T.E. Bethancourt. Belmont, CA: David S. Lake.

It is a curious thing that at my age, and I shall never be sixty again, I should be starting to write a book. I wonder what sort of book it will be when I have finished, if I ever come to the end of it! (p. 1)

Our students do not find such sentences difficult. Notice also how the beginning of this novel arouses the curiosity of the reader.

Even adapted novels that pass a first inspection can turn out to be a disaster in the classroom. We gave a high rating to an adaptation of *Kidnapped* by Robert Louis Stevenson (1988). As we had anticipated, the class thoroughly enjoyed the first half of the book. The second half proved to be much more difficult, however, because students needed to know the complex history of Bonnie Prince Charlie and the political intrigue among England, Scotland, and France. The teacher found herself attempting to teach Scottish history to students who had not yet learned to find the United States on a world map!

We learned that teachers must consider students' background knowledge when selecting a novel. In fact, we found it wise to ask several typical students to read the adapted novel under consideration and to share their reactions with us before we made a final selection.

Guidelines for Selecting Excerpts

We also developed some useful guidelines for selecting excerpts from full-length novels. We found that passages of dialogue were easier for students than passages of description. The sentences in dialogue passages are shorter; the vocabulary is simpler; and the emotional intensity carries the student over a multitude of reading difficulties.

Excerpts of scenes involving exciting action are effective. For example, in *Treasure Island* students enjoy the dramatic scene in which the pirates attack the stockade. No adapted version can match Stevenson's description of the pirates climbing over the wall of the stockade, their daggers in their teeth.

Excerpts yielding deep insights into a major character can bring life to otherwise flat characters. A good example is Miss Havisham's repentance scene in *Great Expectations*. In this scene, Miss Havisham, an elderly half-mad woman who has never recovered from the shock of being abandoned by her fiancé on her wedding day, regrets her lifetime of bitterness and revenge. She sees how her selfishness has hurt the two people she loves, and she cries repeatedly, "What have I done? What have I done?"

We discovered that excerpts need to be brief and to be read with as few explanations as possible. Since students have already read the adapted versions of the episode, they can handle limited exposures to sophisticated reading material. These readings also provide an opportunity to teach students that a good reader does not have to know all the words in order to enjoy a story.

No More Snippets

Adult new readers and other adult students with minimal reading skills deserve more than the snippets of stories ordinarily served up for them. Unfortunately, however, there are not enough whole selections of well written literature to meet their needs and interests. This article has presented one solution which has been successful with ABE students at Project: LEARN in Cleveland, Ohio, for the past 4 years. It has described how teachers can use adapted or abridged classic novels such as *Jane Eyre, Great Expectations*, and *Treasure Island* if they enrich them by reading aloud to students short passages from the full-length novels. By reading silently along with the teacher's voice, students see good reading modeled and experience the novels that more literate readers have read and loved.

References

Allington, R. (1977). If they don't read much, how they gonna get good? *Journal of Reading, 21*, 57–61.

Atwell, N. (1987). *In the middle: Writing, reading, and learning with adolescents.* Portsmouth, NH: Heinemann.

Beder, H., & Valentine, T. (1990). *What motivates adults to participate in the federal adult basic education program?* Des Moines, IA: Iowa Department of Education.

Brozo, W.G., & Tomlinson, G.M. (1986). Literature: The key to lively content courses. *The Reading Teacher, 40*, 288–293.

Commeyras, M. (1989). Using literature to teach critical thinking. *Journal of Reading, 32*, 703–707.

Goodman, K.S. (1986). *What's whole in whole language?* Portsmouth, NH: Heinemann.

Laubach, F.C., Kirk, E.M., & Laubach, R.S. (1981). *The Laubach way to reading.* Syracuse, NY: New Readers Press.

Trelease, J. (1985). *The read-aloud handbook* (rev. ed.). New York: Penguin.

General Teaching Methodology

Writing Workshops: An Experience from British Adult Literacy

ANDREW PATES
MAGGIE EVANS
DECEMBER 1990–JANUARY 1991

The Foxfire Project in the United States has demonstrated vividly that oral history can be a powerful tool in writing education (Thompson, 1988; Wigginton, 1988). Writing workshops, which developed in Britain in the 1970s, exploited this potential of oral work by placing participating students in the roles of both subject and writer. Little has been written, however, about this recent experience (see, however, ALBSU, 1983; Gardener, 1985). The purpose of this article is to describe the phenomenon of the writing workshop as it developed in the early days of the British adult literacy campaign.

History

A writing workshop is essentially a group of learners and tutors coming together for an intensive period (day, weekend, or series of regular sessions) to share writing as a group process. Usually a printed version of the work is produced.

Writing workshops developed in Britain as adult literacy workers explored ways of teaching people in an adult, nonpatronizing, and relevant way. Many were influenced by Third World educators such as Freire and echoed dissatisfaction with remedial models of education expressed by Kohl (1974) and others.

One influential group founded a national newspaper of student writing called *Write First Time*, produced quarterly from 1975 to 1985. (Back issues are available from Avanti Books, 1 Wellington Rd., Stevenage, Herts, England. Avanti also produces a subject listing of student writing, publications on running writing workshops, and numerous other adult literacy publications.) This publication provided both a focus for writing activity and influential exemplars; it offered an opportunity for students to write for print and to be involved in the editorial and production processes. Because it was circulated nationwide, it invited emulation; students could produce one issue of the paper or organize their own local publications.

Write First Time also provided a focus for the first national writing workshop residential weekend in 1976. The model was repeated and reformulated by many other groups nationally and regionally.

Writing workshops developed in a variety of ways according to local circumstances, needs, and resources. Many groups organized their own writing days or ran classes as a sequence of connected writing sessions. These led to the production of a vast array of writing, which was sometimes published in semicommercial format but more often produced on duplicators and photocopiers by the learners during the workshop.

The material produced by these groups offered things for adult learners to read (answering in part the frequent plea for relevant reading material for adults) and was a spur to learners to produce their own reading matter: if other students could do it, why couldn't they? Some educational organizations and publishers developed their own lists of student writing (Basic Skills Unit, undated a, undated b, 1980, 1982a, & 1982b).

The model of writing workshops gradually came to be used in other adult learning programs, especially those which were concerned with reawakening learners' self-confidence and self-esteem. They were particularly effective for work with older people in reminiscence groups (Lawrence & Mace, 1987), unemployed people (Replan, 1988), women's groups (Solity, 1985), and a range of community development activities where the writing provided both a focus and a method for local groups to gather and work together.

Between 1982 and 1984 writing workshops became well-established activities. A survey found that in 154 adult literacy programs, 60 produced books and magazines, 27 organized writing workshops, 25 held writing weekends, 22 had regular writing groups, and 18 were involved with *Write First Time* (Merry, 1988).

How a Writing Event Works

Writing workshops acknowledge that literacy students will usually be as fluent orally as their teachers and, as oral historians have demonstrated, uneducated people can master very rich spoken language. Furthermore, it is this spoken language that is used by learners in their real lives: "The oral traditions reign in the ghetto, for literate and nonliterate alike" (Fingeret, 1983).

The features of successful writing workshops seem to be that they: (1) start with the students' concerns and needs; (2) value the learners' mastered language (spoken or written) and use it as a basis for further learning; (3) generate trust through equal participation of all present in all group processes; (4) use discussion as a medium common to all; and (5) turn discussion into writing as appropriate. There is a sequence of stages through which a writing workshop moves, based on experiences and emotions individuals share, discover, and create together. Although no two workshops are ever the same, the following description is based on the sequence that workshops typically pass through.

Planning: Planning ahead of the workshop is essential. This is the time to identify roles (tutors as well as students need to know what is expected of them). Roles may involve facilitating groups, providing technical help with reprographics, scribing (writing down people's words individually or in groups), and providing help with editing or other aspects of manipulating language. By allocating roles, tutors will not only be able to fit in easily but will also have time to participate as writers.

This stage allows the group members to become comfortable with each other and provides time for checking that all the resources needed are available. The involvement of participants in the planning group means both that learners' needs are properly accounted for and that professional staff become accustomed to different ways of relating to the learners.

Planning does not so much mean preparing the program in great detail as it means paying attention to overall structure, roles, resources, group processes, and planned outcomes. The program needs to allow choices so that people can work together in ways that are comfortable for them, including individual or small group work.

Group forming: The first essential of the workshop is that the people attending should gel as a group. This must start with everyone getting together for a welcome session to acquaint them with what's going to happen, to explore expectations, and to get started. It is important that all participants say something so that they can feel part of what's happening and initial barriers can be broken. They may just introduce themselves, or they may choose to say a few words about how they are feeling at that moment or what they hope to gain from the workshop.

This minimal input can be turned into the first writing as someone writes down what people have said on a flip chart or transparency so that the message that speech can be writing is explicit from the beginning. There can be an audible expression of astonishment as someone ventures "I don't know what I'm doing here" or "I can't wait to get started" that is immediately translated into writing open to all.

If the output of the workshop is to be a printed booklet or magazine, these introductions will also be the first item to be typed ready for printing and can provide a fresh, vigorous introduction to the finished publication.

Agenda setting: The large group can't function productively for long, so it will soon be necessary to divide into smaller groups or pairs for further introductions and to begin setting agendas. In this smaller setting, individuals can formulate what they want to say, with space for everyone to contribute. This may be the time for ice-breaking exercises, which are time consuming in a very large group.

Discussion of possible agendas for the workshop may encompass what to write about, what sort of material to produce, and how to work. Some organizers provide a list of topics for writing, but this is superfluous since people's experiences form their subject matter—and these are also related to their reasons for wanting to write.

Groups just asked to write commonly use the same themes: their feelings about being asked to write; the process of writing; the environment they are presently in; their family, home, relationships, and work; or sometimes an imaginary situation used to distance themselves from the immediate situation. They may write a poem, a letter, or a shopping list.

The agenda setting therefore need not be about topics for writing so much as about the stimuli necessary to get everyone working. One option is to ask participants to bring something to the workshop about which they can talk and write—perhaps a photo or other memento.

Another approach is to use the environment itself. In England, many workshops take place in historic houses that have been converted to residential adult education centers. The history of the house, surrounding village, countryside, or the local economy may offer a topic. Country houses aren't always available (even in Britain!) but the environment is never neutral; familiar surroundings can be seen through new eyes by sharing writing.

Working: Writing then starts in earnest and carries on until the end of the workshop. It happens with groups, pairs, and individuals working on the agreed themes or on their own topics.

Some participants will be entirely independent; others will want help, maybe with proofreading or scribing. (The use of scribes is a supportive way of getting writing moving, and it is not "cheating" as some people think. After all, few business or political leaders put pen to paper themselves; they use scribes called secretaries. Many go further in having letters, papers, or speeches drafted for them.)

Other media: Photography and other media may contribute substantially by providing further stimuli for the writing. For example, one group may form round the video equipment and write a documentary; others may write a radio program for sound recording or a drama script for live performance; others may do a photography project with commentary. If other media are used, it is good to have an experienced person on hand to act as technician, if not tutor.

Media may simply provide an extension of writing (for example, as illustration) or may offer a way of working in their own right. The experience of developing and printing photographs can be as much a revelation to people as is seeing themselves in print for the first time.

How's it going?: About halfway through, it is advisable to have a review session with the whole group. This involves reviewing progress, dealing with problems, sharing the current mood, setting sights on finishing, and facilitating any necessary changes. Changes in mood, confidence, and writing will be evident by now.

More work: Much writing will have been done by this stage. As it progresses, pieces may be shared, for example, by display on a pinboard. But writing is never finished. The processes common to all good writing come into their own at this point, and there will be much changing of drafts, editing, proofreading, sharing, and critical discussion. Although trepidation was apparent early on in the workshop, the mood now will be one of concentration and perhaps anger over being disturbed during periods of intense writing.

Merging into production: As projects near completion, some writers will have moved into production. They may have been typing or wordprocessing their work from the beginning, but if not, it now needs to be turned into a format that can be reproduced.

While some tutors may have been assigned the role of helping with production, this process also involves learners in critical ways. The experience of typing their own work and photocopying, duplicating, or printing it themselves is an essential part of the process of demystifying print, and leaves writers with confidence about their ownership of their finished work. Not all jobs are complex. Collating and stapling can be done by everyone and offer a last intense burst of teamwork.

Together again: The whole group can come together again for a farewell as magazines or booklets are finally stapled together or for a more lengthy session where outcomes—such as dramatic productions or videos—are presented to the rest of the group. This opportunity for goodbyes is an important part of a process in which everyone has been so closely involved in sharing a task.

Afterwards: That may be the end or just the beginning; it may lead to an occasional get-together or to a regular group meeting. The printed product will be in evidence for a long time.

Organizational Concerns

Venue: It is possible to hold a writing workshop anywhere. (It doesn't have to be at an elegant country house.) However, the experience of staying somewhere comfortable, for people who often haven't been away for a residential activity before, can be powerful. A residential program also means that daily distractions are removed and an atmosphere for concentration is provided. On the other hand, working on home territory demonstrates that the people are the fundamental ingredient and that anyone can participate. It may also ease logistical and resource problems.

Participants: All participants should have equal status. Observers often comment that they cannot distinguish tutors and students— a sure sign of a successful workshop. This is achieved by sensitive management (how are people introduced—as tutors, as students, or by names?) and by tutor participation. Writing is difficult for everyone, and it is salutary for students to see tutors struggling alongside themselves. Childcare may need to be organized, but children may want to take part in the workshop; that can lead to some powerful family education.

Numbers: An effective mix of people necessitates at least 12 participants. Any number can be accommodated, dependent on the physical capacity of the building, but a maximum of no more than 60 still allows people to get to know each other.

Technical help: The use of typewriters or word processors can facilitate the creative process as well as the preparation of materials for production. The word processor has been one of the big equalizing forces in adult literacy work because it allows students to write more easily and forces tutors to worry about mastering the technology!

Facilitating techniques: The facilitator is not passive in the group process. The key technique is talk: Everybody can do it, it gets ideas going, and it makes people relax. The most important thing for tutors is learning to let go and not to feel the need to control everything that's happening. "The conversations themselves are the educational process—exchanging ideas, sorting out our opinions, building on our knowledge and the knowledge others have passed on to us" (Solity, 1985).

Outcomes: People like to take away a tangible product. It's preferable that participants take home a simple duplicated booklet rather than having to wait for a glossy printed publication (though that may be the outcome for workshops working over a period of time). The outcome can also be something more intangible. If a group that has been meeting regularly has a writing weekend together, it will certainly be reflected in the way the group works subsequently.

Implications

Two features make writing workshops a powerful educational tool: the articulation of students' own voices reinforced by seeing themselves in print and the sharing of experience and problems possible when working in a group. There are, however, three other important features that make writing workshops attractive as a means of instruction:

1. The writing workshop facilitates work at different levels. There is no reason why beginning and advanced writers shouldn't work alongside each other with equal power. This allows for a continuous focus on the difficulty everyone experiences in writing.

2. Students see the power of print in a new perspective when they learn that they too can be published, that they can be writers. "This is a real achievement. I thought you had to be someone to write, someone highly educated to write a book. It's been a real boost for me" (participant in Eden Grove Women's Writing Group quoted in Solity, 1985).

3. The experience of students controlling their own learning is another powerful by-product of writing workshops, an experience that can be transferred fruitfully to other learning.

In sum, the work starts where the learner is. The writers write what is important to them and thus invest the task with a relevance, immediacy, and potency which dramatically enhance their motivation and commitment to mastery of writing.

By Contrast

This approach contrasts starkly with curriculum models that advocate the teaching of adult literacy as a means to remediate a language problem inherent within the individual. Individual learning programs are devised to rectify this "problem," first by diagnosing the language deficiency and then by putting into practice a series of tutor-led activities concerned with solving the problem. The relationship of the student to the process is controlled by the diagnostician. Writing is used to highlight the deficiency; the learner may be asked to do a piece of writing in order that the tutor may spot spelling errors. Various activities designed to teach correct spelling may follow but the value of writing as an impetus for learning is ignored or missed. This reinforces within learners a sense of deficiency, and this position is validated, organized, and reinforced by the diagnostician.

Using writing as a vehicle for promoting learning enables tutors and learners to be free of a belief in deficiency models. Writing workshops do not, however, supersede other approaches—rather, they complement them. They can act as a catalyst for other learning and assist in such practical matters as completing applications or writing resumes.

Process Plus Outcomes

Writing workshops are as much concerned with process as with outcome. The process offers the chance to explore oneself and one's relationship with language, and to experience the power that comes from sharing and creating printed expressions from common experience. Their power is well summed up by the experience of one writing group:

> Many students came particularly to read and write, to enable them to participate more fully in society. The writing is conversational in style, writing from the personal, the personal being the political in that they gained control over their own lives and independence, whilst at the same time inspiring each other. Writing in a workshop or collective group is an opposite experience to a process of writing done in painful silence and isolation. The support and nurturing in a group allows individuals to clarify their opinions, test knowledge and gain extra knowledge. It often results in a more formulated view of what the learners want to say, how and where she or he wants to say it. It may also result in richer more varied styles of writing (Solity, 1985).

So, in the end, writing workshops have a political dimension about oneself in relation to education and one's daily life.

A recent report on American adult literacy used the title *Jump Start* to highlight the fact that programs needed external energizing, not least through funding (Chisman, 1989). To be effective, however, adult literacy courses also need the involvement of students. Writing workshops are a very effective way of motivating students to articulate their needs and make demands. An alternative metaphor for success in adult literacy work might be "Kick Start" which epitomizes the self-generated energy needed for effective forward momentum.

References

ALBSU. (1983). *Write away from it all: A guide to writing groups*. London: Author.

Basic Skills Unit Student Writing. (undated a). *I wanted to be a mechanic*. J. Coronas (Ed.). Sheffield, England: BSU/COIC. (Out of print.)

Basic Skills Unit Student Writing. (undated b). *I started work*. R. Merry (Ed.). Sheffield, England: BSU/COIC. (Out of print.)

Basic Skills Unit Student Writing. (1980). *Deaf out*. P. Ruddock (Ed.). Sheffield, England: BSU/COIC. (Out of print.)

Basic Skills Unit Student Writing. (1982a). *Braces and boots*. T. Leonard (Ed.). Sheffield, England: BSU/COIC. (Out of print.)

Basic Skills Unit Student Writing. (1982b). *Not a bed of roses*. Sheffield, England: BSU/COIC. (Out of print.)

Chisman, F.P. (1989). *Jump start: The federal role in adult literacy*. Final Report of the Project on Adult Literacy. Southport, CT: Southport Institute for Policy Analysis.

Fingeret, A. (Spring 1983). Social network: A new perspective on independence and illiterate adults. *Adult Education Quarterly, 33*(3), 133–145.

Gardener, S.S. (1985). Conversations with strangers: Ideas about writing for adult students. London: Write First Time/AL-BSU.

Kohl, H. (1974). *Reading: How to*. Harmondsworth, Middlesex, England: Penguin.

Lawrence, J., & Mace, J. (1987). *Remembering in groups: Ideas from reminiscence and adult literacy work*. London: Exploring Living Memory/Oral History Society.

Merry, R. (1988). More than reading and writing: Literacy schemes and other activities. In J. McCaffery & B. Street (Eds.), *Literacy research in the UK: Adult and school perspectives*. Lancaster, England: RaPAL.

Replan. (1988). *Working through words*. Report of an arts education project in Liverpool, Leicester, England, NIACE/Replan.

Solity, J.L. (1985). *Working class women's literacy and publishing*. Master's dissertation, University of London Institute of Education, London, England.

Thompson, P. (1988). *The voice of the past: Oral history* (2nd ed.). Oxford, England: Oxford University Press.

Wigginton, E. (1988). *Sometimes a shining moment*. New York: Doubleday.

General Teaching Methodology

Writing Our Lives: An Adult Basic Skills Program

BIRD B. STASZ
ROGER G. SCHWARTZ
JARED C. WEEDEN
SEPTEMBER 1991

The scene is familiar: adults sitting at tables with sheets of paper in front of them, arduously working on compositions, struggling with the mechanics of language, searching for the appropriate words. The room is like all the rooms across the United States that house Adult Basic Education (ABE) classes. Depending on the economy and the availability of space, the classes occur in firehouses, family counseling centers, converted garages, and church basements.

To the casual observer, it is a wonder that the lure of education is strong enough to capture even an hour out of the lives of busy men and women, never mind the six-hour-a-week commitment that most states require of students who enroll in their programs.

Despite all the apparent similarities to other ABE programs, this particular class is something new. The adults are mostly women who work in animated groups while their children color and eat crackers. There is no easily identifiable instructor, but a number of younger college students dressed in jeans and T-shirts sit at the tables, talking and laughing with individuals and small groups. When one young woman gets up to sneak a cigarette in the ladies' room, her exit is greeted with the hoots and howls of the college students and other mothers.

There are no workbooks—just piles of paper and coffee cans full of pencils and pens. There doesn't seem to be any particular curriculum in place. Rather, one is reminded of a painting studio or a craft workshop: there is an easy atmosphere and sense of community here that belies the seriousness of the task at hand.

These mothers, most of whom are without high school graduation diplomas, are working on a book—their fourth, in fact—that will chronicle their lives and ideas. They plan to send this latest effort to the president of the United States to show him exactly what transpires in this Head Start program. There is no end to their confidence and their energy.

An Innovative Approach

What has been described thus far is an innovative adult basic skills class that is being run through a community Head Start program in conjunction with a federally sponsored Student Literacy Corps grant through Hobart and William Smith Colleges in Geneva, New York. Head Start, a federally supported program for underprivileged children, sponsors parent-involvement meetings. The purpose of these meetings is to encourage parents to become active in Head Start and to learn useful skills for themselves and for their children. Literacy is an important topic here, for parents and children alike. The more literate and aware the parents are and the more they read to or with their children, the greater their children's chances for success in school.

The purpose of the Student Literacy Corps is to put college student volunteers into established adult literacy programs. The students are trained to tutor or assist adults in learning to read and write.

To promote literacy among Head Start mothers, the program's staff had at first suggested offering a traditonal GED (General Equivalency Diploma) class. A survey of the parents showed little enthusiasm, however, and the idea was dropped. At about the same time, a group of college students completed a seminar with Jonathan Kozol and were excited to put some of his ideas into practice with a grassroots literacy project.

They approached the Head Start policy council, which is composed of mothers with children in Head Start, with the idea of getting a parent group together to write a book for their children about their own childhoods. This was the start of a two-year literacy project that had far-reaching effects for the lives of a group of Head Start mothers and the students who worked with them.

The conceptual underpinnings of this project lay in what we know about the way adults learn. The overarching principles are that adults do best when (1) the educational experience is designed from the bottom up, (2) the responsibility for the class rests with the students and not with the instructor, and (3) students and staff believe that all students, regardless of academic level, can be self-directed learners (Cross, 1981; Knowles, 1980).

To translate these concepts into practice at this Head Start site, we decided that the best way for these adults to improve literacy skills was for them to use their own language, write their own material, and structure their own educational experience. This makes sense given what we know about the characteristics of typical ABE students.

In general, ABE students are individuals for whom the educational experience has been confusing and alienating at best. Education is often understood as an external structure created by some "mysterious other," far removed from the life experience and needs of students (Hunter & Harman, 1985; Mezirow, Darkenwald, & Knox, 1975). These adults have experienced programs where students have to run someone else's ideas in someone else's language through their own heads, where the language is foreign and the ideas so remote and strange that it sometimes seems as if students and teachers occupy different times and spaces.

It would seem then that a class designed and orchestrated by the students themselves, conducted in their own language, and producing material that chronicled their lives and ideas would be successful where other more traditional programs had failed.

The Project's Basic Methodology

The basic methodology for the Geneva project combines the whole language approach with the writing process and oral history techniques. Whole language is understood to be teaching reading in as holistic a fashion as possible. Learning to read is not broken down into isolated skills; rather it is seen as an organic process that grows much the way a garden does.

The approach makes sense when we consider how reading operates in our lives. We use print to explore, expand, and make sense of our lives. We read in order to make luscious desserts, pay our income taxes, and lull our children to sleep. We read to sing the praises of heroes and heroines and to celebrate or grieve the viscissitudes of life. We rarely learn to read or process print in a neat, sequential order—it is a much messier process than that, especially at the adult level.

Adult learners in an ABE or GED setting have already completed a number of years of school. As readers, they have strengths and weaknesses. The whole language approach allows adults to use their strengths and improve their weaknesses because the process relies on using print to give voice to their individual ideas.

As a consequence, the learning of skills becomes a natural outcome of the process itself. Rather than listening to a lecture about main ideas or textual organization in isolation and then doing a series of exercises to reinforce the rules, the learner works with those ideas within the context of whatever is being read or written. The need to know drives the lesson and is a logical outcome of the reading process.

Using Oral History As a Springboard

Annie struggled for days with a story about her childhood on a farm in the American South. Her use of language was lovely, and the piece was full of images of folks fishing on a dike by the bayou and making fig preserves, and of gumbo cooking in a pot on her mother's stove. Despite her best efforts, however, the work just didn't sound right. Finally in exasperation she threw down her pen and paper and announced to anyone who would listen, "I've had it. I can't do this anyway."

At this point, Matthew, an English major, ambled over to Annie's table and sat down next to her. "Talk to me, Annie, about this place you're writing about."

"Well, it's where I grew up."

"What are some of the things you remember that you loved best?"

Annie and Matthew then explored the sounds, shapes, and smells of her childhood. Each idea or image was carefully recorded by Matthew until the list filled the page. At some points he would ask for more language or probe for other ideas to help him understand what Annie wanted to say. Those responses were added to the page.

Then Annie and Matthew began to organize and reorganize the phrases and ideas on the list and turn them into paragraphs. They talked about what made sense where, what ideas were most important, and what ideas helped fill in the holes.

What actually took place within this essay framework was a great lesson on paragraph organization and main ideas. The end result was an essay that captured the tone, imagery, and values of life in a small Louisiana town.

We got to meet kindly neighbors, such as the woman who "if you did a chore for her she paid you a quarter." We learned the meaning of self-sufficiency:

> Everybody had a large amount of land around their house where you did gardening, raised chickens, ducks, and geese. Pretty much everything we needed was right there. We had figs, peaches, apples, and a cherry tree. The fig tree was so large it split in half during a hurricane.

As a result of this process, Annie was able to help other students with the notion of main idea. She described it as "how would you tell your mama what this story was about if you were calling her long distance."

Peter Elbow (1973) suggests that writing is a studio craft and should be treated as such. Just as an individual learns to be a watercolorist by watching, listening to, and practicing with an accomplished painter, the adult writer learns to write by observing and practicing with other writers. The classroom becomes a studio, the members are participants in a workshop. Stories, articles, and poems are written, often shared with the group, and rewritten. The emphasis is on writing as a process of musing, discussing, writing, and rewriting. Writing becomes a way for participants to recapture a slice of their lives, articulate ideas, and frame a greater understanding of themselves and their world.

"Oral history is the reminiscences and recollections of living people concerning the past. These recollections may be passed down orally from one generation to another or may be the oral memories of an individual who was present at a specific time" (Beck, 1985). Oral history gets adults involved in the practice of literacy.

The key to using oral histories as a teaching tool is the ability of the tutor to establish rapport with the adult students and tease out narratives. In our Head Start program, the adult learner and the college student work together to record these narratives, smooth out the rough edges, and produce a piece of writing that everyone is proud of.

The end result of the project is a collection of adult narratives that are bound together and published as a small book. The publication is seen as a way of legitimizing and celebrating the learners' work.

Oral history projects can be on virtually any topic and of any duration. They can include reminiscences from childhood about simple events. Annette, for example, wrote about a walk around a lake:

Oh it was so beautiful! My grandmother walked us around the lake to get to the other side. She showed us how rocks skip across the water, she showed us how to fish. We found driftwood and many wonderful things you could put in pots to dry like pussy willows and cat tails. I myself, liked catching creepy crawlers, like grass snakes, grasshoppers, frogs, ladybugs. My grandmother wouldn't let me keep snakes, because my mama is afraid of them.

The stories can be intergenerational, such as a collection of tales about grandmothers. Oral histories can cover almost any aspect of community life from the demolition of buildings to harvesting techniques to playground games. An oral history can focus on a single individual or be a collection of rhymes or superstitions. The point is for adult students to explore their own world and capture the spirit and language of that world in print.

Outcomes

One of the most visible outcomes of this particular project is the four books that the mothers have published. They range in content over a series of stories about their grandmothers, a book of family histories and recipes, a children's play, and a historical account of Head Start in this community. The books were displayed at the public library, featured in the local newspaper and distributed among the Head Start families. Copies were sent to U.S. senators and to the President, all of whom have taken the time to write back to the authors directly. These letters are framed and hang on the parent-room wall as recognition of these mothers' expertise as authors and as validation of their experience.

Lives have changed. Two mothers returned to school to get their GEDs. One has gone on to a community college to train to be an elementary school teacher. Many of the mothers now read routinely to their children; others feel that the educational system isn't so foreign and scary.

Without question, the effect of publishing books for community consumption is an empowering experience for the mothers who participate. Women who were silenced because of their sex, class, or lack of language skills suddenly have a forum to present their ideas and record their lives. Women who felt that they could not write suddenly find themselves the authors of lyrical and poignant stories, stories that are valued, read, and reread. Women who have been in the shadows of a middle-class city find themselves quoted and photographed in the newspaper. Hispanic women, whose language has always set them apart, find their stories translated into English and read with pride in their children's classrooms. Heady stuff.

A less obvious outcome of this project comes from the interaction of middle-class college students and Head Start mothers. The students begin to see life through different eyes. They learn to listen and respect the lives and language of women far different from themselves.

One young college student was surprised to find that the favorite childhood stories of a Head Start mother were the very same stories she enjoyed as a child. By the same token, the mother was surprised to find that the special things she does with her children are not so different from what the student recalls about her own mother. The Head Start women learned that these bright and imaginative young people are full of possibilities and hopes, not unlike the young everywhere. Their dreams for happy lives are not that far from the dreams the mothers have for their own children.

The two groups learn to exchange ideas, support one another, and build reading and writing skills—all without a professional instructor or outside curriculum. Each one acts as both teacher and student regardless of academic expertise or social status.

Finally, the most profound change comes in the mothers' view of knowledge and expertise. In a real Freirean sense, these women became the creators of knowledge (Freire, 1970, 1973); they are the experts.

Rosa described a scene from her life in Puerto Rico:

At this date, I did not have a washing machine and had to wash the clothes in the ravine or the river. In order to dry them we had to lay them on the grates of the wire fence. This time I dried my clothes like I always had, but with bad luck. There were bulls in the field. When I returned for my dry clothes, which to my surprise were scattered in the field and some of the bulls had my clothes on their horns. Tears came to my eyes, in this moment, for I had lost my clothes. But later I laughed to see the bulls running in the field with clothes between their horns resembling small flags.

There is little question that this event belongs to the author. No one knows more about this subject than she does. She is the expert, and her expertise gives her ownership of the information.

Ownership is the crucial ingredient if students are to be empowered by their learning. When one is an expert on a particular subject, one has the power of that information; with that power comes confidence and self-esteem. Rosa is not writing and reading about a distant place; she is communicating a slice of her life to a group of other women. She is no longer outside the learning loop; she is a major player.

This program represents a fine marriage between the best of community-based literacy, current theory, and instructional practice and the best of volunteerism. The successes and glitches of the program belong to the participants. The books are testimony to their accomplishments and to the validity of their experience. Their language has become the fabric of their education. The volunteers have learned how to become comfortable in a collective project where, despite their obvious talents, they act as facilitators rather than lecturers. They have learned the meaning of dialogue.

References

Beck, J. (1985). *On my own: The traditions of Daisy Turner*. Montpelier, VT: Vermont Folk Life Center.

Cross, P. (1981). *Adults as learners*. San Francisco, CA: Jossey-Bass.

Elbow, P. (1973). *Writing without teachers*. New York: Oxford University Press.

Freire, P. (1970). *Pedagogy of the oppressed*. New York: Continuum.

Freire, P. (1973). *Education for critical consciousness*. New York: Continuum.

Hunter, C., & Harman, D. (1985). *Adult illiteracy in the United States*. New York: McGraw-Hill.

Knowles, M. (1980). *The modern practice of adult education*. New York: Cambridge University Press.

Mezirow, J., Darkenwald, G., & Knox, A. (1975). *Last gamble on education*. Washington, DC: Adult Education Association of the USA.

General Teaching Methodology

Using Student Journals in the Workplace ESL Classroom

DOROTHY SOLÉ
DECEMBER 1990–JANUARY 1991

In art, sometimes the most threatening request a teacher can make is to ask students to draw a picture on an empty page with no further instructions. What is true for art, I have noticed, holds for language as well.

I teach ESL both to graduate students at the University of Cincinnati and to employees of a large local firm as part of an extensive after hours training program offered by the company. The graduate students express themselves quite freely in journals, once they have realized that they will not be penalized for technical errors. Although they still have trouble communicating in English, they intuitively recognize the benefits of writing. Their journals are warm, evocative, and interesting.

The workplace ESL students are different. Although the group I teach already speaks relatively fluent, albeit incorrect, English, their first reaction to the journal assignment was a mixture of horror and terror; "You know I can't write" was a general lament, and some of the journals were returned empty.

I was introducing journals as the last activity of a 2½ hour class. The first time I handed out the little empty notebooks, I asked them to write their reactions to the class, ask any questions, or make any comments they wished. The writing would not be judged for technical competence; this was personal mail between them and me and I would answer accordingly. But my students wrote very little.

I then turned to a model described by Joy Reid at the Ohio TESOL Fall Conference, 1989. As a metacognitive exercise, I asked my students to think about the class and list what had been easy or difficult and what they had learned. Given a specific task, and having already experienced my reaction to their entries, the workplace ESL students began to write more. But the writing was still choppy and monotone.

Finally I decided to make the exercise far more personal. Most of my classes are arranged around a general theme. We have dealt with matters as simple as planning vaca-tions to issues as complex as crime preven-tion. The finest journals result when I use the readings and class discussions as a LEA or lan-guage experience base to which the students can relate and react.

Now, as the last activity, I ask a series of specific *wh* questions based on the theme of the class. For instance, after readings and dis-cussion about American education, I asked the class to comment in their journals about their own schooling. I put a series of ques-tions on the board: Where did you go to school? What did you like the best in school? What irritated you the most? Why did it irri-tate you? Who was your favorite teacher? What was so special about him or her?

I told them that not all of the questions had to be answered, but to begin writing. A mira-cle occurred: the entries jumped from short, stiffly composed paragraphs to two-page emotionally charged, coherent accounts of their childhood and school experiences. The writing had voice and meaning.

Evidently workplace ESL students who feel the support of a well defined springboard will find it easier to get started and are able to draw on a wealth of ideas they consider wor-thy of committing to paper. Journal writing seems less painful, maybe even pleasurable, and reading the journals is a joy.

G e n e r a l
T e a c h i n g
M e t h o d o l o g y

A Nondirective Combinatory Model in an Adult ESL Program

ANTHONY D'ANNUNZIO
NOVEMBER 1990

In metropolitan areas containing large populations of immigrants and refugees with limited English proficiency, the typical tutorial programs cannot come near to meeting students' instructional needs. The problem is aggravated by the fact that too few instructors have had professional training.

However, after a short training period, even pedagogically unsophisticated bilinguals can become effective tutors and trainers of other tutors. Employing a Language Experience Approach (LEA) and individualized reading as the mainstay of instruction, bilingual tutors may break the chain of heavy reliance upon professional intervention. The three bilingual tutors used in the project described here were only high school graduates; the assistant tutors had not even attained this milestone, and yet they became very effective instructors.

Using educationally naive bilingual tutors and a combinatory instructional format (described in more detail in what follows) may prove to be not only pedagogically sound but also cost effective, and can even encourage these refugees and immigrants to take more initiative in working out their educational destinies.

Specifics of the Project

The objective of our adult English as a Second Language (ESL) proposal, funded through a grant from the Pennsylvania State Department of Education, was to determine the instructional effectiveness of a combinatory model in an adult ESL program.

The combinatory model included the use of a modified LEA in the initial phase of learning to speak and read in English. The modification consisted of using virtually untrained Cambodian and Hispanic bilingual tutors to accept dictations given in the students' native language and immediately translate these into English, after which standard LEA procedures were followed.

After this initial phase of the model was complete, students were introduced to individualized reading and expressive writing. The procedures were nondirective in the sense that they required the student to take the initiative in the pursuit of speaking, reading, and writing competence in English.

Two groups of approximately 15 non–English-speaking Cambodians and one class of approximately 15 non–English-speaking Hispanics received a maximum of 10 hours of instruction per week. Local social service agencies referred the student population, with an age range of 17 to 67, to the program. These agencies provided space for classes in their own buildings, or in the case of the Hispanics, in a room in a neighborhood public library.

The Cambodians were recent arrivals to the United States who had endured unspeakable hardships and had not, with few exceptions, received any formal schooling in Cambodia. The level of education in the Spanish-speaking population was also low, few students having completed secondary school in their native lands.

Pretest mean scores on the Basic Inventory of Natural Language (BINL) revealed that all the Cambodian students performed at the Non–English-Speaking level. The Diagnostic Reading Scales (DRS) produced no pretest scores, while the Wide Range Achievement Test–Revised (Word Recognition Subtest) (WRAT–R) produced a mean of pre-first grade.

The pretest mean for the Hispanics was also non–English-speaking on the BINL, while the DRS was less than first grade. The mean level of attainment in word recognition was 2.5. The average length of stay in the tutorial program was 4.5 months. Very few of the students were able to attend daily—the average was between 2 and 3 days per week, 2 hours a day.

Getting Started

The use of LEA with ESL adults in the initial phase of the combinatory model is based upon the following assumptions (Ben-Barka, 1982; Cohen, 1981; Dixon & Nessel, 1983; Nessel & Jones, 1981):

1. Their life experiences are of great personal value and are highly meaningful.

2. Learning to read is easiest and most enjoyable when reading materials match language patterns and speaking vocabulary.

3. When allowed to take the initiative, students' self-image and learning efficiency are significantly enhanced.

In addition, the LEA possesses some distinct advantages when used in adult ESL programs: It makes use of the adults' experience and promotes reading as a byproduct of their thinking and oral expression. Also, LEA allows for one-on-one, personalized learning situations.

ESL adults with negligible proficiency in English frequently exhibit stilted syntax and limited vocabulary in their dictations. For these cases, attempts have been made to modify certain aspects of LEA (Moustafa, 1987; Moustafa & Penrose, 1985). With individuals who are non–English-speaking, however, little has been done to incorporate the benefits of the LEA format. The use of bilingual tutors was an attempt to overcome the difficulty of using LEA with a non–English-speaking population.

One Hispanic and two Cambodian bilingual tutors were given two training sessions on the use of LEA. For the first week of instruction, the tutors took whole class dictations, each student being encouraged to provide a sentence or two on a class-selected theme (Figure 1). After each contribution to the story had been translated into English by the tutors, standard LEA procedures were followed.

A week of group LEA allowed the students to become familiar with the procedures. After the first week all the students were introduced to individual dictations. As each student related a personal story in Khmer or Spanish to the Cambodian or Hispanic bilingual tutors, the latter immediately transcribed it into English (Figures 2 and 3).

The tutors then proceeded with the standard LEA procedure (Cohen, 1981; Rigg & Taylor, 1979; Schneiderman, 1978; Stauffer 1980). The tutor pronounced and pointed to each word as it was written, eventually reading the entire selection to the student. The tutor next pointed to each word, pacing the student as they read the story together. At this juncture, the student returned to his or her seat and attempted to read the story silently.

Figure 1

A group story taken during the first week of class to allow the students to become familiar with the LEA procedures:

Why I Came to Class
"I came to class to learn to speak English because I am afraid to answer the phone. It might be an American who does not speak Spanish," said Rosa. "I came to class because I am afraid to go out in the world and communicate with someone who only speaks English. I am shy," said Lydia. Marisol said, "I feel timid and afraid to speak to someone in public because I do not know if I might say the wrong thing."

During the rereading, the student underlined each word that was recognized. This is a positive approach to word recognition since the emphasis is upon what is known. Because the words are of the student's choosing, there is a greater likelihood that she or he will recognize them in the translated account.

When the student later reread the dictated story to the tutor, he or she was again asked to underline any words recognized. If 2 or 3 days later an underlined word was recognized within the context of the story, the word was printed by itself on a separate sheet.

The next day the tutor used a window card to determine ease and accuracy of recall. Words thus recognized in isolation provided the deposits for the student's word bank. Every word recognized in this fashion was printed by the tutors on an index card and placed in random order in the student's small index box. When the word bank exceeded 30 words or so, the student was introduced to alphabetizing and then to the dictionary.

The word bank provided one of the most valuable sources for the development of word recognition skills and sight words, and became a personalized record of words the student had learned. The word bank was used as the basis of a variety of word recognition activities, including the development of visual-auditory discrimination skills, finding word families, composing sentences, and so forth. Group activities, where students worked together to construct sentences, ask questions, identify the words in written contexts such as books or magazines, or develop sentences and stories, provided the greatest aid to word recognition.

LEA stories carried over into group activities that provided the opportunity for verbal interaction in English. These included show-and-tell and group LEA stories that were dictated with a view to dramatizing them for the class. Individual LEA stories were frequently read to the class.

Figure 2

An individual dictation spoken in Khmer and translated by the tutor:

War by Sok Kong
I think no one likes war. War can kill people. The soldiers work hard. The life of a soldier is difficult. When there is war, no one works in the rice fields. There are many sick people during the war because they don't have enough to eat.

Figure 3

An individual dictation spoken in Spanish and translated by the tutor:

Learning English by Juan Berrios
I would like to learn English so that I am able to express myself better with others. When I need to talk to someone, I don't want someone else to speak for me. I would like to speak for myself. I feel bad.

Although hints were given by the tutors, many group activities were self-directed. Words from the students' word banks were constantly being compared, traded, and used for window card recognition games. The classes bustled with paired and group interaction. The encounters among the students had a tone of helpful comradery, with the more seasoned frequently assisting the newer arrivals.

Skills Begin to Develop

Once the immigrants had acquired some fluency in reading their dictated stories and had accumulated approximately 50 word bank entries, they were introduced to individualized reading by the tutors, under the guidance of the reading specialist. As is the case with LEA, individualized reading is a basically nondirective procedure. Through self-seeking, self-selection, and self-pacing, the adults were allowed to take additional initiatives and thereby continue to increase their self-esteem.

The Spanish class was housed in a branch of the Free Library of Philadelphia; the two Cambodian classes were within a block of another branch. As individual students were deemed ready for individualized reading, they were taken to the library to become members.

After books were selected and read, the tutors were given demonstrations on how to conduct an individual conference. Individual and group conferences provided the tutors an opportunity to observe the students' reading interests and skills in word recognition, comprehension, and oral and silent reading. It was another opportunity for personal instruction, guidance, and support, and conferences frequently led to warm personal communication between the tutors and the learners. Tutors spent time discussing current reading choices and what progress was being made, checking

comprehension, and providing individualized instruction in areas of weakness. The tutors tried, under the continuous guidance of the reading specialist, to have a minimum of two to three conferences per week.

These adult ESL students made many false starts, attempting to read books that were too difficult, but quickly learned to select books that they could manage. Some soon became avid readers, completing two or three books a week. Adults need reading strategies that enhance self-esteem by showing practical results in a short time (Schneiderman, 1978). Although there was a great deal of variation, the students began to use English more and more frequently, especially during the individual conferences and group activities. The tutors encouraged this by using English as much as possible.

As the students engaged in individualized reading they gave LEA dictations much less frequently, but continued their story-telling through expressive writing. The basic assumption here was that the most efficient means of developing written expression was to write and write—the more the better (Blot & Davidson, 1984; Parry & Hornsby, 1988; Rockcastle, 1986). The point was to encourage the flow of written expression so that the students naturally acquired syntactical facility and attempted to use more sophisticated constructions. They received continuous feedback and developmentally appropriate minilessons during this stage of instruction.

At one point during the natural development of facility in writing, for example, a student attempted to use quotation marks, however inappropriately. The student expressed a need, and a minilesson on the use of quotation marks was in order for this student. The tutors were guided by the reading specialist into making only those corrections on a completed story that were compatible with the student's level of writing competency. Students frequently read their productions aloud to the tutor, to a group, or to the entire class (Figure 4).

Some of the students became proficient enough in English to become tutor aides and were paid for their services. They were particularly useful in taking LEA dictations. With the continual flow of new students sent to us by the contractual agencies, they helped acclimate new arrivals to what might otherwise have been an intimidating situation.

The combinatory expressive instructional approach included an emphasis on encouraging the students to express themselves through class presentations. It should be kept in mind that LEA, individualized reading, and creative writing are in themselves expressive in nature. The students easily moved into other expressive activities, such as reading their LEA stories to other classmates, relating experiences, storytelling, skits, and dramatizations—all in English. Most of these activities were suggested to the tutors by the students.

The Program Proves Successful

For both the Cambodian and Hispanic populations, the posttest scores on the BINL were substantially higher than their pretest performance. The Cambodian students' posttest performance revealed that they achieved a mean score in the Fluent English Speaking category, roughly comparable to a typical American fourth-grader, which we considered excellent for speakers coming from a totally unrelated language background. The Hispanic population also advanced to the Fluent English Speaking category, roughly comparable to a typical American fifth grader.

The mean posttest score in word recognition for the Cambodian population on the

---

Figure 4

Creative writing by a Cambodian student after 3 months of instruction:

The Snows by Ly Pa Khun
I'm Cambodian. I have lived in America for one year. When the winter comes my health always changes. This year, I have a bad cough. When I work hard, I always cough.

Asian people dislike the climate in America because they have no snow in their countries. American kids like snow.

When the snow falls down at night and I look through the window, it seems like it's daytime. Everything can be seen.

I don't like the snow because I am not used to it. Some American people don't like the snow either.

WRAT–R was at the beginning of the third grade, while their reading performance on the DRS advanced to the 3.7 grade level. For the Hispanics, the posttest word recognition advanced to a mean of 6.9, while their reading mean increased to 3.7.

These significant results were attained despite the fact that instructional time was short. The mean length of stay in the program was 5.5 months for the Cambodians and just less than 4 months for the Hispanic students.

Beneficial Byproducts

Aside from their role as instructors, the bilingual tutors served other essential functions that may have contributed to the students' rapid gains in speaking, reading, and writing. Because they shared the same background with the refugees and immigrants, bilingual tutors helped to assure an accepting, nonintimidating atmosphere that increased the students' desire to remain in the program. The use of such nondirective strategies as LEA, individualized reading, and expressive writing ensured a high degree of personal interaction among the students, tutors, and professional staff. The pedagogical and motivational advantages of such personal involvement have been demonstrated (Boyd & Martin, 1984; Clabby & Belz, 1985; Johnson, 1985; Miller et al., 1985).

Since LEA, individualized reading, and expressive writing fostered the disclosure of personal experiences which revealed the intimate needs, interests, and concerns of the students, the interaction between them and the tutors became, through inservice demonstrations, a Rogerian type of nondirective, incidental counseling (Corsini, 1979). Because of the nondirective nature of the instruction, the content of which was so closely related to personal experiences, the tutors were able to enter into the phenomenal world of the students.

Many of these adult refugees and immigrants have had experiences that undermined their sense of personal worth. These students needed to establish an awareness of, and trust in, their own experiences. Nondirective instructional procedures that allowed the students to take a great deal of initiative for their learning, the opportunity to vent their personal problems in a safe and accepting milieu, and the use of bilingual instructors who shared the students' experiences, all assisted in providing for beneficial growth.

References

Basic Inventory of Natural Language (BINL). (1986). San Bernardino, CA: Checpoint Systems.

Ben-Barka, A.C. (1982). LEA as a methodology for use with semi-literate ESOL adolescents: A case study. A Thesis Report. (ED 239 510)

Blot, D., & Davidson, D. (1984). *Write from the start.* New York: Newbury House.

Boyd, R.D., & Martin, L.G. (1984). A methodology for the analysis of the psychosocial profiles of low literate adults. *Adult Education Quarterly, 34*(2), 85–96.

Clabby, J.F., & Belz, E.J. (1985). Psychological barriers to learning: Approach to group treatment. *Small Group Behavior, 16*(9), 525–533.

Cohen, J. (1981). *A reading and writing program using language experience methodology among adult ESL students in a basic education program.* Washington, DC: Office of Vocational and Adult Education.

Corsini, R. (1979). *Current psychotherapies.* Itasca, IL: Peacock.

Diagnostic Reading Scales (DRS). (1981). Monterey, CA: CIB/McGraw-Hill.

Dixon, C., & Nessel, D. (1983). Language experience approach to reading (and writing). In *Language experience reading for second language learners.* Hayward, CA: Alemany.

Johnson, P.H. (1985). Understanding reading disability: A case study. *Harvard Educational Review, 55*(2), 153–177.

Miller, G.E., et al. (1985). *Helping adults learn: Instruction guide.* University Park, PA: Institute for the Study of Adult Literacy, College of Education, Pennsylvania State University.

Moustafa, M. (1987). Comprehensible input PLUS the language experience approach: A longterm perspective. *The Reading Teacher, 41*(3), 276–286.

Moustafa, M., & Penrose, J. (1985). Comprehensible input PLUS the language experience approach: Reading instruction for limited English speaking students. *The Reading Teacher, 38*(7), 640–647.

Nessel, D., & Jones, M. (1981). *The language-experience approach to reading: A handbook for teachers.* New York: Teachers College Press.

Parry, J.A., & Hornsby, D. (1988). *Write on: A conference approach to writing.* Portsmouth, NH: Heinemann.

Rigg, P., & Taylor L. (1979). A twenty-one year old begins to read. *English Journal, 68,* 52–56.

Rockcastle, V.N. (1986). Nothing succeeds like succession. *Science and Children, 23*(7).

Schneiderman, P. (1978). Active reading techniques systems (ARTS): A method for instruction of functionally illiterate adults. *Urban Education, 13,* 195–202.

Stauffer, R.G. (1980). *The language-experience approach to the teaching of reading* (2nd ed.). New York: Harper & Row.

Wide Range Achievement Test–Revised (WRAT–R). (1984). Wilmington, DE: Jastak.

"*A middle-aged man waves to his friend across the street. 'I'm going for my computer lesson now,' he shouts as he enters the public library. In fact, he is learning basic reading skills with a tutor; in his mind, however, he is learning a modern skill that will help him retrain for the changing job market.*"

– ASKOV & CLARK, 1991, P. 434

Computers offer adult students a new way to learn, a way that was not available to most of them when they were children. This section explores the uses of computers in adult literacy programs. It opens with Askov and Clark's piece, which cites advantages and disadvantages of using computers in adult literacy programs and provides a matrix of available software along with publisher addresses (current as of March 1991, the date of the article's original publication). Next, Howie provides a very different list of software in the context of a discussion of the various functions of literacy in a multiliterate society. Still another distinct list of software is provided by Finnegan and Sinatra, this one differentiated by level.

It is to be hoped that research and literature on adult literacy will soon begin to explore the use of newer technologies such as laser discs, CD-ROMS, *and hypermedia.*

References

Askov, E.N., & Clark, C.J. (1991). Using computers in adult literacy instruction. Journal of Reading, 34, 434–448.

Using Computers in Adult Literacy Instruction

EUNICE N. ASKOV
CINDY JO CLARK
MARCH 1991

A middle-aged man waves to his friend across the street. "I'm going for my computer lesson now," he shouts as he enters the public library. In fact, he is learning basic reading skills with a tutor; in his mind, however, he is learning a modern skill that will help him retrain for the changing job market (Turkle, 1984). Similarly, a single mother of several young children is receiving literacy instruction by computer, right at the welfare office. She, too, is acquiring the basic skills of reading, writing, and math while preparing to enter a word-processing training program. Although learning to read to her children is of paramount importance to her at this time, she eventually wants to enter a clerical career and become self-supporting.

Computers offer these adult students a new way to learn, a way that was not available to them as school children. Advantages and disadvantages of computer-based instruction have been enumerated elsewhere (Askov & Turner, 1989), but the following list offers a summary.

Advantages

Privacy. Only the adult and the teacher or tutor need to know the actual level at which the learner is working. Once the adult student learns how to operate the computer, she or he can work independently without anyone (other than the teacher or tutor) knowing the program's level of difficulty.

Individualization. Instruction can be tailored to the adult student's needs rather than to those of a group. The teacher can individualize not only the pace of learning but also the content and presentation to suit the needs and interests of the student.

Achievement gains. A number of research studies have demonstrated that students make better-than-average gains through use of technology (Askov, 1986; Askov, Maclay, & Bixler 1987; Maclay & Askov, 1987, 1988). Although Clark (1983) cautions that achievement gains may not be related to the medium of instruction but instead to content, adoption of computer technology causes teachers to rethink the curriculum, which is a positive step and generally leads to better instruction (Papagiannis, Douglas, Williamson, & LeMon, 1987).

Cost-effectiveness. An extensive evaluation of an urban technology and literacy center has revealed that instruction with computers is no more expensive than traditional instruction (Turner & Stockdill, 1987). In addition, a larger number of students can be served through using technology in instruction.

Control of learning. Adult students gradually take control of the learning situation as they become familiar with the computer, and subsequent changes in their attitudes about themselves have been documented (Askov &

Brown, 1988; Lewis, 1988). Controlling a computer seems to lead to a sense of empowerment for low-literate individuals who prior to instruction often feel that they have little control over their own lives.

Flexibility in scheduling. While the use of computers may not eliminate the need for group instruction, it can offer opportunities for instruction in a student's open time slots, something which is particularly important for adults who are juggling multiple responsibilities.

Open entry, open exit. While classes may operate on a regular schedule, it is common for adult students to need some flexibility. Instructional use of computers enables teachers and tutors to start where students leave off, saving valuable time for everyone. Student records can be easily stored on computer disk—a confidential and convenient means of retaining student data.

A modern way to learn. Technology is revolutionizing the workplace; business, industry, and labor organizations look to technology to upgrade workers' skills. A faith in technology exists in the modern mind (Turkle, 1984), which can help adult students overcome feelings of inadequacy as they approach the task of learning basic skills (Lewis, 1988). Repeated use of computers leads to computer literacy and provides a means of basic skills instruction.

Disadvantages

Change. Technology is constantly changing. What seemed "state of the art" several years ago is now deemed "primitive." Continual upgrading is necessary to take advantage of the best that technology has to offer (Turner, 1988).

Lack of compatibility. Lack of compatibility between machines makes identification and use of appropriate software difficult. Use of software evaluation guides (described below) helps identify software appropriate for a given computer.

Cost. Cost used to be a major barrier to purchasing computers for instruction. Fortunately, costs have come down, making computers affordable to most literacy programs.

Pressure to make rapid decisions. When money for computers comes from an unexpected windfall, administrators must often "use it or lose it." Instead of making careful plans, which should precede any purchase, they may fall prey to a sharp salesperson who does not always have the best interests of students in mind.

Lack of expertise. A trained resource person needs to be available to set up the equipment, to fix minor malfunctions when they occur, and, most important, to train teachers and tutors in the use of the computer. This person also needs to keep up with what is happening, not only in computer technology but also in adult literacy, so that equipment and software can be upgraded.

Lack of training. Unfortunately, when program administrators decide to adopt technology (especially computers for instruction) the first consideration is usually hardware and not software. Often it is after those initial decisions are made that the administrator realizes that teachers and tutors need to be trained. Instead of training being the first step, it is often an afterthought.

Inappropriate instruction. Most instructional software is designed for children. However, many programs may be adapted for use with adults if care is exerted in the way they are presented. Many instructional games can be used if the graphics are not too obviously childish. As more funding is becoming available for adult instructional programming, vendors are producing more appropriate materials. Adult educators need to be active in making the needs of their students known to vendors.

Curriculum integration. It takes time for any innovation to be adapted and adopted in a local program. As such, use of a new technology is often viewed as a special event rather than part of the ongoing curriculum. Teachers must become so familiar with the instructional materials offered via the computer that these materials can become part of the routine of instruction.

Role changes. When students use computers and have control over their personal learning agendas, they become more independent. Sometimes teachers and tutors feel displaced by the technology. Training can overcome these feelings of displacement and give instructors an important role in instruction (Bixler & Askov, 1988).

The Software

Computers are finding their way into adult literacy programs of all types. Sometimes, however, they are not being used to full capacity. A major complaint from teachers is the lack of appropriate software.

One resource is the Adult Literacy and Technology Project (administered by People's Computer Co. Inc., 2682 Bishop Drive, Suite 107, San Ramon, CA 94583, USA; 415-830-4200), which offers annual software evaluation guides and quarterly newsletters. The project also sponsors an annual conference at which the most recent software is displayed.

Another resource is the index matrix we have created as an aid to teachers of adults who need to identify relatively inexpensive software for use with various types of learners. The matrix appears on pages 171–180.

We particularly favor software that can be customized or that provides mini-authoring systems; this kind of software allows teachers to enter the vocabulary and reading material

needed for the particular target group. For example, some programs can be customized with vocabulary and sentences relating to parenting or to word-processing for the young mother on public assistance. Our middle-aged man preparing for a new career is more motivated to learn when technical vocabulary needed for a job-training program is included in the software. Our workplace literacy program that prepares state transportation workers for the Commercial Vehicle Driver's License exam uses *Word Attack Plus* to teach technical vocabulary. Instead of vocabulary such as *bridal* (which is in the general program), we were able to teach *antenna* and *vehicle* in contextually relevant sentences.

Outstanding Software

Our intent in presenting this matrix was *not* to evaluate the quality of the various software packages. Rather, we intended to create a user-friendly matrix that permits teachers to see at a glance how specific commercial software programs may be used. We suggest that teachers request preview copies before making purchases to determine if the program is applicable to their students and if it is of appropriate quality. Nevertheless, we have identified a few outstanding programs, based on the criteria of being most useful in instruction and least difficult to use. These programs are noteworthy for their design and flexibility, and some offer the option of teacher input.

Individualized lessons. A mini-authoring system allows teachers to create their own computer or print activities. Several good pieces of software with this capacity are *E-Z Pilot II Authoring System*, *Individual Study Center*, TAS, *Teacher Option Organizer*, and *The Semantic Mapper*.

Vocabulary skills. Being able to customize software with the vocabulary of the workplace or family literacy program is a great advantage. Customizing also allows for individualization of the course content to the students' goals and needs. Our selection includes *Create Lessons, Lucky 7 Vocabulary Games, Penn State Adult Literacy Courseware, Square Pairs, Vocabulary Challenge,* and *Word Attack Plus.*

Writing skills. Adapted word-processing or writing software can provide students with real writing experiences, such as letter writing or keeping journals or logs. With *Penn State Adult Literacy Courseware* and *Success with Writing*, the teacher is able to access the students' files to read journal entries and make comments.

Math skills. Math exercises are most relevant and helpful when the students are working with actual problems, such as those from the workplace or those related to life skills. A key to motivating students is to provide relevant and real problems. The following programs are possible selections: *Career Arithmetic, Cooking and Baking Series, Prevocational Math Review, Vocational Math for Automotive Technicians,* and *Vocational Math for Carpenters.*

Teachers might start software review with these programs, keeping in mind that no software program will be useful to every student or all literacy programs. We have chosen to focus solely on instructional software programs in this matrix; simple word-processing, database, and spreadsheet programs can also be used to tailor instruction to the needs of individual students. Publications, such as Pollak's *The Reading/Writing Teacher's Word Processing Companion* (1989), can guide teachers in how to use these tools in adult literacy instruction.

Interpreting the Matrix

In the matrix, the titles of the software programs are listed in the column on the far left. The next column, Teacher/Tutor Tools, indicates whether the program can be customized or whether it has a mini-authoring system: customized programs allow teachers to insert special vocabulary in an already established program such as an electronic game of hangman; mini-authoring systems allow teachers to devise their own lessons, as in the *Individualized Study Center* software which provides on-screen prompts to help those who have no programming experience.

The next column, Assessment & Skills, indicates the skills assessed or taught. The Content column is subdivided as follows:

1. General basic skills content is basic skills material that possesses a literacy or informational content, rather than content derived from a specific occupation.

2. Workplace basic skills refer to those taught in the context of a job. A teacher might give the *Agricultural Math Tutor* to students interested in farming-related occupations, rather than encouraging those adults to learn from an application that provides only general basic skills content.

3. Job-domain related skills refers to content related to a job or profession that is not necessarily basic skills material, such as typing skills for clerks and knowing body parts for healthcare workers and rules of the road for truck drivers.

The rest of the categories should be self-evident. The numbers in the far right column indicate where the software programs can be obtained and correspond to the numbers on the list of publishers in Figure 1. [Note: These addresses were current as of March 1991.]

When using this guide, never automatically disregard software because of possible limitations such as the following:

Figure 1
Adult Software Publishers/Distributors (U.S.)

1. AAVIM
The National Institute for
Instructional Materials
120 Driftmier Engineering
Ctr.
Athens GA 30602
404-542-2586

2. Academic Therapy
Publications
20 Commercial Blvd.
Novato CA 94949-6191
800-422-7249

3. Aquarius International
PO Box 128
Indian Rocks Beach FL
34635-0128
800-338-2644

4. BLS, Inc.
2503 Fairlee Rd.
Wilmington DE 19810
800-545-7766

5. Career Aids
20417 Nordhoff St.
Dept. Z9876
Chatsworth CA 91311
818-341-2535

6. Conduit
The University of Iowa
Oakdale Campus
Iowa City IA 52242
319-335-4100

7. Conover
PO Box 155
Omro WI 54963
414-685-5707

8. Continental Press
520 East Bainbridge St.
Elizabethtown PA 17022
800-233-0759

9. Davidson & Associates, Inc.
3135 Kashiwa St.
Torrance CA 90505
800-556-6141

10. Design Ware
185 Berry St.
San Francisco CA 94107
800-572-7767

11. Educational Activities, Inc.
PO Box 392
Freeport NY 11520
800-645-3739

12. Educational Technologies,
Inc.
1007 Whitehead Rd. Ext.
Trenton NJ 08638
609-882-2668

13. Educulture, Inc.
1 Cycare Plaza
Suite 805
Dubuque IA 52001-9990
800-553-4858

14. EMC Publishing
Changing Times Education
Serv.
300 York Ave.
St. Paul MN 55101
800-328-1452

15. Focus Media, Inc.
839 Stewart Ave.
PO Box 865
Garden City NY 11530
800-645-8989

16. Hartley's Courseware, Inc.
Box 419
Dimondale MI 48821
800-247-1380

17. Houghton Mifflin
PO Box 683
Hanover NH 03755
603-448-3838

18. Ideal Learning, Inc.
5005 Royal Lane
Suite 130
Irving TX 75063
214-929-4201 (TX)

612-445-2690 (MN)

19. Institute for the Study of
Adult Literacy
Penn State University
College of Education
204 Calder Way, Suite 209
State College PA 16801
814-863-3777

20. Island Software
Box 300
Lake Grove NY 11755
516-585-3755

21. Learning Unlimited Corp.
6512 Baum Dr., No. 11
Knoxville TN 37919
800-251-4717

22. Marshmedia
PO Box 8082
Shawnee Mission KS
66208
816-523-1059

23. MECC
3490 Lexington Ave. N.
St. Paul MN 55126
612-481-3500

24. Micro Power & Light Co.
12810 Hillcrest Rd.
Suite 120
Dallas TX 75230
214-239-6620

25. Milliken Publishing Co.
1100 Research Blvd.
PO Box 21579
St. Louis MO 63132-0579
314-991-4220

26. Mindscape, Inc.
Educational Division
Dept. D, 3444 Dundee Rd.
Northbrook IL 60062
800-221-9884

(continued)

Figure 1
Adult Software Publishers/Distributors (*continued*)

27. Morning Star
   PO Box 5364
   Madison WI 53705
   800-533-0445

28. Optimum Resource, Inc.
   10 Station Pl.
   Norfolk CT 06058
   800-327-1473

29. Queue, Inc.
   562 Boston Ave.
   Bridgeport CT 06610
   800-232-2224

30. Scholastic, Inc.
   PO Box 7502
   2931 East McCarty St.
   Jefferson City MO 65102
   800-541-5513

31. Softwriters Development
   Corp.
   4718 Harford Rd.
   Baltimore MD 21214-9968
   800-451-5726

32. South-Western
   5101 Madison Rd.
   Cincinnati OH 45227
   800-543-7007

33. Spin-A-Test Publishing Co.
   3177 Hogarth Dr.
   Sacramento CA 95827
   916-369-2032

34. Sunburst Communications
   39 Washington Ave.
   Pleasantville NY 10570-2898
   800-431-1934

35. Teach Yourself by
   Computer Software, Inc.
   349 W. Commercial St.
   Suite 1000
   E. Rochester NY 14445
   716-381-5450

36. Teacher Support Software
   PO Box 7130
   Gainesville FL 32605-7130
   800-228-2871

37. Ventura Educational
   Systems
   3440 Brokenhill St.
   Newbury Park CA 91320
   805-499-1407

- Made for children—As long as the program is not insulting or childish, it can be used successfully.
- A grade level too high—Many studies show that students can read technical or work-related material at several grade levels above their tested ability (Diehl & Mikulecky, 1980).
- Generic in content—Before deciding against such a package, try to determine if it can be customized to students' needs by inserting specialized vocabulary and content.

We hope that by using this guide teachers will discover that computer software can be an effective tool for enhancing instruction. This matrix will enable adult literacy practitioners to receive the best value from the software purchased.

References

Askov, E.N. (1986). *Evaluation of computer courseware for adult beginning reading instruction in a correctional setting* (Final Report). University Park, PA: Institute for the Study of Adult Literacy, Pennsylvania State University.

Askov, E.N., & Brown, E.J. (1988). Attitudes of adult literacy students and their teachers toward computers for instruction: Before and after use. *Yearbook of the American Reading Forum.* Muncie, IN: Ball State University.

Askov, E.N., Maclay, C.M., & Bixler B. (1987). *Penn State adult literacy courseware: Impact on parents and children* (Final Report). University Park, PA: Institute for the Study of Adult Literacy, Pennsylvania State University.

Askov, E.N., & Turner, T. (1989). Using computers for teaching basic skills to adults. *Lifelong Learning, 12*(6), 28–31.

Bixler, B., & Askov, E.N. (1988). *Use of computer-assisted instruction with displaced workers and volunteer tutors* (Final Report). University Park,

PA: Institute for the Study of Adult Literacy, Pennsylvania State University.

Clark, R.E. (1983). Reconsidering research on learning from media. *Review of Education Research, 53*(4), 445–459.

Diehl, W.A., & Mikulecky, L. (1980). The nature of reading at work. *Journal of Reading, 24*, 221–227.

Lewis, L.H. (1988). Adults and computer anxiety: Fact or fiction? *Lifelong Learning, 11*(8), 5–8, 12.

Maclay, C.M., & Askov, E.N. (1987). Computer-aided instruction for Mom and Dad. *Issues in Science and Technology, 4*(1), 88–92.

Maclay, C.M., & Askov, E.N. (1988). Computers and adult beginning readers: An intergenerational study. *Lifelong Learning, 11*(8), 23–25, 28.

Papagiannis, G.J., Douglas, C., Williamson, N., & LeMon, R. (1987). *Information technology and education: Implications for theory, research, and practice.* Ottawa, ON: International Development Research Centre.

Pollak, P. (1989). *The reading/writing teacher's word processing companion.* University Park, PA: Institute for the Study of Adult Literacy, Pennsylvania State University.

Turkle, S. (1984). *The second self.* New York: Simon & Schuster.

Turner, T.C. (1988). An overview of computers in adult literacy programs. *Lifelong Learning, 11*(8), 9–13.

Turner, T.C., & Stockdill, S.H. (Eds.) (1987). *The Technology for Literacy project evaluation.* St. Paul, MN: St. Paul Foundation.

Index of Workplace & Adult Basic Skills Software

Software	Customize	Mini-authoring systems	Math	Reading/Decoding & Structural Analysis	Reading/Comprehension	Writing/Grammar	Writing/Composing	Vocab./Spell. & Meaning	Problem-solving	Complete B. Skills Prog.	General B. Skills Content	Workplace Basic Skills	Job-Domain Related	Job Search/Career	E.S.L.	Drill & Practice	Tutorial	Simulation	Games & Puzzles	Apple	I.B.M.	Tandy	Commodore	TRS-80	Macintosh	Publisher/Distributor*
ABS										●	●						●			●	●	●				21
Adult Education - Math			●								●									●	●					4
Adult Education - Reading					●						●									●	●					4
Agricultural Math Tutor			●									●					●			●						1
All About Your Body								●			●		●							●						15
Angling for Words in Bits & Bytes				△							□					●				●						2
Base										●										●	●					12
Basic First Aid and Illness													●				●			●						3
Basic Language Units: Parts of Speech						●					●									●	●	●				8
Basic Grammar Units: Sentences						●					●									●	●	●				8
Basic Math Competency Skill Building			●								●						●			●	●					11

Teacher/Tutor Tools: Customize, Mini-authoring systems
Assessment & Skills: Math, Reading/Decoding & Structural Analysis, Reading/Comprehension, Writing/Grammar, Writing/Composing, Vocab./Spell. & Meaning, Problem-solving, Complete B. Skills Prog.
Content: General B. Skills Content, Workplace Basic Skills, Job-Domain Related, Job Search/Career, E.S.L.
Instruction Method: Drill & Practice, Tutorial, Simulation, Games & Puzzles
System Requirements: Apple, I.B.M., Tandy, Commodore, TRS-80, Macintosh, Publisher/Distributor

△ Teacher required

□ Basic Skills keyed to jobs, but content generic

*Numbers in the Publisher/Distributor column refer to the list of publisher on pp. 168–169.

© 1989, Institute for the Study of Adult Literacy, Penn State

Index of Workplace & Adult Basic Skills Software

Feature	Improving Your Vocabulary Skills	Ideal Learning Curriculum	I Love America Series/U.S. Cities	Gapper Reading Lab	Game Power for Phonics, Plus	Foreign Language Vocabulary Games	Food For Thought	E-Z Pilot II Authoring System	Exploring Career Options	ESL Writer	EA Core Vocabulary Worksheet Generator
Teacher/Tutor Tools											
Customize				●		●				●	●
Mini-authoring systems								●			
Assessment & Skills											
Math			●								
Reading/Decoding & Structural Analysis					●						
Reading/Comprehension				●					●		
Writing/Grammar											
Writing/Composing										●	
Vocab./Spell. & Meaning	●			●	●	●					●
Problem-solving											
Complete B. Skills Prog.		●									
Content											
General B. Skills Content	●	●		●	●	●					●
Workplace Basic Skills									●		
Job-Domain Related			●				●				
Job Search/Career									●		
E.S.L.						●	●			●	
Instruction Method											
Drill & Practice			●								
Tutorial											
Simulation											
Games & Puzzles						●	●			●	
System Requirements											
Apple	●	●	●	●	●	●	●	●	●	●	●
I.B.M.	●				●	●				●	
Tandy										●	
Commodore					●						
TRS-80					●						
Macintosh											
Publisher/Distributor*	29	18	20	29	13	33	29	34 29 22	16	30	11

*Numbers in the Publisher/Distributor column refer to the list of publisher on pp. 168–169.

Index of Workplace & Adult Basic Skills Software

	Diascriptive I, II, III Reading	Diascriptive Language Arts Development	Crossword Magic	Create - Medalists	Create Lessons - Advanced	Create Lessons	Cooking & Baking Series	Computational Skills Program	Career Arithmetic	Bones and Muscles: A Team to Depend On	Basic Skills in Math	
Teacher/Tutor Tools												
Customize			●	●	●	●						
Mini-authoring systems												
Assessment & Skills												
Math							●	●	●		●	
Reading/Decoding & Structural Analysis												
Reading/Comprehension	●						●					
Writing/Grammar		●										
Writing/Composing												
Vocab./Spell. & Meaning	●		●									
Problem-solving												
Complete B. Skills Prog.												
Content												
General B. Skills Content	●	●		●				●			●	
Workplace Basic Skills							●		●			
Job-Domain Related										●		
Job Search/Career												
E.S.L.												
Instruction Method												
Drill & Practice								●				
Tutorial		●						●				
Simulation												
Games & Puzzles												
System Requirements												
Apple	●	●	●	●	●	●	●	●	●	●	●	
I.B.M.	●	●	●	●		●	●					
Tandy	●	●										
Commodore	●		●									
TRS-80	●	●							●			
Macintosh												
Publisher/Distributor *	11	11	30	16	16	16	3	17	4	30 22	5	

Index of Workplace & Adult Basic Skills Software

	Print Your Own Calendar	Print Your Own Bingo Plus	Prevocational Math Review	Penn State Adult Lit. Courseware	Nursing	M_ss_ng L_nks	Micro-Computer Simulations in Business	Medical Terminology: General Terms	Math Facts	Make-A-Flash	Lucky 7 Vocabulary Games
Teacher/Tutor Tools											
Customize	●	●		▲		✴				●	●
Mini-authoring systems											
Assessment & Skills											
Math			●						●		
Reading/Decoding & Structural Analysis											
Reading/Comprehension						●					
Writing/Grammar											
Writing/Composing											
Vocab./Spell. & Meaning				●	●			●		●	●
Problem-solving											
Complete B. Skills Prog.											
Content											
General B. Skills Content				●		●			●		●
Workplace Basic Skills			●		●			●			
Job-Domain Related							●				
Job Search/Career											
E.S.L.											
Instruction Method											
Drill & Practice			●	●				●		●	
Tutorial			●					●		●	
Simulation											
Games & Puzzles				●		●					●
System Requirements											
Apple	●	●	●	●	●	✴	●	●	●	●	●
I.B.M.		●			●	●	●				●
Tandy						●	●				
Commodore						●					
TRS-80						●	●				
Macintosh											
Publisher/Distributor*	16 30	16	1	19	3	34	32	13	27	36	13

✴ Only customize Apple software

*Numbers in the Publisher/Distributor column refer to the list of publisher on pp. 168–169.

▲ Module 3 & 6 only

Index of Workplace & Adult Basic Skills Software

Category	Skill	Lucky 7 Spelling Games	Letter Man	Learning Ways to Read Words	Learning to Write	LEA-1 Functional Lit. Using Whole Language	Language Arts: The Rules	Key Game	Keyboard Cadet	Introduction to the Business Office	Interpreting Graphs	Individual Study Center
Teacher/Tutor Tools	Customize	●		■			●	◉				●
	Mini-authoring systems											●
Assessment & Skills	Math										●	
	Reading/Decoding & Structural Analysis			●								
	Reading/Comprehension					●						
	Writing/Grammar				●							
	Writing/Composing					●						
	Vocab./Spell. & Meaning	●		●			●	●				
	Problem-solving										●	
	Complete B. Skills Prog.											
Content	General B. Skills Content	●			●		●	●				
	Workplace Basic Skills											
	Job-Domain Related		●						●	●	●	
	Job Search/Career											
	E.S.L.			●	●	●						
Instruction Method	Drill & Practice							●				●
	Tutorial			●								
	Simulation										●	
	Games & Puzzles	●	●								●	
System Requirements	Apple	●	●	●	●	●	●	●	●	●	●	●
	I.B.M.	●	●	●	●	●		●				
	Tandy				●							
	Commodore							●				
	TRS-80				●			●				
	Macintosh			●								
*	Publisher/Distributor	29	5	13	13	11	27	36	5	13	6	35

Index of Workplace & Adult Basic Skills Software

Software	Teacher/Tutor Tools — Customize	Mini-authoring systems	Assessment & Skills — Math	Reading/Decoding & Structural Analysis	Reading/Comprehension	Writing/Grammar	Writing/Composing	Vocab./Spell. & Meaning	Problem-solving	Complete B. Skills Prog.	Content — General B. Skills Content	Workplace Basic Skills	Job-Domain Related	Job Search/Career	E.S.L.	Instruction Method — Drill & Practice	Tutorial	Simulation	Games & Puzzles	System Requirements — Apple	I.B.M.	Tandy	Commodore	TRS-80	Macintosh	Publisher/Distributor*
Square Pairs	●							●			●								●	●			●			30
States: Geography Study Unit																				●						37
Success With Writing																				●						30
Survival Reading Series					●						●									●	●					29
TAS		●					●						●								●			●		35
Teacher Option Organizer		●																		●						23
The Body in Focus													●							●	●		●			26
The Body Transparent													●						●	●	●		●			13/10/30
The Human Body													●							●	●	●				11
The Human Body - An Overview													●				●			●			●			30
The Human Pump													●							●						34

*Numbers in the Publisher/Distributor column refer to the list of publisher on pp. 168–169.

© 1989, Institute for the Study of Adult Literacy, Penn State

		Soft Text: Word Study	Soft Text: Math	Soft Text: English	Spelling for Careers in Medicine	Spelling for Careers in Business	Skills Bank II	Rules of the Road	Rov-A-Bot	Retailing Series	Read-A-Logo	Project Star
Teacher/Tutor Tools	Customize											
	Mini-authoring systems											
Assessment & Skills	Math		●							●		
	Reading/Decoding & Structural Analysis											
	Reading/Comprehension									●		
	Writing/Grammar			●								
	Writing/Composing											
	Vocab./Spell. & Meaning	●			●	●		●			●	
	Problem-solving								●			
	Complete B. Skills Prog.						●					●
Content	General B. Skills Content	●	●	●			●				●	●
	Workplace Basic Skills				●	●		●		●		
	Job-Domain Related								●			
	Job Search/Career											
	E.S.L.									●		
Instruction Method	Drill & Practice		●									
	Tutorial											
	Simulation											
	Games & Puzzles											
System Requirements	Apple	●	●	●	●	●	●	●	●	●	●	
	I.B.M.						●			●		
	Tandy											
	Commodore											
	TRS-80											
	Macintosh											
*	Publisher/Distributor	8	8	8	14	3	31	4	11	3	36	16

Index of Workplace & Adult Basic Skills Software

Software	Customize	Mini-authoring systems	Math	Reading/Decoding & Structural Analysis	Reading/Comprehension	Writing/Grammar	Writing/Composing	Vocab./Spell. & Meaning	Problem-solving	Complete B. Skills Prog.	General B. Skills Content	Workplace Basic Skills	Job-Domain Related	Job Search/Career	E.S.L.	Drill & Practice	Tutorial	Simulation	Games & Puzzles	Apple	I.B.M.	Tandy	Commodore	TRS-80	Macintosh	Publisher/Distributor *
Vocational Math for Automotive Technicians			●									●				●				●	●					1
Vocational Math for Carpenters			●									●				●				●	●					1
Vo. Math for Construction Materials & Costs			●									●				●				●	●					1
Vocational Math for Welders			●									●				●				●	●					1
Vocational Mechanics			●		●							●								●	●					3
Vocational Metal Trades			●									●								●	●					3
Vocational Welding					●							●								●	●					3
Vocational Survival Words - Carpentry Cluster					●			●				●								●	●					3
Vocational Survival Words - Food Service Cluster					●			●				●								●	●					3
Vocational Survival Words - Mechanics Cluster					●			●				●								●	●					3
What do you do with a broken calculator?			●						●		●										●	●				34

Teacher/Tutor Tools	Assessment & Skills	Content	Instruction Method	System Requirements

*Numbers in the Publisher/Distributor column refer to the list of publisher on pp. 168–169.

© 1989, Institute for the Study of Adult Literacy, Penn State

Index of Workplace & Adult Basic Skills Software

Category	Feature	Vocational Cosmetology	Vocational Construction Trade	Vocational for the World of Work II	Vocabulary for the World of Work	Vocabulary For the World of Work	Vocabulary Challenge	Vocabulary Builder	Typing Keys to Computer Ease	Time Master	Tic Tac Spell	The Semantic Mapper	The Respiratory System A Puff of Air
Teacher/Tutor Tools	Customize						●	●			●		
	Mini-authoring systems											●	
Assessment & Skills	Math		●							●			
	Reading/Decoding & Structural Analysis												
	Reading/Comprehension	●											
	Writing/Grammar												
	Writing/Composing												
	Vocab./Spell. & Meaning				●	●	●				●	●	
	Problem-solving												
	Complete B. Skills Prog.												
Content	General B. Skills Content						●	●		●	●		
	Workplace Basic Skills	●	●	●	●								
	Job-Domain Related								●				●
	Job Search/Career												
	E.S.L.			●	●							●	
Instruction Method	Drill & Practice							●	●	●			
	Tutorial			●	●								
	Simulation												
	Games & Puzzles										●		
System Requirements	Apple	●	●	●	●	●	●			●	●	●	●
	I.B.M.	●	●	●	●			●					
	Tandy												
	Commodore												
	TRS-80											●	
	Macintosh			●	●								
*	Publisher/Distributor	3	3	13 / 29	13 / 29	30	24	13	2	24	30	36	30 / 22

Index of Workplace & Adult Basic Skills Software

Software	Customize	Mini-authoring systems	Math	Reading/Decoding & Structural Analysis	Reading/Comprehension	Writing/Grammar	Writing/Composing	Vocab./Spell. & Meaning	Problem-solving	Complete B. Skills Prog.	General B. Skills Content	Workplace Basic Skills	Job-Domain Related	Job Search/Career	E.S.L.	Drill & Practice	Tutorial	Simulation	Games & Puzzles	Apple	I.B.M.	Tandy	Commodore	TRS-80	Macintosh	Publisher/Distributor
Word Attack Plus!	●							●			●					●			●	●	●		●			9
Wordfind	●							●												●						11
Word Machine	●							●			●								●	●						25
WordMatch	●							●			●					●			●	●						29
Word Parts - Education				●							●									●						3
Wordplay	●							●			●									●						14
Wordsearch	●							●											●	●						16
Workplace Literacy System										●		●								●						7
Writing Skills Improvement Program						●					●					●					●	●				28

Teacher/Tutor Tools · Assessment & Skills · Content · Instruction Method · System Requirements

*Numbers in the Publisher/Distributor column refer to the list of publisher on pp. 168–169.

©1989, Institute for the Study of Adult Literacy, Penn State

Adult Literacy in a Multiliterate Society

Sherry Hill Howie
January 1990

There are those who fear that ours is a postliterate society. They fear that books are being replaced by technology and media. They believe such innovations as computers will replace the need to read books to gain information and to learn. Just as in the *Phaedrus* Plato feared that the invention of the paper and pen to record ideas would destroy the oral literacy tradition, writers such as Neil Postman (1985) fear that the inventions of television and computers will destroy our print literacy tradition.

We once were predominately a preliterate society, but with the invention of the printing press, we became primarily literate. The availability of the computer today is changing us into a multiliterate society, one in which we learn and take in information in many different ways.

Instead of fearing changes and decrying the passing of traditions, perhaps it is wiser to understand technological innovations and prudently use them to facilitate and perpetuate the values we believe in. In other words, computers as language processors can be of tremendous benefit in the learning of language processing in reading and writing.

The urgency for print literacy today is unique in that approximately 70% of contemporary jobs require literacy. Furthermore, at the rate that information doubles today (every 20 months) and the rate it is projected to double by the year 2000 (every 20 weeks), print literacy will be a necessity for mere survival. For adults who are illiterate or semiliterate, the computer has many advantages for improving abilities that could later be transferred to paper and print. With the goal of transference in mind, there is no justification for fearing the demise of the book for primary literacy. In a multiliterate approach, the objective is learning through a variety of ways.

The Differences in Technologies

The technologies of the book and paper and pencil appear to differ from the computer in the ways they require users to think and to solve problems. Print offers activities of deductive reasoning that have the reader proceed from general ideas to details in a linear, sequential manner. Such reasoning is prescribed by an author and is restricted to the limits the writer sets. On the other hand, Norton (1985) argues that certain software offers the opportunity to think in a different way, one that may be closer to the way adults live and solve problems day by day. Problem-solving software asks a user to reason inductively by experimenting and asking "what if" to a problem rather than using "if-then" as in cause and effect sequencing in a linear book.

The experimenter hypothesizing "what if" makes mistakes and learns from them. Seeing patterns and creating patterns and connections allow the computer user to employ synthesis, to determine probabilities, and to use intuitive reasoning. The user operates in an open system that he or she creates rather than in one set down in black and white by the author.

An example of such a software program would be *Where in the World Is Carmen Sandiego?* by Broderbund Publishing. In this simulation, one that semiliterate adults could enjoy with help, the user becomes a sleuth tracking criminals across the world to specific geographic points. During the chase, the user refers to an almanac of facts to uncover information about the clues that are provided to the whereabouts of the criminal. The paperbound almanac included with the program has facts on flags, coins, governments, and all else the sleuth would need to look up. The user formulates patterns to the criminal's behavior, synthesizes information from a variety of sources (both video and book), and makes decisions based on inductive logic. The program is recommended for groups of adult learners of varying abilities, so that using it becomes a social experience as well.

The two systems of thinking are not the dichotomies that Norton (1985) presents. A reader of books in the process of reading asks questions that are "what if," not solely "if-then." A reader searches for patterns to the text that exist and synthesizes information. A reader makes guesses and uses intuition to arrive at solutions to the problems the print poses. A reader tests hypotheses and makes mistakes, correcting as more context becomes available. The reader relies finally on personal experience and background knowledge to compose the meaning the text suggests. Perhaps the theory should be that what Norton suggests as computer-oriented activities are actually ones that occur during a reading process and then are validated by engaging in the print-oriented activities, as shown in Figure 1.

The point is that technologies of both book and computer are compatible in problem-

Figure 1

Print-oriented activities	Computer-oriented activities
if-then	what if
deductive	inductive
linear, sequential	patterns and connections
closed system	open system
active	interactive

Adapted from Norton (1985), pp. 36–40.

solving tasks and may reinforce each other in helping people become literate. The kinds of thinking and problem solving they elicit from a user are not exclusive, but perhaps developmental. That means that if a computer program provides an experience in problem solving that is preliminary to actual reading (a problem-solving process), then the experience may transfer to the actual literate experience with print in the book technology.

Using certain problem-solving software that provides this experience can aid an adult in becoming literate. Certainly, the software program described earlier offers the opportunity to think and solve problems preliminary to reading, but it also provides a relevance and a necessity for reading a book (the almanac) to find information in order to solve the problems posed.

Needs of Adult Learners

The ability to read has a functional purpose for adults, of course, in their jobs, in making decisions on consumer products, in reading safety and health warnings and directions, and in assuring their rights as citizens. Such functional competencies have been detailed in the 1980 Adult Performance Level Study (APL) out of Texas (Kozol, 1985), and they do have their place in teaching literacy to adults.

Beyond just functional purposes, though, is the need to "perpetuate an ongoing communication with life," as Wolf (1977) concludes from his survey of elderly adults. He found that print literacy serves lifelong purposes and fulfills specific needs in the lives of aging persons. Reading satisfies needs for entertainment, curiosity, cultural development, and companionship—not only for the older adults, but for people of all ages. Wolf found, too, that reading was a way to maintain spiritual and community interests. Many adults needed to read in order to read the Bible. Many wanted to read about events and people in communities where they lived.

The most important purpose for print literacy, though, is that it has a social function among adults. Individuals who read do not isolate themselves socially (Steinberg, 1972). Wolf (1977) found that the adults exchanged books, discussed them, and built social contacts around sharing ideas they gained from reading. Such adults were more active and involved socially than those who did not read. Kozol (1985) eloquently describes this social need of adults in his poetic definition of a literate human being: "One soul, reaching out of the loneliness of the human condition to find—through love—another" (p. 162). Books serve to fulfill life needs, not only of adults but of the young as well.

Cautions in Using the Computer

There are cautions to using the computer to teach literacy to adult learners that have to be heeded before one may begin to consider the computer's advantages.

One caution resides in the area of selection of the software itself: the teacher must have software that is compatible with the overall teaching approach. For example, if one takes strictly a skills approach to the teaching of reading, then one will select drill-and-practice programs and tutorials that provide practice and drill in skills already taught.

The second caution is related to the first: remember that the computer is not a substitute for good teaching and does not replace a good teacher. An effective teacher prepares plans, selects relevant materials, and proceeds to teach with educationally sound methods. The selected software should facilitate the plans and be part of a lesson being orchestrated by the teacher, who operates from a clear philosophical approach (Howie, 1988).

One approach, then, is the skills approach. Another is a problem-solving approach to teaching literacy using such software as simulations, text adventures, and problem-solving programs. Teaching literacy as problem solving requires a student to hypothesize, predict, make guesses, and realize patterns to reading and writing (Howie, 1989). These are all mental processes of the mature reader who focuses on understanding and composing ideas in text. This approach to teaching reading is also based on a definite philosophy and is one that is superior to the skills approach with adults.

Figure 2 gives a limited list of current problem-solving programs that are suitable and recommended for teaching reading to adults.

Another caution to heed is that skills and ways of thinking on the computer do not automatically transfer to books. The transfer has to be part of the teacher's plan, and the students must be made aware of this goal of their instruction by computer, not just left to infer it. Good instruction, therefore, will focus on the transference of problem solving, ways of thinking, and acquisition of literacy skills, and will integrate the two technologies for the development of print literacy.

A final caution is that the teacher must be aware of the effects of the software program

Figure 2
Software for Adult Use

Simulations
Oregon Trail—MECC
Lemonade—MECC
President Elect—Micro Media

Problem solving
Where in the World Is Carmen Sandiego?
—Broderbund
Where in the USA Is Carmen Sandiego?
—Broderbund
Memory Match—Hartley
Money! Money!—Hartley
Memory Building Blocks—Sunburst

Drill and practice
Dr. Peet's TalkWriter—Hartley
That's My Job—Hartley
Word Attack—Davidson & Associates

on the learner, both affectively in meeting the learner's needs for self-esteem and cognitively in developing thinking abilities and literacy skills. Usage of the computer should have a positive learning effect. Not every adult will be willing to use machines, particularly computers, and they should never be forced to do so. Most adults, however, will find using a computer a matter of prestige and a boost to their esteem and confidence.

Specific Advantages

Because of the tremendous variety of software, the computer offers a wide variation in techniques that appeal to different ways of thinking and learning. Each individual has learning styles that vary but may be accommodated through the variety of techniques the software offers, from drill and practice to simulations to word processing. For example, one adult student may learn best through role playing and would benefit from a simulation.

Another student may learn best through language experience and would learn most with a word processor. Taylor (1980) described the variations as Tool, Tutor, Tutee, and Toy, the functions of the great array of software programs available.

Another advantage is the sensory involvement provided on the computer. Instead of being entirely visual, as is a book, software can be tactile, visual, and even aural, if one uses a voice synthesizer. People have different learning modalities, and a multisensory approach would benefit the majority of learners as to their learning strengths.

If one ascribes to the theory of hemispheric dominance—that the right side of the brain is primarily visual and spatial while the left is predominately verbal and linear—then one may see that the computer would accommodate hemispheric needs in its graphics and text displays.

In contrast to the static book, most software programs are interactive with the learner. The student has the opportunity to ask the program questions, respond to it, and get immediate feedback. Another advantage is that the learner may control this interaction, its rate and repetition, through self-pacing. Thus, the learner may interact continuously with the program until mastery is achieved and feelings of confidence are given a boost.

Continuous and timely feedback may be a tremendous aid to learning. A book or a test in a class cannot give this kind of feedback; too frequently it is delayed for days so that learning from mistakes is impossible. Because of the interaction possible on the computer, learning from mistakes and subsequent corrections is a strong advantage.

A word processor provides excellent advantages over using paper and pencil or a typewriter. Writers are freed to concentrate on composing, knowing that they may easily scroll back through their manuscript to re-shape and edit their ideas later. Revision is simple with a word processor.

Adult learners will come to appreciate the ephemeral nature of writing that appears on an electronic screen, with the realization that it may be rethought and changed at any time. No longer will language appear unmanipulat-able or unchangeable—all one needs to do is push the delete key or move and replace text to change ideas. Language thus becomes usable, mutable, and dynamic to the adult learner.

Probably the best advantage of the com-puter resides in its social possibilities for learning. Current research in cooperative learning and grouping on the computer reveals that learning is significantly enhanced when two or three students are grouped to share language and experiences in learning (Carrier & Sales, 1987). In such grouping, students use language to generate ideas, become teachers to each other, and enjoy their experiences more. Certainly, grouping could also fulfill adult longing for social interactions with other adults. Such grouping counters a sense of isolation and anxiety regarding formal learning. Furthermore, grouping deals with necessary aspects of adult learning outlined by Mocker (1975) that differ from such aspects of children's learn-ing: (1) providing for student-to-student com-munication that recognizes the experience and knowledge of each; (2) placing responsi-bility for learning on the students to foster independence; and (3) having the teacher assume the role of colearner rather than con-troller of all knowledge.

Cooperative learning may be the best method to meet learning and social needs of adults. The computer, with its screen at a comfortable distance, affords this possibility to a group of people who may share a single screen's output and read at the same rate. This is in contrast to a book that is smaller and is physically inaccessible to a group whose members may not read the same page at the same pace.

Motivational Technology

The computer has many advantages over traditional technologies in learning, thinking, and problem solving. It still is highly motiva-tional because of its novelty. If reading and writing are taught as thinking processes akin to problem solving, then skills and experi-ences acquired on the computer should trans-fer well, with guidance, to the book. Our goal is literacy development with adult learners and, in a multiliterate society, we need to use technology wisely to perpetuate our values of print literacy. The technologies now available are compatible with and mutually supportive of the overall goals.

References

Carrier, C.A., & Sales, G.C. (1987). Pair versus individual work on the acquisition of concepts in a computer-based instructional lesson. *Jour-nal of Computer-Based Instruction, 14*(1), 11–17.

Howie, S.H. (1988). Software evaluation based on reading theory. *CUE* [Computer Using Educators] *NewsLetter, 10*(5).

Howie, S.H. (1989). *Reading, writing and comput-ers: Planning for integration.* Needham Heights, MA: Allyn & Bacon.

Kozol, J. (1985). *Illiterate America.* New York: New American Library.

Mocker, D.W. (1975). Cooperative learning process: Shared learning experience in teaching adults to read. *Journal of Reading, 18,* 440–444.

Norton, P. (1985). Problem-solving activities in a computer environment: A different angle of vision. *Educational Technology, 25,* 36–41.

Postman, N. (1985). *Amusing ourselves to death.* New York: Viking.

Steinberg, H. (1972). Books and readers as a sub-ject of research in Europe and America. *Interna-tional Social Science Journal, 24,* 753.

Taylor, R. (1980). *The computer in the school: Tutor, tool, tutee.* New York: Teachers College Press.

Wolf, R.E. (1977). What is reading good for? Perspectives for senior citizens. *Journal of Reading, 21,* 15–17.

T e c h n o l o g y

Interactive Computer-Assisted Instruction with Adults

ROSLYN FINNEGAN
RICHARD SINATRA
OCTOBER 1991

Adult literacy programs face a multitude of problems: in the United States they attract less than 7% of the illiterate population and they must provide for widely differing reading levels among their adult students (Park, 1987); they suffer from lack of both funding (Askov & Turner, 1989) and age-appropriate materials (Wangberg & Reutten, 1986); their tutors, though dedicated and well intentioned, often lack the skills necessary to teach and motivate adults (Rogers, 1987); and the drop-out rate is extremely high, ranging from 50% to 70% (Park, 1987). Moreover, instruction is strongly skill-based, presented by tutors with little training who are usually encouraged to use only their sponsoring agency's materials (Hunter & Harman, 1979; Rogers, 1987).

This article offers a more modern alternative for adult literacy instruction, one that may keep the adult returning for learning— computer-assisted instruction (CAI) which provides a pragmatic way of developing the emergent literacy skills of adult readers and writers. When computers and appropriate software have been used with adult learners, both increased achievement (Askov & Turner, 1989; Wangberg, 1986) and higher attendance (Turner & Stockdill, 1987) have been reported. In one program at an urban adult literacy center, evaluation revealed that computer instruction was no more expensive than traditional instruction, and that more than the anticipated number of students were served (Turner & Stockdill, 1987).

In this article, we will first discuss types of CAI formats that engage adults in holistic, concept-driven instruction, thereby providing meaningful and useful literacy situations. Next we will describe specific software programs useful for adults functioning at three different levels of reading proficiency.

Computers Meet Adults' Needs

Modern CAI programs engage students in a variety of reading and writing activities, usually centered on themes of high interest and wide social applicability. The inherent privacy of computer use allows adults to work at their own level and proceed at their own pace.

Specific needs of the weakest learners can be met through computer programs that use language experience (LEA). LEA can be used initially to create holistic, age-appropriate text based on the learners' experiences and language patterns. The use of their own oral language facilitates reading of text, while content based on their own experiences provides immediate interest, familiarity, and ultimate success. With LEA, reading and writing are depicted as meaning-making experiences, so adults change their concept of reading and writing as the learning of discrete skills. Skills can be taught as the need arises, naturally and within the context of students' self-generated texts.

In one functional literacy program, the use of software based on the language experience approach with adults reading at about the 5th grade level resulted in an average 1-year gain in ability after just 22 hours of instruction. Eleven adults in the control group completed the same number of hours of instruction without microcomputers and showed no grade-level increase in reading (Wangberg, 1986).

Some software programs allow for branching to differing ability levels, so students are not totally reliant upon a teacher or tutor to check their work before they continue (Askov & Turner, 1989; Turner, 1988). Other programs provide correct answers to prevent frustration, while others will not proceed unless the student inputs the correct answer. In both cases, the student is prevented from proceeding with faulty information and incorrect assumptions. This is an extremely valuable feature, for it prevents the reinforcement of misconceptions (Sloane, Gunn, Gordon, & Mickelson, 1989).

One of the most significant features of using computers in adult literacy programs is the sense of empowerment they provide (Turner, 1988). The adult has control of his or her learning, and accomplishments become more meaningful. By accepting responsibility for educating themselves and by controlling the pace and level of program accomplishment, adults become empowered to succeed.

Learning computer skills also brings the adult learner into the world of the future.

Adults weak in literacy are denied access to so much of the world, and they may be understandably anxious about computers. Once they experience the ease of using a computer, they are eager and highly motivated to continue learning. Furthermore, computer know-how provides opportunities to explore and upgrade job possibilities (Askov & Turner, 1989). This knowledge is useful in daily life as new technology changes everyday functions, from using a bank machine to searching through a library's computerized card catalog.

Benefits of Holistic CAI

Computer-assisted instruction is not designed to take the place of the teacher or of group learning. Computers and software are effective when they are integrated into a more traditional instructional program. Preparatory and follow-up lessons are pertinent to the ultimate success of CAI. For best results, teachers and tutors should receive training in the specifics of a given program and also in ways to integrate programs into job- and life-related language activities.

Computer-assisted instruction can take a variety of formats. Unfortunately, much educational software is based upon misconceptions about the reading process. Many software developers adhere to a bottom-up approach to reading instruction and produce subskill-based programs and reading activities that focus solely on literal comprehension (Reinking, 1988–89) and decoding. These programs often employ a drill-and-practice or tutorial format providing the same sort of reading activities that these students have faced in skillbooks. Instruction that focuses on isolated skills taught out of meaningful contexts may not only frustrate adult learners but will reinforce erroneous beliefs that reading is the ability to sound out words, rather than a meaning-making process (Jones, 1981; Nickerson, 1985).

The software formats which we will now describe engage adult learners in more holistic literacy interactions while promoting higher level thinking skills. Adults become engaged with program scripts and use language to discuss, plan, and solve problems (Bork, 1985). Such holistic, concept-driven formats are ideally suited for an adult literacy program that uses computers. They capitalize on adults' extensive vocabularies and wealth of background experiences, and provide learners with a purposeful context in which to learn. These programs construct meaning within the contexts of both verbal and nonverbal messages, develop higher level thinking skills through language activities that nurture discovery and creativity, and show reading and writing as meaningful modes of communication (Sinatra, 1987).

CAI Formats That Enhance Instruction

Interactive fiction and interactive story collaboration involve readers in programs by allowing them to discover various twists and endings for the same story. Students' choices drive the action, thus fostering motivation. Interactive story collaboration allows the student and the computer to form a composing partnership. The computer presents the story structure, and the student, as reader and writer, composes and alters the final product.

Text adventures engage students in a story, game, or simulation. The student must use reading skills to locate information in a reference book and input the correct answer, or the adventure cannot continue. Because students are focused on completing the text adventure, they perform the tasks eagerly. (Broderbund's popular Carmen Sandiego series, for example, uses this text adventure format.) Simulations model real and imaginary worlds. While they are similar to film and television because they draw the student into an alternate reality, simulations have the added feature of involving the student as a participant, not strictly as an observer. They are also an excellent means of fostering group interaction (Balajthy, 1984).

Simulations generally provide background knowledge for the learners, but they require students to read carefully and to make decisions. They foster prediction and evaluation as students examine the outcomes of their decisions. In one program, students became so fascinated with simulated worlds that they did not realize they were reading (Willing, 1988).

Databases, spreadsheets, and graphs are tools to manage and organize information. Yates and Moursand (1988–89) say these programs provide learners with alternate ways to represent or solve a problem. Adults discover how the representation of information changes one's perspective. In an adult literacy program, these tools can be used for a multitude of practical purposes, allowing for easy transfer. Used in small and large groups, they provide much interaction among students.

Databases can be used to store such things as word banks, traveler's tips, and movie reviews, and to chart individual progress. For instance, students can access a database file to see if anyone in the class has visited a particular area. After reading the traveler's tips, they can write a note to the traveler (using the word processor) requesting more information.

Spreadsheets can be used to assist adults in budgeting their household expenses. Although the computer performs the numerical computations, students must grasp the underlying concepts of mathematical formulas.

Graphs allow students to see familiar patterns so they can determine problem-solving strategies (Yates & Moursand, 1988–89).

A word-processing program is a most valuable asset in the adult literacy classroom. Word processing enriches LEA by providing the instructor with a tool for taking dictation while producing highly readable text. Within minutes of dictating a story, the adult is provided with the written account. Additional copies can be used to create sentence strips.

Incorporating writing into an adult reading program capitalizes on the strong relationship between reading comprehension and written composition while accessing the adults' wealth of information, interest, and experience. By using word processing (and perhaps desktop publishing) to integrate reading and writing, adults become adept with the new technology in a creative atmosphere. The nature of both word processing and desktop publishing programs alters adult learners' views about writing. They learn to focus on the process, not the product. With the computer as partner, writing becomes a painless, recursive process, since the word-processing format allows the writer to revise and evaluate work in progress. The learner becomes far more comfortable with actual composing and thinking because the software is responsible for the many mechanical aspects of writing.

Software for Three Levels of Learners

After successful work at the St. John's University reading clinic with adults functioning at differing reading levels, we have arranged CAI programs into three general levels. (The levels correspond roughly to three levels of reading and writing achievement demonstrated by adults during diagnostic intake.) "Beginning-level software" includes programs appropriate for adults traditionally considered "illiterate"—those scarcely able to read or write. The second level encompasses software useful for those who are "function-

ally literate"—for our purposes, those operating at about an intermediate-grade level of reading (Grade 4 or 5). These adults can read and write with some success, and when challenged with interesting material, they quickly become more proficient. The software at the third level is useful for adults who are quite competent but who cannot meet the requirements of advanced schooling or of a technologically advanced marketplace (particularly in the area of written organization).

Especially at the beginning level, we include only those programs that do not demean or embarrass adult students. Since these programs were generally produced for young novice readers, it is their adaptation for adults that provides the key to successful implementation. Figure 4 (at the end of this article) provides sources for obtaining the specific programs [current as of October 1991] as well as details on the compatibility of the software with various computer systems.

Beginning-level software. Word-processing programs (with and without graphics) can help new adult readers build a sight vocabulary, practice new vocabulary, and use context to read fluently. Although many good word-processing programs are available, the *Language Experience Recorder* (Language Experience Primary series) provides the teacher and student with an analysis of each story written with it. This includes the number of words and sentences used, frequency of repeated words, and the readability level. This information can be used in planning off-computer activities and charting student progress. The stories can also be printed in large type.

The same series' *Make-a-Flash* program allows a teacher or tutor to create individualized printed flashcards to reinforce quick recognition of sight vocabulary. In addition, the computer acts as the teacher by testing and evaluating the student's knowledge of specified target words.

Sentence Starters and *Great Beginnings*, also of the Language Experience Primary series, use pictures to aid the reader's interpretation of text. With *Sentence Starters*, the student inputs words to complete simple sentences on related topics. After choosing a topic through a picture clue in *Great Beginnings*, the student is shown several related words that will be used to generate sentences. Both programs allow students to choose pictures to illustrate their sentences, and the finished product can be printed. Synthesized speech is an option for the entire series; this can help students with limited sight vocabulary to work independently.

Story Builder is a multilevel program that uses an interactive tutorial format to teach sentence elements and the relationship of sentences within a paragraph. As the student selects elements to form an initial sentence, graphics are added to illustrate it and provide a setting for a developing story.

A number of programs designed for children, such as *Story Maker, Once Upon a Time, Monsters and Make-Believe*, the Explore-a-Story series, and *Snoopy Writer*, are nonetheless well accepted by beginning adult readers and will help them become creative writers of stories. These interactive programs also allow for the creation of text from graphics and the matching of graphics with text. Thus, in addition to providing experience in writing extended, illustrated stories, these programs on a simpler level can help adults lacking sight vocabularies match and label concepts to a visual representation. For example, one 19-year-old student in our clinic did not know the meaning of the word *barn*. When she typed in the letters of the word, *Once Upon a Time* provided the picture, enriching both her comprehension and word reading.

Monsters and Make-Believe gives the illiterate adult an opportunity to use vocabulary as body parts are chosen to create a monster. The adult can then write or dictate a story about the monster, which can be printed and later read aloud to the learner's own children.

Snoopy Writer contains a simple word-processing program that offers the student the option of choosing an illustrated setting along with a sentence starter to begin the story. Stories and graphics involve the familiar characters from the *Peanuts* comic strip.

The Explore-a-Story series, *Story Maker*, and *Once Upon a Time* help extremely low-functioning readers develop a sight vocabulary. Learners select words to name objects on the screen. They can also input text to label objects, form sentences, and create ongoing stories. As students become more capable, they can create elaborate scenes using a variety of pictures. Such scenes can serve as the impetus for writing descriptive text. Figure 1 shows how our 19-year-old student created two lines of text to accompany her picture story.

As their sight vocabularies improve, adult beginning readers will enjoy using *The Semantic Mapper* (Package B), which is specifically designed for these learners. This package aids teachers and students in the creation of semantic maps for individualized areas of interest. Students will learn to organize their new words according to central topics and subcategories.

Thinking Networks for Reading and Writing also uses the concept of semantic mapping to develop reading, writing, and thinking skills through high-interest narratives. After reading a short story on a text card, the student helps build a semantic map of the story by choosing the title, major events, and sup-

Figure 1
Using Software to Build Sight Vocabulary and Comprehension

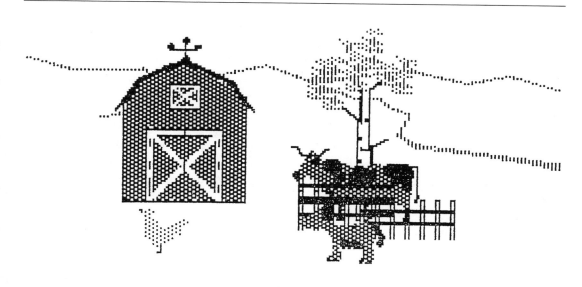

I SEE THE CHICKEN IN FRONT OF THE BARN.
THE CHICKEN IS ORANGE.

Screen from *Once Upon a Time* reproduced by permission of the publisher, Compu-Teach. [The technology has been updated since this illustration.]

porting details in sequential order. As the student makes correct choices, each event is recorded in its proper slot in the map. Through the use of the map configuration, the student learns a format for narrative story structure, which will help later when students write original stories with the program's "Creative Writer" portion.

The "Word Challenge" section of the program helps students develop vocabulary understanding through context, offers practice in remembering new vocabulary through a tachistoscopic flash, and provides an opportunity to use the new words in a cloze passage. During the "Author's Apprentice" and "Creative Writer" program segments, students are asked to retell their original stories in their own words or to compose new stories using the skeleton map as a visual guide. Any word processor can then be used to create and revise students' compositions.

Intermediate-level software. The Storyteller, Tales of Mystery, Tales of Discovery, and *Tales of Adventure* are of the interactive fiction and story collaboration type of software. They provide high-interest stories with multiple twists and endings, chosen by the student through regenerative branching. Because the student inputs his or her name and that of a friend to provide names for the characters, the stories are personalized. They are humorous and engaging, and students will want to plot their choices so they can pick alternate branches when they return to the program.

The Playwriter series also allows the student to collaborate with the computer to create stories. In answering open-ended questions, the student may select from prepared choices or input several lines of text to form a more creative answer. All answers chosen or created are intertwined in a continuing story to form chapters of a book.

Treasure Hunter and *The Secrets of Science Island*, two text adventure programs, require students to use context clues to locate information in accompanying high-interest reference books. Correct answers increase scores and allow text adventure games to proceed to higher levels. While some adults may not find the game approach particularly challenging, they will enjoy searching through reference materials and reading nonfiction passages.

Mystery Mazes is a fun simulation that asks students to become detectives and use clues to find a master criminal. As students read selections to build background information, they learn to extract pertinent clues. They then write these clues in their detective notepads, to be used for decision making.

Super Solvers Midnight Rescue is another challenging simulation. This program requires reading from literary selections, responding to clues, and answering comprehension questions.

The Santa Fe Trail and *The Oregon Trail* allow the student to experience the hardships of life in the United States in the 19th centu-ry. Both programs develop critical thinking skills by asking the student to choose provisions and map routes for the long trek across uncivilized land. This approach requires students to consider potential consequences before they act.

Scholastic's Microzine series provides students with a variety of programs of different styles. Each edition in the series includes one or more simulations plus exercises in other formats such as interactive fiction, electronic billboard, word-picture processing, games, and introductory programming techniques.

Grolier produces a group of programs that instruct students in the use of management tools, followed by practical and creative applications of the tool. They are well planned, effective programs and would be an asset to an adult literacy program's software library. *Graph Master* teaches the use of pictographs, bar graphs, and pie graphs. Students can compare the representation of data in different graphs; in creating graphs, they learn the relationships between verbal and nonverbal representation of data. *Infor-Master* teaches the uses of databases simply and effectively. The practice section offers multitrack branching, and allows students to see if they have mastered the concept. The limited number of fields demands careful decision making, as students choose the pertinent classifications of data to include in a given file. Both programs allow printing of finished products.

Thinking Networks for Reading and Writing offers another level of programs using semantic mapping in conjunction with informational reading (generally pertaining to science, health, or social studies). The "Theme Programs," consisting of reading selections ranging from 3rd to 9th grade levels, model a visual representation of ideas found in expository reading. The map is developed when the adult selects correct answers based on the text reading.

The map displays the main topic of the reading selection in a large center box. The four categories of information relating to the central topic appear in smaller boxes branching out from the center box, and the subordinate information within each category is linked to the appropriate category box. Once the adult has worked through the program, he or she begins to see how expository organization relates superordinate, subordinate, and coordinate ideas.

Following up with the "Author's Apprentice" and "Creative Writer" routines of the program, the adult uses skeleton map outlines to plan and write thematic reports. The word-processing component helps the adult complete the reading, composing, and writing cycle and transform the visual-verbal map into a well-developed, organized essay.

The Children's Writing and Publishing Center offers a menu-driven, desktop pub-

Figure 2
Desktop Publishing

REAL ESTATE NEWS

Real estate is a great business where you can make a lot of money. One of the pleasures of being in real estate is that your routine changes. You meet new people everyday. You meet new people when they want to list their house for sale, or when they want to buy a house. You get to see new properties and you never get stuck sitting in your chair. As a real estate salesperson, you have more freedom than other jobs. Real estate agents' responsibilities are showing people houses and looking for properties to sell. They try to get the seller and the buyer to come to an agreement. They try to get the seller to fix all the problems in the house before

Screen created using *The Children's Writing and Publishing Center*. Reproduced by permission of the publisher, The Learning Company.

lishing program that is ideal for both children and adult new readers. Adults can create and illustrate newsletters, reports, stories, and letters by choosing from many type styles and sizes and from over 150 pictures. The program can also import graphics from several other published sources. Figure 2 illustrates how rewarding this simple-to-use program can be for the adult who is developing literacy skills. Benjamin began in our reading clinic some 7 years ago as an adolescent with a third grade reading level; he is now a young adult searching for career possibilities. He collaborated with his tutor to write, select clip art, and lay out the visual presentation of "Real Estate News," the first page of which is shown.

Advanced-level software. MECC's interactive writing tutorials *Writing a Narrative*, *Writing a Character Sketch*, and *Writing an*

Figure 3
Outline for an Opinion Paper

Topic:
Controlling drunk driving

Various aspects:
The government should pass tougher laws to punish drunk drivers.
People who allow drunks to drive should be arrested.

Question:
Should the government pass tougher laws to punish drunk drivers?

Opinion:
Tougher laws are needed to punish drunk drivers and prevent accidents.

Reasons for opinion:
Most car accidents are caused by drunk drivers.
Most accidents are caused by people who have been stopped many times for driving drunk.
Too many people drink and drive!

Opinion Paper provide extensive practice in strengthening the elements of writing with various types of texts. *Writing an Opinion Paper* has some word-processing capability, allowing students to complete an outline of their first draft on the computer. Figure 3 shows how one adult organized the components of a paper on a controversial topic.

What Do They Do in Ougadougou is an engaging program in game format. Through a variety of cultural, geographic, and economic clues, students learn about the similarities and differences of life in other countries. Understandings of people from various cultures are enhanced, and adults learn information on 20 countries.

Farewell Alaska and *Hospital* are text adventures that require students to locate information in the *Encyclopedia Americana*. Researched information is then entered to continue the text adventure. Each program contains 20 high-interest episodes that focus on the exploits of four characters.

A number of simulations involve adults in different levels of decision making and are excellent for individual or group use. *Annam* asks the student to become the ruler of a mythical Third World country and make difficult decisions affecting personal popularity and the military. The adult has the opportunity to view the U.S. from the perspective of a developing nation.

Lincoln's Decisions and *Washington's Decisions* draw the student into a historical context. The student must "become" each president and make difficult decisions based on the social, economic, and political influences of the time. The programs are challenging and informative and require thoughtful reading.

The Colonial Merchant transports the adult to the explosive years before the American Revolution. In his or her role as a merchant, the adult experiences the economic frustrations that the British imposed on some of the North American colonies in the 18th century.

Note Card Maker and *The Americana Topic and Research Finder* guide students through some of the essential steps in organizing data for research papers. With *Note Card Maker*, students learn to create a bibliography and individual note cards. *The Americana Topic and Research Finder* aids the student in choosing a topic for research and then teaches the necessary steps in focusing on and organizing a paper. After finishing the program, the student has a working outline and a list of sources to examine for further research.

Edu-Calc is an excellent program for teaching the uses of a spreadsheet. Although it is more complicated than any of the other recommended software, it would be of great value to adults and could be taught and practiced in a group setting. In selecting the text for the rows and columns of a spreadsheet and by deciding which mathematical formula to use, adults are involved in determining relationships between items and using appropriate problem-solving strategies.

Wordbench—Student Edition is both a sophisticated, menu-driven word-processing program and an organizing tool for writing. Outlines, note cards, and bibliographies can be created with the software; the outline and note cards can be merged into the text of a document, providing the basis of a rough draft. Four brainstorming techniques are available, as well as a thesaurus and spell-checker. *Wordbench* offers a lot of power for minimal cost.

Publish It! is a sophisticated desktop publishing program. Icons and pull-down menus make the program visually appealing, and a tutorial is included for new users. Students can work together or individually to create newsletters, reports, advertisements, personal letters, flyers, and invitations. By determining page layout, graphics, fonts, and text, students learn to create documents with professional flair.

Many more sophisticated word-processing and tool application programs (*Word Perfect*, *Appleworks*, *MacWrite*, and *MacDraw* are just a few of the good ones) are available for adult learners to use in a literacy center or at home. However, even highly literate adults often need to take courses to learn to master these programs.

Computers Provide Possibilities

Understanding the special characteristics, needs, and interests of adult learners is a necessary component of a successful literacy program. Interactive computer-assisted instruction is not only conducive to providing a holistic, meaningful approach but is also tailormade to fit the many needs of adults at home, in the community, and in the workplace.

It is not necessary to stock each literacy program with all the software recommended in this article. Even a single program from each category will provide many reading and writing opportunities for learners. A simple word processing program or one desktop publishing program can provide a myriad of instructional activities, limited only by the creativity and ingenuity of the instructor. Modern CAI formats can transport emerging adult readers from print impoverishment to an enriched world of communication.

References

Askov, E.N., & Turner, T.C. (1989). Using computers for teaching basic skills to adults. *Lifelong Learning: An Omnibus of Practice and Research, 12*(6), 28–31.

Balajthy, E. (1984). Computer simulations and reading. *The Reading Teacher, 37*, 590–593.

Bork, A. (1981). *Learning with computers*. Bedford, MA: Digital Press.

Bork, A. (1985). *Personal computers for education*. New York: Harper & Row.

Hunter, C., & Harman, D. (1979). *Adult illiteracy in the United States*. New York: McGraw-Hill.

Jones, E.V. (1981). *Reading instruction for the adult illiterate*. Chicago, IL: American Library Association.

Nickerson, R.S. (1985). Adult literacy and technology. *Visible Language, 19*, 311–355.

Park, R.J. (1987). Three approaches to improving literacy levels. *Educational Horizons, 66*, 38–41.

Reinking, D. (1988–89). Misconceptions about reading and software development. *The Computing Teacher, 16*(4), 27–29.

Rogers, J.J. (1987). Readability as a source of perceived failure in adult literacy instruction. *Lifelong Learning: An Omnibus of Practice and Research, 10*(4), 26–28.

Sinatra, R. (1987). Holistic applications in computer-based reading and language arts programs. *Computers in the Schools, 4*(1), 95–107.

Sloane, H.N., Gunn, C., Gordon, H.M., &

Mickelson, V.S. (1989). *Evaluating educational software—A guide for teachers*. Englewood Cliffs, NJ: Prentice Hall.

Turner, T.C. (1988). Using the computer for adult literacy instruction. *Journal of Reading, 31*, 643–647.

Turner, T.C., & Stockdill, S.H. (Eds.). (1987). *The technology for literacy project evaluation*. St. Paul, MN: St. Paul Foundation.

Wangberg, E.G. (1986). An interactive, language experience based microcomputer approach to reduce adult illiteracy. *Lifelong Learning, 9*, 8–12.

Wangberg, E.G., & Reutten, M.K. (1986). Whole language approaches for developing and evaluating basic writing ability. *Lifelong Learning: An Omnibus of Practice and Research, 9*(8), 13–15, 24–25.

Willing, K.R. (1988). Computer simulations: Activating content reading. *Journal of Reading, 31*, 400–409.

Yates, B.C., & Moursand, D. (1988–89). The computer and problem solving: How theory can support classroom practice. *The Computing Teacher, 16*(4), 12–16.

Figure 4
Sources (U.S.) and Compatibility of Software

Program	Publisher	Compatibility
Beginning level		
Explore-a-Story series	W. Bradford Publishing 310 School St. Acton MA 01720 800-421-2009	Apple II family
Language Experience Primary series (*Language Experience Recorder*, *Make-a-Flash*, *Sentence Starters*, and *Great Beginnings*)	Teacher Support Software PO Box 7130 Gainesville FL 32605 800-228-2871	Apple II family
Monsters and Make Believe	Queue, Inc. 338 Commerce Dr. Fairfield CT 06430 800-232-2224	IBM Apple II family Macintosh

(continued)

Figure 4
Sources (U.S.) and Compatibility of Software (*continued*)

Program	Publisher	Compatibility
Once Upon a Time	Compu-Teach Educational Software 78 Olive St. New Haven CT 06511 800-448-3224	IBM (and MS-DOS) Apple II family Macintosh Tandy
The Semantic Mapper (package B)	Teacher Support Software (see Language Experience Primary series)	Apple II family
Snoopy Writer	American School Publishers PO Box 4520 Chicago IL 60680 800-843-8855	Apple II family
Story Builder	American School Publishers (see *Snoopy Writer*)	Apple II family
Story Maker	Scholastic Software PO Box 7502 2931 E. McCarty St. Jefferson City MO 65102-9968 800-541-5513	Apple II family
Thinking Networks for Reading and Writing (Narrative levels 2 & 3; Theme level 3)	Think Network Inc. PO Box 6124 New York NY 10128 201-613-8977	Apple II family
Intermediate level		
The Children's Writing & Publishing Center	The Learning Co. 6493 Kaiser Dr. Fremont CA 94555 800-852-2255	most IBM (and MS-DOS) most Apple most Macintosh most Tandy
Graph Master	Grolier Educational Software Sherman Turnpike Danbury CT 06816 800-243-7256	Apple II family
InforMaster	Grolier Educational Software (see *Graph Master*)	Apple II family

(continued)

Figure 4
Sources (U.S.) and Compatibility of Software (*continued*)

Program	Publisher	Compatibility
Microzine series	Scholastic Software PO Box 7502 E. McCarty St. Jefferson City MO 65102 800-541-5513	Apple II family IBM (from edition 27 on)
Mystery Mazes	Educational Activities, Inc. PO Box 392 Freeport NY 11520 800-645-3739	Apple II family
The Oregon Trail	MECC 3490 Lexington Ave. N. St. Paul MN 55126 612-481-3500	Apple II family IBM (MS-DOS)
Playwriter series	Woodbury Software 42 Nikki Court Morganville NJ 07751 908-972-9695	Apple II family IBM Commodore 64
The Santa Fe Trail	Educational Activities, Inc. (see *Mystery Mazes*)	Apple IBM Tandy
The Secrets of Science Island	Houghton Mifflin Co. 101 Campus Dr. Princeton NJ 08540 800-257-9107	Apple
The Storyteller	Educational Activities, Inc. (see *Mystery Mazes*)	Apple II family
Super Solvers Midnight Rescue	The Learning Co. (see *The Children's Writing & Publishing Center*)	IBM (and MS-DOS) Tandy
Tales of Adventure	Scholastic Software (see Microzine series)	Apple IBM
Tales of Discovery	Scholastic Software (see Microzine series)	Apple II family IBM
Tales of Mystery	Scholastic Software (see Microzine series)	Apple II family IBM

(continued)

Figure 4
Sources (U.S.) and Compatibility of Software (*continued*)

Program	Publisher	Compatibility
Thinking Networks for Reading and Writing (Narrative levels 4–6; Theme levels 3–7)	Think Network, Inc. PO Box 6124 New York NY 10128 201-613-8977	Apple II family
Treasure Hunter	Houghton Mifflin Co. (see *The Secrets of Science Island*)	Apple II family
Advanced level		
The Americana Topic and Research Finder	Grolier Educational Software Sherman Turnpike Danbury CT 06816 800-243-7256	Apple II family
Annam	Educational Activities, Inc. PO Box 461 Coram NY 11727 516-223-4666	Apple Commodore TRS-80
The Colonial Merchant	Educational Activities, Inc. (see *Annam*)	Apple II family
Edu-Calc	Houghton Mifflin Co. 101 Campus Dr. Princeton NJ 08540 800-257-9107	Apple II family
Farewell Alaska	Grolier Educational Software (see *The Americana Topic and Research Finder*)	Apple II family
Hospital	Grolier Educational Software (see *The Americana Topic and Research Finder*)	Apple II family
Lincoln's Decisions	Educational Activities, Inc. (see *Annam*)	Apple IBM Macintosh
Note Card Maker	Houghton Mifflin Co. (see *Edu-Calc*)	IBM Apple II family Commodore

(*continued*)

Figure 4
Sources (U.S.) and Compatibility of Software (*continued*)

Program	Publisher	Compatibility
Publish It!	Timeworks Inc. 444 Lake Cook Rd. Deerfield IL 60015-4919 703-948-7626	Apple IBM Macintosh
Washington's Decisions	Educational Activities, Inc. (see *Annam*)	Apple IBM TRS-80
What Do They Do in Ougadougou	Educational Activities, Inc. (see *Annam*)	Apple IBM Tandy
Wordbench (student edition)	Addison-Wesley Publishing Co. Reading MA 01867-9984 617-944-6479	Apple II family IBM
Writing a Character Sketch	MECC 3490 Lexington Ave. N. St. Paul MN 55126 612-481-3500	Apple II family
Writing a Narrative	MECC (see *Writing a Character Sketch*)	Apple II family
Writing an Opinion Paper	MECC (see *Writing a Character Sketch*)	Apple II family

> " **It is time to stop viewing literacy as merely decoding graphemes and learning facts through text. Literacy should be seen as learning to decode and accommodate multiple levels of meaning through a complex system of social relations.** "
>
> – McCollum, 1991, p. 119

Tutors come with many educational philosophies; they also come in many guises. Purcell-Gates, Meyer and colleagues, and D'Annunzio all write of college literacy centers in which literacy instruction is provided by either graduate students in reading or undergraduate students. Nickse, Speicher, and Buchek describe an intergenerational beginning literacy program for parents and their children. Scoble, Topping, and Wigglesworth use family and friends of adult literacy students. Regardless of the model, all tutors in these articles were in the literacy field or received special training.

Tutoring of illiterate or low-literate adults is perhaps best examined through case studies, and four are included here: Gipe et al.'s story of Arthur, a nonspeaking adult male with cerebral palsy; Purcell-Gates's ethnographic study of Jenny, an Urban Appalachian mother; Scully and Johnston's use of an educa-tional therapy model with Chad, a first-generation Italian American; and Meyer et al.'s story of Norman, a 44-year-old described in school as "slow." I found myself analyzing these four studies for keys to success. All the students learned after establishing a personal relationship with a tutor who worked hard on bolstering the student's self-esteem; all showed great persistence; most learned by focusing, at least initially, on deficits or materials identified by themselves. Arthur reached a 6th- or 7th-grade level by starting with a great desire to learn to use a microcomputer, finding a personal friend in a tutor who—like himself—was a black male in his 30s, and participating in varied methods in 180 hours of instruction over 3 years. Jenny, over a 2-year period, learned through the use of a journal that she could write and read her own words. Through an acceptance of her "countrified words," the tutor was able to help

Jenny move to a level of functional reading. Chad was allowed to begin as he wanted to: with "sounding out and vowels." Over fifteen 90- to 120-minute sessions of educational therapy, he established a personal relationship based on trust with his therapist. Following work on phonics and sight vocabulary and more than 10 hours a week of independent practice, Chad's anxiety was relieved and, with that, he was able to read his own mail, a series of short stories, and more. Norman, as opposed to the other three, was never asked to memorize sight vocabulary. His tutor approached instruction from a whole language theory base. In less than one year Norman moved to a 6th- or 7th-grade level and to reading 7 to 12 hours on his own each week.

As with the history of methods studies (see, for example, Bond & Dykstra, 1967), these three case studies do not point to a single "correct" method. They do, however, fit in nicely with some of Cambourne's (1988) conditions for learning. Always present were serious attention to student choice, expectations for success, and ample opportunity to apply skills.

References

Bond, G.L., & Dykstra, R. (1967). The cooperative research program in first-grade reading instruction. Reading Research Quarterly, 2, 5–142.

Cambourne, B. (1988). The whole story: Natural learning and the acquisition of literacy in the classroom. *Richmond Hill, Ontario, Canada: Scholastic-TAB.*

McCollum, P. (1991). Cross-cultural perspectives on classroom discourse and literacy. In E.H. Hiebert (Ed.), Literacy for a diverse society (pp. 108–121). New York: Teachers College Press.

College Students as Tutors for Adults in a Campus-Based Literacy Program

ANTHONY D'ANNUNZIO

MARCH 1994

The Pennsylvania Literacy Corps, under the auspices of the Pennsylvania Department of Labor and Industry, has provided 3 years of funding to 13 competitively selected colleges and universities throughout the state to develop innovative literacy projects involving college students as tutors. These efforts needed to include the development of partnerships with local literacy-providing institutes to offer standard credit-bearing courses on literacy for volunteer college students and to provide classroom and tutorial space on campus.

Within this mandated structure, Drexel University, located in the city of Philadelphia, developed a model literacy corps program. Salient features included the use of three nonintrusive instructional procedures, the language-experience approach (LEA), individualized reading, and expressive writing. The procedures were nonintrusive in the sense that they encouraged the learners to take considerable initiative in their pursuit of reading and writing competency. These were combined with the pervasive use of nondirective counseling procedures in an attempt to establish an experiential, meaningful, whole-person learning situation. The adult learners were encouraged to set their own goals and determine how they should proceed. As is consistent with experiential learning, the tutors maintained a nondirective stance of unconditional positive regard in their partnership with the adult learners.

Specifics of the Project

The course, called Literacy Training and Participation, was limited to 15 undergraduate university students and was offered once each year for 3 successive years by the Department of Psychology/Sociology/Anthropology. The tutors, from second- to fourth-year, included a roughly equal distribution of academic majors with both sexes about equally represented. The offering was a standard, 10-week credit-bearing course in which 3 hours were spent in a classroom and 3 hours were devoted to volunteer tutoring each week. The Center For Literacy (CFL), the neighborhood literacy provider that offers a range of literacy services throughout the greater Philadelphia area, was selected as the Drexel partner since its own pedagogical philosophy was also nonintrusive.

The CFL arranged to have 15 adult learners come to Drexel for tutoring. Over the 3-year program the learner population consisted of inner city African Americans, ranging in age from 17 to 82, with both sexes about equally represented. They were mostly working in low-paying jobs that required few academic skills. They came for tutoring to "learn to read and write" and "better themselves."

After the Drexel tutors were interviewed to determine what sort of learner they'd prefer to work with (age and sex), each tutor was tentatively matched with an adult learner whose own preferences had been determined during an admission interview conducted by the CFL.

The first 3 weeks of the course were devoted to presenting the CFL's standard tutor and learner training program. During the first classroom session, only the tutors came. They were given an overview of selected chapters in a CFL handbook (Pomerance, 1988) dealing with the discovering of student goals, using the language experience approach (LEA), using individualized reading, and facilitating expressive writing.

During the second week, after the tutors and learners were paired and had gotten acquainted, the CFL staff guided the pairs through each chapter's procedures by demonstration and actual tutor and learner practice. The setting of learner goals and use of the LEA were completed.

During the third session, the pairs were exposed to individualized reading and expressive writing procedures. Each of the steps in the individualized reading format was practiced by the tutors and paired learners. This was followed by a get-acquainted introduction to expressive writing, including an attempt by the tutors and learners to set down a topic of their choosing in writing. Those learners who did not feel comfortable writing were encouraged to copy the LEA story they had just dictated to the tutors.

Finally, both the learners and tutors were introduced to the keeping of portfolios and journals. Samples were provided. Each tutor was encouraged to use the portfolio, containing all of the student's dated work, as the basis for a weekly appraisal of learner performance. The tutor journals contained a short rendition of each tutorial session as well as tutor thoughts and reactions to each week's encounters with the learners.

Tutoring Gets Underway

After the two training sessions, the tutors and students met twice each week for 1.5 hours of tutoring. The pairs were encouraged to meet, at least initially, in a student lounge where the project director was available to provide assistance. In many instances the pairs continued working toward the tentative goals they had set in the two training sessions. The tutors were encouraged to plan a part of every lesson reviewing the adult learners' interests or goals.

For the duration of the 10-week tutorial program, the tutors attended classes with the project director. During these classes the tutors were given thorough exposure to the LEA, individualized reading, expressive writing, and nondirective counseling. Also, during each college class, the tutors reviewed the week's tutorial sessions. Discussions, demonstrations, and comments concerning the procedures and tutor–learner interactions followed. During a class segment the tutors took turns presenting their journal summaries of the weekly tutoring sessions. This was followed by class discussions during which the tutors asked the project director for additional suggestions and demonstrations on the use of the four nondirective procedures. More will be said of these sessions later.

Examples of tutoring sessions and the procedural steps that were followed with three different learners are provided to exemplify the idiosyncratic nature of learner needs and interest.

The first learner. The learner in the first example, Jim, was raised in a sharecropping family. At age 82, he had never learned to read. He quickly relayed to the tutor how important the Bible was in his life and how wonderful it would be if he could read it. Jim brought in his Bible and the tutor read requested stories from it.

The tutor asked Jim if he would like to dictate his favorite stories. This introduced LEA (Cohen, 1981; Schneiderman, 1978; Stauffer, 1980). After Jim had dictated a story, the tutor pronounced and pointed to each word as it was written, reading the entire selection aloud. The tutor next pointed to each word, pacing Jim as they read the story together. Jim then attempted to read the story to the tutor while Jim underlined each word that was recognized. During their next session, Jim reread his story and again underlined words he had recognized. Any word that was recognized on two occasions was printed by itself on a separate sheet.

At the next session, the tutor used a window card to determine the ease and accuracy of recall. Words recognized in isolation provided the deposits for Jim's word bank. Each word was printed by the tutor on an index card and placed in random order in Jim's index box. When the word bank exceeded 30 words or so, Jim was introduced to alphabetizing and then to the dictionary. His word bank was used as the basis for a variety of word recognition activities, including the development of visual-auditory discrimination skills, finding word families, composing sentences with the word cards, and so forth.

The LEA possessed some distinct advantages for Jim. It made use of his own experience and promoted reading as a byproduct of his thinking and oral expression. Reading became easier and more enjoyable since the reading materials matched his language patterns and speaking vocabulary (Ben-Barka, 1982; Dixon & Nessel, 1983). This one-on-one personalized learning situation, in which Jim was permitted to take the initiative in determining his goals, significantly enhanced his learning efficiency and self-image.

Once Jim was able to recognize 50 or so words at sight, he was encouraged to select a book he might be interested in reading, which introduced him to individualized reading. Jim and his tutor met at a neighborhood public library where Jim became a member. Finding a number of books relating to the Bible, he leafed through each book to determine which he would read, selecting one that did not appear "too hard." Jim read it to himself. At this point the tutor engaged Jim in an individual conference, which gave the tutor the opportunity to observe Jim's skills in word recognition, comprehension, and oral and silent reading. Within a week Jim selected another book and presented it to the tutor for a conference the following week.

The conferences provided the opportunity for instruction in areas of weakness, as well as for guidance and support. Jim's tutor spent time discussing current reading choices and the progress being made. As is the case with the LEA, individualized reading is a basically nondirective procedure. Through his self-seeking, self-selection, and self-pacing, Jim was allowed to take additional initiatives, which continued to increase his self-esteem and academic progress.

The second learner. Another learner, Frank, brought in maps of his statewide truck routes the first time he met alone with his tutor. After spending some time with his tutor on map interpretation, Frank dictated a story concerning the difficulties he had in accessing unfamiliar truck routes and locations. Frank knew most of the words in his experience story at sight. Frank had already, during the two sessions with the CFL staff, selected a book to read. He took it home to read, and a conference was conducted by the tutor at the next session. Having joined the public library,

Frank brought a completed book each week for a conference. During this time, he continued to give LEA dictations.

The tutor asked if Frank would like to write his own story, thus continuing Frank's storytelling through expressive writing. The basic assumption here was that the most efficient means of developing written expression was to have Frank write and write, the more the better. The point was to encourage the flow of written expression, unhampered by spelling or correct English usage, so that Frank would naturally acquire syntactical facility and gradually attempt to use more sophisticated construction (Blot & Davidson, 1984; Parry & Hornsby, 1988; Rockcastle, 1986).

Frank enjoyed rereading his initial paragraph-length stories aloud to his tutor. He did not write in sentences and his spelling showed phonetic guessing. As Frank read his stories the tutor would point out that periods should be placed whenever he came to a natural halt in his oral reading, thus providing a quick minilesson. Developmentally appropriate minilessons continued as Frank rapidly gained in syntactical facility. At one point, for example, Frank attempted to use commas; he expressed a need, and a minilesson was in order.

In college class sessions, of which still more will be said later, the project director guided the tutors in making only those corrections on a student's written story that were compatible with the level of writing competency. It would have accomplished little to give Frank a lesson on quotation marks when he could not yet write complete sentences. Correcting all of his mistakes would have been overwhelming. Within 8 or 9 weeks, additional minilessons were given on compound sentences, quotation marks, and so forth, as he continued to progress.

Frank and his tutor also continued their map reading, and within weeks Frank reported that he was having less difficulty using maps to find new locations. He continued reading one, and sometimes two, books each week, with reading conferences during and at the end of each book. During the conference the tutor spent time discussing current and future reading choices, reviewing Frank's reading records, checking comprehension of silent reading, and providing individualized instruction in reading skills (Spache & Spache, 1986). Here too, developmentally appropriate minilessons were given as the need for them arose, including lessons on such thinking skills as getting the main idea, sequencing, noting detail, summarizing, and so forth.

The third learner. The learner in the last example, Louise, could read and write with fair proficiency. She readily admitted to her tutor that her major problem was herself. Now in her early 40s, Louise saw little hope of ever getting out of her present rut, having been a cleaning lady in a business office for the past 15 years. At the instigation of her daughter, she finally decided to "get some help with my reading and writing so maybe I could get into a business school and do good." She was never a success in school and "just got passed along and graduated." She was quite apprehensive about coming to a tutor, believing herself to be out of place.

Through nondirective, incidental counseling, Louise was provided the opportunity of venting her personal problems in a safe and accepting milieu. The tutor was able to enter into Louise's phenomenal world. It became clear that Louise was suffering from a profound sense of inferiority concerning academic pursuits and needed to establish a trust in her own experiences in the tutorial setting (Rogers, 1983).

It seemed important to the tutor that Louise be given the opportunity to experience immediate success in reading and writing. To this end she was encouraged to dictate the feelings she had expressed about schooling to her tutor. This became the basis for an experience story. She continued giving dictations for the next 2 weeks and then decided to write down her feelings on her own.

Developmentally appropriate minilessons were given by the tutor whenever the need arose, although Louise exhibited well-developed writing skills. She continued her writing until the seventh week when, accompanied by her tutor, Louise became a public library member and selected an easy book to read. Conferences revealed that Louise read with little difficulty. She stated that she would try to "read something harder." By the last tutorial session, Louise decided she would enroll in a General Education Diploma program as a refresher and then enter a business school. "Talking out my problems," she stated, "helped me gain more confidence."

Tutors in the College Classroom

In addition to monitoring the progress being made in these tutoring sessions and offering suggestions and demonstrations on how to proceed methodologically, an important classroom task for the project director was to engender within the tutors an attitude of empathetic understanding and genuine, unpossessing caring. This was attempted by highlighting the following (Corsini, 1979; Rogers, 1970):

1. Understanding the world of the literacy student as he or she sees it.

2. Avoiding any behavior toward the student that was overtly or covertly judgmental.

3. Avoiding any behavior toward the learner that expressed approval or disapproval or that was unnecessarily probing or interpretive.

4. Completely trusting the learner's resources for self-understanding and positive change.

5. Allowing the learner's experiences to be the tutor's for a moment, and feeling what it would be like to live the experience of the learner.

During the remaining sessions the tutors practiced nondirective counseling with each other and with their literacy students during tutoring. Rather than being superimposed, nondirective counseling was a natural outgrowth of the intensely interpersonal relationships between the tutors and students, fostered by the LEA, individualized reading, and expressive writing. Each learning interaction became, in effect, an incidental nondirective counseling opportunity where the learners were able to vent their personal problems safely. The pedagogical and motivational advantages of such personal involvement have been demonstrated (Boyd & Martin, 1984; Clabby & Belz, 1985; Johnson, 1985).

Another class presentation to the tutors included the use of the Fernald-Keller approach (Fernald, 1943; Wilson & Cleland, 1985). Students who made little progress after a trial with the LEA were introduced to the LEA combined with visual, auditory, kinesthetic and tactile (VAKT) stimulation. With this nonintrusive technique, LEA procedures were followed, but words with which the learner experienced continued difficulty were printed on paper and traced by the student as each syllable was pronounced. Wilson and Cleland (1985, p. 222) have defined the VAKT procedure. Finger tracing the word while pronouncing its syllables was repeated until it appeared that the word had been mastered. The student was then directed to reproduce the word without the copy, while again pronouncing each syllable. Since this is a whole word technique, the student neither spells the word nor sounds out the letters. Four of the adult learners, who continued to experience unusual difficulty in acquiring a basic sight vocabulary in the context of their LEA stories, were introduced to this procedure and began to make slow but certain progress.

Class time was also devoted to presenting the Laubach (Meyer & Keefe, 1988) method of literacy training to the tutors to interface with their nondirective reading formats. The Laubach method is fundamentally different, a "bottom-up" approach in which reading is seen as a series of steps beginning with the letters of the alphabet that stand for specific sounds. These letters and sounds are put together to form words. Words are practiced in short sentences and paragraphs emphasizing phonic regularities. Reading is viewed as essentially a process of phonics mastery and the learning of specific skills.

The Program's Effectiveness

Having carefully reviewed 19 successful adult literacy program descriptions, Padak and Padak (1991) provided questions to guide program evaluation. These questions were paraphrased under six rubrics, three of which were particularly relevant to the Drexel program (p. 348):

1. Academic achievement—To what extent do learners and tutors believe that academic progress has been made?

2. Quality of life—To what extent has learners' self-confidence as readers and writers increased? To what extent have learners achieved their own goals? To what extent has learner self-esteem increased?

3. Program content—To what extent does the program content meet learners' functional and academic needs and interests? What is the quality of the social context for instruction such as interactions between learners and tutors? What theoretical principles about reading, writing, and learning underlie program content? What are tutor perceptions of program effectiveness?

The Drexel program's effectiveness was evaluated under these three rubrics.

Academic achievement. Weekly observations and analysis by CFL supervisors and the project director provided increasing evidence that the learners were making substantial academic progress toward their stated goals. As suggested by Biggs (1992), this monitoring focused on an analysis of learner reading performance and writing samples, as well as learner portfolios and tutor journal entries.

The learners were also asked to participate in the evaluation by interpreting their own reading and writing behavior each week with their tutors: "I think I can now use periods in the right place," or "I see now that I have to read something easier." Learners were asked to evaluate their own progress since routine self-evaluations encouraged ownership in literacy learning (Padak & Padak, 1991). The learners were continually informed about strengths and weaknesses through conferences about their reading and writing. In this way, as suggested by Padak and Padak (1991), assessment both informed and enhanced instruction.

Another indication of the extent to which learners and tutors believed progress was being made was obtained through questionnaires and interviews. Staff, learners, and tutors completed a questionnaire developed by the Pennsylvania Governor's Office of Citizen Service (PennSERVE, 1991) to monitor the qualitative and quantitative progress of literacy programs funded by the Pennsylvania Department of Labor and Industry.

Over the 3-year period, more information was obtained through term-ending 2-hour discussions with the learners and 2-hour discussions with the tutors, conducted by two CFL supervisors and the project director. An analysis of their audiotape responses revealed that the tutors and the learners were unanimous in stating:

- that learners had made considerable progress in working toward their stated goals,
- that their collaboration in assessing progress provided learners with continuous feedback,
- that the learners' interests and functional literacy needs were met as a natural outgrowth of the nonintrusive learning procedures, and
- that rapid progress had been made in reading and writing.

Many learners believed their academic growth was so obvious that "anyone can see it." For many, progress in reading and writing was so rapid that it could not be explained along the lines of skill enhancement. Although the majority of the learners initially claimed that their reading and writing abilities were nonexistent or marginal, their performance, as their self-confidence became enhanced, belied their initial self-depreciation.

Since 10 weeks did not provide sufficient instructional time for an evaluation by standardized test performance, such testing was conducted on those learners who continued with the Drexel tutors and remained for at least 1 year. This included 5 students from the first year (1989–1990), 6 from the second year, and 7 from the third year. Combining the 3-year totals for the 18 learners revealed a mean pretest level of first grade on the Diagnostic Reading Scales (DRS) and a 2.1 grade level on the Wide Range Achievement Test–Revised (WRAT-R) word recognition subtest. Posttest scores improved to Grade 4 in comprehension (DRS) and to 5.6 in word recognition. These results were contrasted with a typical growth expectation of 1.5 reading grade levels per year, cited by Diekhoff (1988) and based on a follow-up study of literacy program effectiveness.

It should be noted that many of the learners did not remain in the program after the 10-week period, having stated that they were reading and writing well enough to go directly into a GED program. Thus those students who made some of the most rapid academic strides were not available for the 1-year posttesting.

Quality of life. An analysis of the questionnaires and audiotaped interview data confirmed what the tutor and staff observations had discerned during the program: a dramatic increase in learners' self-confidence as readers and writers, as well as their self-esteem as persons. The major reason given by the learners for this positive attitudinal change was the climate of acceptance and tutor willingness to listen and encourage the learners to talk out their personal problems. The majority of the learners and all of the tutors expressed the belief that using the LEA, individualized reading, and expressive writing fostered a high degree of personal involvement.

The tutors were unanimous in stating that the nondirectiveness of the tutor-learner encounter was instrumental in increasing the effectiveness of instruction. This aligns with Reder (1992), who stated that program designers and policy makers should carefully consider whether participation in activities besides formal course instruction facilitates literacy development.

The majority of the tutors noted that the learners had more or less accepted distorted beliefs about African-American ability to achieve academically. Biggs (1992) offered that African Americans accept this stereotype as a reflection of reality. When interviewed, the learners admitted to this perception of themselves but had begun to positively modify this self-image. The learners cited the personal involvement with their tutors that encouraged them to discuss their needs, interests, and problems, as the most conspicuous feature of their image modification.

The tutors were unanimous in stating that the nondirective, incidental counseling skills that they had developed encouraged them to listen to their learners in a more intense and empathetic way. And this empathetic listening had an unexpected carryover into all of their interpersonal encounters.

Program content. An essential beginning point for program development was to have, as Padak and Padak (1991) have suggested, a clear focus of what constitutes learning. Any detailing for the design of practice needs to begin with such a focus (Lambert, 1986). The program exemplified what Rogers (1983) called experiential learning. Such learning has the quality of personal involvement, is self-initiated, is pervasive, is evaluated by the learner, and has meaning as its essence. The learners established their own instructional goals and continuously evaluated their progress. This helped assure that the program content met learners' functional academic needs and interests. The social context for instruction was one of complete openness and unconditional positive regard. As Padak and Padak (1987, pp. 495–496) stated, "Effective adult reading programs address literacy in light of learners' cognitive, affective, and social needs."

A major objective of the project was the involvement of college students as adult literacy tutors. In their questionnaire responses and end of program discussion, all the tutors expressed the desire to continue as volunteer tutors. Records kept over the 3 years of the project revealed that of the 11 tutors from the first year who could be reached, 9 were still engaged in some tutorial capacity. For those college students who began in the second and third years of the project, responses accumulated thus far revealed much the same retention rate. Many of the former project tutors expressed the belief in year-end questionnaires that their continued tutoring effort added a new dimension to their lives, one of responsible service to those in need.

References

Ben-Barka, A.C. (1982). LEA *as a methodology for use with semi-literate* ESOL *adolescents: A case study* (A thesis report). ERIC ED 239 510.

Biggs, S.A. (1992). Building on strengths: Closing the literacy gap for African Americans. *Journal of Reading, 35,* 624–628.

Blot, D., & Davidson, D. (1984). *Write from the start.* New York: Newbury House.

Boyd, R.D., & Martin, L.G. (1984). A methodology for the analysis of the psychological profiles of low literate adults. *Adult Education Quarterly, 34*(2), 85–96.

Clabby, J.F., & Belz, E.J. (1985). Psychological barriers to learning: Approach to group treatment. *Small Group Behavior, 16*(9), 525–533.

Cohen, J. (1981). *A reading and writing program using language experience methodology among adult* ESL *students in a basic education program.* Washington, DC: Office of Vocational and Adult Education.

Corsini, R. (1979). *Current psychotherapies.* Itasca, IL: Peacock.

Diekhoff, G.M. (1988). An appraisal of adult literacy programs: Reading between the lines. *Journal of Reading, 31,* 624–630.

Dixon, C., & Nessel, D. (1983). Language experience reading for second language learners. In C. Dixon (Ed.), *Language experience approach to reading (and writing).* Hayward, CA: Alemany.

Fernald, G.M. (1943). *Remedial techniques in basic school subjects* (pp. 320-329). New York: McGraw-Hill.

Johnson, P.H. (1985). Understanding reading disability: A case study. *Harvard Educational Review, 55*(2), 153–177.

Lambert, H.M. (1986). Engineering new designs for school psychological service delivery. *Professional School Psychology, 1*, 295–300.

Meyer, V., & Keefe, D. (1988). The Laubach way to reading: A review. *Lifelong Learning, 12*, 8–10.

Padak, N.D., & Padak, G.M. (1987). Guidelines and a holistic method for adult basic reading programs. *Journal of Reading, 30*, 490–496.

Padak, N.D., & Padak, G.M. (1991). What works: Adult literacy program evaluation. *Journal of Reading, 34*, 374–379.

Parry, J.A., & Hornsby, D. (1988). *Write on: A conference approach to writing.* Portsmouth, NH: Heinemann.

PennSERVE, The Governor's Office Citizen Service. (1991). Harrisburg, PA: Pennsylvania Department of Labor & Industry.

Pomerance, A. (1988). *Center For Literacy basic training handbook* (3rd ed.). Philadelphia, PA: Center For Literacy.

Reder, S. (1992). Research raises several important issues. *Mosaic: Research notes on literacy, 2*(2) 3-4.

Rockcastle, V.N. (1986). Nothing succeeds like succession. *Science and Children, 23*(7), 20–21.

Rogers, C.R. (1970). *Carl Rogers encounter groups.* New York: HarperCollins.

Rogers, C. (1983). *Freedom to learn.* Columbus, OH: Charles E. Merrill.

Schneiderman, P. (1978). Active reading techniques systems (ARTS): A method for instruction of functionally illiterate adults. *Urban Education, 3*, 195–202.

Spache, G.D., & Spache, E. (1986). *Reading in the elementary school.* Boston: Allyn & Bacon.

Stauffer, R.G. (1980). *The language-experience approach to the teaching of reading* (2nd ed.). New York: HarperCollins.

Wilson, R.M., & Cleland, C.J. (1985). *Diagnostic and remedial reading for classroom and clinic.* Columbus, OH: Charles E. Merrill.

An Intergenerational Adult Literacy Project: A Family Intervention/ Prevention Model

RUTH S. NICKSE
ANN MARIE SPEICHER
PAMELA C. BUCHEK
APRIL 1988

Several theorists and observers in the field of adult literacy suggest the importance of an intergenerational instructional approach (Fingeret, 1984; Fox, 1986; Harman, 1987; Sticht, 1983). Descriptions of creative programs which combine adult and children's literacy efforts are entering the literature (Nickse & Englander, 1985, 1986). And the federal government of the United States, alerted to the possible connections between adult and child literacy, has attempted to influence adult and child literacy policy by introducing Even Start legislation.

Adult literacy programs that are combined with efforts to improve early childhood literacy are overdue and gain support from several complementary lines of current research: concern with parental roles in schools and schooling (Cochran & Henderson, 1986; Lightfoot,

Figure 1
Parents' Effects on Children's Reading Achievement

Research Topic	Authors	Summary of Findings
A. Home environment	Chandler et al., 1983 Chall et al., 1982 Heath, 1980, 1983 Hewison & Tizard, 1980 Smith, 1971 Teale, 1978, 1986	Availability and range of materials in home are important; ("everyday print,"—labels, magazines, newspapers—necessary; many ways parents can arrange for children to come into contact with print; homes devoid of books and lacking curiosity about world inhibit child's enthusiasm for learning in school.)
B. Shared reading activities	Chall et al., 1982 Chomsky, 1972 Clay, 1979 Smith, 1971 Taylor, 1983 Teale, 1984, 1986	Parents' reading to children is important; being read to is fundamental to early literacy development; demonstrates concept of print, books, reading, and form and structure of written language; is major correlate with language maturity and reading achievement; creates shared bond as base for positive literacy experiences in home which support reading and writing practices.
C. Parents as reading models	Chall et al., 1982 Duff & Adams, 1981 O'Rourke, 1979	Parents are child's first and most influential teacher; parents act as models for reading behavior; "printworm" parents' children test higher in word recognition and reading comprehension; early reading preparation and supportive home environment promote reading as natural life process; children of mothers with higher literacy levels outperform children of non-reading mothers at 6th-grade level.
D. Parents' attitudes toward education	Anderson & Stokes, 1984 Chall, 1979, 1982 Coleman, 1966 Durkin, 1964 Laosa, 1978 Lengyel & Baghban, 1980	Parents' aspirations and attitudes toward children's education create positive environment that supports literacy development; parents with high expectations more likely to have children who achieve; as children grow, parental expectations have greater impact; positive parental behavior encourages children's school achievement; non-literate parents can be aware of importance of literacy and supportive because of constraints of limited literacy in own life; one mother became role model, improving own basic skills and teaching them to child; mother's education related to how she thinks about and behaves toward her children, which affects their school achievement; educated parents provide more materials and activities which promote literacy and become more involved in children's school instruction.

1973; Sinclair et al., 1980); the importance of family literacy in preparing children to read (Heath, 1983); parents' roles in encouraging school achievement (Clark, 1983); and findings that adults in tutoring programs who have children in school tend to stay longer in tutoring programs (Heathington, 1984). The research suggests that further study would be fruitful to determine whether a literacy program aimed at parents *and* their children would improve literacy for both groups. Reading aloud to children is the single most important factor in preparing them to read (Anderson, 1985), yet millions of parents with poor reading skills cannot engage in this effort because of their own reading deficiencies, and millions of others have neither the knowledge of its importance nor the skills to read to their children.

The short-term effects of the illiteracy cycle are felt daily by individuals and families. The long-term consequences of this continuing cycle include the lack of parental reading models, in-school reading problems, and poor attitudes toward reading and education in general. The case for improving family literacy seemed sufficiently strong to warrant the design of an intergenerational adult basic education and literacy program at Boston University. In 1983, at the request of the U.S. Department of Education, Nickse (Nickse, 1985; Nickse & Englander, 1986; Staryos & Winig, 1985) developed the Collaborations for Literacy model, which seeks to develop a new format for adult literacy services, action research, and materials development. It employed college students as literacy workers and paid them through the Federal College Work-Study program (Nickse, 1984). The newly established Family Learning Center (1987) subsumes the part-time program at a newly renovated site provided by the university. In the past 4 years, more than 50 undergraduates supervised by graduate students and faculty from the School of Education have been trained, paid, and have received optional academic credit for work as literacy tutors. They have provided reading instruction to more than 150 ethnically, educationally, and socioeconomically diverse urban adults in a part-time, intergenerational, one-on-one tutoring program.

In 1986, the Boston University project began collaborating with the Boston Public Schools to identify and focus recruitment on parents of Chapter 1 children in a comprehensive adult literacy intervention-prevention model. With a grant from the Office of Educational Research and Improvement, the staff is exploring the effectiveness of this intergenerational approach to family reading instruction. A brief literature review, the design of the study and some preliminary data follow. It is hoped that our experiences in this pilot program can guide others in similar action research.

Literature Review

At present, there is no coherent body of research available that directly addresses the intergenerational literacy instruction of adults through the use of special literacy techniques. Figure 1 summarizes evidence from a variety of research reports about parents' activities and home environment factors that seem to impact children's reading achievement.

The Study

With a grant from the U.S. Department of Education Office of Educational Research and Improvement, the co-principal investigators (Nickse & Paratore) were exploring the effectiveness of an intergenerational approach to adult literacy instruction. Two research questions were being examined: Does an intergenerational approach have a positive impact on adult beginning readers' progress and retention? Do children of parents enrolled in an intergenerational reading project show gains in reading and language arts achievement and improved attitudes toward reading and learning? Preliminary data on the first question are reported; the analysis of the effects on children were incomplete at this writing.

Study subjects were recruited from a targeted pool of parents with children in federally funded Chapter 1 reading programs who lived in multicultural, urban sections of Boston. A school-based coordinator, familiar with school district reading programs and with the community, contacted parents and informed them of the purposes and requirements of the intergenerational program. The demographic profiles of the 30 adult participants studied as of June 1987 are reported. These individuals completed 30, 40, or 50 hours of tutoring in 2- or 3-hour weekly sessions over 5–8 months and completed pre- and posttests on a standardized reading test.

Minority parents represented 83% of the adult participants (Asian, 23%; Hispanic, 23%; and black, 37%) and white parents the remaining 17%. Women participants (70%) outnumbered men participants (30%) more than two to one. Only 20% of subjects were unemployed, but nearly three-fourths (70%) had dropped out of school before earning a high school diploma. English was a second language for 40% of the subjects. The 30 subjects had a total of 44 children of school age—59% of their children were in primary school. Only a few subjects had preschool children; the remaining children were already in middle school or high school. Almost half of the adult program participants (47%) were between the ages of 35 and 44. Their reasons for program participation show the benefits of targeted recruitment: 40% gave "helping their children" as a primary motive for enrollment; 40% mentioned "improvement of their own reading and writing skills"; and 30% mentioned "self-improvement" as an important factor in participation.

Intervention Techniques

For the 1986–1987 year, the Family Learning Center staff incorporated several procedures to strengthen and support its basic teaching curriculum, focusing on creating a supervised, supportive teaching environment for the adults while modeling literacy prevention and intervention techniques for the parent and child. The procedures in use during the weekly sessions follow:

1. Tutors design lesson plans and use a four-step model (demonstration, guided practice, independent practice, and evaluation) identified as important to successful teaching (Rosenshine & Stevens, 1984). The focus is on decoding (phonics or structural analysis), vocabulary, reading and listening comprehension, study skills, and writing.

2. Staff observe tutors and learners during instruction and provide weekly consultation. Tutors model learning activities for parents to use with children and frequently design lessons for parent and child; tutors model these lessons for the parent and observe the parent teaching the child. Tutors encourage parents to practice independently at home and demonstrate the advantages of shared parent and child activities by taking field trips with them to local libraries and area museums.

3. The Center provides literacy events ("socials") for parents and children concerning shared reading and home activities (for example, showing the Jim Trelease "Read Aloud Handbook" movie or holding a Parents and Children Reading Together Workshop).

4. The Center provides weekly inservice sessions for tutors on topics related to literacy, prevention and intervention techniques, and teaching strategies (for example, Teaching Basic Reading and Math Skills or Selecting Appropriate Life Skills Materials).

Literacy Tutors

The tutors are the primary providers of instruction to adult participants. Boston University tutors are work-study students who are paid US$7 an hour, 12 hours a week for two semesters. For 1986–1987, tutor retention for the 9-month academic period was 90%. Tutors often return for a second or third year to their tutoring positions and may elect optional college credit. They are socially committed, mature, patient, and motivated to teach adults and children to improve reading skills and attitudes. They are 19–23 years old; 92% are undergraduates; 8% are graduate students; and 35% are education majors.

Each work-study student receives about 112 hours of training by professionals in reading and adult education: 18 hours of initial training; mandated 2-hour weekly inservice training (for two semesters or 56 hours); and weekly personal observation and supervision (two semesters, 28 hours). Intergenerational methods are stressed in all training and inservice. Tutors individually instruct two adult learners in weekly 3-hour sessions.

While tutors have considerably more training than most volunteers, the 3-hour weekly instructional session is typical of many volunteer literacy programs.

Results and Discussion

Preliminary data are reported on the effects of participation by adults ($n = 30$) on two dimensions: reading progress in vocabulary and comprehension and retention in the program. Results to date seem to indicate that reading gains (ABLE, 1986) on vocabulary and comprehension increase as a factor of the number of hours of tutoring (see Figure 2).

The lowest level learners are pretested on ABLE (Level 1) normed at the 1.0–5.3 level. If those learners score at a 6th level grade equivalent on the comprehension section, they are posttested on ABLE (Level 2) normed at 5.4–11.11. This change in forms may affect individual scores and thus the average gains.

Retention

Nationwide, only 30–50% of those in Adult Basic Education (ABE) programs stay in the program for 1 year (Balmuth, 1985). Enrollment officially begins after the learner has received 12 hours of instruction. For those "enrolled" in the program, the retention rate is 73.3%. Of the 26.7% who left after "enrollment," 50% withdrew because they were able to find new or better employment (which cre-

Figure 2
Adult Reading Progress

Number of tutoring hours	Number of SSs (N = 30)	Vocabulary average gain	Comprehension average gain
50-41	13	0.8	1.0
40-31	9	0.5	0.7
30-25	8	-0.2	0.5

Gains as estimated by the Adult Basic Learning Exam (ABLE), Levels 1 and 2; given as portion of a year in grade level.

ated scheduling difficulties) or felt qualified to pursue more advanced ABE education or training.

Learners in the study are parents of children who already are identified as having reading difficulty; they have a high interest in and concern for helping their children. The program design fits individual needs and also stresses continued focus on activities related to improving children's literacy. This observation seems to confirm that of Heatherington (1984), that adults in tutoring programs who have children in school tend to stay longer in tutoring programs. A number of parents expressed pride in their children's progress in school based on teachers' comments to them. The parents attributed this growth to their increased work with their children.

A primary objective of the project is to change behaviors to improve the literacy climate in the home. The staff responds positively to progress by the adult and the family as a learning unit. Through direct conversation, activities, and special events, plus positive examples and modeling, tutors let parents know they share their concern for improved literacy at home. These factors also seem to contribute to retention of adult learners in the program.

As a condition for acceptance into the program, we asked parents to read to their child for 10 minutes a day. When tutors reported that parents were not reading to children, we realized our expectations were unrealistic, and we substituted an expanded list of literacy-related activities. The results were exciting (see Figure 3). Although in use for only 6 weeks, the expanded idea of "reading" seems to be both better understood by the adult learners and more within their capabilities and current lifestyles. Tutors who had suggested activities on this list reported a gradual increase in these kinds and occurrences of home literacy events.

Conclusions and Recommendations

This pilot study focuses on the improvement of adults' literacy in support of their own improved reading skills and the subsequent effects on their children who are in Chapter 1 reading programs. The work is in progress, and not all research results collected have been analyzed. However, based on 4 years' experience using an intergenerational tutoring approach, some preliminary conclusions can be drawn and several recommendations made.

1. Support for the concept of intergenerational learning must be built and marketed in the local community through calculated and direct messages. Such targeted recruitment is best done in cooperation with local and public schools.

2. At both national and local levels, policy should stress intergenerational learning as an

Figure 3
Checklist of Literacy-Related Activities

Read to child	Listened to child read a book
Helped with homework	
Asked about homework	Looked at homework
Wrote note or message to child	Bought a book
Played a word game	Visited a library with child
Viewed TV together and discussed it	Helped child write letter or send letter or greeting card
Other shared activity	Asked child about school or reading

intervention-prevention strategy, and such programs should be funded.

3. Intergenerational curriculum should be mixed with personal and career-related tasks and literacy events. Adults need to build self-confidence through work on their own learning agendas as well as improving their children's literacy. A mix of both kinds of assignments will maintain adult enthusiasm and provide an important social element.

4. Adults can model literacy-related behaviors only when they have been successful with these behaviors and feel confident that they can accomplish them in their current home environment. Their increased self-esteem as readers and improved shared activities in the home appear to them to transfer to their children.

5. Project experience has confirmed our opinion that literacy is more than the teaching of specific technical skills in reading, writing, and math. Particularly in a multicultural community context, where parental attitudes and values about literacy, schools and schooling, and education in general are varied and where discourse is limited and reading is not a family habit, direct instruction in increasing literacy events must be accompanied by constant reminders and support by tutors for changed parental behaviors. If they haven't been read to, children may reject parental overtures, preferring to watch television; many parents need modeling and coaching by tutors to help them know how to improve communications with their children before attempting to read to and with them.

6. Tutors need to be well-trained for one-to-one and intergenerational tutoring. To be effective in teaching reading to adult literacy students, they must be supported and constantly supervised by professionals. There cannot be "too much training" when the range of individual reading problems among adults in the population is so vast and complex.

7. The bonding relationship so valued between tutors and learners has to stretch to include children and other family members in order to improve the family's attitude toward reading. We have found that this is important for participant retention, motivation, and shared reading activities.

8. A broad perspective on the concept of literacy and the home and school events which promote it is imperative. Attitudes and values about education provide the context for basic skill improvement. They are not byproducts of instruction but the primary focus of direct instruction in families where literacy is undervalued.

9. In our experience, any instructional model relying on 2–3 hours of reading instruction a week is insufficient for beginning or new adult readers. For measurable reading progress in these learners, hours of direct instruction must be doubled as a desirable minimum with daily practice. This is a considerable time commitment for busy adults.

10. While the phrase "the only degree you need is a degree of caring" perhaps describes the personal relationships so important in literacy tutoring connections, its effects should not be confused with the effects of skilled professional reading instruction. There are no "quick fixes" in literacy. This intergenerational project is a first effort in working at the heart of literacy improvement—the family and its home.

References

Anderson, A.B., & Stokes, S.J. (1984). Social and institutional influences on the development and practice of literacy. In H. Goelman, A. Oberg, & F. Smith (Eds.), *Awakening to literacy*. Portsmouth, NH: Heinemann.

Anderson, R.C., Hiebert, E.H., Scott, J.A., & Wilkinson, I.A.G. (1985). *Becoming a nation of* readers: The report of the Commission on Reading. Washington, DC: National Institute of Education, U.S. Department of Education.

Balmuth, M. (1986). Essential characteristics of adult literacy programs: A review and analysis of the research. Unpublished paper. (ED 273 823)

Chall, J. (1979). The great debate: Ten years later with a modest proposal for reading stages. In L.B. Resnick & P.A. Weaver (Eds.), Theory and practice of early reading. Hillsdale, NJ: Erlbaum.

Chall, J., & Snow, C. (1982). Families and literacy: The contribution of out-of-school experiences to children's acquisition of literacy (National Institute of Education Final Report). Cambridge, MA: Graduate School of Education, Harvard University. (ED 234 345)

Chandler, J., et al. (1983). Parents as teachers: Observations of low-income parents and children in a homework-like task (NIE Contract #G-80-0086 Technical Report). Cambridge, MA: Graduate School of Education, Harvard University. (ED 231 812)

Chomsky, C. (1972, February). Stages in language development and reading exposure. Harvard Educational Review, 42, 1–33.

Clark, R. (1983). Family life and school achievement: Why poor black children succeed or fail. Chicago, IL: University of Chicago Press.

Clay, M.M. (1979). Reading: The patterning of complex behavior (2nd ed.). Portsmouth, NH: Heinemann.

Cochran, M., & Henderson, C.R. (1986). Family matters: Evaluation of the parental empowerment program (NIE Final Report; Contract #400-76-0150; Comparative Ecology of Human Development Project). Ithaca, NY: Cornell University. (ED 262 862)

Coleman, J.S. (1966). Equality of educational opportunity. Washington, DC: U.S. Government Printing Office.

Duff, R.E., & Adams, M.E. (1981, January). Parents and teachers: Partners in improving reading skills. The Clearing House, 54, 207–209.

Durkin, D. (1966). Children who read early. New York: Teachers College Press.

Fingeret, A. (1984). Adult literacy education: Current and future directions. Columbus, OH: ERIC Clearinghouse on Adult, Career, and Vocational Education. (ED 246 308)

Fox, M. (1986). Personal communication.

Harman, D. (1987). Illiteracy: A national dilemma. New York: Cambridge Book Company.

Heath, S.B. (1980, Winter). The functions and uses of literacy. Journal of Communication, 30, 123–133.

Heath, S.B. (1983). Ways with words: Language, life, and work in communities and classrooms. Cambridge, UK: Cambridge University Press.

Heathington, B.S., Boser, J., & Satter, T. (1984, February). Characteristics of adult beginning readers who persisted in a volunteer tutoring program. Lifelong Learning: The Adult Years, 7, 20–28.

Hewison, J., & Tizard, J. (1980, November). Parental involvement and reading attainment. The British Journal of Educational Psychology, 50, 209–215.

Laosa, L. (1978, December). Maternal teaching strategies in Chicano families of varied educational and socioeconomic levels. Child Development, 49, 1129–1135.

Lengyel, J., & Baghban, M. (1980). The effects of a family reading program and SSR on reading achievement and attitudes. (ED 211 925)

Lightfoot, S.L. (1978). Worlds apart: Relationships between family and school. New York: Basic.

Nickse, R. (1984, September). The college work-study adult literacy project: A survey by the National Association of Student Employment Administrators.

Nickse, R., & Englander, N. (1985, Spring). At risk parents: Collaborations for literacy. Equity and Choice, 1, 11–18.

Nickse, R., & Englander, N. (1985). Administrator's handbook. Collaborations for literacy: An intergenerational reading project. Boston, MA: Trustees of Boston University.

O'Rourke, W.J. (1979, January). Are parents an influence on adolescent reading habits? Journal of Reading, 22, 340–343.

Rosenshine, B., & Stevens, R. (1984). Classroom instruction in reading. In P.D. Pearson (Ed.), Handbook of reading research. White Plains, NY: Longman.

Sinclair, R.L. (1980). A two-way street: Home-school cooperation in curriculum decision making. Boston, MA: Institute for Responsive Education.

Smith, C.B. (1971). The effect of environment on learning to read. Newark, DE: International Reading Association.

Staryos, M., & Winig, L. (1986). *Tutor's hand-book. Collaborations for literacy: An intergen-erational reading project.* Boston, MA: Trustees of Boston University.

Sticht, T. (1983). *Literacy and human resources development at work: Investing in the education of adults to improve the educability of children.* Alexandria, VA: Human Resources Research Organization.

Taylor, D. (1983). *Family literacy: Young children learning to read and write.* Portsmouth, NH: Heinemann.

Teale, W.H. (1978, November/December). Positive environments for learning to read: What studies of early readers tell us. *Language Arts, 55,* 922–932.

Teale, W.H. (1984). Reading to young children: Its significance for literacy development. In H. Goelman, A. Oberg, & F. Smith (Eds.), *Awakening to literacy.* Portsmouth, NH: Heinemann.

Teale, W.H., & Sulzby, E. (1986). Home back-ground and young children's literacy develop-ment. In *Emergent literacy: Writing and read-ing.* Norwood, NJ: Ablex.

T u t o r i n g

Training Family and Friends as Adult Literacy Tutors

JOHN SCOBLE
KEITH TOPPING
COLIN WIGGLESWORTH
FEBRUARY 1988

The proportion of adults who are dis-advantaged in their daily lives by a lack of functional reading skill is alarmingly high. Yet the severe eco-nomic and social effects of this widespread problem rarely hit the headlines. In adults, illiteracy is the hidden handicap. In the United Kingdom, it is estimated that 1.3 million ad-ults (6% of the population) have difficulty in reading (ALBSU, 1983). In the United States, Hunter and Harman (1979) estimated that there were at least 23 million adult illiterates, while the Office of Education puts the figure at 27 million—20% of the population. Very few of these are ever recruited into adult edu-cation basic skills courses—in the United Kingdom the proportion is estimated at 15% and in the United States at 5%.

Even for those enrolled in courses, owing to "the very part-time nature of the service, most students can only benefit from a severe-ly limited amount of tuition, despite the fact that many of them need intensive courses" (ALBSU, 1986). Nevertheless, in a U.K. study it is reported that over a period of 3 months, 25% of adult students made "rapid progress," 50% made "measurable progress," and 25% made "no progress" (ALBSU, 1981). Students commencing with higher levels of achievement who were "well supported by family or friends" gained most. However, no follow-up results are reported, so it is not known to what extent gains endured in the longer term.

Although in recent years provision has included the widespread use of volunteers, greater variety in the type of remedial courses offered, establishment of drop-in advice centers, packages for distance teaching, and computer assisted learning, much of the help available for the adult of low literacy remains very traditional in organization and methodology. Current approaches seem to hold little hope of solving this huge problem. New directions and radically different patterns of service delivery are needed. For these, new techniques may prove necessary.

The Paired Reading Technique

There has been a growing interest in the United Kingdom over the last decade in a variety of means for involving parents in the reading development of their children (Topping & Wolfendale, 1985). Some of the techniques articulated in this context have proved effective in the hands of other nonprofessional tutors, such as adult volunteers and peer tutors (Topping, 1987a, 1987b). The Paired Reading technique is probably the best researched of these innovations, and has demonstrated applicability and effectiveness with a very wide range of target children (see the bibliography in Topping, 1986a).

In Paired Reading, tutees are encouraged to choose their own reading material at *any* level of readability, provided this is within the competence of the *tutor*. Tutees can thus select books and other material of high interest to themselves irrespective of difficulty. The frequently reported problem of finding appropriate reading materials for adult literacy students is virtually eliminated, since no special materials are usually required. At its simplest, Paired Reading involves two phases. On sections of text that are difficult for the tutee, both tutor and tutee read out loud together, establishing synchrony with practice. When the tutee makes an error, the tutor merely repeats the word correctly and requires the tutee to do likewise before proceeding. When the tutee has selected an easier text that is more within her or his independent readability level, the tutee can choose to silence the tutor by a prearranged nonverbal signal. When the tutor becomes silent, the tutee continues to read out loud, until there is a failure to read a word correctly within 5 seconds, at which point the tutor corrects the error as described and the pair resume reading together. Praise at very regular intervals for correct reading and specific positive reading behaviors is emphasized throughout. Discussion of the text is an essential part of the method to ensure tutee comprehension, but this flows much more naturally with high interest materials. The method is outlined graphically in the figure. Further details of its application in practice will be found in Topping and Wolfendale (1985) and Topping (1986a).

Some of the features of the Paired Reading technique are of course found in other approaches to reading which bear different names, for example, Heckelman's (1986) "Neurological Impress Method (NIM)," the associated "Prime-O-Tec" strategy described by Meyer (1982), and the methods known as "Reading-While-Listening," "Assisted Reading," and "The Lap Method." However, the

Paired Reading Procedure

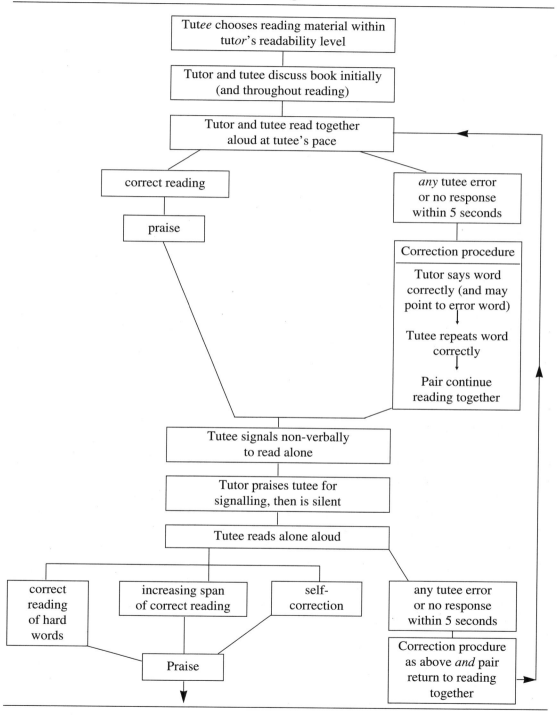

Tutee chooses reading material within tutor's readability level

Tutor and tutee discuss book initially (and throughout reading)

Tutor and tutee read together aloud at tutee's pace

correct reading

praise

any tutee error or no response within 5 seconds

Correction procedure

Tutor says word correctly (and may point to error word)

Tutee repeats word correctly

Pair continue reading together

Tutee signals non-verbally to read alone

Tutor praises tutee for signalling, then is silent

Tutee reads alone aloud

correct reading of hard words

increasing span of correct reading

self-correction

any tutee error or no response within 5 seconds

Correction procdure as above and pair return to reading together

Praise

value of Paired Reading is that within this technique many of the most valuable features of other methods are blended into a coherent package which permits widespread and successful use by nonprofessionals. One possible method of service delivery to adults of low literacy is to use Paired Reading within a college of further education, utilizing able students as tutors for adults involved in basic skills courses. Substantial success with the deployment of Paired Reading in this form of organization has been reported by Booth and Winter (1987). However, the technique clearly has the potential to be deployed effectively in open community settings, as has been widely demonstrated in the case of literate parents working with their own children. Thus, the organizational parameters for service delivery of Paired Reading to low literacy adults *in the natural environment* were delineated (Topping, 1986b), and after some weeks of discussion and planning, the Ryedale Adult Literacy Paired Reading Project commenced.

Training Procedure

Students who were already in some way in touch with the Adult Literacy organization in the rural Ryedale area of North Yorkshire were approached by their existing contacts to see whether they would be interested in participating in the "experiment." The importance of using existing relationships in communication networks was therefore evident right from the start. As tutees and their potential tutors were to be trained together, both needed to attend the initial training meeting. Tutees were asked to bring along someone they *already* met frequently, who would be prepared to help them with reading for a minimum of 5 minutes for 5 days each week during 6 weeks. Twelve "pairs" attended, and some tutees brought more than one potential

tutor. The eventual main tutors comprised 4 wives, 3 mothers, 1 daughter, and 1 friend.

In a group meeting, the project leaders acted out "How Not to Do It," demonstrating every possible form of bad practice. The group was then told about the aims and methods of the project, and the two phases of the Paired Reading technique were described in detail and demonstrated via role play between the project leaders. Questions were answered, and diary cards for each pair to record their efforts were distributed together with a pamphlet to remind them about the technique.

It had originally been hoped that it might be possible to have the pairs practice the technique under the supervision of the project leaders that same evening, but the group members not surprisingly demonstrated little enthusiasm for this, and this part of the training procedure was therefore omitted on this occasion. (For subsequent training meetings, graduates of the first project would be available to demonstrate the technique, live or on video, thereby creating a more relaxed atmosphere in which new tutors and tutees would feel more willing to practice the technique.)

Monitoring

The pairs were asked to use Paired Reading regularly for a minimum of 6 weeks, this being the shortest time during which the project leaders felt that a discernible improvement might become evident. Of the 12 pairs, 2 dropped out during the 6 weeks, in one case owing to the disinclination of the tutee, and in another case owing to a more generalized disagreement. Ten pairs thus completed the project. All the pairs were visited at home at the end of the first and second weeks by one of the Adult Literacy Organizers involved with the project. In some cases more visits were made. During the visits, each pair's use of the technique was observed and praised or remediated as necessary. Checklists of good practice were used by the visitors when monitoring quality of technique. General encouragement was given, and problems specific to particular pairs were discussed.

A number of problems in use of Paired Reading were encountered. In some pairs it proved difficult to establish the required rate of praise, particularly for cases in which a wife was tutoring her husband. Some tutees became so engrossed in their chosen text that they forgot to signal for independent reading even when the text was well within their independent readability level. In these latter cases, the visitors suggested a variety of minor modifications in the technique (extra rules) to get around these difficulties. It proved very difficult to find suitable reading material for two students who were virtually totally illiterate, and this problem was resolved by the tutor writing materials using a language experience approach.

The tutoring was disrupted by the usual round of domestic events, and thus one student had a 2-week holiday in the middle of the project and had difficulty getting back on task, while in another family a wife who was tutoring her husband separated from him towards the end of the project. (The latter student subsequently reported much greater confidence levels and a determination to carry on his reading on his own.) In many cases, however, the tutoring was going well and considerable enjoyment was reported by the pairs and, indeed, was evident during the visits.

Evaluation

In addition to the evaluation of the process by observation in the home, evaluative evidence was also available from pre- and post-project norm referenced reading tests and subjective feedback from the participants which was both verbal and written. The New Macmillan Reading Analaysis (Vincent & de la Mare, 1985) was used as the "objective" test, in parallel forms. This test has the advantage of reasonably modern text and illustrations, although the standardization proved to have too high a floor for some of the students to register at pretest. For the 5 students who did register on the scale at pretest, the average gain in reading age was 10.4 months in reading accuracy and 13 months in reading comprehension. For the students who did not register on the standardization scale at pretest, it was more difficult to quantify the gains made. In any event these were more erratic and not quite so encouraging, although these students had more domestic problems and their use of the technique was less perfect.

However, *all* students made some measurable progress in either reading accuracy or reading comprehension, though this was small in some cases. These results compared favorably with those of more traditional methods of helping adults with reading difficulties. Furthermore, they were achieved in a short space of time, with a modest input from professional agents. The cost effectiveness of the deployment of the Paired Reading technique in this way was clearly substantial.

Tape recordings of students' pre- and post-test performance on the Macmillan Analysis were available for 7 of the 10 participants. (It is not always reasonable to expect adults who are highly conscious of their reading difficulties to function remotely adequately in a test situation while simultaneously being tape recorded.) Using the miscue analysis categories incorporated in the Macmillan test, 6 of the 7 students showed a striking increase in self-correction, and the overall proportion of self-corrections increased by an average of 115% from pre- to post-test. Of the 7 students, 2 showed markedly reduced hesitations coupled with markedly increased substitutions, suggesting that these participants had greater confidence in guessing at unknown words. These results compare favorably with those of Lee (1986), who found that self-corrections in his Paired Reading group of children increased by 135% over a longer period.

Feedback

At the end of the initial intensive phase of the project, tutors and tutees gathered together with the project leaders for feedback. The intention of the project leaders was not that the pairs should see the project as having a finite end after 6 weeks, but rather that this intensive period of use of the technique should render them fluent in its use and able to see some significant change in the reading progress of the tutees which would motivate the pairs to continue using the technique in the long run.

At the feedback meeting, therefore, it was necessary for the project leaders not only to thank the pairs for their cooperation and give them the highly encouraging results from the reading tests (in terms of group averages rather than individual scores), but also (most importantly) to solicit the views of the pairs as to what improvements could be made in the way such projects were organized and to air questions of where the pairs might wish to go from there. Views about the relevance of the "How Not to Do It" role play at the training meeting were various, some students finding the drama amusing and relaxing, others exaggerated and unrealistic, and yet others very pointed and eliciting identification by members of the audience. Most students felt that the "How to Do It" aspect was reasonably well presented. However, once they arrived home, a number had difficulty with signaling for independent reading, and it was felt that more attention should be devoted at the training meeting to

informing tutors as to what to do if the tutee failed to signal, for whatever reason. Some students had had difficulty in finding appropriate reading materials, and in two cases these had been specially written. The opinions of the pairs on the usefulness of the diary cards were mixed, some feeling that they were a chore while others found them useful. The group consensus seemed to be that some form of recording was desirable but that it should be done over longer periods rather than daily. Some pairs reported initial difficulty in establishing synchronous reading together, but in virtually all cases this resolved itself with practice.

The tutees had a variety of opinions about the impact their Paired Reading had on them. An improvement in confidence when reading was widely reported, as was increased inclination to read signposts and other natural reading material. For those who reported it, the latter was a new experience. Some students reported feeling considerably more fluent when reading, and one tutee reported feeling more independent. In general, the pairs had got along well with each other, one pair reporting being delighted with their joint experience. Pairs tended to wish in the longer run to find more convenient times for reading, and the intention seemed to be to fit Paired Reading in even more easily with everyday life.

The tutors were also asked to complete a questionnaire about changes which they had seen during the project in their tutee's reading performance, and 9 of the 10 did so. All reported their tutees were more confident in reading, and 7 tutees were reported to be more willing to read and more interested in reading. Six of the tutees were reported to be understanding books more, enjoying reading more, and keeping a steadier flow when reading. Five of the tutees were felt to be reading more widely; 4 of them were reading more in absolute volume. However, only 2 tutees were felt to be reading with more life and expression. Of the tutors, 6 wanted to continue tutoring with the same frequency as during the project, while 2 wished to continue tutoring but with a lesser frequency. The remaining 2 tutors wished to continue to tutor reading but in a different way. A few (4) were also interested in tutoring in another area such as math or spelling.

A simpler questionnaire was also completed by the tutees, and all 10 of these were returned, although in some cases they must have been completed with the assistance of the tutors, and therefore there may have been a degree of bias in the responses. All 10 tutees reported that they liked doing Paired Reading. Virtually all reported that it was easy to find a good time and place to do the reading. All but 1 reported that they had improved their relationship with their tutor. Eight of the 10 felt their reading had improved and wished to go on using the technique. Seven tutees said they would tell other people about Paired Reading. However, opinions were more divided on other matters. Half of the tutees found it easy to learn the technique, and half found it difficult. Half felt the record sheet was a help, while half felt it was of no use. Generally, the tutees reported liking all kinds of reading better, but this view was not unanimous.

The Longer Term

Despite the good intentions of the majority of tutees to continue doing Paired Reading, the summer came, and the importance of the harvest in this rural area took over. Many of the project participants did *not* do much reading after the initial intensive period. When Paired Reading projects are carried out with children, it is usual for the participants to show continued though lesser acceleration in the months following the end of the intensive period (Topping, 1987b). However, children are typically surrounded by books, at least at school, and enjoy continuing encouragement to read. This was not the case with the adults participating in the Ryedale Project, who found it difficult to regain the reading habit after years of nonactivity.

Follow-up testing was carried out approximately 7.5 months after the end of the initial phase of the project. Continuing acceleration was found in very few students. The average further gain in reading comprehension for the students who had registered on the scale at pretest was only 4 months, while there was actually a slight decline in accuracy scores. (The results were skewed by one student who did particularly badly at follow-up.) The picture was even less optimistic for those students who had not registered on the scale at pretest, although these results were more difficult to quantify. Furthermore, the proportion of self-corrections had shown no further change since posttest.

Continued Use Imperative

The project demonstrated the feasibility of using the Paired Reading technique with non-professional tutors who are in daily natural contact with students in need of help with basic reading skills. Gains in reading ability were evident in students during a period of intensive use of the technique as short as 6 weeks. In the long run, however, when use of the technique was not maintained, the rate of gain in comprehension declined markedly for the more able students, while accuracy did not improve. For the less able students, there was evidence of "wash out" of experimental effects. It is clear that no matter how enjoyable the Paired Reading technique might be, and however easy it is to insinuate it regularly and frequently into everyday life, neither feature guarantees that the technique will continue to be used by students in the long term in a way that sustains the striking gains which can accrue in the short term.

For future projects, the importance of ongoing practice, perhaps 2 or 3 times a week, will need to be stressed and perhaps formalized in some kind of written contract. The continuation of some form of self-recording seems inevitable, although not favored by all tutorial pairs. Gathering project participants together for a booster meeting at regular intervals must also be tried. A more structured long-term approach is being adopted with subsequent groups of students.

The deployment of the Paired Reading technique in an open community education format clearly holds great promise and merits wide dissemination. Paired Reading enables *anyone* who can read to transmit their skill to somone she or he sees regularly. Furthermore, it could be particularly useful in those innovative programs that support parents of low literacy in their attempts to help their own children learn to read. The method may also have implications for education services in Third World and other developing countries. The effectiveness of the technique even in its pilot form compares favorably with traditional methods in the adult literacy field. Methods of service delivery can now be refined to make the use of this technique even more effective and efficient.

References

Adult Literacy and Basic Skills Unit. (1981). *A survey of attainment and progress of students in adult literacy schemes*. London: Author.

Adult Literacy and Basic Skills Unit. (1983). *Literacy and numeracy: Evidence from the National Child Development Study*. London: Author.

Adult Literacy and Basic Skills Unit. (1986). *Annual report 1985–86*. London: Author.

Booth, S., & Winter, J. (1987, Spring). Peer tutored paired reading in a college of further education. *Paired Reading Bulletin, 3,* 2–5.

Heckelman, R.G. (1986, March). N.I.M. re-visited. *Academic Therapy, 21,* 411–420.

Hunter, C.S.J., & Harman, D. (1979). *Adult illiteracy in the United States*. New York: McGraw-Hill.

Lee, A. (1986, Spring). A study of the longer term effects of paired reading. *Paired Reading Bulletin, 2,* 36–43.

Meyer, V. (1982, March). Prime-O-Tec: A successful strategy for adult disabled readers. *Journal of Reading, 28,* 512–515.

Topping, K.J. (1987b, March). Paired Reading: A powerful technique for parent use. *The Reading Teacher, 40,* 608–614.

Topping, K.J. (1986b, Spring). Paired Reading for adults with literacy problems. *Paired Reading Bulletin, 2,* 44–52.

Topping, K.J. (1986a). *Paired Reading training pack* (2nd ed.). Huddersfield, England: Kirklees Paired Reading Project.

Topping, K.J. (1987a). *The peer tutoring handbook: Promoting co-operative learning*. London: Croom Helm.

Topping. K.J., & Wolfendale, S.W. (Eds.). (1985). *Parental involvement in children's reading*. London: Croom Helm.

Vincent, D., & de la Mare, M. (1985). New *Macmillan reading analysis*. Basingstoke, England: Macmillan Education.

Helping a Nonspeaking Adult Male with Cerebral Palsy Achieve Literacy

JOAN P. GIPE
CHARLES A. DUFFY
JANET C. RICHARDS
FEBRUARY 1993

This is the story of how Arthur, a black adult American with cerebral palsy, learned to read and write. Arthur was referred to the University of New Orleans Reading/Language Arts Tutorial Center at the age of 33. It was not until this point in his life that someone finally recognized that Arthur was bright and could learn. As a result of cerebral palsy, he was nonspeaking and was confined to a wheelchair. Although he had some minimal sound production, those sounds were mostly unintelligible. On occasion one could hear his "thank you" (that is, "ank ou"). Also as a result of the cerebral palsy, Arthur exhibited difficulty with fine motor skills and had no control of his right hand but good control of his left. His vision was poor even with corrective lenses. Up until the time he came to the university tutorial program, he had never been sent to school or taught any form of sign language.

When we met Arthur, he let it be known through his own personal alternative means of communicating, mostly gesturing and answering yes-no questions, that he wanted to learn to read and write. He also demonstrated a very independent attitude and maneuvered his wheelchair quite well. In addition, he came to the tutorial sessions with a great desire to learn to use a microcomputer. Thus, it was determined that Arthur could be taught to use a computer, since he would be able to hit the keys with his left hand and his desire to learn was so great.

In addition to noting his physical capabilities, we made an initial inventory of Arthur's academic accomplishments. He knew how to print his name, knew his age, and could print his birthdate in numerical form. He could identify approximately 60 single words (see Figure 1) but only if presented in all capital letters as they appeared on his communication board; thus he did not have a concept of these items as words. He had simply learned each word's configuration and location on the communication board. A well developed sense of humor was a strong indicator that Arthur was bright and that tutoring might be successful.

Understanding Arthur's Literacy Needs

Approximately 70% of persons with cerebral palsy do not develop speech due to severe neuromuscular impairments (Hagen, Porter, & Brink, 1973). They are denied the practice and experience necessary for the development of language abilities and effective social interaction such as participating in a conversation with another human being. Communication boards have provided some means for two-way interaction (McDonald &

Figure 1
Words as They Appeared on Arthur's Communication Board

ALARM	SMOKE	GAS	USE	SELECT
HOLD	PRESS	THIS	BUTTON	WHICH
CONNECT	CONTINUE	WAITING	THANK	NOT
SAFE	ATTENTION	TURN	DIAL	CHANGE
STATION	ADJUST	LOCK	BRAKE	SIDE
FORWARD	REVERSE	COMPLETE	OPEN	DOOR
OR	WINDOW	EXIT	DEPOSIT	QUARTER
CALL	GET	REACH	MICRO	RANGE
FAST	SLOW	BUY/BYE	KEY	ENTER
PLACE	WATER	YES	NO	INCORRECT
ADD	ALL	MORE	TOTAL	FIRST
NEXT	FLOOR	ROOM	HELLO	

Schultz, 1973); however, in general these boards are limited to a finite number of words and phrases. Newer devices dedicated to voice output communication, such as the PRC Touch Talker/Light Talker (1989, Prentke Romich Company, Wooster, Ohio, USA), use pictures, computer technology, and synthesized speech to allow an individual to communicate in complete sentences. Nevertheless, nonspeaking individuals with cerebral palsy have many more thoughts, ideas, and feelings that can only be further developed by communicating with others through reading and writing.

There are three systems of language critical to reading and writing ability: the semantic, the syntactic, and the graphophonemic systems. Briefly, the semantic system reflects the background knowledge, prior experiences, concepts, attitudes, values, skills, and procedures a reader or writer brings to the reading or writing task. The syntactic system refers to knowledge about how the language works. Readers and writers use this knowledge of the meaningful arrangement of words in sentences to help construct meaning in text. The graphophonemic system refers to

the print itself. The graphic symbols represent the relationship between the speech sounds and the letters of the language. For the non-speaking individual, these three systems are underdeveloped—not because of any deficit in mental capacity but because of nonuse or use of another necessary alternative or augmentative means of communication (Lahey, 1988). Nonspeaking individuals have *received* language input but have not been able to *produce* language in a traditional sense. As a result, they have not had opportunities to use language structures in natural, real life contexts or to experiment with language to discover its functions (for example, getting things done, controlling others, maintaining personal relationships, expressing individuality, conveying information, and finding things out [Halliday, 1975]). Such experimentation is what helps children form the basic rules of language structure (that is, syntactic and graphophonemic systems).

Arthur's Instructional Program

In order for Arthur to achieve literacy, a personalized way to develop his language abilities was needed. Since he wanted to learn how to use a microcomputer, and because of his physical impediment for handwriting, an IBM-compatible microcomputer was the basic piece of equipment used. Because of his relatively good control of the left hand, a standard keyboard was used. The microcomputer was initially equipped with a speech synthesizer to provide Arthur with verbalization of sounds; however, due to its robotic-sounding speech, Arthur preferred not to use it. Initially, a large screen display monitor was employed, but it was later replaced with a standard (12"/30 cm) monitor because the resolution of the text on the large screen was poor and gave Arthur difficulty. A printer was attached to the system for printed feedback. The word processing software WordPerfect® (WordPerfect Corporation, Orem, Utah, USA) was used by both Arthur and his student-tutors for text production.

Reading and writing instruction by undergraduate student-tutors enrolled in a corrective reading course has been provided for Arthur 4 days a week, 1 hour per day for two fall, two spring, and two summer semesters, totaling approximately 30 hours of tutoring each semester, or 180 hours of instruction. At this writing, Arthur had begun his third year of the tutoring program.

The following beliefs, as delineated in *Whole Language: Theory in Use* (Newman, 1985), have guided all the activities planned for Arthur's instructional program.

- Language and language learning are social activities; they occur best in a situation which encourages discussion and a sharing of knowledge and ideas.

- Language learning necessarily involves the risk of trying new strategies; error is inherent in the process.

- Reading and writing are context-specific; what is learned about reading and writing is a reflection of the particular situation in which the learning is occurring.

- Choice is an essential element for learning; there must be opportunities for students to choose what to read and what to write about.

- "Whole language" activities are those that support students in their use of all aspects of language; students learn about reading and writing while listening; they learn about writing from reading and gain insights about reading from writing.

- Our role as teachers is best seen as "leading from behind" by supporting the language learning capabilities of students indirectly through the activities we offer them (p. 5).

Arthur's Progress During the First Year

Fall semester. Upon entering the tutorial program, Arthur demonstrated strength in the semantic system through the auditory modality. It was evident that Arthur was able to understand spoken language well because he would respond appropriately (for example, he would laugh at jokes and indicate yes or no by shaking his head to questions asked). He was also a successful participant in the Volunteers of America Independent Living program, which meant that he lived in his own apartment and took care of all his personal needs such as cooking. To come to the university as well as to visit his doctors, he arranged to ride a bus modified for persons with physical disabilities.

Due to his clear independence, an instructional program that used his strength in the auditory modality and that focused on his life experiences was devised to teach reading and writing. Initially, a language experience approach was attempted, since it was apparent

Arthur had ideas he wished to express about the events in his life. The difficulty came because those working with Arthur could not understand what he was trying to communicate. Since Arthur was never taught any form of sign language, he had limited means for communicating his ideas.

It quickly became evident during tutoring sessions using the computer that Arthur also had no knowledge of the graphophonemic system, since he would not even attempt to produce any of the letters in the words (for example, invented spellings), nor could he identify on the keyboard individual letters called out by the tutor. At first, he could only recognize the capital forms of most letters but did not know their names. He could only respond in writing (typing) by answering yes or no questions or by being given multiple-choice questions that were read orally, to which he would type the letter of his choice. Through these yes or no and multiple-choice questions, Arthur's tutors discovered his interests in sports, music, and cooking; they discovered he had no concept of days, weeks, and months or that words have spaces in between them; he had never experienced Halloween; he had no reading ability whatsoever; and he possessed a sight vocabulary of four words (that is, his name, *door, yes*, and *no*).

When given the 1985 Analytical Reading Inventory (3rd ed.), which was modified to questions in a multiple-choice format, Arthur demonstrated a listening comprehension level of primer. This was interpreted as revealing a deficiency in understanding the task of listening to a story and then listening and responding to questions presented in a multiple-choice format, rather than in his ability to understand the text. This interpretation should be viewed with some caution since this informal reading inventory was not designed specifically for use with persons with cerebral palsy or the nonspeaking. However, because it is an informal instrument, modifications in its administration, such as those employed in Arthur's program, are more easily justified than for standardized instruments.

Arthur's initial semester was spent focusing on sight vocabulary and basic concepts about print and about the world. For example, a calendar was introduced and holidays noted; a personal dictionary of new words was begun; signs labeling objects (for example, "This is a red chair") were posted around the room; and lots of language experiences were provided and written about (for example, carving a pumpkin at Halloween, going trick-or-treating at Arthur's request, flying a kite, and visiting the university bookstore). It should be noted that Arthur worked extremely slowly because he was also becoming familiar with the computer keyboard. But there was progress. By the end of his first semester, Arthur's listening comprehension level was fifth grade and his sight vocabulary increased to 50 words. These results were encouraging, and Arthur was given some materials to work with over the Christmas break.

Spring semester. When Arthur returned to the program in the spring, we administered the 1985 Ekwall Reading Inventory (2nd ed.) and the 1981 Peabody Picture Vocabulary Test–Revised (PPVT). With the informal reading inventory, Arthur read silently and answered questions modified to a multiple-choice format. On the word lists, he circled the words he could read. Arthur was unable to demonstrate measurable levels for reading or for sight vocabulary. His listening comprehension level was eighth grade. The PPVT required no modification in administration because Arthur was able to point to the pictures in the test booklet with ease. Results for the PPVT revealed a mental age score of 12

Figure 2
Sample "Conversation" Between Arthur and His Tutor—First Spring Semester

Tutor:	what happened to our work?
Arthur:	gone
T:	yes it is gone. I wonder what happened? we did not do it.
A:	do i no i yoa
T:	do you mean do i know where the words went?
A:	yyyyes
T:	no. I never had that happen before and dr. gipe will think that we messed up.
A:	y3s
T:	what will we say happened?
A:	i do noot no
T:	oh well, we are writing now, right?
A:	yes
T.	what will you eat tonight?
A:	hamb
T:	do you mean hamburgers?
A:	yes
T:	who will make them?
A:	i
T:	you will cook?
A:	yes
T:	what else will you eat?
A:	i icecream
T:	what will you drink?
A:	it

years. The Language Experience Approach was continued. Emphasis was also placed on learning the graphophonemic system using a multisensory phonics program (J.C. Richards, personal communications, 1989).

A breakthrough seemed to occur when Arthur's tutor created a set of key word cards to use for communicating what letters or sounds he was trying to write. Thus, Arthur was taught a key word and signing method that combined his ability to gesture with words representing key sounds of the language (for example, a picture of a baby with the word *baby* written below, accompanied by Arthur holding his arms as if to rock a baby). Learning these key words with ges-tures allowed Arthur to spell out what he was thinking. As he became more adept with his "signing," he was better able to invent spellings, thus providing a written record of his language and a source for reading materi-al. Written conversations were carried out often to give Arthur as much practice as pos-sible using real language in a social situation (see Figure 2). He was also instructed to read along while the tutor read stories aloud to him, in the style of the neurological impress method (Heckelman, 1969). He especially liked material about dinosaurs, sports, and entertainers.

Summer semester. In his first summer semes-ter, Arthur's tutor was a black male of approximately his age, now 34. (All previous and subsequent student tutors were white females in their 20s). The rapport between the two men was wonderful, and Arthur made great progress. The instructional program consisted of working on letter recognition using his key word cards and gestures as well as emphasizing writing using complete sentences with attention to syntax, word endings, and parts of speech. At this point, Arthur's ability to use function words reflected that of a very young child (for example, "I, Arthur, go, UNO."). Although Arthur had heard English spoken for 34 years and understood spoken language, when he was finally able to produce language himself he omitted function words as do very young children. Fry's "instant words" (1980) were the source of function words used to write complete sentences, and Arthur was given daily homework to handwrite sentences using these words. The 1989 Informal Reading Inventory: Preprimer to Twelfth Grade (3rd ed.) results revealed a listening comprehension level of 11th grade and an instructional reading level of preprimer. Sight vocabulary increased but was still not measurable using the inventory. But now Arthur had a firm basis for improving his reading. He was asked to continue reading books, given to him as gifts, during the semester break.

Arthur's Progress During the Second Year

Fall semester. The second fall semester revealed that Arthur had indeed practiced his reading over the summer break. The 1985 Analytical Reading Inventory (3rd ed.) results in September, reflecting 1 year of instruction, showed an instructional reading level of third grade, with frustration at fourth. Arthur had mastered letter recognition for names of letters but not for sounds. Language experience

was continued and cloze passages made from his written productions. The emphasis was on developing knowledge of syntax and sight vocabulary. Directed Listening/Reading Thinking Activities were conducted using folk and fairy tales, newspaper articles, dinosaur books, and material on music and sports.

Toward the end of this semester Arthur had some health problems and became somewhat depressed. As a result, his mental health became of more concern than his academic program. The tutor helped Arthur tremendously by taking him to the gym for weight lifting and swimming and, in the evenings, to basketball games. Arthur's mental health improved 100%, but there were no measurable improvements in his reading levels. More importantly, Arthur found a friend. This tutor continued a personal relationship with Arthur and got him involved in the national organization for persons with cerebral palsy, where he attended all the local meetings and became a member of their sports team, the Hurricanes (the team competed in such events as wheelchair races and boccie).

Spring semester. The second spring semester indicated considerable progress in all areas of Arthur's program. According to the 1988 Basic Reading Inventory: Preprimer Through Grade Eight (4th ed.) and the 1990 Secondary and College Reading Inventory (2nd ed.), Arthur's independent reading level was at the 3rd grade, instructional reading level ranged from 4th–6th, and frustration reading level was 7th. His listening comprehension level remained 11th. Arthur's sight vocabulary for words in isolation was primer. He had definite reading interests; he enjoyed legends, folktales, animal stories, and articles and books about sports. The emphasis during the semester was on writing, specifically syntax and sentence structure. Editing was introduced using language experience produc-

Figure 3
Final Revised Copy of Arthur's Letter of Complaint to the RTA

[Home address]
July 12, 1990

Regional Transit Authority
c/o [addressee]
101 Dauphine St.
New Orleans, LA 70112

Dear Ms. [name]

I am very angry with the RTA. On July 3, 1990 I had to sit on the bus for four hours. Because the bus made me late, I had to miss school. I am not stupid, I have a good brain and I enjoy going to school. I am angered over having been made to pay the one dollar fee for nothing! I would like my money back.

Sincerely,

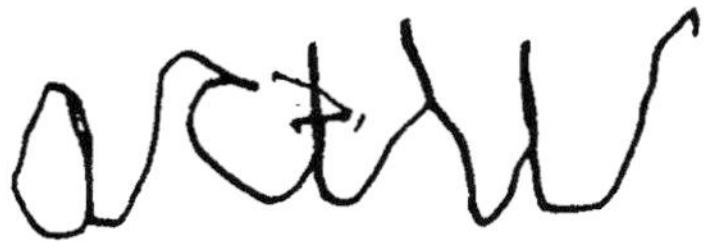

[surname]

Arthur
[surname]
[RTA ID#]

---

tions. Arthur still relied on his key word cards to help with that spelling. Spelling tests were given often using words from his personal dictionary.

Summer semester. The second summer session showed that Arthur maintained his reading levels while his listening comprehension level improved to college (1990 Secondary and College Reading Inventory, 2nd ed.). Sight vocabulary improved to second grade level for words in isolation. The PPVT revealed a mental age score of 20 years, consistent with the listening comprehension level. During this summer session, Arthur wanted to focus on improving his spelling, so he was introduced to WordPerfect's® spell-checker capability. His writing had improved to the point where he was spelling words well enough to make use of the spell-checker function. This summer session was another breakthrough in terms of Arthur's writing progress. He demonstrated understanding of the function of writing to get something done when he had cause to write a letter of complaint to the bus service that provided his transportation to and from school (see Figure 3).

Arthur's Progress During the Third Year

Fall semester. When Arthur began his third year of literacy instruction, in his third fall semester, his silent reading comprehension ability was assessed using the 1989 Analytical

Reading Inventory (4th ed.). The multiple-choice format for comprehension questions was continued so that he would not have to write out his responses. His writing ability was still not developed enough to warrant the time and effort it would take to produce an understandable response. The multiple-choice format, then, assessed Arthur's recognition of a correct response, and not the generation of a response that might better reveal his own thinking with regard to questions that require integration of information. Nevertheless, this type of response format had been used previously, so these results could be directly compared to previous results. Arthur was able to demonstrate an independent reading level of 5th grade, an instructional reading level of 6th–7th, and a frustration reading level of 8th. His sight vocabulary for words in isolation remained much lower than his ability to read words in context. His listening comprehension level remained at the college level (1990 Secondary and College Reading Inventory, 2nd ed.).

Arthur's reading levels seemed quite dependent on the content, or topic, of the passages read. He had difficulty with narrative passages such as the excerpt from *The Incredible Journey* (Level 4 passage) and the bicycle race story (Level 5); however, he had little difficulty with the expository passage about Dr. Charles Drew and his work in blood transfusions (Level 6) and the narrative passage taken from *The Outsiders* (Level 7). It is difficult to interpret these results other than as they are related to the number of passages read at one sitting, or what may be more likely, the presence of appropriate background knowledge or interest on Arthur's part for the passage's content.

Arthur still exhibited extreme difficulty spelling, even when copying from a model. He demonstrated little knowledge of syntax and no knowledge of paragraph structure or punctuation in his writing. He continued to express a wide range of reading interests, including the categories of mystery, comedy, sports (for example, basketball), history (for example, medieval times), fact, and fiction. Arthur believed that his major weakness was in the area of writing. He was determined to improve his spelling, and informed his tutor, in no uncertain terms, that this was what he wanted to work on that semester. With this kind of attitude and level of motivation, Arthur had the potential to continue improving in his goal to achieve literacy. While communication with Arthur remained difficult, this obstacle was being overcome through the use of Arthur's personal sign language, some minimal handwriting, and a computer system. Through these means, Arthur was now able to answer and ask questions, as well as initiate conversation and express his opinions.

Computer Technology and Holistic Instruction

The availability of computer equipment for experimenting with language provides a great opportunity for the nonspeaking person. A wide variety of computer equipment is available for instructional use. While the speech synthesizer used by Arthur was chosen because of its relatively low cost, the speech was highly robotic and its phonetic abilities were marginal. More expensive synthesizers are able to produce more natural sounding speech (in both male and female voices) with enhanced pronunciation capabilities. Unfortunately, speech synthesizers, by and large, do not work with graphic intensive or graphic-interface software. Use of newer communication devices such as Touch Talker® may be a viable alternative. For persons with cerebral palsy and little motor control, there are a number of alternate input devices.

Keyboards can easily be remapped to perform as either left- or right-handed Dvorak keyboards (instead of the standard QWERTY keyboard). Additionally, software can be used which will either remap or substitute for keystroke combinations that usually require two hands. Students with even less motor control can make use of "sip and puff sticks" or thumb clicker devices for input. With the appropriate software, full use of the computer is possible.

Working with Arthur afforded a perfect opportunity for providing holistic instruction through the use of computer technology. Many aspects of Arthur's learning could be observed and directly addressed, as the semester his mental health became the primary focus demonstrates. Arthur was always an active participant in his own learning. His instruction was totally student centered. He learned to read and write using the computer just as a young child learns from interacting with print in his or her environment. Activities were employed that incorporated his interests and events in his daily life (for example, his first Halloween and the bus incident).

The graphophonemic connection to reading and writing had to be taught through the use of pictures, hand signals, and songs. All of these efforts showed Arthur that reading and writing are meaning-based activities. He read, or was read to, and wrote every day, but not for some contrived reason. His reading and writing always had real purpose and a real audience (for example, to converse with the tutor or to complain to the RTA). Through this holistic approach, Arthur's schemata about the world, along with his knowledge of how our language works, were expanded. For Arthur, writing was talking, and writing, along with his gestures and grunts, was his most effective and efficient way of communicating. To conclude, there could be no packaged program that would have helped Arthur learn to read and write. His level of literacy could only have been achieved in such a short time by adhering to holistic beliefs.

References

Fry, E.B. (1980). The new instant word list. *The Reading Teacher, 34*, 284–290.

Hagen, C., Porter, W., & Brink. J. (1973). Nonverbal communication: An alternative mode of communication of the child with severe cerebral palsy. *Journal of Speech and Hearing Disorders, 38*, 448–455.

Halliday, M.A.K. (1975). *Learning how to mean: Exploration in the development of language.* London: Edward Arnold.

Heckelman, R.G. (1969). A neurological-impress method of remedial reading instruction. *Academic Therapy, 4*, 277–282.

Lahey, M. (1988). *Language disorders and language development.* New York: Macmillan.

McDonald, E.T., & Schultz, A.R. (1973). Communication boards for cerebral palsied children. *Journal of Speech and Hearing Disorders, 38*, 73–88.

Newman, J.M. (Ed.). (1985). *Whole language: Theory in use.* Portsmouth, NH: Heinemann.

I Ain't Never Read My *Own* Words Before

VICTORIA PURCELL-GATES
NOVEMBER 1993

Learners are cultural beings; they exist, move, relate, and make sense of their world within a specified cultural and social context (Ferdman, 1990). They develop literacy concepts and skills within their own sociocultural frames. To better study and understand literacy practices and learning, we professionals must acknowledge the link between literacy development and culture (Ferdman, 1990). I prepared this report on Jenny with this charge in mind. I describe a woman, Jenny, who sought to learn to read and write within her Urban Appalachian culture and the culture of her home, where no one could read or write. Her earlier attempts are viewed through a sociocultural lens, particularly the ways in which her language, her words, served both to deny and then later to provide her access to the world of print.

My second intention is to document carefully Jenny's growth toward conventionality through functional, holistic literacy practices. Many educators dedicated to improving adults' access to literacy have called for contextualized, meaning-centered instruction that

respects the learners' language, experience, and culture (Auerbach, 1989; Fingeret, 1991; Freire & Macedo, 1987; Kazemek & Rigg, 1985). This accompanies the parallel interest in meaning-based instruction for K–12 learners (Calkins, 1986; Goodman, 1986; Harste, Woodward, & Burke, 1984; Smith, 1988). A developmental view of literacy is at the base of these practices, but we have yet to agree on ways in which to document growth.

I describe a case here that supports the conclusion that involving learners in literacy practices that validate their experiences and language will move them toward full, conventional literacy more effectively than the more traditional skills-based, decontextualized instruction still found in most U.S. adult education programs.

The Study

This article comes from a 2-year ethnographic study of Jenny and her son, Donny (not their real names), their community and culture, and the ways in which their becoming literate was influenced by their culture and vice versa. This is not a report of the entire study. Rather, this piece focuses on Jenny's growth as a reader and writer as she invested herself in literacy events directed at connecting her world and language to print.

Data for this article, as for the entire study, were gathered through field notes recorded after each interaction, audiotapes of most meetings that were transcribed and integrated with field notes, collection of literacy artifacts like writing and reading attempts, and structured and spontaneous interviews. Much of the data was collected during Jenny and Donny's literacy instruction at the literacy center of a large urban university in the midwestern United States. The center is the site for the practicum aspect of the graduate-level sequence of courses on diagnosis and remediation of literacy problems. Graduate students work one-on-one in the center with children two times a week, each session lasting an hour. Data were also collected at Jenny's home and during various shopping trips around the city.

Jenny and Her World

When I first met Jenny, I was immediately impressed with her strength of character, her forthrightness, her candor, and her determination. "I cain't read," she stated clearly and unequivocally, meeting my gaze with her own clear blue-eyed one. "It's hard not knowin' how to read. A lot of these women, you know, they think it ain't that hard to read. Just sit down and read.... It's not easy." Jenny's husband, she informed me, also could not read or write and worked part time as a roofer. She had two children—Donny, age 7, and Timmy, age 4. Jenny worked part time as a housecleaner.

Jenny had applied for help for her 7-year-old from the university-based literacy center I directed. He was failing to learn to read in school. She asked if she could sit alongside him in the center to try to pick up enough information to be able to help him with his homework. I accepted her and Donny as students, and she agreed to let me collect data for research as I worked with them both on learning to read and write.

Jenny is a member of the U.S. minority group called Urban Appalachian. This group makes up a significant portion of the low-income population of several mid-size to large cities in the Midwest and Mid-Atlantic states. These people are migrants or descendants of migrants from the Appalachian mountains who came to the cities looking for work, many times not finding any for which they were suited, and who for the most part continue to regard their mountain origins as "home." While many descendants of this population have successfully assimilated into the mainstream cultures of the cities, a sizable portion have not, preferring their mountain homes and lifestyles. As a group, they suffer many ills—poverty, poor health, low educational attainment, and, to some degree, high crime rates.

One characteristic of the unassimilated Urban Appalachians is their retention of characteristic language patterns and usage. Other groups often use these language patterns to stereotype and make fun of the "hillbillies," a discriminatory practice that Appalachians and Urban Appalachians suffer nationwide. Jenny was clearly aware of this focus on her language and by the time she was in her early 30s (when I met her), she was fully prepared to take the blame upon herself and her language for her failure in school: "That's why it was a little hard for me startin' to like...sound my words out...'cause I talk different...'cause I'm, you know...countrified. And my words don't come out the way they're supposed to."

From the beginning of our association, I enjoyed and perceived Jenny's words as part and parcel of the many qualities I admired in her: her ability to cut verbally to the quick of any situations, her honesty and her straightforward way of living and relating to people, her self-deprecating humor, and her strength and grace as she dealt with one setback after another in her attempts to provide for her family.

The reason I have made a point of this is that, as I begin to talk and write about Jenny and her family, I find myself using her voice and her words as she did. I do this out of my respect for her—her language is a part of her—but I am aware of dangers inherent in this. These Appalachian voices and words have been used for so long by bigots and ethnocentrists for purposes of mockery and deprecation that it is possible that when I use this language it will be interpreted as another example of this mockery. If this impression is formed irretrievably then I will stop using her words and voice, but for me that will entail an incredible loss of the power of this story.

Jenny's Conceptual Skill Base

Jenny's initial desire to sit alongside while I taught Donny proved unworkable because Donny needed to do a great deal of listening to literature, exploring writing, and other self-directed activities to build emergent literacy concepts. We weren't *teaching* Donny in any didactic way at that time, and Jenny's conceptual level regarding reading and writing was beyond her son's.

Jenny was typical of many adult low literates: she had dropped out of school in her 7th-grade year after struggling with reading and writing from the beginning; she had created a life for herself in which print played few functions; she decided to try to learn to read when she became concerned about her children's ability to succeed in school; and she had attended various adult programs for several years (Irwin, 1985; Newman & Beverstock, 1990; Northcutt, 1975; Sticht, 1988). Initial informal assessments revealed that Jenny was not *illiterate*—she could read some things with a great deal of struggle— but rather she was more *nonliterate* in that she did not read anything.

In Figure 1 is a list of words she copied off items in her cupboard that fit the criteria I set for her: Find words on labels in your house that you know you can read. When she read this short list to me in the literacy center, she struggled with each word. Aside from this, Jenny did not—in her view, could not—read (in the sense of processing print for meaning) anything in her environment except for one simple children's book she had mastered to

Figure 1
Words Jenny Copied off Items in Her Kitchen That She Felt She Could Read

Words I Know
Cost cutter Apple Juice
A safe crossing
Crisco
Peanut Butter
Maxwell House
SELF-RISING-FLOUR
BEANS

read to her children and a few reminders penciled on the calendar on her kitchen wall. These calendar notations consisted of numbers for the times of appointments and only a few letters which were usually enough to remind her of the nature of the appointments.

As a teacher, I knew that she needed to read text in order to learn to read, but I could find no texts she could read. Since I was primarily Donny's teacher and could not attend to her exclusively, I had to think long and hard for activities for her that would move her beyond the nonliterate stance she had assumed.

Adult Education Classes

Jenny's experiences with adult education classes were also typical of those of many low literate adults (Auerbach, 1989; Fingeret, 1991; Irwin, 1985). She had been attending an evening adult literacy class for 4 years. While she was determined to attend as often as she could, real life problems prevented her from going regularly.

During the third session in the center, she brought a stack of materials with which she had been working at her adult class before she had to quit due to lack of transportation. These were workbooks, with page after page of short passages on a variety of topics followed by questions to test comprehension. Most of the questions called for filling in the blanks of sentences with words taken from the passage. Others called for choosing among several items for the correct answer.

There was no writing in them—Jenny said they were supposed to write their answers on paper—but she said that she had learned to read these passages. I asked her to read one for me and she did with a great deal of struggle—pausing often to try to recall a word as if from some sort of memorized list or spelling it out to see if she could get it that way. When she was finished I was truly surprised. "You *can* read!" I exclaimed, noting to myself that this looked to be on about the 4th-grade level. She looked at me—straight in the eye as usual—and said matter of factly, "I can read these words if they're in this book, after someone helps me, but I cain't read 'em if they're anywheres else!" And this was true; none of this hard-won knowledge transferred—anywhere.

In terms of learning to write, the closest her adult education instruction came to dealing with this was the ubiquitous language arts workbooks and lessons, as she showed me about 3 months after I began working with her. When her family's truck was fixed and she began attending adult school again, she brought me the workbook she had been assigned. The skills addressed included parts of speech (nouns, verbs, adjectives, adverbs, pronouns, prepositions, etc.), paragraphing (one idea per, and remember to indent), and punctuation conventions. Jenny, however, had little use for or understanding of these skills; she had never written anything for her own purposes in her life aside from her name, those notations on her calendar, and her address on the few occasions she was required to do so.

Literacy Experiences in the Center

Clearly, Jenny needed to engage in some authentic reading and writing. I suggested to her that she write in a journal during her times in the center, telling me about her day or about anything at all that would help me learn about her and her own thoughts and feelings. I told her that I would type what she had written and she could then read her own words—words she had written in the preceding session. She looked at me with an expression of stunned awareness. "Why, I ain't never read my *own* words before!" she exclaimed softly. "See, I cain't write!"

"Well, I think you can write more than you think you can," I said. "The writing will come…as you start writing your own thoughts and your own feelings down and not just copying somebody else's words."

Jenny shook her head back and forth slowly as she acknowledged, "That's all I ever really did was copy stuff, you know, from a book." Jenny continued to try to convince me that she was not up to this task, focusing on her inability to spell. "See, I don't…the reason I blew up [I'm not sure what this referred to] was I couldn't spell stuff!" she insisted. Her strength and determination won the day, though, as she finally agreed to begin the arduous task of trying to record her thoughts and feelings onto paper…*in her own words*. She was amazed, and continues to be amazed, at my ability to read her writing that was filled with so many misspellings. The basic concept that someone could read what she wrote was completely new to her.

As Jenny acquired a larger sight vocabulary and accumulated time reading real text for meaning from reading my typed versions of her journal, I began responding to her individual entries, providing her with her first meaningful text from an author other than herself. Jenny was successful at reading these entries from me, usually asking later for confirmation on one or two words. Figure 2 displays one page of her first journal entry. My typed version with standard spelling and punctuation constituted her first text. I always had Jenny read the journal entry to me after she had finished so that I could rely on her intonation for punctuation and the reading of a few of the words I could not decipher. Figure 3 displays one page from the last piece of writing she did for me. This is a four-page letter she wrote to me after I wrote to her from my new home, asking about how she and her family were doing and telling her about my new home and job. Over 2 years I collected 22 journal entries and this one letter from her. The remainder of this report is an analysis of these writings and her reading of them.

Move Toward Conventional Writing

One can see by comparing the writing in Figure 2 and Figure 3 that Jenny's writing moved from very nonconventional to close to conventional text. This can be documented on several different levels.

First, because Jenny herself equated her inability to write to her inability to spell, I analyzed her spellings to check the impression that she became more accurate as she continued to write and then to read her own writing and, later, mine. This analysis was based on the first 6 and the last 10 journal entries and the letter in Figure 3. Although I have my typed versions of journal entries 7–12, Jenny's original drafts were lost during a long period of illness during which she took her journal home.

To analyze for an increase in accuracy from beginning to end, I averaged the percentage of words per journal entry (or letter) spelled conventionally for the first three and last three entries, which included the letter. Figure 4 shows the results. There was a 24% increase in words spelled accurately. A more qualitative look at her move toward accurate spelling did indeed reveal a move, or process. First, the entries reveal an increasing complexity to the words she could spell (see Figure 5). The impression from her early entries is that she had learned only a preprimer list of sight words. Over time, though, she was accurately encoding more difficult words.

Figure 2
Jenny's First Journal Entry

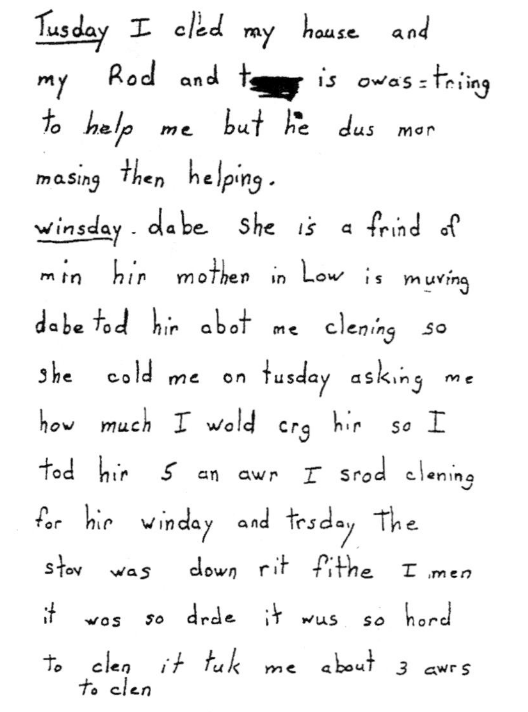

Tusday I cled my house and my Rod and t____ is owas=triing to help me but he dus mor masing then helping.

winsday. dabe she is a frind of min hir mother in Low is muving dabe tod hir abot me clening so she cold me on tusday asking me how much I wold crg hir so I tod hir 5 an awr I srod clening for hir winday and trsday The stov was down rit fithe I men it wos so drde it wus so hord to clen it tuk me about 3 awrs to clen

Figure 3
Jenny's Letter to Her Instructor after 2 Years of the Study

The weather is nice it's not to
hot and not to cold. I like it
the way it is. the days weather was
67 to nit it's 30 something. is your
weather nice. I have 5 women that
I work for. I have one on friday
and one on monday. and the uthers
call me when thay ned me. when I
was working for Sanndy the woman nix
door saw me clening the windows and
she ask me if that is all I do
is windows I sad no I do ine kid
of clening and so she ask me to

Second, a process of increasing approximation shows in words that were initially misspelled but eventually encoded correctly. In Figure 6 is a list of those words, with her spellings in the order in which they appeared over time. Also in Figure 6 is a list of words that she never spelled correctly in the entries I had available but that all showed a move toward convention over time. This analysis confirms that as Jenny encoded her own words, read them in standard form, and then read my words to her, she moved inexorably toward conventional control of written text.

I next looked at appropriate use of punctuation, a skill area she had repeatedly encountered in instruction during her first 7 years in school and 4 years in adult education classes (see Figure 7). I again used the first three journal entries and the last three pieces. She moved from the virtual absence of punctuation (8%) to a near-standard use of periods (94% used appropriately). In the first three entries, she used no commas at all, while in the last three she indicated a sense of the need for a comma by using three periods where commas should go. Two of the periods used in the letter to indicate the end of a complete

Figure 4
Increase in the Correct Spelling Between Jenny's First Three and Last Three Writing Entries

Writing entry	Number of words	Number correct	Percentage correct	Mean percent correct
1	169	91	54%	
2	158	97	61%	
3	156	89	57%	
				57%
21	55	44	80%	
22	77	60	78%	
23	374	316	84%	
				81%

Figure 5
Samples Showing Increasing Complexity of Words Jenny Could Spell Correctly

First writing sample				Last writing sample		
I	went	to	the	new	sent	it's
she	had	me	some	quiet	sleep	nice
in	and	we	house	Literacy	Center	kids
out	of	day	up	hope	off	Spelling
cans	big	do	not	called	yet	says
my	a	bath	home	new	met	times
is	but	he	help	much	weather	hot
so	on	how	helping	cold	way	days
much	an	down	mother	women	call	working
hard	about	asking		door	saw	windows
				keep	friend	

sentence should have been question marks. Periods were the only punctuation marks she used in all of her writing entries.

Given Jenny's ascription of her illiterate status to her "countrified words," which in her eyes—and I suspect the eyes of more than one of her former teachers—prevented her from learning to sound out words, I decided to look at all of her misspellings for indications of phonemic awareness and influences from her dialect. Phonemic awareness is the knowledge that English can be perceived at the level of the phoneme, roughly a letter-to-sound match. Adams (1990) has synthesized a vast amount of research which indicates that learners must possess this knowledge in order to become fluent readers but that many poor readers do not have this knowledge. Without this knowledge, a reader cannot sound out words in print, the skill Jenny reported she was unable to master.

One way of measuring the extent of phonemic awareness is to examine invented or creative spellings. If individual phonemes are represented in regular ways, then it can be said that the speller is aware of the phonemic basis of English spelling. When I examined Jenny's misspellings for phonemic representation, I found that 90% had every single phoneme represented. Some of these are listed in Figure 8. The few inventively spelled words that did not have all of the phonemes represented each contained over half of them, as also illustrated in Figure 8. When I next looked at her misspellings for dialect influence, I found that exactly one third of them reflected her phonological system (Wolfram & Christian, 1976). A selection of these spellings appear in Figure 9. So Jenny was very good at encoding language at the phonemic level as she heard it.

Moving to a different level, analysis of her comments during writing and the content of her writing showed a shift in focus away from a simple listing of a day's events to a struggle to *compose* a representation of an event, complete with tone and voice. As this move occurred, her journal entries began to spill over from one day to another so that the unity of the composition spanned several entries. Her comments during and after each writing episode changed from the "I wrote everything

Figure 6
Words Showing Development of Jenny's Spelling over 2 years, in Order of Appearance

Words Jenny eventually spelled conventionally

abot, abad > about
asting > asking
cold > called
ded > did
frind, firend > friend
hir, hr > her
ked > kid
kep > keep
kies, kis, keds > kids
luk > look
Muday > Monday
pra > pray
red > read
saleing > spelling
sowl, sol, sool > school
tem, thm, thim > them
thek > think
tod > told
wemen > women
win, wen, whin, wen > when
windos > windows
wint, wit, wnt, wint > went

Words still moving toward conventional spelling

becs, becols, be calls, becols ≈ because
ces, sens ≈ since
Dabe, Dabbe ≈ Debbie
Juhov, Juhova ≈ Jehova
pepol, peopl ≈ people
qelt, qwelt ≈ quilt
rember, remmber ≈ remember
srod, stred, strd, storded ≈ started
trsday, tusday ≈ Tuesday
winday, winsday ≈ Wednesday

> became
≈ approximated but did not yet become

I could think of" type to comments such as "...it's hard to say it so that it's like it really was." This last comment was in regard to her

account of the terrifying night that the police broke into her apartment and arrested her husband for selling marijuana to friends, a fairly common practice in their mountain community. The typed version of that entry appears in Figure 10. Comparing it to the first entry (Figure 2) reveals marked progress in tone, voice, and compositional unity.

Move Toward Functional Reading

In terms of reading progress over this 2-year period, Jenny moved from being a total nonreader to a level of functional reading. Soon after she began to read my responses in her journals, I observed her attempting to read environmental print for the first time. She also began to puzzle out more and more of the notices that Donny brought home from school. I was soon able to leave her notes that I knew she could read and respond to, and after I moved, I wrote her a long letter that she read and responded to in writing—a big move toward functional literacy.

Discussion

Jenny's case is not an idiosyncratic one. The level of functional illiteracy among adults is too high for an industrialized nation such as the United States. Stedman and Kaestle (1987) concluded from a review of seven different studies of adult literacy that "about 20 percent of the adult population, or around 35 million people, have serious difficulties with common reading tasks" (p. 34). All of these functionally illiterate adults are cultural beings, and in more cases than not their cultures and mores differ from those of the middle-class bureaucracy of the schools that failed them.

This look at Jenny focused on the issue of people's words. For those of us who have been active in process writing and reading instruction (Atwell, 1987; Buchanan, 1989;

Figure 7
Increase in the Appropriate Use of Periods Between Jenny's First Three and Last Three Writing Entries

Writing entry	Number of spots where a period was appropriate	Number of periods used in those spots	Percentage appropriate period use	Mean percent appropriate period use
1	16	2	13%	
2	8	0	0%	
3	17	2	12%	
				8%
21	3	3	100%	
22	5	5	100%	
23	41	34	83%	
				94%

Periods were the only punctuation marks used in the writing entries.

Calkins, 1986; Cunningham, 1991; Goodman, 1986; Rhodes & Dudley-Marling, 1988), it is hard to believe that Jenny had *never*—in 7 years of school, 4 years of adult school, and 31 years of life—*never* written or read her own words at the text level. However, 2 years' worth of data collected on her validates this statement. Many years of teaching and research in schools lead me to suspect strongly that the majority of literacy programs at the elementary, secondary, and adult levels operate on a workbook-level skills approach to literacy learning. This, of course, needs to be confirmed by research.

From a skills point of view, Jenny should have been able to create her own text, given the amount of practice she received working on the bits and pieces of the type of idealized language represented in the curricular materials. But clearly she did not. So Jenny was right in a way. Her words did act as a wall between her and functional literacy. That is because her words were never acknowledged and affirmed, never allowed. Since people think, conceptualize, and learn with their language—with their words—Jenny was effec-

Figure 8
Selection of Jenny's Spellings Revealing Phoneme Approximation

Jenny's spelling	Standard spelling
Spellings in which every phoneme was represented graphically	
awr	hour
clening	cleaning
Levs	leaves
min	mine
mustak	mistake
muvd	moved
out sid	outside
papr	paper
rit	right
triing	trying
tuk	took
Spellings which did not represent every phoneme graphically	
Bas	baskets
Box	boxes
cled	cleaned
grbe	garbage
kied	kids
Muday	Monday

Figure 9
Selection of Jenny's Spellings that
Reflected Her Appalachian Dialect

Jenny's spelling	Standard spelling
Athos	Ethel's
dines	dentist
famlee	family
fir	far
haf	have
har	hair
ho	whole
masing	messing
mustak	mistake
rast	rest
sterl	still
thar	there
thin	then
war	where
worsh	wash

tively shut out of the literate world. The fact that she was allowed to fail year after year until she finally dropped out of the system in frustration is part of the immorality of this story.

Jenny's world and Jenny's language did not fit with the language of the schools. When she tried to match her own phonological system to the one taught in the phonics lessons, she failed, not because she could not hear the system at the phonemic base but because her system was different. However, it is true that everyone's dialect varies from the phonological system inherent in phonics programs. Jenny needed to see that her words did map onto standard orthography just as others' do; she needed teachers to show her how that happened.

Jenny needed to read real text in order to learn to read. However, the texts given to her to read were not real to her. Not only could she not relate to them on a content level, she was so stuck at the word level that she was effectively paralyzed. She continued year after year trying to memorize words, trying to memorize rules, trying to memorize terms like *adverb* and *pronoun*. None of these words, these rules, these linguistic terms, were hers, related to her in any way, and thus she could not succeed.

That she is beginning to read and write is, I believe, due to the fact that for the first time in her life she is allowed in; she is allowed access to the Literacy Club (Smith, 1988). She is acknowledged as a reader and a writer with the tools to communicate through print. These tools are her words, her thoughts, her needs to read and write. This doesn't make her different from anyone else. We all learned to read and write using our words, our thoughts, our own functions for reading and writing.

Fingeret (1991) issues a powerful call for situating the practices of adult literacy programs in the experiences and cultures of the participants:

> We must be clear that the construction of meaning is at the heart of literacy, and it is rooted in experience, culture, and language. Respect for cultural and linguistic background is not simply a matter of motivating, recruiting, or retaining students. It has to with dignity, power, strength, and authority. Cultural and linguistic diversity must be celebrated, respected and incorporated into the relationships among teachers and learners. We cannot separate literacy from experience, culture, and traditions (p. 10).

This story of Jenny's experience and the analysis of her development as a writer and reader illustrate the promise inherent in the stance Fingeret proposes.

Figure 10
Jenny's Journal Entry Describing the Night Police Broke into Her Apartment

April 5, 1990

Vicki, I hope you do not think I'm a bad person for what I'm going to tell you. Donny smokes pot, and he would sell some to his friends, and one night, the narcotic men came in. I was sleeping, and Donny and Timmy was sleeping; but big Donny was awake. The men came running in the living room. That is where we sleep; the bedroom is too cold to sleep in. Right then the men hollered something. I do not know what they hollered. I cannot remember what they said, but I can remember hearing the guns click as they came running in. They told Donny to get up and go in the kitchen. Donny was sitting on the couch, watching TV. I was on the pallet. A woman told me to get up and come in the kitchen so I did, and I was so scared. That man was asking Donny where he had his pot at. Donny told him. While he was talking to me and Donny, the other men was tearing my house apart. There was nothing I could do but just sit at the kitchen table like they say. Donny had 3 bags of pot. I did not know how much pot he has. I do not pay attention to how much pot he has because I do not ask him and he did not tell me nothing about it. I had told Donny many times to stop smoking pot, but he would not listen to me. So because of Donny's mistakes, I have to pay for it too because I live in the same place, and I know about him selling to his friends and him smoking pot. The law says you cannot do that. When we went to court, Donny got 3 to 6 months in jail. He had stayed in the Justice Center for 2 weeks, and his lawyer got the judge to send him to a drug center. I hope that it can help Donny stop smoking pot because if he don't, I will leave Donny. I love him, but I love my kids and I will not let that happen again because they can take my kids away from me. Just because I know about it, and I got 20 hours of working for the city and had to go to a drug and alcohol and got 5 years of probation for doing nothing but knowing what was going on. I do not smoke pot, and I do not drink, but they had made me go there. It was very embarrassing to me. And with Donny getting caught, he might see how wrong he is for doing what he was doing. I hope so anyway. That is all I can talk about right now and I hope you don't get mad at me.

References

Adams, M.J. (1990). *Beginning to read: Thinking and learning about print.* Cambridge, MA: MIT Press.

Atwell, N. (1987). *In the middle: Writing, reading and learning with adolescents.* Portsmouth, NH: Heinemann.

Auerbach, E.R. (1989). Toward a social-contextual approach to family literacy. *Harvard Educational Review, 59,* 155–181.

Buchanan, E. (1989). *Spelling for whole language classrooms.* Winnipeg, MB: Whole Language Consultants.

Calkins, L.M. (1986). *The art of teaching writing.* Portsmouth, NH: Heinemann.

Clay, M.M. (1975). *What did I write?* Portsmouth, NH: Heinemann.

Cunningham, P.M. (1991). *Phonics they use: Words for reading and writing.* New York: HarperCollins.

Ferdman, B. (1990). Literacy and cultural identity. *Harvard Educational Review, 60,* 181–204.

Fingeret, A. (1991). Meaning, experience and literacy. *Adult Basic Education, 1,* 4–11.

Freire, P., & Macedo, D. (1987). *Reading the word and the world.* South Hadley, MA: Bergin & Garvey.

Goodman, K. (1986). *What's whole in whole language?* Portsmouth, NH: Heinemann.

Green, J.L. (1990). Reading is a social process. In J. Howell, H. McNamara, & M. Clough (Eds.), *Social context of literacy* (pp. 104–123). Canberra, Australia: ACT Department of Education.

Harste, J., Woodward, V., & Burke, C. (1984). *Language stories and literacy lessons.* Portsmouth, NH: Heinemann.

Irwin, P.M. (1985). *Adult literacy issues, programs, and options*. Washington, DC: Education and Welfare Division, Congressional Research Service. Issue Brief (Order Code IB85167).

Kazemek, F.E., & Rigg, P. (1985, April). Adult illiteracy—America's phoenix problem (Occasional Paper). Tucson, AZ: University of Arizona, Program in Language and Literacy.

Newman, A.P., & Beverstock, C. (1990). *Adult literacy: Contexts and challenges*. Newark, DE: International Reading Association.

Northcutt, N. (1975). *Adult functional competency: A summary*. Austin, TX: University of Texas.

Rhodes, L.K., & Dudley-Marling, C. (1988). *Readers and writers with a difference*. Portsmouth, NH: Heinemann.

Smith, F. (1988). *Joining the literacy club*. Portsmouth, NH: Heinemann.

Stedman, L.D., & Kaestle, C.F. (1987). Literacy and reading performance in the United States from 1800 to the present. *Reading Research Quarterly, 22*, 8–46.

Sticht, T.G. (1988). Adult literacy education. *Review of Research in Education, 15*, 59–95.

Wolfram, W., & Christian, D. (1976). *Appalachian speech*. Arlington, VA: Center for Applied Linguistics.

The Use of an Educational Therapy Model with an Illiterate Adult

MARY J. SCULLY
CHRISTOPHER L. JOHNSTON
OCTOBER 1991

The individual who is illiterate is part of a system within the family and society and cannot be considered in isolation (von Bertalannfy, 1968). That person has failed to learn to read, and any attempt to teach him or her must address the failure and resulting anxiety and loss of self-esteem. What he or she experienced in attempting to learn to read, any special efforts that were made to help the individual, how the person has compensated for not being able to read, what efforts were made to hide the inability to read, and how this affected the person's life academically, socially, and emotionally are critical factors in determining the psychological scars the individual carries into adulthood because of the inability to read.

This case study describes how a functionally illiterate adult coped with the disabling effects of not being able to read and how, once he was involved in an educational therapy program, the treatment influenced his attitude towards reading, his self-esteem, interpersonal relationships, coping strategies, and actual progress in reading. This is a descriptive study of an individual who had for most of his adult life developed coping strategies that enabled him to function without learning to read. While there is evidence that many others like him have managed to function in society without being discovered (Fairservis, 1986), much of the literature reports on adults who have not been able to enter the mainstream of society. Determining how an individual has managed to cope with and compensate for his illiteracy while remaining gainfully employed in responsible positions, what the impact has been on his self-esteem, and assessing his progress using an educational therapy approach appeared to be topics worthy of consideration.

Illiteracy

The dictionary defines illiteracy as the "inability to read and write." However, in a practical sense, people who cannot read and write sufficiently to use these skills to function in their job, in their family, and in society suffer the handicap with or without the label. Thus the term functional illiteracy refers to those individuals whose reading and writing skills are so minimal that their opportunities for finding secure and meaningful employment are limited (Harman, 1986). Park (1987) states that as the level of proficiency required to be literate has increased, more individuals are falling into the category of the functionally illiterate. Literacy standards range widely, but an 8th-grade reading level appears necessary now to perform in even the most menial service occupations (Park, 1984). By the 1990s, individuals not reading at a 12th grade level may be unable to function adequately.

In addition to economic and social ramifications, lost productivity, unrealized tax revenues, welfare costs, and the bill for remedial training in business and the military, there are personal implications. Functionally illiterate individuals often feel inadequate and ashamed (Richek, List, & Lerner, 1983). They cannot look up numbers in a telephone directory, depend almost exclusively on label recognition, cannot travel freely, must always trust others, and live in daily fear (Kozol, 1985).

Living with anxiety, these individuals develop strategies to hide their inability to read, such as trying to act intelligently or asking for the help of a trusted adult in filling out forms. They tend to keep their disability hidden from their children and are often unable to provide them with the early learning opportunities that are a necessary preparation for school. In addition, even if these parents realize that their children are having difficulty, they do not have the political powerbase to effect a change. The problem then transfers from one generation to the next (Kozol, 1985). There is a consensus that a traditional academic program built on a developmental perspective concerned with normal growth of the reading process should not be the focus of instruction for reading disabled adults (Park, 1981; Richek, List, & Lerner, 1983). Remedial reading must take into account the educational, psychological, social, cultural, cognitive, and physical factors of the person in planning an individual program for each adult (Harris & Sipay, 1980).

Educational Therapy

Because of the emotional vulnerability of the adult illiterate, a strictly pedagogical approach has generally not been effective. In contrast, an educational therapy model addresses the psychological and educational variables affecting the individual. Educational therapy is an approach to remediating learning problems through the establishment of a personal relationship between the therapist and the individual with the learning problem. The strengths and weaknesses of the individual are considered in planning an appropriate program, and the client is directly involved in that planning. Issues such as resistance and coping with the problem are dealt with as they occur (Johnston, 1986).

Adults, even more than children, have experienced considerable failure in their efforts to learn to read. Strategies must be developed that reduce anxiety sufficiently to allow the individual to focus on overcoming the deficit. The establishment of the "therapeutic milieu" (Dreikers, Brunwald, & Pepper, 1982; Redl, 1966) helps relieve the anxiety associated with repeated failure. The development of a therapeutic relationship allows the individual to begin to trust the person with whom she or he will be working. The therapeutic milieu is essential to the learning process. When the psychological as well as the academic needs of the individual are in focus, the emotional issues related to the academic difficulty can be addressed, thus relieving anxiety and freeing the individual to focus on remediation (Johnston, 1986). The use of an educational therapy model helps to accomplish this goal because it "involves the application of diagnostic results to specific educational and therapeutic interventions that will enable the therapist to intervene more effectively with the psychological resistance to emotional acceptance and understanding of the disability which frequently emerges during the a course of treatment" (Johnston, 1986, p. 72).

There are four stages involved in the educational therapy relationship: (1) initial contact, when the therapist comes to understand the nature of the individual's perception of his or her problem, learns about his or her interests, and develops a mutually agreed upon plan of action; (2) integration of the treatment, during which the therapist evaluates the accuracy of the individual's perception and develops strategies for integrating the remedial and therapeutic techniques to deal with the specific problems; (3) focusing on the relationship between the therapist and client, in which issues such as resistance to or avoidance of reading are discussed; and (4) "termination" in which the therapist and client deal with the issues of imminent separation.

Adaptation, defense, mastery, and coping are critical concepts to understanding how individuals function under stress. People develop defenses to protect themselves against anxiety, strive for mastery through successful task performance, and continue to develop adaptive processes under difficult conditions (Hamburg, Coelho, & Adams, 1974). They "cope, compensate, and conceal" while enduring fear of discovery and a constant feeling of impending disaster (Janis, 1974). How they perceive and respond to the threat and the anxiety depends, in part, on past life experiences (Coelho & Adams, 1974; Hamburg, Coelho, & Adams, 1974). Over time, individuals develop mechanisms to deal with the discrepancies between their assessment of themselves and their environment (French, Rodgers, & Cobb, 1974). Defenses that block painful emotions make learning all but impossible (Abrams, 1968). Withdrawal, denial, rationalization, and projection may be used constructively for a short time, but over a long period, there is the danger that the anxiety-provoking situation will not be reexamined and that a change to more positive problem-solving strategies may be resisted (Lazarus, Averill, & Opton, 1974). Successful adaptation involves compromise while preserving some degree of autonomy or flexibility of action (White, 1974) plus the ability to focus on reality (Adams & Lindemann, 1974).

Individual Case Study

Chad was the functionally illiterate adult who is the focus of this case study. He was a first-generation Italian-American who went to work immediately after completing eighth grade. Chad was 49 years old when he was referred by his supervisor to the Center for Learning at National College of Education (now National-Louis University) in Evanston, Illinois, because of an acute crisis in his workplace caused by his inability to read. There had been many other situations in which Chad changed jobs or refused promotions because he was afraid it would be discovered that he could not read. Although he was unable to read street signs, a restaurant menu, or the names of patients on a computer list at the hospital where he worked, he had developed numerous compensatory strategies over the years to conceal his disability.

Other than family members, Chad did not tell anyone that he could not read. Only one friend of 25 years discovered that he could not read and has helped him through the years by filling out forms for him, reading his mail, and helping him get a job as a salesman in a clothing store where he worked for 13 years. Chad memorized the words he needed to know before he started the job, so that he would not have to read. According to Chad, he was very successful as a clothing salesman and was offered the position of manager at another store. He knew he would not be able to handle the necessary written reports, so he refused the promotion. Chad was in show business as an entertainer for 7 years with a well known singing group that traveled all over the United States. He sang, danced, and played the trumpet. Although he could not read, he was able to memorize the act and all of the songs. Although Chad has never been married, he seriously dated a woman at one time. He felt she was too intelligent for him because he could not read. Chad never told her this, although it was the reason he finally broke off the relationship.

For the past 3 years, Chad had been employed as an assistant to eight physical therapists at a suburban hospital. He used various strategies to avoid having to read patients' names, and initially no one at the hospital was aware of his difficulty. He would get the computer printout, go to the appropriate floor of the hospital, walk into the patient's room, match up the printout with the name on the bed to be sure he had the right patient and then say, "How do you pronounce your last name?" He enjoyed talking to patients and they really seemed to like him. One of the patients wrote a letter to his supervisor and said, "He sure knows how to make an old lady feel like a spring chicken." Chad had recently begun having difficulty getting along with his supervisor because of a change in procedures that again threatened to expose his inability to read. He had trouble sleeping at night and was irritable at work. He finally confided in his supervisor, who suggested that he might be able to get help through National College of Education. At this point the initial contact was made with the Center for Learning by Chad's supervisor. According to results of the initial case study evaluation, Chad was unable to read comfortably beyond the midprimary level. Although he made good use of context clues, sight vocabulary was limited, and word attack skills were almost nonexistent. However, there were good prognostic indicators: average intellectual ability, a high degree of determination and motivation, and no signs of obvious perceptual deficits. Chad appeared to be an emotionally stable, self-sufficient individual who generally had a positive outlook on life. He had good interpersonal skills and demonstrated responsibility and sensitivity to others, although at times he had difficulty expressing his emotions. Chad had concerns for the future but felt that he could be successful if he could overcome his disability in reading and was willing to put forth whatever effort was necessary if someone would just tell him where and how to begin.

Establishing Trust

Chad was seen for 15 sessions of 1.5–2 hours' duration over 4 months. The treatment was based on an educational therapy model, which is an approach to remediating learning problems through the establishment of a personal relationship between the therapist and the individual with the learning problem. The strengths and weaknesses of the individual are considered in planning an appropriate program, and the learner is directly involved in that planning. Issues such as resistance and coping with the problem are dealt with as they occur in the remediation of the problem area.

A personal relationship based on trust between the therapist and the client was established gradually from the time of the initial testing session. Chad was willing to try whatever was asked of him because of that trust. In order to relieve the anxiety associated with reading, constant support was provided so that he could feel successful and know he was not alone in his efforts to acquire basic reading skills. Verbal cueing, positive reinforcement, and help in generalizing from a familiar to an unfamiliar word were used during every session to provide support and relieve anxiety.

Methods

Remedial strategies were developed based on initial testing, but in sessions with Chad,

intervention procedures were often changed when it was apparent that he had a real need at that particular time to work on other issues. For example, when it was first determined that Chad had not developed any word attack skills, the plan was to emphasize sight words. However, Chad wanted to learn "sounding out and vowels," so the emphasis of instruction changed to meet his needs. In certain respects it was the therapy that gave Chad confidence in already existing abilities. However, the educational program enabled him to integrate sound and symbol for the first time and provided considerable incentive to continue reading on his own.

To provide Chad with a sense of independence and relieve his anxiety at the same time, books and words were taped so that he could do his homework independently and could organize his time in preparation for the following week. Although we used word sorts, word families, word lists, picture and vowel associations, and oral reading in context, the amount of time spent on each area depended in part on his interests and needs during that session. As personal concerns relating to work, family, interpersonal relationships, or reading emerged during the educational therapy sessions, they were discussed. There were often instances where an issue occurring in the instruction triggered a memory that needed to be addressed at the time. It was important to help Chad understand how old fears diverted so much energy from the actual process of learning to read.

Sessions were audiotaped and transcribed. Transcriptions of the sessions, as well as additional information obtained from the researcher's journal, process recordings, interviews with staff and a close friend, and a questionnaire filled out by Chad's brother were used as data sources for triangulation. The data were then analyzed. Triangulation, the corroboration of data sources, was achieved by comparing information Chad shared during initial testing, the remedial sessions, and during the final interview. Additional information was obtained as time went on. Some data on Chad's early history were triangulated using information from his brother's interview. For information concerning the last 25 years, Chad's friend Lou was the primary source. Staff interviews were used to support data regarding Chad's reading difficulties, his self-esteem, and anxiety regarding the reading process, which had been reported in the researcher's journal and the initial testing and conference.

Gaining Confidence

Chad's unsuccessful school history, his varied but often self-limiting work experiences, his previous attempts to get help in reading, and the strategies he was forced to develop to compensate for his inability to read appear to be important patterns in understanding his reactions as a functionally illiterate adult. Some of the strategies he developed included "forgetting" his glasses, eliciting sufficient clues to make an educated guess about what information was contained in what he was supposed to be reading, getting others to read for him without realizing what they were doing, memorizing his music, learning by watching and doing, and color coding equipment at work.

From the initial educational therapy session, Chad did not exhibit the extreme anxiety that had been noted during the testing sessions. As he began to gain confidence in himself and his reading skills, he was challenged by the reading process and worked long hours to develop his decoding skills. Chad became enthusiastic about reading, was highly motivated, and began to read for pleasure. He especially enjoyed reading his first paperback novel. Far from avoiding reading, Chad started sounding out the names of patients, almost had a car accident trying to read a street sign, began reading the newspaper and trade papers, read a letter from his nephew, and generally approached reading with enthusiasm. He put in significant amounts of time during each week on homework, generally from 7 to 10 hours per week. He went so far as to put a "Do Not Disturb" sign from a hotel on his door so that he would not be interrupted during his allotted study time. He asked friends to leave early so he could study and kept a book in the glove compartment so he could read in the car while waiting for a friend.

Making Progress

Because he was ready to learn and had developed a therapeutic, trusting relationship with the examiner, he concentrated intently and was receptive to who was being presented. Although decoding was always a challenge for Chad, he worked hard in spite of the frustration he experienced and improved dramatically in his ability to decode unfamiliar words. The use of picture and vowel cards, word family flip charts, and the word sort technique gave him the tools he needed to decode unfamiliar words. Chad's sight vocabulary improved not only because he was studying a list of the 1,000 most commonly used words but because he was reading constantly and had always made good use of context clues. The more words he knew, the more easily he could read a story; and the more exciting it was to read, the more he read. Once he learned to decode words, he would spend more than 10 hours a week practicing what had been mastered in the tutorial sessions. Hence the total time he directed towards learning to read was considerably more than the time recorded in tutorials.

Pre- and posttests suggested that Chad had made significant progress in representing short vowels correctly and marking long vowels as well as being better able to sound his way through a word. In addition, he had made significant progress in word recognition as well as word attack. Chad self-corrected several times. Many of the words he did not know by sight but was able to decode. He was very pleased that he was able to identify correctly so many of the fourth-grade words that he had not even attempted in April. However, it was not the formal assessment of reading proficiency that was the real indicator of the progress Chad made in reading. He was able to read a children's book, a series of short stories (at the second-grade level), his first high-interest, low-vocabulary paperback novel of over 250 pages, newspapers and trade magazines, and his own mail plus identify patients' names, figure out street signs, and generally challenge any reading task he came across. Although progress with word attack skills had been slow by his standards, he had new tools for decoding unfamiliar words and was no longer avoiding reading. This was what opened up new horizons for Chad.

Chad had always demonstrated a strength in interpersonal skills. He was an outgoing, friendly individual. Although on the surface this did not change, as Chad began to make progress in reading, he began to share information about being unable to read with increasing confidence. He confided first to one friend, and then to a few more, that he could not read and expressed amazement at their positive reaction. Comments like "God, you got a good start—I give you a lot of credit" and "Anything we can do to help, Chad" enabled him to realize that his friends were not going to reject him because of his admission that he could not read.

Chad admitted to feeling more "comfortable" in those relationships once he had been able to reveal that he could not read. He no longer had to feel like a fake but could take the same pride in his reading accomplishments as he did in other aspects of his life. In addition, Chad developed a better working relationship with his supervisor. So what finally happened to Chad? When it became necessary for him to continue his work with a different tutor, Chad had some difficulty in making the change. Also, he felt he had made significant progress in his ability to read and believed he could master more advanced skills on his own. He indicated that he could now manage daily living activities more effectively because he could read street signs, decode simple directions, and—most important—derive great pleasure from reading primary grade books on his own. He therefore left the center's program. Chad's progress in his 15 sessions of educational therapy had been remarkable, and we believe that the therapy model could be even more effective if a long-term relationship between the learner and the tutor could be sustained.

Implications

It would appear that the importance of the therapeutic relationship has been validated in this study. In knowing an individual's processing strengths and weaknesses, an appropriate remedial program can be developed, but unless a relationship is established in which the individual trusts the therapist and can share his or her anxieties and fears, it will be difficult to break through the avoidance of reading and the anxiety associated with the reading process. In addition, unless the learner knows she or he is respected as an individual regardless of the amount of progress being made, that there is someone who really cares and is willing to listen as the individual shares his or her life and how traumatic it has been to be unable to read, it will prove difficult to get beyond the past. Because it appears that the person's self-esteem is so closely linked to the inability to read and that this has affected interpersonal relationships with significant others in his or her life, the therapeutic relationship becomes especially important. Methodology is one aspect of teaching reading skills, but the process that emerges between the educational therapist and the client is extremely powerful and cannot be ignored. There must be an acknowledgment of life history and the struggles undergone to reach this particular stage in the person's life. Establishing a therapeutic relationship on a one-to-one basis during the initial stages to allow for the development of trust, the desire to please the "teacher" and ultimately oneself, appears to mandate this type of approach for real, significant growth to be achieved in a relatively brief time. From a pragmatic perspective, group treatment might be considered once the initial therapeutic relationship has been established during the first 8–10 sessions.

Although with Chad lesson plans were not rigidly adhered to, there were some instructional techniques and materials that appeared to be more effective than others: picture and vowel cards, word family flip charts, word sort, and taped word lists and stories. Plans were changed based on Chad's needs and interests at the time. Chad made considerable progress in reading achievement during the 15 educational therapy sessions. The therapeutic nature of the relationship as well as the instructional strategies and techniques used contributed to that progress. Relieving anxiety appeared to be a critical factor in breaking through the years of failure he had experienced in his previous exposure to reading.

Summary

This study has important implications for literacy programs for adults. Focusing on the psychological aspects of reading and the issue of providing support for the functionally illiterate adult who is struggling to learn to read appears to be at least equal in importance to whatever strategies and techniques are used in teaching specific reading skills. The educational therapy model addresses these issues because it takes into consideration the emotional and psychological elements involved in the reading process. Results of this case study strongly suggest that programs working with functionally illiterate adults need to account for the psychological ramifications of being unable to read. For Chad, the acquisition of specific reading skills was only one aspect of his growth during the educational therapy sessions. Of equal importance was the development of greater self-esteem and improved social relationships as he gained more confidence in himself and his abilities.

References

Abrams, J.C. (1968). The role of the personality defenses in reading. In G. Natchez (Ed.), *Children with reading problems* (pp. 77–79). New York: Basic.

Adams, J.E., & Lindemann, E. (1974). Coping with long-term disability. In G.V. Coelho, D.A. Hamburg, & J.E. Adams (Eds.), *Coping and adaptation* (pp. 127–138). New York: Basic.

Coelho, G.V., & Adams, J.E. (1974). Introduction. In G.V. Coelho, D.A. Hamburg, & J.E. Adams (Eds.), *Coping and adaptation* (pp. xv–xxiv). New York: Basic.

Dreikers, R., Brunwald, B., & Pepper, F. (1982). *Maintaining sanity in the classroom: Classroom management techniques* (2nd ed.). Cambridge, MA: HarperCollins.

Fairservis, W.A. (1986, Spring). Illiteracy in America. *The Wilson Quarterly, 2*, 94–103.

French, J.R., Rodgers, W., & Cobb, S. (1974). Adjustment as person-environment fit. In G.V.

Coelho, D.A. Hamburg, & J.E. Adams (Eds.), *Coping and adaptation* (pp. 316–333). New York: Basic.

Hamburg, D.A., Coelho, G.V., & Adams, J.E. (1974). Coping and adaptations: Steps toward a synthesis of biological and social perspectives. In G.V. Coelho, D.A. Hamburg, & J.E. Adams (Eds.), *Coping and adaptation* (pp. 403–440). New York: Basic.

Harman, D. (1986, Spring). Keeping up in America. *The Wilson Quarterly*, 118–133.

Harris, A.J., & Sipay, E.R. (1980). *How to increase reading ability* (6th ed.). New York: David McCay.

Janis, I.L. (1974). Vigilance and decision making in personal crises. In G.V. Coelho, D.A. Hamburg, & J.E. Adams (Eds.), *Coping and adaptation* (pp. 139–175). New York: Basic.

Johnston, C.L. (1986). Educational therapy and psychotherapeutic treatment of the learning disabled. In A.R. Stiffman & R.A. Feldman (Eds.), *Advances in adolescent mental health* (pp. 61–77). Greenwich, CT: Jai.

Kozol, J. (1985). *Illiterate America*. Garden City, NY: Anchor.

Lazarus, R.S., Averill, J.R., & Opton, E.M. (1974). The psychology of coping: Issues of research and assessment. In G.V. Coelho, D.A. Hamburg, & J.E. Adams (Eds.), *Coping and adaptation* (pp. 249–315). New York: Basic.

Park, R. (1981). A critical review of developments in adult literacy. In M.L. Kamil & M.M. Boswick (Eds.), *Directions in reading: Research & instruction* (pp. 279–289). Washington, DC: National Reading Conference.

Park, R. (1984). Overcoming the illiteracy barrier. *Training and Development Journal, 38*, 77–80.

Park, R. (1987). Three approaches to improving literacy levels. *Educational Horizons, 66*, 38–41.

Redl, F. (1966). *When we deal with children*. New York: Free Press.

Richek, M.A., List, L.K., & Lerner, J.W. (1983). *Reading problems: Diagnosis and remediation*. Englewood Cliffs, NJ: Prentice Hall.

von Bertalannfy, L. (1968). *General system theory: Foundations, development and applications*. New York: Braziller.

White, R.W. (1974). Strategies of adaptation: An attempt at systematic description. In G.V. Coelho, D.A. Hamburg, & J.E. Adams (Eds.), *Coping and adaptation* (pp. 47–68). New York: Basic.

T u t o r i n g

Norman: Literate at Age 44

VALERIE MEYER
SHARON L. ESTES
VALORIE K. HARRIS
DAVID M. DANIELS
SEPTEMBER 1991

This is the story of a remarkable man. At 44, Norman decided he wanted to learn to read and write. In less than one year, he had progressed from being a man who could not read or write his own address to a man who enjoys reading the newspaper and social studies books. This is also the story of a team of adult educators and a Student Literacy Corps volunteer who nurtured, supported, and learned from Norman.

To adult educators, Norman's history is familiar. He has a slight speech impediment and when he entered first grade in 1951, this was mistaken for a learning disability. Within weeks he was labeled "slow." By second grade, he said, "My teachers just gave up on me. No one even tried to teach me. They just ignored me. They thought I was dumb." Beyond learning the alphabet, Norman did not learn to read in school. He was taught to work with his hands. He remembered making pot holders and baskets. He now works full time as a meat cutter, as a janitor on weekends, and also bales hay for local farmers in the summer.

Norman is an industrious man and, like other illiterate or low-literate adults, he was ingenious in disguising his lack of reading skills (Brozo, 1990; Johnston, 1985). His wife, Colleen, occasionally read to him. She paid the bills and did all the shopping and other family tasks that required reading. Norman obtained his driver's license by having the questions read to him but, he stated, "I didn't travel very far from home without my wife or someone." He said he rarely really tried to read. "Once in a while I would pick up a newspaper and act like I was reading. The only thing I knew was to look at a picture."

Despite his unpleasant memories of formal education, Norman never lost his desire to learn to read: "I knew there was something I was missing." His desire centered on economic, family, and religious needs. His current job paid only US$8.00 per hour, with few fringe benefits. He planned to pass the GED (general equivalency dimploma) exam, attend trade school, and become a machinist. A new job would give him the economic security he lacked. He also wanted to read to his 10-year-old daughter, Sheila, who is in a wheelchair and paralyzed from the waist down; and as a devoutly religious man he wanted to read the Bible by himself.

The Beginning

In September 1989, Norman enrolled in a local adult education program. Fortunately for him, his first teacher, Sharon Estes, was completing her master's degree with a major in reading. Sharon's classroom, like those of most adult education programs, was not the ideal place for a man who needed as much help as Norman. The class's 10 students had reading levels ranging from below first grade

to about sixth grade. Despite the problems posed by the diverse abilities of the class members, Norman and Sharon were determined and persistent.

Sharon recalls her first class with Norman: She read a story to the group about a woman who received a promotion at work but was very worried that someone would discover her secret—illiteracy. After the story the class discussed how it felt not to be able to read and how prevalent a problem illiteracy is. During a break, Norman approached Sharon. "You know the story we just read and the people you were talking about? I'm one of them people. I can't read." Sharon was startled—the other class members *could* read at at least a basic level—but she maintained her composure and replied, "It's okay. I know how to help you." She says now that "my biggest challenge was to build up Norman's self-esteem and confidence."

There was a pile of old magazines at the back of the room. She invited Norman to flip through the magazines and cut out advertisements for products he recognized. Environmental print (Goodman, Smith, Meredith, & Goodman, 1987) was the beginning. Sharon and Norman spent the evening cutting and taping the ads to blank paper (Figure 1). Sharon wrote the product's name or a description of it next to each ad and began to emphasize to Norman that he could read some things (even though he was relying primarily on familiar pictures). They reviewed the words associated with each picture.

In the weeks that followed, Norman's environmental print book grew larger with advertisements he added at home. Sharon and Norman spent many hours going through this book, attempting to build his sight vocabulary. Then they began to drop the pictures and transfer the words to flashcards. Norman had created his first word bank. He was very

Figure 1
Environmental Print

MACARONI

AND CHEESE

excited and called this his reading material. In addition to environmental print and word banks, Norman was introduced to language experience stories (Van Allen, 1976). He enjoyed basing these on his wife and family life: "When I got up this morning the first thing I did was eat breakfast. I had eggs and sausage and toast and coffee. Then I brushed my teeth. I kissed my wife and went to work." Sharon recalls: "We practiced reading Norman's stories. This gave Norman ownership of his reading material. It was easy for him to recognize and remember his own words. We added new words to his word bank and practiced them often."

Norman made great gains during the first 3 months. From September until December, he advanced from a nonreader to reading at about the first- or second-grade level. His curiosity and enthusiasm were infectious. He felt free in Sharon's class—free to express himself, talk about his life, and dictate his own thoughts. He had a wealth of background knowledge to draw from. Sharon says, "What I remember most about Norman was his genuine desire to learn to read." In December, Sharon left the community college to concentrate on finishing her master's degree. In January, Norman had a new

instructor named Val Harris. Again, he was fortunate—his new instructor was also completing a master's degree in reading.

Writing and Reading

Val was eager to build on the success Sharon had had with Norman. Although Norman had previously shied away from writing, she urged him to try. Val stated, "I knew he had to begin writing if he was going to continue to make progress." She began by simply asking him to copy short passages. Although Norman could read very little independently, he was immersed in a supportive environment that encouraged risk taking. Daily journals were added to his curriculum. Writing did not come easy for Norman. One of his first independent stories reveals his determination and frustration: "If I had my life to live over I would be a good reader and a good math" (Figure 2).

"When we started together," said Val, "Norman didn't like to write—at all! He just

Figure 2
A Writing Sample

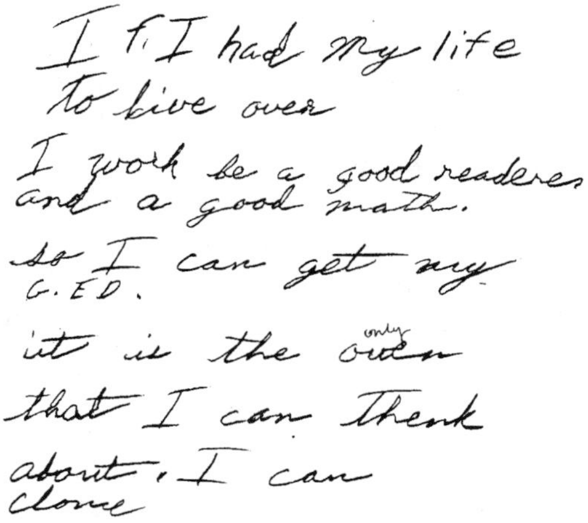

I f I had my life
to live over
I work be a good readeres
and a good math.
so I can get my
G. E D.
its is the onlyover
that I can Thenk
about, I can
close

did not yet see himself as a writer. He would either copy what I wrote or make half-hearted attempts at writing, until one night in math class. He was very upset, almost in tears. It was as if he needed to get something off his chest but couldn't tell me face to face...so he wrote down his feelings. Wow! From then on his writing began to improve." Val continued Norman's environmental print activities and began to include simple sentence stems such as "I like to eat _____, but I don't like to eat _____" and "I like _____ on my pizza, but my wife likes _____ on her pizza." This type of reading and writing was predictable and repetitive. Val stated, "Norman was very concerned about his spelling. I constantly reassured him that his invented spelling was acceptable. Gradually, he began to view himself as a writer."

Val also read to Norman and introduced alternating reading (Meyer & Keefe, 1990). Norman selected a story he wanted to read. Sometimes it was one of his language experience stories; other times it was something simple from a newspaper. Both Val and Norman first read the material silently. Then they read out loud in an "alternating" manner. Val would begin by reading a few sentences, then Norman would read a sentence or two, then Val again and Norman again. The power of this activity was that Val demonstrated for Norman: "I wanted to provide him with a sense of what reading should sound like." Norman continued to progress with Val's encouragement. He practiced at home and enlisted the support of his wife, who helped him with his writing.

Norman's Tutor

In March 1990, Norman began to receive even more assistance. A local university had received a Student Literacy Corps grant. The services of undergraduate students trained as literacy tutors were made available to the community college where Val worked. Norman enthusiastically requested a tutor to work with him outside class. Thus, David Daniels and Norman began their relationship. David stated, "I had been introduced to a whole language theory base and was armed with lots of reading strategies, so I felt reasonably competent as a tutor. I found Norman to be the quintessential learner; he not only wanted to read better, he was convinced this was possible. My job has been to support his intentions compassionately with reading strategies he can adopt for himself. My guess is that he was reading somewhere between second- and third-grade level when I came into the picture."

Val and David worked in tandem to ensure continuity. Their agenda was to reinforce constantly what Norman already knew, that wealth of knowledge gleaned from 44 years of being a productive member of society. Norman and David focused on reading materials selected by Norman—things Norman decided he needed and wanted to read. David recalled, "Norman was able to discover words in print which he used every day, and those little discoveries became a natural expansion of what he already knew. He didn't feel obliged to memorize some alien list of new words." Norman was encouraged to skip words he did not immediately recognize and to gather context clues. Whenever he made an ill-fated guess at a word he did not know, David's response was "Does it make sense to you? Don't try to please me; satisfy yourself." Invariably Norman arrived at a meaning that made sense. Gradually his confidence increased as he realized the benefits of figuring things out by himself.

Each tutoring session included reading *to* Norman, reading *with* him, writing, and sustained silent reading. Norman especially enjoyed articles from the local newspaper and various U.S. tabloids. He usually selected a headline that interested him. He then was encouraged to guess what the article might be about. Finally, he would read the article to determine the validity of his predictions. According to David, "The single most important strategy used before, during, and after each reading session was to support, encourage, and reflect back to Norman—in ways he knew were sincere—the wonderful progress his hard work produced." During a period of approximately one year, Norman, with the assistance of three individuals, had progressed from a nonreader with little confidence to a man with disarming optimism. His most recent writing attempts demonstrated his ability to generate "brainstorming maps" independently. "We continue to bombard Norman with the importance of 'making meaning'," Val said. "He's always talking about making sense and predicting. All this has made a difference—along with his determination and hard work" (Figure 3).

Today, we estimate that Norman is reading at about the sixth- or seventh-grade level, and he continues to improve. He's reading 7–12 hours on his own each week in addition to attending adult education classes and receiving individual tutoring. Recently, Norman wrote this story:

The Man Who Wanted to Read

The man didn't know how to read. One day he decided to do something about it. So he went to school to learn how to read. And he had three good tutors to work with him, to teach him to read. His teacher gave him a little book to bring home to read. Now he can read. He didn't know what he was missing from not reading. Now he wants to read everything he sees.

Indeed, Norman told a group of graduate students, "When I drive somewhere, I have to be

Figure 3
A Brainstorming Map

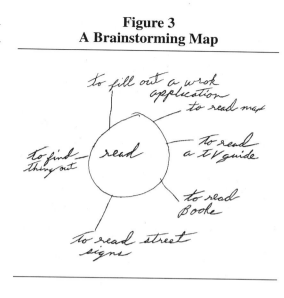

careful because I'm looking and reading everything."

What Made It Work?

Kazemek (1990) has described adult literacy instruction as a field possessing a "meager theoretical base...dealing with rather primitive notions of what it means to be literate...." Stories such as Norman's are not typical in adult education (Kavale & Lindsey, 1977; Lindsey & Jarman, 1984). Why is our story different? First and foremost, credit for Norman's success lies within him and his extraordinary determination. Perhaps a second reason for his success is that his instruction reflected a whole language theory in an adult context. The theories of Cambourne (1988), Smith (1985), and Goodman et al. (1987) were manifest in five ways:

1. *Norman's reading and writing always had a purpose and an audience.* His journal writing with Val was real; he used it to express his joy, his anger, and his feelings. He was immersed in language and print that had meaning for him.

2. *Norman was provided with lots of*

demonstrations of how language works. Sharon, David, and Val constantly read and wrote to Norman. In doing so, they provided him with role models of reading and writing.

3. *The context of Norman's instruction always included the expectation that he would be successful.* The responsibility for learning was always in his hands. When Sharon invited Norman to cut out ads he recognized, she stressed that ads are "real" reading. She suggested to him that he already had a lengthy mental word bank. By the time David began working with him, Norman was convinced he could be a better reader. Norman, not his instructors, always decided what would be read and what needed to be written.

4. *Norman's approximations in reading and writing were accepted and rewarded.* When he wrote "I did nuting but get mat," Val responded to his anger, not his spelling.

5. *Norman spent ample time employing his new skills.* He became actively engaged in reading. Norman first requested a tutor because he wanted additional time to learn. He spent many hours reading independently. Many literacy volunteer projects provide only 90 minutes to 2 hours of tutoring per week (Bowren, 1990). Thus, the amount of engaged time Norman spent cannot be ignored.

Norman was never asked to memorize high frequency vocabulary words from a sight word list. He was never subjected to workbooks and skill sheets. His reading and writing were always in the context of his life. In his discussion of adult literacy instruction, Kazemek (1990) states, "We do not learn from others too readily it seems" (p. 58). Norman's experience has much to teach us. His story is a work in progress, about progress. For those wrestling with the dilemma of confronting illiteracy, let us repeat Norman's bit of advice: "You gotta have the 'want to', 'cuz if you don't have the 'want to' you ain't got nothin'." As Norman will readily attest, "want to" goes a long way.

References

Bowren, F. (1990). *An evaluation of reading gains within Illinois literacy projects: FY '89.* Springfield, IL: Office of the Secretary of State, Illinois State Library Literacy Office.

Brozo, W.G. (1990). Hiding out in secondary content classrooms: Coping strategies of unsuccessful readers. *Journal of Reading, 33,* 324–328.

Cambourne, B. (1988). *The whole story: Natural learning and the acquisition of literacy in the classroom.* Richmond Hill, Ontario, Canada: Scholastic-TAB.

Goodman, K.S., Smith, E.B., Meredith, R., & Goodman, Y.M. (1987). *Language and thinking in school: A whole-language curriculum.* New York: Richard C. Owen.

Johnston, P.H. (1985). Understanding reading disability: A case study approach. *Harvard Educational Review, 55,* 153–177.

Kavale, K.A., & Lindsey, J.D. (1977). Adult basic education: Has it worked? *Journal of Reading, 20,* 368–376.

Kazemek, F.E. (1990). Adult literacy education: Heading into the 1990s. *Adult Education Quarterly, 41,* 53–62.

Lindsey, J.D., & Jarman, L.T. (1984). Adult basic education: Six years after Kavale and Lindsey's literature review. *Journal of Reading, 27,* 609–613.

Meyer, V., & Keefe, D. (1990). *Reading for meaning: Selected teaching strategies.* Glenview, IL: Scott, Foresman.

Smith, F. (1985). *Reading without nonsense.* New York: Teachers College Press.

Van Allen, R. (1976). *Language experience in communication.* Boston, MA: Houghton Mifflin.

" **It may take several hundred hours of instruction before a worker who can barely read a product label is able to troubleshoot by using a manual for computerized equipment.** "

– MIKULECKY & DREW, 1991, P. 686

Most attempts to define literacy or establish a criterion for determining what is "basic functional literacy" tend to become muddled since literacy is not easily defined (Mikulecky & Drew, 1991). Mikulecky and Drew also point out that literacy demands vary among occupations and from job to job within occupations. They clearly remind us of the increasing amount and complexity of literacy demands in most sectors of the workplace.

These authors point to five areas of workplace literacy in need of further research: developing workplace literacy process models, determining the generalizability and limits of transfer for literacy strategies in the workplace, examining the cost-effectiveness of workplace literacy training efforts, technology's role in workplace literacy training, and economic and political issues related to race and social class. Most articles in this section address the first of these issues. Askov's piece on assessment in workplace literacy programs is a model for diagnostic assessment and program evaluation. DeStefano describes a lesson plan format to move from the "diagnosis" of literacy needs in a workplace to working with specific students. Anziano and Terminello's model describes workplace literacy through a teacher training program. Miller recognizes the issue of limits of transfer in her piece on using annual reports as a tool for business literacy. It is to be hoped that future Journal of Reading *articles will address Mikulecky and Drew's other suggested areas of research.*

References

Mikulecky, L., & Drew, R. (1991). Basic literacy skills in the workplace. In R. Barr, M.L. Kamil, P. Mosenthal, & P.D. Pearson (Eds.), Handbook of reading research: Volume II *(pp. 669–689). White Plains, NY: Longman.*

Approaches to Assessment in Workplace Literacy Programs: Meeting the Needs of All the Clients

EUNICE N. ASKOV
APRIL 1993

Assessment in workplace literacy programs must satisfy multiple stakeholders or clients, each with different interests in the outcomes of the program; multiple approaches to assessment are necessary to satisfy these various information needs. In community adult literacy programs an instructor usually has only one client—the learners. In the case of workplace literacy programs, however, two additional clients emerge, namely, the union (if one exists) and the management of the company. In the case of a unionized workforce, the union must be involved from the beginning as a decision maker representing the workers who potentially may join the program. If the business or industry is offering the program on-site and releasing workers from their jobs on company time, the instructor clearly has the business or industry partner as a client. A fourth client—namely, the literacy organization—may also be requiring assessment information in response to some regulatory or funding agency, such as a state department of education.

What are the assessment information needs of each client? The learners may have very specific goals for the literacy instructional program that may or may not pertain to their jobs. For example, some workers may be primarily interested in learning to read the Bible or newspaper and helping their children with homework. In some cases they may want to improve their literacy skills so they may leave their jobs, and even the company. Workers' goals for the instructional program must be assessed individually. This is accomplished best through confidential conferences.

The second client, the union, is usually interested in assessment that focuses on the welfare and development of the workers (Education Writers Association, 1991; Sarmiento & Kay, 1990). In contrast to the very specific objectives of the individual learner, the union may have more global goals for the workplace literacy program, such as empowering workers to become more active decision makers in the company. Assessment for the union client should be designed around the goals of the union at the particular workplace.

The business or industry management client, on the other hand, usually offers a workplace literacy program, especially if it is "on the clock" (on company time) out of concern for workers' skills (Carnevale, Gainer, & Meltzer, 1990; Johnston & Packer, 1987;

U.S. Department of Labor and U.S. Department of Education, 1988). Sometimes management wants to upgrade workers' basic skills to enable them to do their current jobs better or to prepare them to use new technology, such as computers. Assessment information for the business or industry client should focus on job-related basic skills.

Finally, the instructor may have to satisfy funding requirements or state mandates. Some states, for example, require the use of a specific standardized test. Some programs prohibit serving learners who score above a certain grade-equivalent level. The instructor may be required to assess learners with a standardized test that is irrelevant to the curriculum and to the assessment information needs of the learners, the union, and the company! While these observations represent generalizations, many exceptions exist (Jurmo, 1991). The intent is not to prescribe but to suggest what may be appropriate to satisfy the information needs of the various stakeholders in a workplace literacy program.

Assessment Tools in Workplace Literacy Programs

Meeting the assessment information needs of the different clients within a workplace literacy program requires different tools. The needs of the various clients, in fact, could be portrayed as on a continuum ranging from informal, qualitative assessment to formal, standardized testing that yields quantitative information. Taken all together, the assessment process becomes a holistic look at learners' skills, abilities, and interests. The figure that follows is a graphic presentation of the tools that might be used for the various clients in a workplace literacy program.

Learner-Centered Assessments

Learners often have unique goals for entering a workplace literacy program—goals that may or may not be similar to those of the other clients. These goals must be determined during the initial assessment process to make instruction meaningful to the learners; accomplishment of these goals should be reassessed periodically. Learners also differ in prior knowledge, which affects their ability to learn (Farr, Carey, & Tone, 1985); assessment of prior knowledge of occupational and basic skills can also occur informally in individual interviews. Since most workplace literacy programs are voluntary, even when offered on company time, it is important to meet these unique needs along with delivery of the workplace literacy curriculum. Periodic individual conferences are advisable, during which the learner's goals and progress in meeting those goals are reviewed.

Workplace Literacy Assessment Continuum

Informal qualitative		Formal quantitative	
Learner centered	Union centered	Management centered	Provider centered
Portfolios	Retrospective interview	Curriculum-based assessments	Cloze tests
Alternative assessments	Attitude assessments	Criterion-referenced tests	Standardized tests
Participatory approaches			

There are numerous alternative assessments. One type that meets the information needs of the learners is portfolios (Tierney, Carter, & Desai, 1991; Wolf, 1989), in which the learner's work samples are collected over time. Approaches in which learners read a variety of everyday (or job) materials (Lytle & Wolfe, 1989), may also be useful to learners because these approaches emphasize learners' strengths rather than deficits. Participatory approaches (Jurmo, 1991), in which the learner and instructor plan together the assessment and instruction processes, are also appropriate. An instructional approach like the language experience approach may also assess individuals' learning needs, especially for those functioning at beginning reading levels (Frager, 1991; Soifer, Young, & Irwin, 1989).

Union-Centered Assessments

Unions are concerned that learners' individual needs be met. But unions are also concerned about the general welfare and development of the workforce as a whole. Workers in workplace literacy programs can be assessed for growth in positive attitudes toward further education and lifelong learning by using attitude scales (Brown, 1990). Structured interviews should follow up written attitude inventories to gain further information about the impact of the program. Retrospective interviews, in which learners state what they can do now that they couldn't do before the program, also provide information about workers' development. Similarly, self-rating scales of competence in various work- and literacy-related tasks can indicate growth.

Management-Centered Assessments

Management is typically concerned about mastery of job-related basic skills that will result in improved job performance. While management and human resource personnel frequently speak of grade equivalents when referring to workers' skills (for example, a customer service representative needs to read at an 11th-grade reading level), grade equivalents do not easily translate into workplace competencies. In fact, Diehl & Mikulecky (1980) found that workers can read at several grade levels higher than their assessed reading levels (on standardized tests) when reading familiar materials such as those found in the workplace.

Curriculum-based assessments (Bean & Lane, 1990; Fuchs & Fuchs, 1988), however, can provide more meaningful assessment information because they reveal the workers' progress in learning the curriculum. These assessments, which are often in the form of short check tests embedded in the instructional materials, serve as frequent gauges of learning as workers progress through instruction.

Criterion-referenced tests (Popham, 1978) also provide meaningful assessment information by indicating mastery or nonmastery of skills targeted for instruction. Criterion-referenced assessments should focus on the skills—both reading-to-do and reading-to-learn—that were identified as being essential in the literacy task analysis and therefore taught in the curriculum, such as job-related vocabulary.

While it has been reported that job-related basic skills assessments (curriculum-based assessments and criterion-referenced tests) are becoming used more widely in workplace literacy programs (HR Strategies, 1991) and are now encouraged in the National Workplace Literacy Grants program, a concern exists about the validity and reliability of these instruments. Potential legal problems could arise if quantitative information is used without correct test development procedures (Douglas & Williams, 1992).

One solution to this problem is to use standardized criterion-referenced tests such as CASAS (Comprehensive Adult Student Assessment System, 1989), which ties workplace competencies to criterion-referenced tests that have been validated and checked for reliability. Unfortunately, the CASAS tests do not measure the specific job-related vocabulary and other skills needed in the workplace.

Provider-Centered Assessments

Cloze tests (Dupuis, 1980; Jongsma, 1980), which are commonly used by classroom teachers, are becoming more widely used in workplace literacy programs. They allow the instructor to assess quickly the reading abilities of the workers in a workplace literacy program by using materials from the workplace. The instructor is able to see who can handle materials from the job independently (independent level), with some help (instructional level), or not at all (frustration level). Cloze is particularly useful in workplace literacy programs that are open to all volunteers. While some programs are using cloze tests as pre- and posttests for program evaluation, this use is inappropriate if test reliability has not been established or if during instruction learners use the job materials from which the cloze test is drawn, thereby invalidating the posttest cloze score.

While many literacy providers are using alternative assessments, such as the cloze, Ehringhaus (1991) found that most programs relied on the Tests of Adult Basic Education (1987) for assessment and accountability. While the limitations of standardized testing have been discussed (Lazar & Bean, 1991; Tierney, Carter, & Desai, 1991), and alternatives for adult literacy that could be used in workplace programs have been suggested

(Scales, 1987), standardized achievement tests do provide useful information in workplace literacy programs. Sticht (1990, 1991) points out that standardized tests permit comparisons among workplace literacy programs, while curriculum-based assessments, criterion-referenced tests, and cloze tests, being specific to the content and job tasks of the particular workplace, do not. Pelavin Associates (1991) reports this as one of the difficulties in trying to evaluate the impact of workplace literacy programs.

Standardized tests also offer another benefit in showing the amount of transfer of learning from a job-related curriculum to general literacy tasks. Both Sticht (1987) and Brown (1990), evaluating different types of workplace literacy programs, report that job-related basic skills instruction resulted in increased general functioning in literacy skills as measured by standardized achievement tests.

A Final Note

Looking at assessment from different viewpoints is not intended to be restrictive. Fortunately, management personnel in some workplaces are considering qualitative information from informal assessments. Educators are recognizing the limitations and problems of using grade equivalents from standardized tests. A holistic approach to assessment provides the most information. Furthermore, assessment must be an ongoing process. While this discussion has focused primarily on assessment for diagnosis and program evaluaton, the instructor should be collecting ongoing assessment information of interest to all clients throughout the instructional program. Assessment is crucial to the success of workplace literacy programs because only through accurate information can learners be taught effectively and the value of these programs be demonstrated.

References

Bean, R.M., & Lane, S. (1990). Implementing curriculum-based measures of reading in an adult literacy program. *Remedial and Special Education, 11*(5), 39–46.

Brown, E.J. (1990). *Evaluation of the R.O.A.D. to success program.* University Park, PA: Institute for the Study of Adult Literacy, The Pennsylvania State University.

Carnevale, A.P., Gainer, L.J., & Meltzer, A.S. (1990). *Workplace basics: The essential skills employers want.* San Francisco, CA: Jossey-Bass.

Comprehensive Adult Student Assessment System (CASAS). (1989). *Employability competency system: An assessment and curriculum management system for JTPA programs.* San Diego, CA: San Diego Community College District Foundation.

Diehl, W., & Mikulecky, L. (1980). The nature of reading at work. *Journal of Reading, 24,* 221–227.

Douglas, B., & Williams, C. (1992). *Selected legal considerations regarding employee literacy and aptitude testing.* Dallas, TX: Jackson & Walker.

Dupuis, M.M. (1980). The cloze procedure as a predictor of comprehension in literature. *Journal of Educational Research, 74,* 27–33.

Education Writers Association. (1991). Myth #15: Management and labor agree on literacy goals. *The Literacy Beat, 4*(3), 1–4.

Ehringhaus, C. (1991). Testing in adult basic education. *Adult Basic Education, 1*(1), 12–26.

Farr, R., Carey. R., & Tone, B. (1985). Recent theory and research into the reading process: Implications for reading assessment. In J. Orasanu (Ed.), *Reading comprehension: From research to practice* (pp. 135–150). Hillsdale, NJ: Erlbaum.

Frager, A.M. (Ed.). (1991). *Teaching adult beginning readers: To reach them my hand.* Oxford, OH: The College Reading Association.

Fuchs, L.S., & Fuchs, D. (1988). Curriculum-based measurement: A methodology for evaluating and improving student programs. *Diagnostique, 14*(1), 3–13.

HR Strategies. (1991). *The HR Strategies 1991 survey of human resource trends.* Grosse Pointe, MI: Author.

Johnston, W.B., & Packer, A.H. (1987). *Workforce 2000: Work and workers for the 21st century.* Indianapolis, IN: Hudson Institute.

Jongsma, E.A. (1980). *Cloze instruction research: A second look.* Newark, DE: International Reading Association.

Jurmo, P. (1991). Understanding lessons learned in employee basic skills efforts in the U.S.: No quick fix. In M.C. Taylor, G.R. Lewe, & J.A. Draper, (Eds.), *Basic skills for the workplace* (pp. 67–84). Toronto, Ontario, Canada: Culture Concepts.

Lazar, M.K., & Bean, R.M. (1991). *Alternative assessment measures in adult basic education programs.* Pittsburgh, PA: University of Pittsburgh, Institute for Practice and Research in Education.

Lytle, S.L., & Wolfe, M. (1989). *Adult literacy: Program evaluation and learner assessment.* (Information Series No. 338). Washington, DC: Office of Educational Research and Improvement. (CE 054 812)

Pelavin Associates, Inc. (1991). *A review of the national workplace literacy program.* Washington, DC: Author.

Popham, W.I. (1978). Case for criterion-referenced measurements. *Educational Researcher, 7,* 6–10.

Sarmiento, A.R., & Kay, A. (1990). *Worker-centered learning: A union guide to workplace literacy.* Washington, DC: AFL-CIO Human Resources Development Institute.

Scales, A.M. (1987). Alternatives to standardized tests in reading education: Cognitive styles and informal measures. *The Negro Educational Review, 38*(2–3), 99–106.

Soifer, R., Young, D.L., & Irwin, M. (1989). The academy: A learner-centered workplace program. In A. Fingeret & P. Jurmo (Eds.), *Participatory literacy education.* San Francisco, CA: Jossey-Bass.

Sticht, T.G. (1987). *Functional context education: Workshop resource notebook.* San Diego, CA: Applied Behavioral & Cognitive Sciences. (Available from University Park, PA: Institute for the Study of Adult Literacy, The Pennsylvania State University.)

Sticht, T.G. (1990). *Testing and assessment in adult basic education and English as a second language programs.* San Diego, CA: Applied Behavioral and Cognitive Sciences.

Sticht, T.G. (1991). *Evaluating national workplace literacy programs*. El Cajon, CA: Applied Behavioral & Cognitive Sciences.

Tierney, R.J., Carter, M.A., & Desai, L.E. (1991). *Portfolio assessment in the reading-writing classroom*. Norwood, MA: Christopher-Gordon.

U.S. Department of Labor and U.S. Department of Education. (1988). *The bottom line: Basic skills in the workplace*. Washington, DC: Author.

Wolf, D.P. (1989). Portfolio assessment: Sampling student work. *Educational Leadership, 46*(7), 35–39.

Workplace Literacy

Workplace Literacy Lessons: From Literacy Audit to Learner

JOHANNA S. DESTEFANO
OCTOBER 1992

In our workplace literacy program—a joint partnership between faculty and staff of the College of Education, the Inland Fisher Guide division of General Motors, and the United Auto Workers Union Local 969—Sandra Prinz, Verna Terminello, and I devised a lesson plan format for two major curricular strands: communications and math. The communications strand was based on an integrated approach to oral communications, reading, and writing. The plan provides for language and literacy activities, a literacy skills section including metacognitive skills, pre- and post-reading and writing activities, and a section for both teacher and student follow-up. The lesson based on this plan was a crucial component in the curricular chain from the "diagnosis" of literacy needs in a workplace to working with a specific student.

In our project, this chain began with a DACUM (acronym for Developing A Curriculum) which was done with selected workers in the plant for the job of All Purpose Operator (APO), a new job configuration that was called for by synchronous manufacturing of auto body parts. The DACUM procedure yields a series of "duties" which are then broken further into component tasks, each of which is numbered. Thus, at the very top of the lesson plan form (see figure) the DACUM Task Reference is entered to indicate how that lesson plan is clearly tied to an on-the-job task, not to some generic job skill as commonly found in published material.

After the DACUM was completed, some of us did literacy task analyses of many of the duties revealed by the DACUM. For each sub-job within the APO category, such as packer (of auto parts), and for each job duty (such as "pack parts"), the subtasks were identified in a from-start-to-finish manner. For each sub-task, literacy skills embedded in the job were identified, including higher order metacognitive skills. These skills formed the pool from which more specific skills were drawn from each lesson and written out in the "Skills highlighted" section.

To determine which employees might benefit from instruction on the literacy skills identified by the analysis, the teacher conducts a diagnosis. After needs are identified, plans are created by the teacher or collaboratively by the teacher and student. At the top of each lesson plan are three categories: (1) learning objectives addressed, (2) learning activities, and (3) learning materials (see figure). The objectives come from the teacher's and student's knowledge of what needs to be accomplished by the employee. For example, performance outcomes might be "parts packed will not be damaged and will be packed in proper alignment at plant."

Lesson Plan Format for Workplace Communication Strand

Packer DACUM task reference: 14.0 (pack products); 14.1 (follow pack spec)

Learning objectives addressed	Learning activities	Learning materials
Work context—Given X number of parts and packaging material	**Reading**—Read routing sheet and spec sheet	Routing sheet Spec sheet Highlighter
Work task—Pack X number of parts	**Writing**—See follow-up	Pencil Paper
Performance outcomes—Parts will be quickly packed, not damaged, and in proper alignment at plant.	**Oral language**—Discuss	

Skills/processes highlighted—Recognizing/comprehending abbreviation (LTA 1.3—sets up packing routine, 3.3—packs parts); improving vocabulary skills; improving metacognitive skills (promoting awareness of task of recognizing/understanding abbreviations)

Before reading—Discuss: Why are abbreviations used? What are some common abbreviations you use every day on the job? What are the abbreviations used in the packer job? Elsewhere? What are some problems abbreviations might or do cause? Have they caused problems for you? (Setting purposes; activate schema: What I know, What I don't know)

While reading—Skim through the routing sheet and the spec sheet. Read through them again more slowly and highlight all abbreviations. (Study method—to develop metacognitive strategy awareness)

After reading—Discuss and write out the words the abbreviations stand for. Arrange a key to the abbreviations used. How do they help on the job?

Learner follow-up	**Instructor follow-up**	
Journal assignment: For several days, keep a diary of all abbreviations you encounter at work, in the home, and elsewhere. Write down the words the abbreviations stand for and explain how you figured out the "codes" (metacognition).	This lesson (After lesson is done)	Next lesson (After lesson is done)
	Long range: Group creates a glossary of plant abbreviations.	

For each lesson, reading, writing, and oral language activities are created. These are based on job tasks, skills, and actual job materials revealed by the literacy task analysis. These activities are usually integrated, often with the math strand, which has the same category in its format. The activities emphasize self-questioning to promote awareness of the reading process and on-the-job reading demands while the employee is working with the materials. We also try to include as much reading and writing of continuous text as possible, although some job tasks don't include continuous text.

The third part of the lesson plan may look exclusively geared to reading, but it isn't, in practice—it just focuses the teacher's attention on these critical elements. The oral and written aspects of the communications strand are integrated with reading at this point. The "Before reading" directions help the employee activate schema to provide a cognitive framework for what follows, which is enhanced by the employee's knowledge of the job itself. This is accomplished in a variety of ways in our lessons where the reader may skim, predict content, and so on. "While reading" is designed, in part, to help the student keep in mind the purpose for reading or writing, to check predictions, and so on. "After reading" is a crucial part of each lesson, designed to help the student employ a variety of strategies such as clarification, self-questioning, summarizing, and monitoring reading strategies. This middle section looks quite different for lessons in the math strand. Included there are identifying the purpose, selecting an approach, gathering needed data, calculating, and checking the solution as the steps in each lesson.

At the bottom of each lesson plan is a crucial section which not only provides for practice by the student, but also links the various lessons together into the larger unit encompassed by the job itself and the skills needed to perform it well. The "Learner follow-up" portion can be determined by the teacher before working with the student or in conjunction with the student. It often includes having a student write in a journal and rewrite various job materials such as routing sheets and spec sheets. It also can include practice activities such as more reading of related materials.

After the lesson, the teacher fills in "Instructor follow-up" on the form. "This lesson" is a place where she or he can critique and note the need for more work on a specific skill or strategy. Under "Next lesson," the teacher includes something that ties the lessons together into a coherent unit. This last step is important to our emphasis on individualized educational plans for each student. This format for lessons plays a central role in our ability to deliver a quality workplace literacy program in a company that heavily emphasizes quality in all aspects of its manufacturing process. I'd argue that such a format is applicable to virtually any employment setting, because it enables teachers and students to create a curriculum that can close the gap between the demands of the jobs and the skills of the employees.

Note: I would like to acknowledge the help of the three instructors in our project, Janet Collins, Patricia Connor, and Margaret Girkins, whose feedback and implementation were an important part of the creation process.

Navajo Head Start: Teacher Training and Adult Literacy in a Local Context

Michael C. Anziano
Verna Terminello
February 1993

One of the most interesting problems in education is how to ensure the transfer of skills from one situation to another. The question arises equally among single-language learners and among bilinguals who are thinking and working in a second language. And it applies to all sorts of academic skills, including the useful language skills of comprehending what one reads and writing down what one thinks. While the issue of transfer of reading comprehension skills from a native language to a second language has recently been investigated by Royer and Carlo (1991), we have been working on a related problem: writing in a second language when the writer's native language is based largely on an oral, rather than a written, modality, as is true for speakers of Navajo.

Literacy instruction in English for Navajo Native Americans has been an ongoing challenge that we have been fortunate to experience. The approach to "literacy in the workplace" that we will describe here involves literacy training in the context of teacher education for Head Start teachers. The results from this project replicate the approaches and findings of others—but in a context which is substantially different from those where previous work on adult literacy has been carried out. In our work in remote areas of the Navajo Reservation in the southwestern United States, we have observed that effective schools and effective teaching depend on the specific local circumstances.

In 1990 Project Head Start celebrated its 25th anniversary. In accordance with the continuing effort to provide comprehensive child care to children of poor families, a mandate was issued to all Head Start centers: In order to maintain U.S. federal funding, each classroom must have at least one teacher who has earned an Associate of Arts (A.A.) degree or a Child Development Associate (CDA) credential by 1994. The CDA credential is a professional certificate awarded by the Council on Early Childhood Professional Recognition to preschool teachers and child caregivers who have demonstrated their competence in working with young children. This policy mandate is critical, since federal funds for the preschool centers will be tied to the teachers' credentials.

In the fall of 1989, San Juan College received a grant from the New Mexico Department of Labor–Job Training Partnership Act (JTPA) to provide teacher training on the Navajo Reservation which would prepare Head Start teachers for the National CDA assessment process and to provide instruction in adult basic education (ABE) for teachers whose writing skills had generally been absorbed by an oral tradition. The project began with 22 teachers, 11 from each of the Eastern Navajo and Shiprock Agencies in New Mexico.

Each agency consists of vast open spaces characterized by rugged plateaus and high desert vegetation. Of the estimated 8,255 miles of roads on the reservation, only about 27% are paved; the remainder are dirt roads of varying quality, many of which become impassable in bad weather. The Navajo reservation encompasses 26,000 square miles in Arizona and New Mexico with an average population density of 5 persons per square mile (Commission for Accelerating Navajo Development Opportunities, 1988). One of the agencies we served (Eastern Navajo) is extremely isolated with only 2.2 persons to the square mile. The Navajo Nation reports an average household size of 4.7 persons per household, compared to a national U.S. figure of 3.17 persons per household in 1988. The typical living quarters are small and relatively modest, and risk factors for both teachers and children associated with living in geographic isolation are considerable (see Anziano, 1991).

Teacher Characteristics

The 22 Head Start teachers in our project are Native American men and women who live and work in rural New Mexico. It is interesting to note that these teachers grew up in the same remote areas and share the background characteristics of the children they teach in Head Start. Most of these individuals were unsuccessful in school, and several were high school dropouts who eventually earned a GED. The typical teacher in our program comes from a low income family and has children who are or were students in Head Start. Many of the teachers began their association with Head Start as classroom volunteers, and one individual had volunteered for 9 years prior to getting hired as a teacher assistant. The following are characteristics of the teachers, their family environments, and their living conditions.

Teacher characteristics ($n = 22$)

Ethnicity: Navajo	22
Female	17
Male	5
Mean age	32.1
Mean years in Head Start	4.5

Family background ($n = 14$ respondents)

Language spoken at home		
English	1	7%
Navajo	1	7%
Navajo and English	12	86%
Teacher's own home has electricity	12	86%
Teacher's own home has running water	8	57%
Mean household size (number of persons)	4.67	

The majority of these individuals speak Navajo as their first language, but in order to go through the CDA assessment process, they were required to document their work in English. For many who had been away from formal education for years, the requirement brought to mind a series of negative experiences with writing. Most were initially fearful of judgment by yet another critical teacher.

To assess the teachers' levels of reading and language proficiency in an academic context, we administered the Test of Adult Basic Education (TABE) at the start of the literacy program. Across the two agencies, 13 of 22 teachers were reading English at or below the 7th-grade level, and 15 of 22 had English language scores at or below seventh grade (in the Eastern Navajo Agency all those tested scored below seventh grade in language, with a mean grade level of 5.75). These scores must be interpreted cautiously, since the Head Start teachers had generally been out of high school for more than 10 years, and none of them spoke English as his or her first language. The TABE Reading and Language levels, score means, and standard deviations for the 22 people are as follows:

Eastern Navajo Agency ($n = 11$)

Reading score at or below 7th-grade level	8	
Reading score above the 7th-grade level	3	
Mean reading grade level	6.54	(SD 2.16)
Language score at or below 7th-grade level	11	
Language score above the 7th-grade level	0	
Mean language grade level	5.75	(SD .73)

Shiprock Agency ($n = 11$)

Reading score at or below 7th-grade level	5	
Reading score above the 7th-grade level	6	
Mean reading grade level	9.64	(SD 3.23)
Language score at or below 7th-grade level	4.	
Language score above the 7th-grade level	7	
Mean language grade level	9.18	(SD 2.57)

It became clear to us that these individuals, who may have been fine practitioners, would need a specialized approach to literacy in order to write about their teaching practices. Recent theorizing and research in adult literacy strongly suggest that literacy skills need to be taught within a context that is meaningful to the adult as reader and writer (Cornell,

1988; Smith, 1989). Since Head Start had mandated the acquisition of the CDA or an A.A. degree by teachers, the writing context was immediately meaningful, but an approach to writing for individuals who were used to conveying information by speaking had to be developed. The next section of this article describes the CDA process and the storytelling method used in the project to encourage our teachers to write.

Writing from Experience

Since 1971, the CDA credentialing program has worked closely with Project Head Start to evaluate and improve the skills of teachers in classrooms and home-based programs. To receive the CDA, a person must combine academic experience (usually in the form of college coursework), practical teaching experience, and the ability to write about one's own effectiveness in six general areas of competence. Figure 1 gives the six competency goals which a preschool teacher is evaluated against.

Figure 1
CDA Competency Goals for Preschool Caregivers

1. To establish and maintain a safe, healthy learning environment.
2. To advance physical and intellectual competence.
3. To support social and emotional development and provide positive guidance.
4. To establish positive and productive relationships with families.
5. To ensure a well-run, purposeful program responsive to participant needs.
6. To maintain a commitment to professionalism.

Source: Child Development Associate National Credentialing Program, *Preschool caregivers in center-based programs*. Washington, DC, 1988.

These six general goals are subdivided into 13 specific functional areas. For example, under goal number 2, "To advance physical and intellectual competence," the functional areas are physical, cognitive, communication, and creative. Under each functional area the candidate must demonstrate her or his competence both in writing and in action with children. For example, under "cognitive" the teacher is expected to demonstrate evidence of providing "opportunities for children to try out and begin to understand the relationships between cause and effect" or to "help children understand concepts such as space, time, shape and quantity" (CDA National Credentialing Program, 1988). One condition of receiving the CDA, then, is the teacher's ability to demonstrate competence in each of the 13 functional areas before a review committee of professionals and parents.

However, the teacher must also produce written documentation of her or his competence in the form of a portfolio. The portfolio contains an autobiography and a description of the teacher's program setting (for example, a center-based Head Start classroom that might be 30 miles from the nearest paved road). In addition to this, the teacher must write entries which describe her or his own competent planning and behavior in each functional area. A total of 39 entries are required which state in detail *what* the teacher does (for example, to promote cognitive development), *why* she or he does it that way, and *how* the materials, space, and routines used are developmentally appropriate for children between 3 and 5 years of age.

A total of about 50 pages of the teacher's own original writing is required for the portfolio, and many are lavishly illustrated with photographs, examples of children's work, or lesson plans created by the teacher. It is the writing process itself which has presented the greatest obstacle to Navajo teachers in the past. The task of providing a 50-page portfolio appeared insurmountable to many, even though they were excellent teachers and could easily demonstrate their competence through their activities with children in the classroom. Writing about their approaches to teaching was not something ordinarily expected in the primarily oral cultural tradition of the Navajo. Our approach to this problem draws from two seemingly disparate sources: cognitive psychology and the Navajo tradition of telling stories.

According to researchers in cognitive psychology, what we learn depends largely upon what we already know (see, for example, Anderson, 1980). Psychologists use the idea of a schema to represent an internalized, organized set of experiences. Schemata allow individuals to encode and relate complex new information to an existing base of knowledge. For example, some teachers who recognize traditional Navajo stages of child development consider children between the ages of 4 and 6 to be in Stage II, "One Becomes Self-Aware" (McCarty, Bia, & Lynch, 1982). Here the child is expected to become progressively more aware of the environment through stories told about the hogan, the elements, and Mother Earth. The child comes to appreciate respectful relationships with others and nature. The teacher might use her or his existing knowledge base to help in understanding Erikson's (1963) ideas about psychosocial autonomy, shame, initiative, and guilt, which characterize the 4- to 6-year-old in Western and European theorizing.

In a similar fashion, we encouraged the teachers to use their experience as they approached the task of writing. Since the CDA portfolio involves writing down what one does in the classroom, we asked teachers to draw on the oral tradition of their culture by telling stories (Beers, 1989) about their classroom activities as they pertained to the 13 functional areas. If a teacher was struggling with written expression, the CDA advisor might ask her or him to describe orally what she or he does in a particular area such as "cognitive." The advisor listens to the teacher and writes down what she or he says, handing the description back, saying "Here, this is a rough draft of a portfolio entry—I wrote down your story for you."

This oral description allowed the candidate to access her or his knowledge base by activating schemata for functional areas like "learning environment," "cognitive," or "social." Through the process of description, schemata facilitate understanding of events as well as memory of past events (Small, 1990). The storytelling method, then, is a fairly simple extension of one's drawing upon experiences. The Navajo teachers were encouraged to write descriptions of what they did in their classrooms only after they had given the same descriptions orally to our CDA advisors. The process begins with the traditional oral mode and moves to the more difficult written mode.

As Gray (1988) points out, writing not only reflects the teacher's thinking, but it also generates further thought. When our candidates wrote entries about what they do in the classroom and why they do it that way, they often noted variations or modifications in activities which they kept as lesson plans to be carried out in the future. We believe that our candidates' schemata for the 13 functional areas might be conceptualized as expectations for, and knowledge about, appropriate learning activities for children.

Strategies for Writing Down Stories

When the CDA advisors began writing down the teachers' oral descriptions in rough drafts, the teachers saw the power of their own words. The project then developed five specific strategies designed to encourage the persistence of writing.

1. *Establishing a writing rapport.* The two advisors in the project not only visited the teachers' Head Start classrooms for observation and feedback sessions but also held weekly writing workshops on campus. Advisors met with the teachers each Friday for 1–2 hours to practice portfolio entries.

2. *Establish trust.* The Head Start teachers were treated as colleagues by our faculty advisors. The Friday sessions were informal, nonthreatening workshops where advisors and teachers came to value each other's input. The fact that the advisors also met the teachers at the Head Start classrooms on the reservation created a sense of trust in that the advisors were familiar with the teachers' local context.

3. *Respect students' writing.* We respected our Head Start teachers' attempts at writing by postponing the correction of English grammar and spelling errors. Advisors asked each individual to read his or her work aloud in one-to-one tutoring sessions. If the teacher's writing did not make sense, the advisor asked her or him to "tell me what is wrong." Teachers identified errors in voice, person, thematic organization, and so forth. Only at this point would the advisor offer suggestions to correct written structure or to clarify meaning.

4. *Brainstorming.* Since many of the teachers had difficulty writing a single English sentence, we worked on brainstorming activities to stimulate expression. For example, the first functional area defined by CDA is "safe." Advisors would ask the teachers "What do you do in your classroom that demonstrates you have provided a safe environment for preschool children?" Our teachers eventually

responded to these questions because we were beginning to identify the issues they dealt with each day. Sometimes the advisor wrote down the teacher's response, other times the teacher wrote.

5. *Write about specific behaviors.* As the Head Start teachers began to respond to important issues in their classrooms, we began to focus more precisely on their own behaviors. If a response to the topic of "safe" was "we hold a fire drill at the preschool," we carefully led the candidate through an approach designed to produce specific behavioral descriptions. The advisor asked who, what, where, why, and how regarding the activity. Depending on the skill level of the individual, we determined how much or how little to assist in the brainstorming, writing, and revising of the portfolio entries.

Implications

We began CDA training with 22 individuals, and 16 completed a CDA credential at the end of 7 months, a success rate virtually unheard of on the Navajo Reservation prior to this project. (By our best efforts to uncover data pertaining to CDA, it appears that in the 10 years prior to this project, fewer that 20 CDA credentials were awarded to Navajo Head Start teachers.) Our own internal evaluation of the project's success can be demonstrated by a variety of performance factors. Figure 2 gives a structure for assessing the teachers' performance in the project.

Adults who can write about their competence are more effective teachers. Writing about one's competence requires that the individual reflect upon what he or she actually does in the classroom, and why she or he does it that way. Even though our candidates were fine teachers before the project began, anecdotal reports from teachers themselves, parents, supervisors, and early childhood education professionals concur that these individuals are better teachers now than they were a year ago (Anziano, 1991). Inspired by the confidence in themselves gained from new levels of literacy, and more aware of teaching methods due to their reflection on what they do with young children, the teachers' skills have improved. Their teaching practices have become more developmentally appropriate as they recognize and write about the need to vary a particular activity to suit the developmental level of the children who engage in that activity.

Other program outcomes include affective dimensions of the Head Start teachers themselves. In a postproject interview, 14 individuals responded to a number of survey questions, including "How has earning a CDA credential changed your life?" In response to this question, (a) a 40-year-old female and (b) a 30-year-old male replied:

(a) "After I finished high school I didn't believe I could go any further in my education. I never felt good about writing and I never wrote anything. Now I write letters to my daughter in California. I wrote a letter to the tribe and I got a scholarship. Now my writing gets things done!"

(b) "I'm able to read and write more now, and the CDA brought me up to a point where I know how to teach children. I felt proud of that. I felt that the CDA was more than just for me—it is for the kids, the community, for my family, and for Head Start. If I can do it, others can also."

Not only did these individuals realize that they had the ability to write respectable prose, but they also became better Head Start teachers in the process. Moreover, these teachers are now empowered with the confidence to share their skills with others. An important outcome of this project is seen in the increased self-sufficiency of these geographically isolated programs. When our teachers

Figure 2
Evaluation of workplace literacy program for Navajo Head Start teachers

Program outcome	Purpose	Strengths
Teacher reaction: Higher self-esteem—comments: "I didn't know I had it in me." "You showed me I could do it." "All of this time I thought I was really stupid, but I really can write."	**Measure teacher feelings about program/course:** Qualitative survey data indicate high levels of teacher satisfaction, improved self-confidence.	Easy to administer Provides immediate feedback on instructors
Teacher learning: Writing subskill acquired: 1. Knowledge of voice and person. 2. Journalistic style (who, what, where, when, why, how) 3. Identification of theme/topic 4. Organization—introduction, body, conclusion. 5. Use of pictures and other visual aids to inspire descriptive writing. 6. Writing process: brainstorming, writing, revising 7. Chronological order. 8. Lesson plan design. 9. Use of reference materials (CDA *Handbook*, curriculum guides, early childhood textbook journals). 10. Peer- and self-evaluation of written work, including feedback sessions.	**Measure the amount of learning that has occurred in a program/course:** 1. Documentation in the form of the CDA porfolio; lesson plans. 2. Distinct improvement in trainees' writing skills. 3. Teachers encouraged to teach others through this writing approach. 4. Improvements in teachers' knowledge and confidence.	Provides objective data on the effectiveness of training. Data can be collected before students leave training program. Data can be used to further program goals. Data can be used in formative and summative evaluation process. Writing is viewed by teachers as purposeful—They wrote in order to achieve specific goals.
Teacher performance: 1. Improved writing and thinking. 2. Improved teaching skills 3. Empowerment to be CDA advisors to others.	**Measure the transfer of training:** 1. Oral tradition becomes documented in written English. 2. Writing leads to improved teaching.	Provides objective data on impact to job situation. Writing acts as a tool to stimulate thinking about curriculum for children.
Organization results: 1. Sixteen teachers have earned CDA credential. 2. Several teachers received promotions.	**Measure impact of training on organization:** Head Start children's improved skills, attitudes.	Provides objective data for cost/benefit analysis and organizational support.

Adapted from U.S. Department of Education; U.S. Department of Labor. *The bottom line: Basic skills from the workplace*. Washington, DC, 1988.

wrote down what they do in the classroom, their words in print helped to validate for themselves the fine work they are performing. Sharing these practices with other Head Start teachers will be the next step.

References

Anderson, J.R. (1980). *Cognitive psychology.* San Francisco, CA: W.H. Freeman.

Anziano, M. (1991). Approaches to early intervention on the reservation. *Early Education and Development, 2*(1), 68–76.

Beers, C.D. (1989, March–April). Storytelling and Native American CDA's. *Children Today,* 24–25.

CDA National Credentialing Program. (1988). *Preschool caregivers in center-based programs.* Washington, DC: Author.

Commission for Accelerating Navajo Development Opportunities. (1988). *Navajo nation fax: A statistical abstract.* Window Rock, AZ: Author.

Cornell, T. (1988). Characteristics of effective occupational literacy programs. *Journal of Reading, 31,* 654–656.

Erikson, E.H. (1963). *Childhood and society* (2nd ed.). New York: W.W. Norton.

Gray, D.J. (1988). Writing across the curriculum. *Phi Delta Kappan, 69,* 729–733.

McCarty, T., Bia, F., & Lynch, R. (1982). *Title IV-B Navajo materials development project.* Rough Rock, AZ: Rough Rock Demonstration School.

Royer, J.M., & Carlo, M.S. (1991). Transfer of comprehension skills from native to second language. *Journal of Reading, 34,* 450–455.

Small, M. (1990). *Cognitive development.* New York: Harcourt Brace.

Smith, F. (1989). Overselling literacy. *Phi Delta Kappan, 70,* 352–359.

Workplace Literacy

Using Annual Reports for Adult Literacy Improvement

Phyllis A. Miller
October 1988

For adults, the world of work involves considerable and varied kinds of reading. Often people in job settings face reading materials unlike any they experienced in school. While a majority of young adults have mastered the basic literacy demands, for the most part they cannot handle literacy tasks of increased complexity—the type of reading needed in much of the workplace (Kirsch & Jungeblut, 1986; Mikulecky, 1986). Much work-related reading is complex and requires inferential thinking and application of the information for decision making and problem solving (Mikulecky, 1982, 1986; Miller 1982).

A challenge to educators is to help adult learners bridge the gap between competence with basic reading tasks and competence with more difficult and complex ones. Part of that challenge involves finding practical instructional materials that require more than locating and identifying information. One such material is the annual business report. An annual report is prepared by a company for public information. It gives an overview of that company during a particular year. This formal report to stockholders includes the general philosophy, business thrusts, and a financial statement (certain disclosures are required by law). See Figure 1.

Why Use Annual Reports?

To bridge the gap existing for many adults between levels of literacy competence, I have used annual reports as instructional materials in reading improvement classes. The reports are practical for several reasons. First, annual reports provide an opportunity to apply the three distinct types of literacy characterized by the National Assessment of Educational Progress (Kirsch & Jungeblut, 1986):

Prose literacy—the literacy involved in using texts such as editorials, news stories, and so on.

Document literacy—the literacy required to locate and use information in forms, tables, and so forth.

Quantitative literacy—the knowledge and skills needed to apply arithmetic operations, either alone or sequentially, that are embedded in printed materials.

Second, annual reports provide an introduction to material that is not typical school material but is similar in nature to the material adults face in many work settings. Also, because companies spend considerable sums on these reports for public relations purposes, the reports look appealing and inviting.

Figure 1
Typical Content of Annual Reports

Letter from the company chairman—Tells how the company is doing and why that is so; gives the company's stance on economic, social, or political climates affecting the company; provides thoughts about the company's future.

A review of operations—Often includes a statement of what is new in the business.

Management review of financial conditions

Income statement—Includes sales, cost of goods sold, expenses, and net income.

Balance sheet—Gives assets (current and longterm operating assets), liabilities (current and longterm), and stockholders' equity (paid-in capital and retained earnings).

Statement of changes in financial position—Gives working capital, which is the difference between current assets and current liabilities.

Accounting policies—Include a report of certified public accountants and any other accounting premises, such as whether the report refers to a family of corporations (in a footnote).

Other footnotes or simply notes—Provide other disclosures which do not fit in the main body of the report (they help explain profits); examples include maturity dates on loans, interest rates, the amount spent for research and development, any pending lawsuits, retirement plans, businesses sold or purchased.

Comparison to earlier years (often in graphs)

Officers of the company

Note: The annual reports called 10K reports, filed with the U.S. Securities and Exchange Commission, may contain certain additional information.

From *Managing Your Reading*, copyright by Phyllis A. Miller. Littleton, CO: Reading Development Resources, 1987, p. 134. Used with permission.

Yet, while the look of annual reports is nonthreatening, the contents provide a range of difficulty levels and offer opportunity to teach varied reading strategies and skills to master more complex reading tasks. Some areas for instruction include:

- Recognizing and using the structure of material to gain an overview of its message. (The reports are generally consistent in structure and content. See Figure 2.)

- Establishing a specific reading purpose to make the task more manageable (for example, to discover the areas of company growth).

- Developing a strategy for accomplishing the reading purpose (a process important in dealing with many kinds of technical materials).

- Analyzing the position and bias of the writers and noticing how writing styles carry out an apparent intent to communicate or to obscure information (for example, seeing the difference between the chairman's letter and any footnotes which might try to downplay a pending lawsuit).

- Comparing various parts of a report (or several reports) to reach a general understanding of the whole.

- Asking questions of the report, which requires reading charts, doing arithmetic, and reading prose material (for example, is the working capital rising?).

- Building new vocabulary.

Adults in my classes give several additional reasons for the appeal of these materials. Annual reports offer a broader look at a company or its competitors than an employee usually receives; they let people see large local companies in a new way; they provide a perspective on national firms whose products consumers buy; they allow people to analyze a company in which they might want to invest. In a nutshell, the reports open a whole new world of reading matter.

Figure 2
Typical Structure of Annual Reports

An annual report is arranged in three basic parts—a beginning, a middle, and an ending. The arrangement is predictable, as follows:

Beginning: Here are the chairman's letter, a general review of operations, and an introduction to what is new in each line of business. (Many reports begin with a summary of financial highlights.)

Middle: The numbers and their analysis by management are here. Either may precede the other.

Of the numbers (financial statement), first is the income statement. It starts with sales and then lists the cost of goods sold and various expenses, ending with the net earnings.

Then comes the balance sheet (a snapshot of the company at a single point in time) which begins with the assets. On the top are the current assets—things which can be quickly turned into cash, such as accounts receivable. Below those are longterm operating assets, such as property or equipment (what the company owns). Next are the liabilities, including the current liabilities (debts due in 1 year) and longterm liabilities. Following is the stockholder equity section.

Changes in financial position are in the middle, too.

Ending: The footnotes are here.

From *Managing Your Reading*, copyright by Phyllis A. Miller. Littleton, CO: Reading Development Resources, 1987, p. 135. Used with permission.

How to Use Annual Reports

To use the annual report as a teaching material with adults, I recommend following these steps.

1. Become familiar with the general content and structure of annual reports by reviewing a number of them. (See Figures 1 and 2 again.) Public libraries keep files of these reports (usually noncirculating, so you need to review them at the library), or the library

---

Figure 3
A Strategy for Reading an Annual Report

Get an overview. Know the general content and structure of the report.

Decide purpose(s) and questions. Think about your purpose. Then get questions in mind to "ask" of the report. Included below are some pertinent questions to consider.

Check terms. Look up the meaning of financial terms which might be unfamiliar to you.

Start at the end. In a particular annual report, start your reading at the ending, by skimming over the footnotes. Look first at the accountant's report. Note anything there which says "subject to." This suggests doubt about a particular piece of business. Look at the other footnotes too, because they can help explain the profits.

Some footnotes disclose information about sensitive issues (for example, about abandoned business ventures due to losses). Beware that the writing may be poor or highly legalistic. (That may be intentional to obscure the information.) Note questionable items briefly as you try to comprehend this footnote material, because you may find key insights about the company there.

Go to the beginning. Next, turn back to the front part to find the chairman's letter. It is addressed to the stockholders. Its tone likely reflects the vitality and personality of the company, as the chairman tells you how the company is doing now and what is anticipated for the future. Compare the writing style to that in the footnotes. Also page through other parts that tell you about new or interesting directions the company is taking. They could be written by a public relations person, and will reflect a particular position the company wants to portray publicly.

Move to the numbers. Now move to the section of numbers, beginning with the balance sheet. Once you look at the current assets and the current liabilities, notice the difference between the two, which is the net working capital.

Note: Here is an example of where it is helpful to compare an annual report of one year with that of the year before. (Reports usually contain summary graphs of prior years.) Comparisons are crucial when you look at the numbers. For instance, is the working capital shrinking or expanding? Look at the balance sheet to see the stockholders' equity (the difference between all assets and liabilities). That should be growing from one year to the next. Again, compare.

Notice the longterm debt. Is it high (perhaps fine if the business is growing, perhaps not so fine if the business is leveling off)? Potential creditors may want the ratio of that debt to the company's equity less than one to one. Compare that to earlier years or to other companies in the industry.

Now look at the income statement. First note the sales at the top of it. Compare the sales to the year before. Are they rising, staying the same, or falling?

Look at the expenses and then the net income. (Here is where the footnotes may offer some explanation for what is going on, for example, if the net income is high yet sales are not significantly changed. Perhaps the company sold off a business.)

From *Managing Your Reading*, copyright by Phyllis A. Miller. Littleton, CO: Reading Development Resources, 1987, pp. 136-7. Used with permission.

will have information on where to write for reports they do not carry.

2. Select a couple of reports in a similar industry and compare them (for example, I find publishing companies interesting).

3. Pick a particular report and follow the strategy in Figure 3. (I have learners do this once they are familiar with report content and structure.)

4. Choose some reports to use with students. Contact the company for your own copy (try the public relations department). Often the reports are free or the small charge is waived if you tell the company you are using the report for educational purposes. Depending on your request, some companies will give you a number of copies.

5. Build up a collection of annual reports to use with students. Keep old ones. (Then you can compare a current year with a past year or various companies within an industry.)

6. Develop teaching plans involving the reports.

As a consultant, I have taught reading classes within particular companies. Here are suggestions which have worked for me as I incorporate the annual report as one of my teaching materials. All the participants first use the report of the specific company. However, to place the company within a broader perspective, I bring in reports of competitors or, when possible, of other local companies. I also tell participants how to acquire their own copies of reports. In using the reports, I do not attempt to be a financial expert. When following the learning strategy fails to help me comprehend some part of a report, I tell participants and then we analyze the difficulty. Sometimes I must gain more background. Sometimes I do not understand a term or conceptual base. Sometimes the writing is confusing or vague. Talking through my own process of trying to comprehend is in itself instructive.

The annual report can be used to build higher levels of literacy competence among adults who possess the basic levels. Because it calls for the three aspects of literacy—prose, document, and quantitative—its use is consistent with the objectives of many reading educators. Since the annual report is an appealing and a relatively easily available type of nonschool technical material, it is a practical yet valid instructional material to use with adults in reading improvement classes.

References

Kirsch, I.S., & Jungeblut, A. (1986). *Literacy: Profiles of America's young adults.* Princeton, NJ: National Assessment of Educational Progress, Educational Testing Service.

Mikulecky, L. (1982). Job literacy: The relationship between school preparation and workplace actuality. *Reading Research Quarterly, 17*(3), 400–419.

Mikulecky, L. (1986, December). The status of literacy in our society. Paper presented at the National Reading Conference, Austin, TX.

Miller, P.A. (1987). *Managing your reading.* Littleton, CO: Reading Development Resources.

Miller P.A. (1982, November). Reading demands in a high-technology industry. *Journal of Reading, 26,* 109–115.

C i t a t i o n   I n d e x

Note: An "f" following a page number indicates that the reference may be found in a figure.

Subject Index

classroom format, 110; combinatory expressive approach, 157–162; computer-assisted, 186–200; decision making, 60; for disabled readers, 95–100, 227–235; Geneva (NY) projects, 150–155; holistic, 234–235; inappropriate, 165–166; intergenerational projects, 211–219; international rural projects, 43; for nonspeaking adult male with cerebral palsy, 227–235; pragmatic, 104–105; Ryedale Adult Literacy Paired Reading Project, 222–226; strategies, 103–105; training for family and friends, 219–226; workplace, 267–269, 270–277. *See also* Teaching; Tutoring

C o n t r i b u t o r   I n d e x